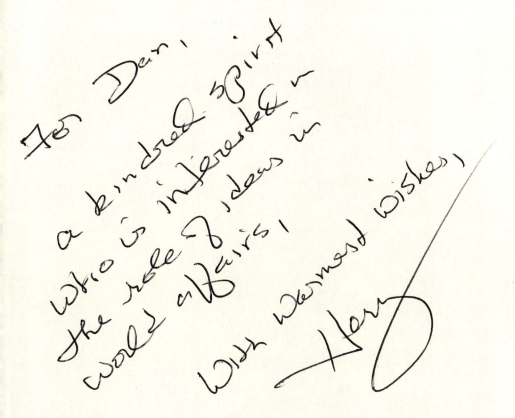

For Dan,
a kindred spirit
who is interested in
the role of ideas in
world affairs!

With warmest wishes,

Henry

Also by Henry R. Nau

Perspectives on International Relations: Power, Institutions and Ideas, 4th edition, CQ Press

Worldviews of Aspiring Powers: Domestic Foreign Policy Debates in China, India, Iran, Japan and Russia,
Oxford University Press, co-editor and contributor

At Home Abroad: Identity and Power in American Foreign Policy,
Cornell University Press

Trade and Security: U.S. Policies at Cross-Purposes,
American Enterprise Institute

The Myth of America's Decline: Leading the World Economy into the 1990s, Oxford University Press

Domestic Trade Politics and the Uruguay Round,
Columbia University Press, editor and contributor

Technology Transfer and U.S. Foreign Policy, Praeger

National Politics and International Technology: Nuclear Reactor Development in Western Europe,
Johns Hopkins University Press

Conservative Internationalism

Armed Diplomacy
Under Jefferson, Polk, Truman, and Reagan

HENRY R. NAU

Princeton University Press
Princeton and Oxford

Library of Congress Cataloging-in-Publication Data
Nau, Henry R., 1941–
Conservative internationalism :
armed diplomacy under Jefferson, Polk, Truman, and Reagan / Henry R. Nau.
p. cm.
Includes index.
Summary: "Debates about U.S. foreign policy have revolved around three main
traditions—liberal internationalism, realism, and nationalism. In this book, distinguished
political scientist Henry Nau delves deeply into a fourth, overlooked foreign policy
tradition that he calls "conservative internationalism." This approach spreads freedom,
like liberal internationalism; arms diplomacy, like realism; and preserves national
sovereignty, like nationalism. It targets a world of limited government or independent
"sister republics," not a world of great power concerts or centralized international
institutions. Nau explores conservative internationalism in the foreign policies of
Thomas Jefferson, James Polk, Harry Truman, and Ronald Reagan. These presidents
did more than any others to expand the arc of freedom using a deft combination of
force, diplomacy, and compromise. Since Reagan, presidents have swung back and
forth among the main traditions, overreaching under Bush and now retrenching under
Obama. Nau demonstrates that conservative internationalism offers an alternative way.
It pursues freedom but not everywhere, prioritizing situations that border on existing free
countries—Turkey, for example, rather than Iraq. It uses lesser force early to influence
negotiations rather than greater force later after negotiations fail. And it reaches timely
compromises to cash in military leverage and sustain public support. A groundbreaking
revival of a neglected foreign policy tradition, Conservative Internationalism shows how
the United States can effectively sustain global leadership while respecting the constraints
of public will and material resources"— Provided by publisher.
ISBN 978-0-691-15931-7 (hardback)
1. United States—Foreign relations—Philosophy. 2. United States—Foreign
relations—1801–1809. 3. United States—Foreign relations—1845–1849. 4. United
States—Foreign relations—1945–1953. 5. United States—Foreign relations—1981–1989.
6. Jefferson, Thomas, 1743–1826. 7. Polk, James K. (James Knox), 1795–1849.
8. Truman, Harry S., 1884–1972. 9. Reagan, Ronald. I. Title.
E183.7.N378 2013
327.73009'034—dc23
2013019882

British Library Cataloging-in-Publication Data is available

This book has been composed in Sabon and Kozuka Gothic

Printed on acid-free paper ∞

Printed in the United States of America

1 3 5 7 9 10 8 6 4 2

For my friends who became family and know who they are

Contents

Acknowledgments

WRITING A BOOK IS MUCH LIKE running a marathon, with one difference: the finish line never arrives. You just stop writing before the book is ever completed. This book is no exception. I began running with it some fifty years ago, long before any of my other books. I arrived in Washington as a graduate student and discovered quickly that the world around me at that time was almost completely liberal. I attended seminars at the Brookings Institution and Carnegie Endowment for International Peace and heard little that resonated with my predispositions toward liberty, small government, low taxes, religious faith, and competitive markets. It was never a kind of in-your-face liberalism; it was always more subtle—a matter of topics chosen and conclusions reached, not ideology. For example, no one studied *government* failure only *market* failure, and no one concluded that stronger families and churches, personal responsibility and savings were the solution to social problems; they simply advocated new government welfare programs. And in my field of American foreign policy, everyone talked about liberal internationalism but never mentioned conservative internationalism or even imagined such a thing could exist.

I accepted my environment and have loved every minute of my academic marathon ever since. Indeed I adore the contemplative profession. It fits my temperament "to a T." My colleagues, most of whom are liberal, have treated me splendidly, even if at times they are bewildered by my political predilections. Early on Joe Nye, Bob Keohane, and Ernie Haas drew me into their intellectual projects and supported my work on energy, technology transfer, food, and U.S. foreign economic policy. I passed Joe on my way out of the State Department as I left the Ford administration and he entered the Carter administration. There were always more academic colleagues in Democratic than Republican administrations. I don't think there was another *one* (with the exception perhaps of Jeane Kirkpatrick) in the Reagan administration. Bob, who invited me to teach at Stanford after I left government the first time, stayed in touch with me during my White House years, perplexed to be sure by what I was doing there but always supportive of my academic research on a more conservative (or domesticist, as I called it then) approach to international economic policy. Ernie Haas also reached out to me, a gentle and powerful intellect with whom I had practically nothing in common politically.

My environment since then has improved substantially, especially in Washington. The American Enterprise Institute, sleeping contentedly in the backwaters during the 1960s, rose to compete with Brookings and Carnegie. The Heritage Foundation and CATO Institute burst onto the Washington scene and now fortify conservative causes in public policy debates. Today Congress is also more competitive, no longer the preserve of the Democratic Party, as it was for fifty to sixty years after 1930. But there are still big gaps. The capital city of the world's leading democracy has only one consequential newspaper. Outside Washington, Fox News battles valiantly against multiple liberal channels to provide a better balance of daily news reporting, and the blogging and tweeting tsunamis have flooded the political universe, amply flowing from both liberal and conservative wellsprings.

Conservatism still sleeps in the academic universe, but its day will come there, too, because there is always further evidence and alternative explanations for any conclusion that social or natural science may reach, however ironclad that conclusion may seem. If the Madisonian democracy we cherish means anything, it means endless spirited intellectual and, yes, partisan debate about every issue, a debate held together only by our common belief in individual liberty and an accessible public square in which, as Thomas Jefferson proclaimed, "error of opinion may be tolerated where reason is left free to combat it."

I run my marathon, as all of us do, only with the help of countless colleagues. I start with those who read the current manuscript at various stages from stem to stern: Peter Berkowitz, Michael Desch, Colin Dueck, Mark Haas, Peter Katzenstein, David Lake, Robert Lieber, Tod Lindberg, John Owen, Peter Trubowitz, and Stephen Walt. Over an evening and a day, nine of these colleagues waylaid my analysis at a review seminar hosted in Washington by the Hoover Institution. Mark Haas and John Owen provided intellectual life support when I was ready to collapse in my latest race. I'll never forget my delight at reading Mark's first book, *The Ideological Origins of Great Powers*, and finding so many of my ideas formulated and developed better than I could have ever imagined. And John's work is, in my judgment, monumental not only for its breadth but also for its counterconventional contributions on the role of ideas in world affairs. No one of these colleagues, however, contributed more to this book than Peter Katzenstein. He gave me unqualified emotional and intellectual sustenance throughout the marathon of this race and earlier ones. I gave him more than one justification to dismiss the study and me, even forgetting once to honor an appointment I had made with him only to arrive an hour later and find him still waiting in the designated place. He disagrees deeply with some parts of the book, but he is one of those colleagues who idolizes the public square and inclusiveness. He not only writes about ecumenism; he lives it.

For this latest race, I express a special debt to the Hoover Institution at Stanford University and only wish that I had discovered this impressive institution, or it had discovered me, earlier in my marathon. Hoover is the one institution in the world of premier universities that proudly accepts the label of conservative. In the academic universe, the c-word not the l-word is in disrepute, and but for Hoover it might be utterly homeless. Hoover's standards of scholarship are unsurpassed, and the academic public square would be blessed bountifully if there were more Hoovers on university campuses examining topics and drawing conclusions from a conservative rather than just a liberal worldview. The Bradley Foundation, which supported a previous book of mine, and the Rumsfeld Foundation provide fellowships for Ph.D. students and labor earnestly to improve the fortunes of conservative scholarship in academe.

At Hoover, I am grateful, in particular, to Dave Brady, who runs the National Fellows Program and numerous other activities at the institution. I spent a year at Hoover as a National Fellow in 2011–12 and will always remember Dave's greeting when I arrived: "You are here because we like what you are doing; so go do it even if we don't see you again." That kind of trust in individuals personifies the conservative faith, not only in the academic square but among ordinary people at large. Jefferson (my favorite, as you will soon discover) honestly believed that uneducated whiskey farmers had the right and ability to govern themselves. I also owe special debts to Tod Lindberg and Peter Berkowitz, both senior fellows at Hoover. Tod helped me establish contact with Hoover for the first time some seven years ago, and Peter led the effort to organize the review seminar that ripped my manuscript apart.

George P. Shultz, the Thomas W. and Susan B. Ford Distinguished Fellow at Hoover and Ronald Reagan's secretary of state, has supported my work ever since I met and worked with him briefly in the Reagan administration. He consented to numerous interviews and never retracted his support even when I openly dissented from his conclusions. Martin and Annelise Anderson, senior research scholars at Hoover, contributed mightily to my understanding of Ronald Reagan. They have written, in my judgment, the best books so far on Reagan's stewardship, and they are not done writing yet. Allan Meltzer, another Hoover fellow and colleague from the Reagan administration, tutors me diligently on economic matters and understanding Reagan's economic legacy. Larry Diamond, Frank Fukuyama, Judith Goldstein, Paul Gregory, Stephen Haber, Tom Henrikson, Charles Hill, Steve Krasner, Peter Robinson, Henry Rowen, Kori Schaki, Peter Schweizer, and Amy Zegart are other Hoover and

Stanford colleagues who critiqued my work and brightened my associations at Hoover. Finally the Hoover staff was exceptional in every way, easing my daily life at the institution: Denise Elson, Marianne Jacobi, Mandy MacCalla, Emily Messner, Cheryl Weissbart, and Eryn Wichter. Susan Schendel played a special role, providing me with a truly idyllic cottage next to her home as my daily residence during the fellowship year.

I am especially indebted to David C. Hendrickson for a very careful reading of the chapter on Thomas Jefferson. Robert Merry provided valuable insights on the Polk chapter, as did Denver Brunsman, Tom Zeiler, Joseph (Andy) Fry, and Michael Landis. Elizabeth Edwards Spalding wrote one of the best books I've ever read on Truman, from which I borrowed shamelessly. Martin and Annelise Anderson contributed mightily to the Reagan chapter. Paul Kengor, Jeffrey Chidester, Stephen Hayward, Tom Mahnken, Lou Cannon, and Doug Brinkley also assisted. Ed Meese, Reagan's counselor and attorney general, extended steady friendship and advice. Richard V. Allen, Reagan's first national security advisor, not only gave me the chance of a lifetime to serve in the Reagan White House but also encouraged me to get in touch with Hoover. And William (Bill) P. Clark, Allen's successor from 1982 to 1983, did more to erect the scaffolding of Reagan's foreign policy, coordinating more than one hundred National Security Decision Directives, than any other single advisor. I interviewed Bill on his ranch in Paso Robles in 2011, was transfixed by the majesty of the little mission church that stands on the top of the hill at the entrance, and left with a much deeper understanding of the simple faith and sophisticated serenity of this man who was so close to Ronald Reagan.

Others colleagues who read, discussed, or contributed to parts of the study include: Paul Avey, Michael Bardo, Matthew Baum, Nicholas Bouchet, Alan Buckley, Dan Caldwell, Ralph Carter, Mike Chandler, Elizabeth Cobbs-Hoffman, Eliot Cohen, Mick Cox, Dan Deudney, David Ettinger, Amitai Etzioni, Aaron Friedberg, Payam Ghalehdar, Roy Ginsberg, Charles Glaser, Jim Goldgeier, Steven Hook, Chris Jones, Stuart Kaufman, Jun Kurihara, John Ikenberry, Ash Jain, Bruce Jentleson, Paul Lettow, Jim Liebovic, Charles Lipson, Dieter Mahncke, Hal Malmgren, Matteo Martimucci, Walter Russell Mead, John Mearsheimer, Mike Mochizuki, John Morris, Mitch Muncy, Donette Murray, DJ Nordquist, Deepa Ollapally, Rob Paarlberg, Wiegand Pabsch, Tom Pangle, Walter Reich, Thomas Risse, Jonathan Rynhold, Elizabeth Saunders, Dianne Sehler, Zachary Selden, David Shambaugh, Josh Shifrinson, Kristin Silverberg, Tony Smith, Duncan Snidal, Abe Sofaer, Charles Waldorf, and Jay Winik.

Students assistants are invaluable and I have had some of the best: Michael Wain, Alex Forster, Mark Romaniw, Maiko Ichihara, Shannon Powers, Eduardo Cortazar Perez, and Sandy Snider-Pugh.

The staff at Princeton University Press was especially pleasant and helpful. I owe a great deal to Charles (Chuck) T. Myers, the longtime executive editor at Princeton for political science, law, and American political history who recently became associate director and senior editor at the University Press of Kansas. He took an early interest in my project and cared deeply about intellectual diversity. This was the third book I offered to Princeton for publication; the other two were published by Oxford and Cornell. Chuck is a big reason I did not strike out on a third swing at Princeton. Jennifer Backer was a superb copyeditor, and Karen Carter, Eric Crahan, and Eric Henney steered me effortlessly through the production process.

I dedicate this book to my friends who over the years became family and enlarged my relatively small circle of life. My wife and daughter, to whom earlier books were dedicated, remain the core of that circle. For almost fifty years (in 2014), Marion, or Micki as I call her, has been there for me, through all sorts of celebrations and crackups. Kimberly is a strong and accomplished businesswoman and remains in my eye always that little girl who gave me the supreme happiness of being a father. From the beginning friends expanded my little circle and added untold happiness. They know who they are and how grateful I am.

Conservative Internationalism

Introduction

Traditions of the Eagle

IT WAS EARLY MARCH 1946. The presidential train rumbled along the Ohio River Valley. President Harry Truman was taking Winston Churchill to Fulton, Missouri, where Churchill would deliver his famous "iron curtain" speech at Westminster College. On the train, Truman showed Churchill the new American presidential seal.

The seal had just been redesigned. Prior to 1945, the American eagle faced toward the left talon holding the arrows symbolizing American arms. In the redesign, ordered by President Franklin Roosevelt, the eagle's head was moved to face the right talon holding the olive branches symbolizing American diplomacy.

Fraught with political meaning, this change was made for purely technical reasons. According to George Elsey, Truman's aide assigned to redesign the seal, the chief of heraldry for the U.S. Army suggested the change to comply with heraldic traditions. In a coat of arms, the eagle's head facing toward the left was "sinister" or an indication of illegitimacy. The correct position of the head was "dexter," to the right, the direction of honor.[1]

Pointing to the new design mounted on the wall of the train car, Truman explained the change to Churchill: "we have just turned the eagle's head from the talons of war to the olive branch of peace." Churchill thought for a moment and said: "the head should be on a swivel so that it can turn to the talons of war or the olive branch of peace as the occasion warrants." Then, mischievously, Churchill added that the berries on the olive branches looked to him like atomic bombs.[2]

The different positions of the eagle's head on the presidential seal represent in many ways the various traditions of American foreign policy. Churchill was expressing the archetypical *realist* view that American foreign policy should combine force (arrows) and diplomacy (olive branches), in whatever measure external circumstances require, to ensure national security. He anticipated the realist response to nuclear weapons:

a diplomacy of deterrence that brandished the threat of atomic bombs to preclude their use (the berries on the olive branches).

The original seal with the eagle facing the arrows and war represented the *nationalist* orientation, the idea that America should remain strong and non-entangled in world affairs, a posture popular in the country's early history and again in the 1930s. The eagle's head fixed on the olive branches in the redesigned seal identified the *liberal internationalist* tradition, America's leadership of world affairs through international institutions like the League of Nations and United Nations.

This is a book about these standing American foreign policy traditions: realism, nationalism, and liberal internationalism. But it is about something much more, a further and until now neglected interpretation of America's foreign policy experience: the *conservative internationalist* tradition. This tradition mixes in different ways America's responsibility to reform world affairs stressed by liberal internationalism, America's power to maintain global stability emphasized by realism, and America's respect for national sovereignty preferred by nationalism. It features three key tenets:

- the liberal internationalist goal of spreading freedom, but disciplined by threat and priorities to spread freedom primarily on the borders of existing freedom, not everywhere in the world at once;
- the realist means of armed diplomacy to counter gains by adversaries *outside* negotiations in order to move freedom forward by timely compromise *inside* negotiations, not just using force *after* negotiations fail; and
- a conservative vision of limited global governance, a decentralized world of democratic civil societies or "sister republics," as Thomas Jefferson called them, not one of centralized international institutions as Woodrow Wilson and Franklin Roosevelt advocated.

The world envisioned is a conservative nirvana. States remain separate and armed; national culture, sovereignty, defense, and patriotism are respected; civic virtue and democracy are widespread; the global economy is mostly private; and global governance is limited. Such a "republican" world will always be more competitive and risky than a "liberal" world of centralized international institutions. Freedom and the availability of force to defend it are in some sense inseparable.

Today in the foreign policy literature and public discourse, conservative internationalism does not exist. Liberal thinking dominates the internationalist tradition, and conservative thinking has been classified historically as either nationalist or realist. More recently, liberal critics have tried to conflate conservative foreign policy with neoconservatives (neocons) and George W. Bush. But important tenets of conservative internationalism, such as small government, limited priorities, and armed diplomacy to achieve timely compromise, not unconditional surrender, are not synonymous with neoconservatism; and despite his liberal internationalist rhetoric, George W. Bush had the instincts of a nationalist and realist, not a neocon. His freedom agenda did not exist before the 9/11 attacks, and that agenda was undermined after 9/11 chiefly by his nationalist focus on victory and realist aversion to nation-building.

Conservative internationalism is a separate and distinct foreign policy tradition. It goes back to the earliest days of the republic and was revived most recently by Ronald Reagan. Reagan startled all of the standing American traditions as well as much of the world when he pursued an unabashed agenda of freedom, through a very risky foreign policy of military and economic rearmament, that brought the Cold War to an end and spread liberty across Europe and a good part of the rest of the world without firing a single shot or relying on centralized international institutions.

This study develops this conservative internationalist tradition. It distinguishes clearly between conservative and liberal thinking, identifies multiple types of conservatives—social, libertarian, economic, and reform conservatives, including neoconservatives—and shows how conservatives, too, are internationalists, not just realists and nationalists, but differ significantly in the kind of internationalism they envision. The study develops more enduring distinctions among the foreign policy traditions, rooted in history and logic, not in quotidian political passions stirred by recent wars, and investigates in depth the foreign policies of four American presidents—Thomas Jefferson, James Polk, Harry Truman, and Ronald Reagan—who pioneered the conservative internationalist tradition. The study fills a gaping hole in the foreign policy literature, where there is currently no tradition that emphasizes the spread of freedom, armed diplomacy, and a world republic without big government.

To understand this revived tradition, the presidential seal needs further redesign. The head of the eagle would be turned to face outward, not inward left or right, peering toward the rest of the world, not just toward America's military and diplomatic assets. Peering outward would signify the hope of freedom for the rest of the world, not just for America. Since its inception, even during the era of slavery, America has been the world's leading constitutional or liberal republic. It offered more freedom—a wider franchise, initially to white males but eventually to people of all colors and genders—and more economic opportunity—initially landownership and later entrepreneurial opportunity—to more people than any other country in the world.[3] In this sense all Americans today, both liberal and conservative, are "classical liberals." They accept the idea that individual human beings, regardless of race, religion, or gender, are free and equal and that America offers a political and economic model of society that, however imperfect, is special, indeed *exceptionalist*, which the rest of the world wants and needs.[4]

Exceptionalist does not mean perfect. At inception, America was a racist society, religiously Protestant and anti-Catholic and ethnically British and monocultural. The "classical liberal" consensus that launched the American experiment excluded slaves, women, Catholics, Mormons, Jews, and native Americans. But that consensus also included determined abolitionists, courageous suffragettes, defiant native Americans, and a haunted white male elite, including Presidents Jefferson, Polk, and Abraham Lincoln, who could not reconcile prejudice with commitments to self-government and the Declaration of Independence. These elites, split from the beginning between conservatives favoring local government and liberals favoring national government, spawned struggles that progressively widened the consensus. The Civil War ended slavery and ignited "a new birth of freedom." Jim Crow, segregation, gender, and religious bias persisted. But the consensus widened again in the twentieth century as women's suffrage, the civil rights revolution, and religious diversity broadened American freedom.

A further foreign policy tradition, the radical or revisionist tradition, rejects American exceptionalism. It argues that America remains a racist, militarist, and imperialist society, aggressive and lacking in self-restraint, morally equivalent to other great powers, and therefore not exceptionalist. This radical critique makes an important statement and is in one sense enduring. America falls short of its promise and probably always will. But if America's model for the world is bad, a model that has enabled widening freedom at home and expanding democracy and prosperity abroad, what model is better? Until revisionists come up with another alternative, other than counseling America to come home and hoping that other countries will do no worse and possibly better, the mainstream traditions promise more progress, and they disagree enough among themselves to hold America accountable.

The debate among mainstream foreign policy traditions, like that between conservatives and liberals, is part of the exceptionalist American system. Each tradition emphasizes different aspects of American freedom and tracks different dimensions of real-world events. Each has a logic and historical record of its own. If American foreign policy is to succeed, all traditions have to be involved in the debate. Thus the argument in this book does not seek to discredit liberal thinking or the established foreign policy traditions—nationalism, realism, and liberal internationalism. Just the opposite; it argues that liberals and conservatives and the four mainstream traditions, with conservative internationalism now added, need each other to continue to widen the consensus of freedom at home and around the world.

The mainstream traditions disagree about *how* not whether to make wider freedom and economic opportunity a reality. Nationalists and realists prefer to keep the focus inward, balancing commitments and resources and letting each country or alliance worry about its own freedom and growth. They believe that defending and stabilizing the international status quo—in short, peace—will do more to nurture freedom than any foreign policy that explicitly seeks to export freedom.

Internationalists, by contrast, prefer to focus outward. They want to change the status quo in favor of free countries, not just defend or stabilize it in cooperation with despots. They see the eagle of freedom gathering the rest of the world slowly under its wings. It won't be exactly American freedom that uplifts other nations, but it will be the freedom of individual independence and self-government, which believes that "all" not just American "men [people] are created equal." As Ronald Reagan once put it, "what sets America apart [is] not to remake the world in our own image, but to inspire people everywhere with a sense of their boundless possibilities."[5] And once the eagle "slips the surly bonds" of global tyranny, it tames the use of military force in world affairs, subjects it to the reciprocal constraint of democratic societies, and ushers in the democratic peace. Liberal internationalists have long dominated this tradition, clutching the olive branches of diplomacy while holding the arrows of war in reserve if diplomacy fails.

Conservative internationalists also believe that freedom is spreading. But they are more doubtful that it can spread primarily by diplomacy and international institutions while limiting the use of force to a last resort after diplomacy fails. Conservative internationalists see a world in which despots persist. Despots use force daily to stay in power at home, and they use it readily to gain power abroad. Indeed, they use force not just *after* negotiations fail but also *before* and *during* negotiations. And if they know that democracies will use force only after negotiations fail, they negotiate until they have achieved their objectives by force *outside* negotiations. Thus diplomacy without the use of force does not reduce the role of arms in world affairs; it simply enables the use of arms by despots. Despots are the source of repeated violence in world affairs, not anarchy as realists believe or diplomatic misunderstandings as liberal internationalists assume. The road to freedom is bumpy, conservatives warn. Despots do not go peacefully.

To counter the greater force field created by despots, conservative internationalists see the likelihood that military force will be needed sooner and more often than liberal internationalists expect. It will be needed *during* negotiations and *before* an attack when it is a choice, not just *after* negotiations and *in retaliation* to an attack when it is a necessity. Thus conservative internationalists are more reluctant to restrict the use of force prematurely by disarmament or by commitments to global organizations that include despots. They arm their diplomacy from the beginning, believing that the threat or use of force does not disrupt negotiations but gives them the best chance to succeed. A position of military strength influences the agenda, timing, and bargaining chips associated with negotiations, *and*, most important, shuts off aggressive alternatives that opponents might pursue outside negotiations.

The purpose of armed diplomacy, however, is not to defeat adversaries in some conventional military showdown, as some neoconservatives may envision, or to coexist with them indefinitely in some morally ambivalent status quo, as realists accept. It is rather to succeed in negotiations that move freedom forward. When armed diplomacy works best, no force is actually used. But it is a mistake to assume therefore that the arms were not necessary. Ronald Reagan's risky arms race was essential to raise the cost to the Soviet Union of options outside negotiations and make Soviet leaders pay attention to the peaceful future Reagan was offering inside negotiations—the elimination of offensive nuclear weapons and the chance to join the information age and globalized world economy. If you read what the Soviets said at the time, not even the Soviet leader Mikhail Gorbachev believed that Reagan's arms buildup did not matter.

To write a book about the use of military force in world affairs is not appealing. It would be easier and certainly more popular to write a book about eliminating the use of military force in world affairs, especially nuclear weapons, and solving all the world's contentious issues by economic sanctions, diplomatic isolation, and at most selective strikes from over the horizon, like stealth raids and drone attacks, that kill only bad guys, such as Osama Bin Laden and Anwar al-Awlaki. To think about the use of force is not only distasteful; for some people it is equivalent to advocating the use of force.

If that is the reaction to this book, so be it. It might be easier to ignore the topic of armed diplomacy but it would not be wiser—especially now. America is passing through another historical cycle in which it is pulling back from world responsibilities. Having overextended under George W. Bush, it is now coming home under Barack Obama. If, as some argue, America lacks self-restraint, it also, on occasion, indulges in it. And in each cycle of retreat, it leaves the world at its own peril. When it left Europe in 1919, World War II followed. When it left Europe again in 1945, the Cold War followed. And when it retreated from Vietnam, the Soviet Union established naval bases in Cam Ranh Bay, invaded Afghanistan, and projected Soviet military power for the first time into Africa.

As America leaves Iraq and Afghanistan, different but equally dangerous events are likely to follow. America is ending its involvements in wars, but wars themselves are not ending. Indeed, they are getting worse—witness Syria, Lebanon, and Pakistan. The country enjoys a brief and false respite of peace, but when it returns to the fight, as history predicts it will, the costs will be much higher and more blood will be shed because the United States failed to arm its diplomacy throughout.

Conservative internationalism does not advocate the use of *more* or *unrestrained* force. It advocates the *earlier* and perhaps more frequent use of *smaller* force to deter, preempt, and prevent the *later* use of much *greater* force. As George Shultz, Reagan's secretary of state, once noted, it is "better to use force when you *should* rather than when you *must*; *last* [resort] means no *other*, and by that time the level of force and the risk involved may have multiplied many times over."[6] In a world where tyrants use force congenitally, using force too late can be just as costly as using it too soon. Iraq in 2003 is thought to be a case of using force too soon. But dealing with Nazi Germany in the 1930s is a clear case of using it too late. And the failure to unseat Fidel Castro in the Bay of Pigs invasion in the early 1960s brought the world closer to the brink of nuclear Armageddon in the Cuban Missile Crisis than it has ever been before or since. Using force too soon risks unnecessary wars because preemption can never be perfectly clairvoyant. But using it too late risks bigger and more costly wars because the stakes compound in the meantime. Conservative internationalism may be a more *risky* strategy in the short run, but liberal internationalism may be the more *costly* strategy in the long run.

The presidents studied in this volume pursued foreign policies that are better explained by conservative internationalism than by any of the other traditions. They succeeded by championing the three central pillars of conservative internationalism: spread freedom disciplined by threat, always integrate the use of force and diplomacy, and be ready to compromise to respect the will of the people both at home and abroad.

Jefferson and Polk were ardent advocates of self-government, even though they were slave masters. They wanted more citizens to vote, even as they were haunted by the people to whom they denied the vote (nonwhites and women). They knew that America did not have to be perfect to be exceptionalist. Nor did it have to be preeminent. They led when America was both flawed and weak. Today America is more free and strong, but many still counsel it to hold back. They say others will do more as America does less. Perhaps, but imagine what the world might be like today if America had led "from behind." How might the Cold War have ended or terrorism after 9/11 fared? The question is not just rhetorical. After World War II, the United States deliberately created a world in which it not only accepted other powers but assisted them to become relatively stronger and wealthier. It continues to do so today—consider China. So as America grows relatively smaller, by its own choice, when will it share and to whom will it pass the baton to lead a world that remains both free and prosperous? Britain passed the baton to the United States at the end of the nineteenth century. Who will pick it up from America at the beginning of the twenty-first century?

The obvious candidate is the European Union. Helped by the United States, particularly under the leadership of Truman and Reagan, Europe is now whole and free. It supported America in Afghanistan, was there in the case of Britain in Iraq, and took the lead under France and Britain in Libya. But Europe has no independent security arm. And its history makes it hesitate to speak out confidently for freedom. So if Europe demurs, authoritarian rivals may step up. They did so before, when free nations stepped back—Wilhelmine Germany and imperial Japan. If they do so again, America remains the only champion freedom has to stay oppression in Russia, China, Venezuela, the Arab Spring, and elsewhere around the world.

The four presidents studied in this book also armed their diplomacy. They never used force without follow-up diplomacy or diplomacy without backup force. Polk escalated the threat or use of force four times against Mexico, and each time he offered Mexico a diplomatic way out. Reagan never opposed negotiations with Moscow, as some supporters believed; he opposed negotiations with Moscow from weakness. Force was essential to his diplomacy, but diplomacy in turn disciplined his use of force. Reagan knew where he wanted to go with the Soviet Union without having to defeat them militarily.

The four presidents also disciplined their use of force by prioritizing freedom where it was most consequential and likely to succeed: on the borders of existing freedom. If freedom fails there, the threat looms nearer. On the other hand, because freedom is difficult to achieve, it has the best chance to succeed in areas next to strong existing free societies. Jefferson and Polk secured self-government first on the American continent, not in Europe or Latin America. And Truman and Reagan secured freedom in Europe and East Asia (Japan and South Korea), not in Indochina or the Middle East.

Today the borders of existing freedom stretch in Europe from Turkey through Greece, Bulgaria, Romania, and Poland to the Baltic states and in Asia from India through Bangladesh, the Philippines, Indonesia, Australia, New Zealand, and Taiwan to South Korea. The greatest threats along these borders come from the major authoritarian states of Russia and China, not from rogue states and terrorists. Rogue states and terrorists pose dangers, to be sure, especially the possibility that they might collude to acquire and proliferate weapons of mass destruction. But they do not rise to the level of existential threats to the United States and the free world unless they are used, directly or indirectly, by Russia and China to undermine Western democracy and markets.

Hence the United States should think twice before it fights rogue states and terrorism in remote regions such as the Middle East and southwest Asia while it ignores or placates efforts by Russia and China to extend their influence along the central borders of free Europe and Asia. Instead it must counter Russian and Chinese efforts to expand in border regions *outside* negotiations—Russia's sphere of privileged interest in the former Soviet area and China's backstop of North Korea and claim to island territories in the Pacific—if it hopes to convince these countries to fight terrorism and proliferation in more remote regions *through* negotiations.

That does not mean that the United States does not respond vigorously to threats from whatever regions they may come. It means simply that the United States does not prioritize democracy promotion in remote regions. When threats come from areas that do not border on existing democracies, the United States defeats the threat and gets in and out as quickly as possible. It employs what I call a *ratchet strategy* to replace governments, if necessary, but not to install democracy and build nations. Then, if another attack comes, it does the same thing again, "ratcheting" local institutions toward greater openness and stability. Such a strategy retains public support, whereas the long wars in Iraq and Afghanistan exhausted public patience and preclude any return to those countries under almost any circumstances (as the long war in Vietnam did after the United States left).

It is not that nations in remote regions are unfit for democracy; it is just that they are not first in line for democracy. First in line are countries that border on existing democracies—Egypt and Jordan next to Israel more than Libya, Turkey next to European members of the North Atlantic Treaty Organization (NATO) more than Iraq, Ukraine next to Poland more than Georgia, Pakistan next to India more than Afghanistan, and Taiwan and South Korea next to Japan more than China or Southeast Asia. In these cases, an *inkblot strategy* applies—spread freedom by proximity. If circumstances allow, in Ukraine and Turkey for example, mobilize powerful trade and investment resources as well as people exchanges of all sorts to draw these countries inexorably toward existing freedom that flourishes nearby, as the European Union did to secure democracy and markets in Eastern Europe.

Without such priorities, any policy to spread freedom is Pollyannaish and quickly exceeds the limits of the public will. Conservative internationalist presidents always acted within the constraints of what the public would tolerate. Despite embargoes and wars, Jefferson and Polk left office as popular as they entered. Reagan did, too. And Truman won a smashing electoral victory in 1948 when he rallied America to defend Europe, although he lost public confidence later in Korea when he allowed General MacArthur to ignite a wider and unending war in Asia.

So what will the American public bear today? It is unlikely to support another invasion like Iraq to prevent nuclear weapons in Iran. Under present circumstances, that threat is simply not credible, especially at a time when the United States is downsizing its military to fight only one war at a time and is simultaneously pivoting its forces from the Middle East to Asia. So unless America is attacked again, its presence around the world steadily recedes. It is not just the defense pullbacks; it is also the weak American recovery and beleaguered global economy. The European Union and NATO no longer beckon to Ukraine, Turkey, and Georgia the way they did two decades ago, and Russia and China face a much less impressive America than the Soviet Union did in the 1980s. Decline of a leading power, however well-meaning, has never augured well for global peace and well-being. The declining power has less to offer in negotiations, and rising powers have more space to roam outside negotiations.

After ten years of war, America yearns for another false retreat. Can it be dissuaded before it is attacked again? Conservative internationalism says yes. It offers a middle way between a realist retreat to offshore defense, which spurns the advance of freedom, and a liberal internationalist commitment to open-ended diplomacy, which spurns the assertive use of force. It rearms American diplomacy to pursue the goals of American exceptionalism at a cost that the American public can bear. Which threats take priority and where on existing borders is freedom advanced at least cost? What are the smaller uses of force today that might prevent the larger uses of force tomorrow? And what peaceful outcomes can the United States accept by compromise inside negotiations once the adversary is precluded from achieving its objectives by force outside negotiations? These are the questions this study seeks to understand. Until now, conservative internationalism has not been treated as a distinct and deeply rooted tradition separate from that of liberal internationalism and realism. Perhaps, after this book, that will no longer be the case.

Chapter 1

What Is Conservative Internationalism?

THE SCENARIO WAS FAMILIAR. I was on my way to a major American university to give a talk on the topic of this book, "conservative internationalism." I had prepared diligently to confront the challenges that I knew I would get from my liberal colleagues. How is "conservative internationalism" different from "liberal internationalism"? Liberal internationalism is, of course, the only, all-encompassing tradition of internationalism in the study of American foreign policy. America has a mission to change the world by spreading freedom and doing so in a way that builds up international institutions and diminishes the role of force and the balance of power in world affairs. If you agree with that, you are a liberal internationalist, and if you don't, you are a realist or a nationalist. Realists believe in the balance of power to promote stability in the world but not to spread freedom, and nationalists believe that countries value their sovereignty and independence above everything else and some may never wish to be free. Conservatives are usually realists and nationalists. Hence there is no such thing as "conservative internationalism."

I intended to argue against this common view, to contend that many conservatives are also internationalists, that is, they, like liberal internationalists, believe that the world can be changed and freedom spread. However, they also believe that this can be achieved only through the realist's commitment to the use of force and the nationalist's commitment to respect and preserve national sovereignty. Conservatives, therefore, are more inclined to expect the use of force in international affairs and less sanguine about the role of centralized institutions, foreseeing a world in which nations remain armed even as they become democratic. I had identified the basic tenets of an overlooked tradition of conservative internationalism and backed up my argument with historical examples from the foreign policies of four American presidents: Thomas Jefferson, James Polk, Harry Truman, and Ronald Reagan. I entered the room brimming with confidence and gave my lecture.

Little did I expect that my principal challenge would come from a fellow conservative, not the more numerous liberal colleagues who have always dominated my intellectual surroundings.[1] As the question period opened, a skeptical conservative friend intoned: "Henry, what is so conservative about spreading freedom? Conservatives do not support such revolutionary aims; they value stability." Suddenly I realized I was as unhappy with the conventional definition of conservative as I was with the liberal definition of internationalism.

So let me begin with some definitions. They never satisfy anyone, not least because they pin labels on people and we all prefer to be considered as objective. But we can make no distinctions without definitions.[2] Definitions are not categorical; they are comparative and identify *relative* not *absolute* differences. With that caveat, what do I mean by liberal and conservative? What are the different strands of conservatism? And, finally, what do I mean by nationalist/realist and internationalist?

Liberal versus Conservative

Louis Hartz got it right when he said that all Americans are liberals.[3] He meant, pure and simple, we are all children of the Declaration of Independence, of the revolutionary idea that "all men are created equal."[4] This idea is liberal in the sense that it challenges both the traditional authorities of ancient times and the rationalist utopias of modern times. Traditional authority, rooted in religion and monarchy, restrained freedom from Roman times on and was often identified as conservative. Rationalist dogma, an outgrowth of modern times, shackled freedom to the dictates of reason and was often identified as radical. At the extreme, traditional authority led to fascism and the exaltation of myth, culture, and race; rationalist dogma led to socialism and communism and the exaltation of the intelligentsia, expertise, and the state. But the American Revolution yielded neither fascism nor socialism let alone communism. Unique among modern Western countries, the United States experienced no fascist (except fleetingly perhaps in the Old South) or socialist extremes. There was no monarchy or state church to destroy and hence no fascist or socialist utopias to build. "By and large," as Russell Kirk aptly puts it, "the American Revolution was not an innovating upheaval, but a conservative restoration of colonial prerogatives."[5] American colonialists claimed the rights they possessed as Englishmen. In that sense, the American Revolution was not a revolution but an evolution, a continuation of the experiment in self-government running from classical times to the Magna Carta, to the Glorious Revolution, to the Whig politics of the late eighteenth century.

In short the American Revolution was conservative. It built on the liberal antecedents of Western and English thought and advanced freedom incrementally, not radically. The Declaration did not liberate black slaves or white women, and it extended the franchise only to white male property owners, who comprised roughly 60 to 70 percent of the white male population at the time.[6] And the Constitution did not legislate change; in fact it did just the opposite. It divided powers and made it difficult to legislate change—hence the protracted struggle against slavery and on behalf of women's suffrage. While both advances, franchise and constitutional, went beyond what existed in England at the time, they were not radical. The American Revolution conserved as much as it changed, legitimating progress by precedent rather than by dogma. If the American academy were conservative rather than liberal, Hartz might well have written, "all Americans are conservatives."[7]

Either way, whether all Americans are liberals or conservatives, America's traditions reject political extremes. Indeed, once we define these traditions, we see that they collaborate to rule out radical outcomes. In America, liberals and conservatives compete for the center of the political spectrum, not the polar extremes.

I am well aware that by defining America's core identity in classical liberal terms, I risk marginalizing racial, religious, and cultural accounts of American history.[8] I do not discount these approaches. In chapters 4 and 5 I deal with them directly in examining the America of Jefferson and Polk. But America's traditions are neither singular nor multiple; they are both *simultaneously*.[9] The republic began with a singular set of declared beliefs in liberty and equality. Otherwise it would not have come into existence as a distinct entity. However, these singular beliefs were not shared or interpreted by all Americans in a similar way. They were multiple and contested. Otherwise the country would not have evolved. Traditions of freedom and equality struggled against traditions of racism, religious intolerance, and gender discrimination.

History provides some record of how this tug-of-war fared, at least until the present day. By any empirical measure, American society today is less racist, less Anglo-Saxon, less Protestant, and less male dominated than it was two hundred years ago. Through all the strife, including civil war, America came out a more and more liberal society, indeed the leading liberal society in the world. Something more basic than race, culture, or religion must be at work and responsible for this blossoming of freedom. And I have no difficulty arguing that that something is the core classical liberal belief in individual liberty and equality that binds all

Americans, conservatives and liberals alike. This creedal conviction not only freed slaves, emancipated women, ended Jim Crow and segregation, and embraced multiculturalism, it unites America today more than any other single factor.[10] There are continuing, even serious, racial and social issues in America, but history suggests that these fissures can be overcome if we build on the progress and do not obsess on the problems of the past or present.

How, then, do American liberals and American conservatives differ? Both embrace the liberty of the individual drawn from the Declaration and of the separation of powers affirmed by the Constitution. And both believe in equal opportunity under the law. Lincoln called this the "sheet anchor of American republicanism": "The doctrine of self-government is right—absolutely and eternally right. . . . No man is good enough to govern another man, *without that other's consent*."[11] But beyond this right of *self*-government, liberals and conservatives differ on the relative emphasis to be placed on liberty versus equality. Liberals believe that equal opportunity requires more or less equal *conditions* that affect individual ability to take advantage of equal opportunities. They then expect roughly equal conditions to yield roughly equal results. As Lyndon Johnson argued on behalf of his Great Society vision, "we seek . . . not just equality as a right and a theory but equality as a fact and equality as a result."[12] Conservatives believe that once equal opportunities exist, results depend more on individual *character* and *choice*. Natural distinctions exist among individuals in heritage, talents, and energy, and unequally endowed individuals need room to realize these differences—not just for self-fulfilling reasons but also for the benefits that ambition, creativity, and progress bring for the rest of society. As Aristotle pointed out long ago, there are two types of inequality in life: treating equal individuals unequally—that's the liberal concern—*and* treating unequal individuals equally—that's the conservative concern.[13] Liberals seek *social* justice, conservatives *individual* justice. Liberals accept less liberty to guarantee equality; conservatives accept less equality to guarantee liberty.[14]

Two further differences follow. Liberals, because they privilege equality, opt for activist government. Conservatives, because they privilege liberty, opt for limited government. Liberals fear private power that breeds inequality and embrace public power that promotes social equity; conservatives fear public power that stifles liberty and embrace private competition that stimulates individual initiative. Thus liberals support centralized institutions, both at the national level and through common institutions at the international level; conservatives support decentralized institutions, both at the state level and in the form of national sovereignty at the international level. Liberals have greater confidence in state initiatives, conservatives in civil society and free market initiatives.[15]

This preference for activist versus limited government is not about the *absolute* size of government. The size of government grows with industrialization, and at least since the days of Teddy Roosevelt, conservatives have accepted the need for more government. The issue is about the size of government *relative* to civil society. Thus the government's share of GDP, a frequent focus of contemporary conservative concern, is a signature feature of conservative thought. This concern is partly about effective or efficient government. Conservatives believe that government cannot produce wealth as efficiently as the private sector and therefore at some disproportionate size the government diminishes the capacity of civil society to support necessary social programs. But the concern over the relative size of government is also about freedom. Conservatives do not reject progressive taxation or means-tested social programs. They reject social programs that breed dependency and eviscerate individual responsibility.[16] The thing conservatives fear most is an effective government *that is large*. It is the ultimate form of monopoly. Large private sector corporations face competition; large public sector government does not.

The argument about the relative size of government is also one about the *purpose* of government and how governments are put together within society. For liberals, the purpose of government is to achieve community and solidarity; for conservatives, it is to enhance individual fulfillment and self-reliance. The liberal believes that man cannot govern himself without the help of others; it takes a village.[17] The conservative believes that if man cannot govern himself, he has no business governing others. Jefferson crafted this memorable idea in his first inaugural: "Sometimes it is said that man can not be trusted with the government of himself. Can he, then, be trusted with the government of others?"[18] To achieve their objectives, liberals favor a top-down approach to government heavy on expertise and bureaucratic direction, conservatives a bottom-up approach heavy on common sense and civil society institutions. For liberals, government compensates for the failures of civil society—prejudice, monopoly, ignorance, and intolerance. For conservatives, civil society—families, churches, markets, volunteer organizations, and personal responsibility—preempts the vices of big government—corruption, oppression, omniscience, and elitism. The liberal's focus is on the *community* of individuals (equality), which is mostly a matter of institutions and law; the conservative's focus is on the *character* of individuals (liberty), which is mostly a matter of civil society and civic virtue. The size and purpose of government will always loom larger in liberal thought, the independence and vitality of civil society in conservative thought.

A further difference between liberals and conservatives follows from their understanding of human knowledge. Liberals adopt a more rationalist and secularist understanding of human knowledge, while conservatives retain a greater philosophical and religious skepticism.[19] Liberals are generally positivists who believe that knowledge is objective and science yields universal truths, eventually about social as well as natural affairs. They look to objective academic and public policy studies to guide legislative and government intervention. Conservatives are more dubious about the objective nature of human knowledge, particularly social knowledge in which human beings study themselves. Natural scientists do not study things—planets, quarks, and so on—that they like or dislike or that have minds of their own. Social scientists, on the other hand, do study things that they like or dislike—individual leaders, political parties, labor unions, corporations, the military, and churches—and these things do have minds of their own. Thus values and uncertainty influence social knowledge much more than scientific knowledge.[20] For conservatives, policy studies evaluate objective realities from different moral and political perspectives; they do not provide uncontested scientific prescriptions.[21] The difference in the understanding of human knowledge makes liberals more optimistic and impatient about progress, conservatives more dubious and cautious.

The two traditions are different and pull against one another. In that sense partisanship is a staple of American politics. It has been around since the earliest days of the republic.[22] But partisan politics in America plays out in the middle of the political spectrum. Each side pulls the other toward the center, not toward the extremes. If either side were not there, the two traditions might go off the rails. Liberals, left alone, might succumb to the leveling influence of equal status and bureaucratic centralism, which eventually snuffs out individual liberty and meritorious competition. Social *equality* dumbs down human *quality*, as life under communism did or as programs that encourage dependency do today. Conservatives, left alone, might succumb to the authoritarian allure of individual avarice, which appropriates material or moral dominance and suppresses the liberty of others. *Liberty* becomes *license* to enslave or segregate, as life in the Old South and under Jim Crow did or as voter discrimination does today. Americans have avoided the extremes of socialism and fascism primarily because in comparison to other countries with communist and fascist pasts, American liberals and conservatives are centrist and fight over the middle.[23] Maybe we need both and should be less hasty to decry and diminish the healthy partisanship of liberal and conservative politics in America today.[24]

In advancing conservative internationalism, therefore, I am not rejecting liberal internationalism. I hope that my liberal colleagues will not reject conservative internationalism. This book would not be necessary if the American academy were more diverse and more of my colleagues had a healthy appreciation of the limits of liberalism. All of us are better-off with each other than without, and spirited and perpetual disagreement is not the evil but the essence of "scientific" scholarship.[25]

Types of Conservatives

Just as liberals and conservatives differ, so do each within their own community. Since this is a book about conservatives, what do I include under this label? Conservative thinking is as old as the classics and entails two major strands or traditions. The first stems from religion and classical philosophy. Divinity and ancestry were primary sources of wisdom in ancient societies. Religion and mystic cults illuminated what the human mind could not comprehend. Starting in Greek and Roman times, classical philosophy applied human reason to these unanswered questions. Reason searched for the good or virtuous in society while recognizing in most cases that anything that might be universal might also be divine. In this sense classical philosophy supplemented rather than supplanted religion. Classical scholarship helped structure the early texts of Western religions such as Judaism and Christianity.

But the classics and Christianity also clashed. Was reason available to all human beings or only to a select group of philosopher kings and high priests? With the marriage of Christianity and the state in ancient Byzantium, religion became political. The Catholic Church suppressed classical knowledge for centuries, well into the Middle Ages,[26] and the strand of conservative thought associated with the Church became identified with hierarchy and authority, not individual freedom—the authority of popes and monarchs. Traditional conservatism in this milieu stressed the fallibility of man and the wisdom of inherited institutions. Another revolution was needed before conservatism embraced the redemptive qualities and self-governing capacity of individual human beings.

That revolution came with the Reformation and Enlightenment and generated the second strand of modern conservative thought. The Reformation and Enlightenment liberated the human mind from the Middle Age shackles of political and religious authority. These movements produced the emancipatory or "classical liberal" themes of modern conservative thinking—individual dignity, freedom, independence, responsibility, and political equality. Individuals acquired the capability not only to rule themselves and dispose of monarchy but also to think for themselves morally and dispense with religious intermediaries. Classical liberalism eroded the traditional authority of the church and the natural aristocracy of monarchy and philosopher kings. It championed rule by consent and opposed the concentrated power of elites.[27] But it also opened up the specter of radicalism—unchecked individual appetites and unbridled human reasoning. Individuals were now free to create their own oppressive ideas and institutions.

In Europe, classical liberalism succumbed to two extremes. Continental liberalism embraced rationalist dogma and became radical. It produced the god-less, man-made utopias of socialism and communism. Continental conservatism rejected rationalism and became reactionary. It took refuge in the myths of the master-less man and fascism. In this struggle between extremes, classical liberalism in Europe all but vanished.[28] What emerged after World War II was not liberal democracy but social democracy. Today in Europe, socialist parties on the left and confessional parties on the right lock arms across an empty classical liberal center to affirm that they will never repeat the catastrophic extremes of the past. They prefer stability and solidarity, not new experiments in freedom and entrepreneurship. European parties of all stripes favor much more intrusive and centralized government than does either party in America. Indeed, Europe has no classical liberal conservative party like the Republican Party, while the Democratic Party in the United States is a *liberal* democratic party, not a *social* democratic party as is dominant across most of Europe.[29]

American liberalism and conservatism not only helped Europe vanquish fascism and communism; America revitalized its own political center in the process. Postwar American liberalism rejected the utopianism and anti-religious phobia of continental radicalism. And American conservatism never resorted to the fatalism and anti-Enlightenment rant of continental conservatism.[30]

Conservatism in America achieved a new synthesis between ancient and modern wisdom.[31] Conservatives in America today consist of four groups that combine in varying degrees the two historical strands of conservative thought: the strand of philosophy and religion (the classical conservative strand) and the strand of individualism and limited government (the classical liberal strand). Figure 1.1 juxtaposes these two dimensions. Remember: definitions are relative, not categorical; the axes are spectrums, not opposites. Some conservatives, like Thomas Jefferson, are located in the upper-middle part of the figure sharing both libertarian and classical liberal conservative views. Others, such as George W. Bush, are located in the lower-middle part sharing both traditional and reform conservative sentiments. Liberals and conservatives overlap to some extent in the upper right-hand corner of the matrix. For most liberals, however, as Figure 1.1 suggests, the matrix shifts off sharply toward the top and right. Liberals substitute group for individual identities (race, multiculturalism, etc.) and centralized for limited government along the horizontal axis, and secularism for tradition and scientific truth for reason along the vertical axis.[32]

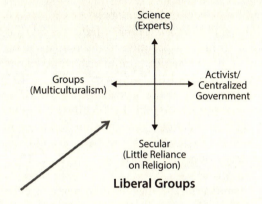

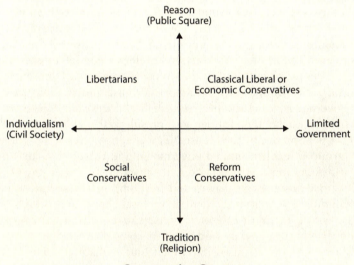

Figure 1.1. Types of conservatism.

The first group (upper left-hand box) prioritizes both individualism and reason. Known as libertarians, this group maintains that individuals are free to do whatever their own reasoning requires so long as they do not deny the right of others to do the same. Of all conservative groups, libertarians prefer the least government and the least moralizing in the public square. Their lodestar is the protection of private preferences and property, not government reform or civil society virtue.[33] They fear the infringement of civil rights by excessive domestic or foreign policy ambitions. In the past, Thomas Jefferson and James K. Polk, though majoritarian in their devotion to the public square, were also more libertarian than most American presidents. More recently, Senator Barry Goldwater, Congressman Ron Paul, and Senator Rand Paul represent this group.

A second group prioritizes individualism and religion. This group, known as traditional conservatives (or paleo-conservatives in pejorative labeling), includes today's social conservatives, the Christian (Catholic and Evangelical) and Tea Party communities that supply much of the energy of contemporary conservatism. They believe that individuals are free, to be sure, but that true freedom consists in self-restraint and must be guided by the ancient wisdom of the classics and the divine. This wisdom resides in natural rights and religion and must be nurtured by families, churches, schools, and other institutions of civil and local society.[34] Such wisdom informs government through individuals but is not itself a product of government or in need of government support. Most American social conservatives, for example, do not advocate a state church. They are not continental or European conservatives. They support multiple denominations, not a single state version. But they also believe that religion is a central pillar of civil society and prefer individuals in government who are people of faith rather than those who are not.[35] Abraham Lincoln was a person of open faith, as are social conservatives today such as former governor Mike Huckabee, Senator Rick Santorum, Congresswoman Michelle Bachmann, former vice-presidential candidate Sarah Palin, and former Speaker of the House Newt Gingrich.

A third group prioritizes limited government and reason. Unlike libertarians, it assigns important functions to government (to ensure defense and remove obstacles to growth and freedom), but these functions are sharply limited by institutional and procedural checks and balances. Known as classical liberal or economic conservatives, this group champions the open pluralist society and the free competitive marketplace. It indulges a utilitarian and majoritarian calculus—whatever serves the interests of individuals acting through competitive politics and markets serves the interests of all—and believes, like Thomas Jefferson, that ordinary people, especially with some education, can make good judgments about public policy through open debate in the public square using reason more than moral standards. Classical liberal conservatives share more in common with liberal groups than any other conservative group.[36] Calvin Coolidge and Ronald Reagan in the past and Mitt Romney and Paul Ryan today represent this group.

A fourth conservative group prioritizes limited government and religion or natural rights. This group worries that majoritarianism may destroy freedom, not to mention divided and limited government, unless it is guided by a "higher law than the Constitution," something that precedes government and trumps majority rule.[37] That something derives from religion and natural rights (rights that derive from nature), not just from reason and deliberative decision making. Not only does a higher law guide individuals in government but government now has an obligation to uphold that law if civil society threatens it. In contrast to libertarians and classical liberal conservatives, this fourth group of conservatives believes government can intervene to defend specific moral values or human rights, even against a considerable minority or indeed majority. This is the basis on which Abraham Lincoln ultimately justified the federal government's role in the Civil War, not just as a majoritarian maneuver to preserve the Union but also as a moral imperative to expand freedom. President George W. Bush, who advocated expansive government programs in education and health care, and Richard Nixon, who championed the Moral Majority and embraced policies of affirmative action and environmental protection, may be typical examples of this conservative group.[38]

This last group, known perhaps as good government or reform conservatives (progressive is usually reserved for liberals although it applied to reform-minded conservatives like Teddy Roosevelt), is as interventionist as conservative thinking gets. When some Christian extremists go further and call for government intervention to enforce religious or social views, they betray their radicalism, not their conservatism. But such conservatives are relatively few in number.[39] For most conservatives, intervention by the central government in state or local government and civil society happens only rarely, usually in times of severe disorder, is undertaken slowly and agonizingly, much the way Lincoln proceeded before issuing the Emancipation Proclamation, and always entails significant costs, such as Lincoln's suspension of habeas corpus.[40] And, in contrast to classical liberal conservatives as well as liberals more generally, reform conservatives see such intervention guided more by moral than secular reasoning.[41]

As this discussion reveals, neoconservatives are a part of the conservative community but in fact a relatively recent and small part. By origin, most of them are Democrats, not Republicans.[42] When they defected, fellow Democrats labeled them "neoconservatives" to highlight their apostasy. Neoconservatives are among the most reform-minded conservatives, least committed to limited government. They favor activist government programs to advance conservative values such as family, order, and individual responsibility. As James Piereson writes, "unlike the classical liberals and traditional conservatives, the neoconservatives were not in principle opposed to the welfare state but only to a liberal welfare state that did not uphold the ideals of family, order and community."[43] Their reform zeal sometimes opens a large gap between their objectives and

their means and makes them impatient with the cautious and more skeptical approach to social reforms and nation-building held by most conservatives.[44] Neoconservatives are also less troubled by supporting large
military forces or ambitious foreign policy goals because they do not fear
a garrison state, as libertarians and economic conservatives do.[45] They see
bigger foreign policy and bigger government complementing one another,
renewing republican zeal both at home and abroad. Neoconservatives
strongly supported Ronald Reagan and George W. Bush on foreign policy
grounds, namely opposition to America's enemies and support for Israeli
security, and were less offended than other conservatives by Reagan's
fiscal deficits and George W. Bush's big-government, compassionate, or
heroic conservatism.

The various groups account for divisions in the conservative community today. Libertarians reject social conservative efforts to legislate
issues such as abortion or gay marriage and denounce reform conservatives when their national security agendas threaten civil rights.[46] Social
conservatives question the utilitarian ethics of classical liberal conservatives, while classical liberal conservatives bemoan the conservatism of
faith espoused by social conservatives and the big-government propensities of reform conservatives.[47] And reform conservatives, including neoconservatives, lament the fear of change that afflicts social conservatives
and the lack of a purposeful agenda that characterizes classical liberal
conservatives.[48]

Internationalist versus Nationalist/Realist

How, then, do liberals and conservatives differ on foreign policy? How
should America go about representing and defending the republic abroad?
Two questions stand out. Should it seek primarily to project or protect
American values? That's the question of internationalist versus national-
ist/realist. And should it rely principally on military and economic power
or the development of international institutions? That's the question of
force versus diplomacy.

On the first question, what do I mean by internationalist? This definition is easier but perhaps more crucial. Usually conservatives are identified as realists and nationalists.[49] That means essentially that they accept
the world as it is and do not seek to change or reform it. That's what my
conservative interlocutor at the seminar was getting at. The world consists of many cultures, nations, religions, and civilizations. These cultures
are deep-seated and persisting. It is unlikely that any one political ideology, culture, or religion would ever prove acceptable to all and therefore
spread or dominate. In good conservative thinking, all cultures and hence

politics are local, and seeking agreement at a higher level inevitably diminishes diversity and freedom.

European or continental conservatism *is* mostly realist and nationalist. Realpolitik, hatched in the bowels of the Renaissance, preached accommodation to reality, not change or reform of it.[50] European realism thus accepts a morally neutral anarchy and seeks to make it stable through the exercise of the balance of power. Nationalists believe that the balance of power is mostly automatic; realists believe that it has to be managed. But both believe that, in such a world, the character of domestic regimes is immaterial.

American conservatism, however, is not European conservatism.[51] American conservatives are as committed to the quest for freedom as American liberals. The Civil War was all about the character of the domestic regime, not just about the preservation of the Union.[52] Almost all Americans absorbed this experience. To be sure, many conservatives and liberals remain nationalists and realists.[53] But they are *libertarian* nationalists or *classical* (meaning classical liberal) realists. They embrace individual freedom, not state or church privileges.

Internationalist in the American case thus refers to a commitment to spread freedom abroad and move beyond the balance of power to a world of democracies. It does not mean simply a change in the balance of power among existing democracies, which realists may favor, or a transformation of international institutions, which liberal internationalists envision. It means an increase in the number of domestic regimes that become free. Freedom as used in this study means in initial stages the recognition of individual self-worth (human rights) and self-government (voting rights). Democracy then implies further steps toward regular and fair elections between opposing parties that rotate in power, institutional checks and balances that fragment and hold power accountable, especially military power, and development of civil society that protects individual liberties—independent courts, media, markets, churches, and so on. Sophisticated scales now exist that measure how free democratic countries may be on these and other dimensions.[54]

Liberal internationalists like Woodrow Wilson champion the spread of freedom through international institutions. Conservative internationalists seek it through a more loosely organized, decentralized world of independent and competitive democratic republics. Nevertheless, Wilsonian internationalism defines a broad common ground in American foreign policy where conservative and liberal internationalists sometimes meet. It was the basis of Cold War anti-communist coalitions under Harry Truman and Ronald Reagan and of the post–Cold War consensus under Bill Clinton and George W. Bush, which enlarged democracy and expanded free trade. Among internationalists, whether liberal or conservative, the goal of foreign policy is the same: a commitment to human rights, democratic institutions, and civil society. However, the two types of internationalism differ significantly on the means to achieve this goal: the balance of power versus international institutions.

Force and Diplomacy

The major means of state action in world affairs are force and diplomacy. What is the right combination of these instruments in foreign affairs, and when is the right time to employ one or the other? Leaders have vied with one another for centuries to find the right mix and moment for using force and diplomacy.

Conservative and liberal internationalism mix force and diplomacy in different ways. Conservative internationalists use force to make diplomacy work; liberal internationalists use diplomacy to make force less necessary. These differences are not preferences. Liberal internationalists are not by nature doves or conservative internationalists hawks. The role of force derives from the way the two traditions see the world. Each emphasizes a different aspect of that world, and for this reason the two traditions exist better in competition with another than if one or the other were absent.

Liberal internationalists see the world largely in terms of interactions—communications, negotiations, interdependence, and institutions. Countries behave toward others more or less as others behave toward them. Cooperate and others are more likely to reciprocate. Threaten and others are more likely to retaliate. Misunderstandings and conflicts derive generally from the absence or breakdown of communications. Small powers and marginalized peoples suffer because they lack sufficient voice to defend and represent their interests. Great powers generate unintended consequences because they brandish weapons that threaten or disrupt negotiations. From a liberal perspective, the exclusion of small powers from negotiations and the threat, let alone use, of force by great powers during negotiations almost always exacerbate conflicts and provoke the escalation of violence. Diplomacy has to compensate for these deficiencies, to reach out to the dispossessed to assuage their isolation and to the powerful to diminish their reliance on the use of weapons.

Relative power and the character of regimes continue to matter, to be sure, but their influence attenuates as states deepen their contacts with one another and lose themselves in the labyrinth of interactions and negotiations. This labyrinth ensnares states like a flytrap. It eventually compels them to resolve their differences without resort to force or ideology. They learn the habits of compromise and mutual respect. Process influences outcomes more than the power or domestic identity of states. As one liberal internationalist scholar aptly describes it: "Conflicts will be captured and domesticated in an iron cage of multilateral rules, standards, safeguards, and dispute settlement procedures."[55]

Thus, from the liberal internationalist perspective, diplomacy takes priority; and arms control and reduction, not arms balancing, lead the way. The objective is to include everyone (poor and rich, small and large, enemies and friends), reduce arms, and spotlight collective goods or economic and global activities where interests are shared and everyone has a chance to gain. With repetition, diplomacy transforms the role of force from interstate military conflict to criminal police action; it "domesticates" world affairs. And with enough time, diplomacy inculcates pluralism and the rule of law; it "democratizes" world affairs.

For conservative internationalists, threats emerge primarily from the nature of internal regimes, not from external relationships. Countries have different domestic ideologies and cultures. Some countries are tyrannies, others are free. Tyrannies rule by force, democracies by consent. The two political systems threaten one another whether they relate extensively or not. In fact, their internal differences limit their relationships. Tyrannies use force against their own people and expect to use force in relations with democracies. Democracies practice popular consent at home and press for it in relations with tyrannies. Force in tyrannies threatens democracy; consent in democracies threatens tyranny. Diplomacy plays a role, but it can never resolve fundamental differences. Regime types limit understanding and trust, even with maximum communications.[56]

Given the differences in internal regimes, security for both regimes requires the use of force and the balance of power. Neither country can feel safe in a world in which the other exists unless it is able to defend itself. The balance of power exists not as a preference or consequence of anarchy but because internal regimes differ. Thus, as long as domestic regimes diverge, world affairs plays out more like a realist than a liberal internationalist game. Nations compete more than they cooperate.

Now comes a different twist from realism, however. For conservative internationalists, the purpose of the balance of power is not just to stabilize and perpetuate anarchy, as realists believe; it is also to narrow those differences. Why narrow the differences? Because that's the best way to reduce regime disparities, make countries feel more comfortable with one another, and end anarchy, the balancing of arms, and the threat of war. For all countries, therefore, the balance of power aims at altering the balance of regimes, not just stabilizing the balance of power. Tyrannies seek to tilt the balance toward despotism, democracies toward freedom. This dual struggle for both power and ideas creates a more contentious world than either realism or liberal internationalism envisions.[57] It also limits what diplomacy can achieve without the assertive use of force. For repeated compromise in international institutions may advance the goals of tyranny as easily as those of democracy, or it may simply make international institutions irrelevant as tyrannies use force to achieve their objectives outside these institutions. Thus while conservative internationalism, no less than liberal internationalism, foresees the day when the international system changes and democracy spreads, it arrives at that day by recognizing that force will play a greater role and that it could be more dangerous to use less force, as realism recommends, or to disarm prematurely, as liberal internationalism recommends.

The varying assessments of the use of force by liberal and conservative internationalists are not just theoretical. Political science studies show that presidents who see threats emerging from domestic regimes, like conservative internationalists, are more likely to attempt military interventions than presidents who see threats emerging from international interactions and circumstances, like realists and liberal internationalists.[58] Similarly, studies show that conservatives support the use of force in international affairs more often than liberals do. An index developed by Ole Holsti and others correlates liberal and conservative ideologies with support for the use of force versus the use of diplomacy in world affairs. A preference for the use of force is called militant internationalism (MI), for the use of diplomacy cooperative internationalism (CI). Around three-quarters of respondents who identify themselves as conservatives support militant internationalism or both militant and cooperative internationalism, while less than one-quarter of liberal respondents do.[59]

Conservative Internationalism: A Neglected Tradition

Most disagreements about U.S. foreign policy, both contemporary and historical, trace back to the distinctions outlined earlier between the *goals* of foreign policy—nationalist/realist (security) versus internationalist (spread democracy)—and the *means* of foreign policy—force versus diplomacy. These distinctions are not categories or absolutes; they are matters of relative preference or priority and they interact with one another. Security may be pursued, for example, as the best means to bring about democracy (a realist version of the democratic peace), or democracy may be pursued as the best means to bring about security (a liberal version of the democratic peace). Either way, there is a clear distinction between foreign policies in which security takes the lead and democracy follows, and foreign policies in which regime change takes the lead and security follows. The causal arrows run in opposite directions. Similarly, military force may be used to empower diplomacy (an arms race to convince an

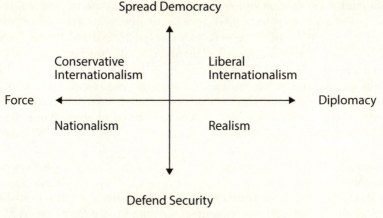

Figure 1.2. Types of foreign policy traditions.

adversary to negotiate), or diplomacy may be used to reduce the role of military force (arms control agreements to increase trust). Once again, there is a clear distinction between foreign policies that prioritize the use of arms and those that prioritize the control of arms. In the first case, arms are believed to facilitate diplomacy; in the second they are seen to impede it.

Figure 1.2 aligns the two dimensions in a single matrix. Four foreign policy traditions result: nationalism, realism, conservative internationalism, and liberal internationalism.[60] Chapter 2 compares these traditions in detail, drawing out the multiple types of each tradition and isolating the key features of the conservative internationalist tradition.[61]

Nationalists, realists, and liberal internationalists are all amply represented and explored in the American foreign policy literature. According to conventional interpretations, the founding fathers were Federalist nationalists (Alexander Hamilton, George Washington) and Republican isolationists (Thomas Jefferson); nineteenth-century presidents were nationalists (Andrew Jackson) and realists (Teddy Roosevelt); and interwar leaders were liberal internationalists (Woodrow Wilson) and conservative nationalists/isolationists (Calvin Coolidge). After World War II isolationism and nationalism receded, and the debate seesawed back and forth between realism and liberal internationalism. Generally speaking, conservative or Republican presidents were considered defensive realists—Eisenhower, Nixon, and Ford—while liberal or Democratic presidents were seen as liberal internationalists—Truman, Kennedy, Johnson, and Carter.

This postwar picture changed, however, with Ronald Reagan. He opposed both the defensive realist containment strategy of Richard Nixon and the liberal internationalist human rights campaign of Jimmy Carter. He adopted a strategy that used force or the threat of force assertively, as realists (especially offensive realists) recommend, but sought the demise of communism and the spread of democracy, as liberal internationalists advocate. However, he did not do so by strengthening international institutions, as liberal internationalists would recommend; and although he advocated the elimination of nuclear weapons, he did not champion a world of "zero nukes" unless it was accompanied by space-based defensive missile technology (strategic defense initiative [SDI]) and the sharing of that technology among adversaries. Reagan's prescriptions shocked all existing foreign policy strategists—realists, liberal internationalists, and neoconservatives.

Reagan's distinctive approach succeeded brilliantly.[62] The Cold War ended, the Soviet Union disappeared, and the United States emerged as the first preeminent "global" power in the history of the world. Even former critics now concede that Reagan was on to something.[63]

So what tradition did Reagan represent? Realists and liberal internationalists try to claim him but they do not succeed. Reagan was no cynic about the spread of freedom, as realists sometimes are. Nor was he a dove, reluctant to build up and use force, as liberal internationalists sometimes are.[64] Others conclude Reagan is unique and "has become a transcendent historical figure," not terribly relevant to contemporary debates.[65] Still others argue Reagan's foreign policy had nothing to do with ending the Cold War and wound up subsequently in the hands of Reagan imposters, the neoconservatives in the George W. Bush administration, who ran it into the ground in Iraq.[66]

This book rejects all of these conclusions. It seeks to put Reagan and recent foreign policy disputes into a broader and more lasting theoretical and historical context. Figure 1.2 reveals a glaring, indeed stunning, omission in the American foreign policy literature. There is practically no literature, historical experience, or president identified with the box in Figure 1.2 labeled conservative internationalism. That box is for all practical purposes blank. This lacuna alone justifies the present book. Logically, conservative internationalism represents an independent tradition similar to liberal internationalism in terms of goals but more akin to realism in terms of force and nationalism in terms of outcomes. It uses force and diplomacy not to defend the status quo, as realism does, or to create centralized institutions, as liberal internationalists expect, but to leave in place a world of decentralized nations, as nationalists prefer.

Neoconservatism, some may say, fills this box. But that's the equivalent of saying that one type of liberalism, such as that identified with socialist Henry Wallace, Franklin's Roosevelt's vice president during his third term, fills the liberal internationalist box. Wallace was left of Roosevelt, who was right of Woodrow Wilson, but they were all liberal internationalists. Similarly, there are varieties of conservative internationalists. Some are multilateralists and closer to liberal internationalists such as Truman, others integrate force and diplomacy tightly such as Reagan, and still others are more hawkish and unilateralist such as the neocons.

Conservatives, like liberals, occupy all the boxes in Figure 1.2. When we map domestic differences among conservatives (Figure 1.1) against foreign policy traditions (Figure 1.2), we see this further complexity. Nationalists divide between conservatives who are more traditional (Patrick Buchanan) and those who are more secular (Ron Paul and his son Rand). Realists split between conservatives who are unilateralist and offensive minded (Dick Cheney) and those who are more diplomacy oriented and defensive minded (George H. W. Bush, Henry Kissinger). Social conservatives, especially Tea Party activists and Evangelicals, tend to be more ideological and militant and support Israel unequivocally (Sarah Palin, Newt Gingrich, Michelle Bachmann, Rick Santorum), while economic conservatives emphasize markets and are more internationalist minded, especially toward free countries (Ronald Reagan, Rudy Giuliani, Mitt Romney).[67] Reform conservatives are perhaps the most internationalist oriented, promoting foreign aid (George W. Bush) and democracy (neoconservatives) aggressively.[68]

Ronald Reagan fits the conservative internationalist tradition squarely. In Reagan, the three distinguishing features of conservative internationalism came together. First, he stood unabashedly for the spread of freedom, not after an attack as in the case of George W. Bush but long before he arrived in office. He was internationalist but conservative, a classical but not social liberal, and he did not envision a free world of "sticky" or centralized international institutions. Second, he was realist but not wedded to the status quo of existing domestic regimes. He used force and diplomacy aggressively to change domestic regimes and to end, not coexist with, communism. He set priorities to spread freedom on borders where it already existed (central Europe), not in remote outposts such as Lebanon and the Middle East or Central America. And, while he amassed and threatened force, enough to scare to death his adversaries and many of his own countrymen who thought he intended war, he combined it with a plan to give his adversaries a peaceful way out, a world of defensive rather than offensive arms and economic benefits for all. Third, Reagan respected the limits of domestic politics when it came to the pursuit of freedom. Nation-building, he believed, was a long, difficult, organic process; freedom could not be grafted onto another society by force or timetables. Modernization was the best way to go, but it may or may not lead to democracy. And the people abroad and at home always knew best how far they could go to adopt or promote democracy. Reagan expected foreign cultures to find their own way to democracy and knew when to compromise to keep the American people onboard. He left office as popular as he entered, chastened only by the Iran-Contra affair, which came closest to breaking his trust with the American people.

Ideas and Reality

Is Reagan unique? This study explores that question. It conducts an historical probe to see if other presidents pursued similar approaches with resulting success. In selecting presidents, I asked which presidents did the most to advance freedom in American history—first in terms of expanding the most liberal republic in the world at the time and then in terms of defending and nurturing liberty abroad—and did so by a combination of ambitious ideological aims and assertive use of military force (Lincoln doing as much or more to deepen freedom domestically by assertive use of force). Four presidents stood out: Thomas Jefferson, James K. Polk, Harry Truman, and Ronald Reagan.[69]

Thomas Jefferson doubled the size of American territory, and although this expansion took place when America was militarily weak, he used all the military—especially naval—power that the United States had at the time and combined threats and diplomacy deftly to seize the opportunity to grab Louisiana. James Polk expanded American territory by another 60 percent. And although a slave owner like Jefferson, he expanded American freedom, namely the right of white males to own land and participate in self-government. In hindsight, as I explore in chapters 4 and 5, both Polk and Jefferson are racists. But in foresight, they inspired and led a republic that moved faster over the next hundred years to emancipate minorities than Mexico or any European power might have if they had prevailed in the western territories. Polk was also a pioneer in orchestrating a tight minuet of reciprocal interaction between force and diplomacy—a particular emphasis, as I will show, of conservative internationalist thinking.

Harry Truman expanded the cause of freedom for the first time beyond the confines of the western hemisphere and inspired the Cold War policy of militarized containment that incubated democracy in Germany, Western Europe, and Japan. Ronald Reagan then transformed Truman's containment policy into a competitive strategy to defeat, not just coexist with, the Soviet Union and bring democracy to Eastern Europe.

I then asked which tradition could best explain the approach of these presidents to foreign policy. I use the traditions as alternative interpretations (hypotheses) of how presidents think and act.[70] Do they see the world as realists or liberal internationalists and act accordingly? I trace their thinking not only in terms of prior speeches and writings but also in terms of their interplay with contemporary rivals. Jefferson, for example, is contrasted with the realist Hamilton, Polk with the realist John C. Calhoun and liberal internationalist Henry Clay, Truman with the realist George Kennan and liberal internationalist Henry Wallace, and Reagan with the realist Richard Nixon and liberal internationalist Jimmy Carter. Presidents and policymakers use traditions (theories) to make sense of the real world (facts) and to contest policy. Theory and policy are never far apart, and the traditions, as I show in chapter 2, uniquely combine theory (logic) and policy (history).

But how do I know whether traditions (ideas) or other factors are more important in determining outcomes? Ideas compete with other factors, such as presidential ambitions and personalities, domestic interests and institutions, public opinion and culture, and foreign leaders and events. My expectation is that ideas matter more than these other factors when outcomes are congruent with those ideas. It can then be argued that the ideas countered or overrode other influences that might have produced different outcomes. For example, when the Cold War ended, communism disappeared. That was a result expected and acted upon beforehand by policymakers who held conservative internationalist ideas, which spotlight changes in domestic regimes. It was not the outcome envisioned and acted upon by realists, who expected the Soviet Union to become weaker or stronger but not dismembered, or by liberal internationalists, who expected the arms race initiated by Reagan to exacerbate not end the Cold War. The end of communism was also an outcome not expected by Gorbachev, suggesting that his ideas did not track realities as well as Reagan's.[71]

It is still possible that other factors caused the same outcome, complementing or acting alongside ideas. The collapse of the Soviet economy coincided with Reagan's ideas. But which *caused* the other? If all factors caused each other, we have an overdetermined outcome. On the other hand, if ideas that are advocated today predict or conform to outcomes that occur tomorrow, and events along the way follow the logic or causal path prescribed by those ideas, I have a strong case to conclude that the ideas helped shape (cause) the outcomes. Leaders in any historical setting debate how the world works and take actions based on that thinking. They do not know if their actions will succeed or not. That is determined by the realities against which they are acting. But if leaders only *reacted* to circumstances and never *shaped* them, strategy and leadership would be meaningless. James Buchanan, Polk's secretary of state, flip-flopped repeatedly on both the Oregon and Mexican issues. In his case, other factors, such as political ambition, drove ideas, which were merely instrumental. Later, not surprisingly, Buchanan was one of the weakest presidents in American history. Successful leaders shape circumstances; they don't just react to them. They take actions today intending, on the basis of their ideas, to create circumstances tomorrow. If they succeed, they channel events and policy in certain directions and not in others. Over some medium-term time period, they create new facts that then constrain future options.

A few examples from the case studies in chapters 4–7 illustrate the point. Reagan had ideas about competing with the Soviet Union through an arms race long before he came into office. He expected to show the Soviets that they could not win, and they would then make a deal to end the military confrontation. Had Reagan accepted the "walk in the woods" proposal in 1982 to cap intermediate-range nuclear forces (INF) weapons, which almost all of his advisors recommended he do, the Soviet Union might have never faced the full military and economic pressures that followed in the years ahead and radical reformers like Gorbachev might have never come to power in the Soviet Union. Reagan's ideas told him it was too soon to compromise. He was taking actions to create added constraints on the Soviet Union, and those actions—revive the American economy and deploy Pershing missiles in Europe—had not yet been fully realized.

Similarly, if Polk had accepted earlier agreements with Mexico negotiated by Moses Beach and Nicholas Trist, he might have lost control of the war to extremists in Congress. In winter 1847 Beach negotiated the acquisition of most of what is today northern Mexico, pleasing the extreme expansionists. In fall 1847 Trist was ready to recognize the Nueces River border and give up a significant part of New Mexico in return for the acquisition of California, pleasing the opponents of the war. Facing both annexationists and peaceniks in Congress, Polk stuck with his original and intermediate position to acquire California *and* New Mexico but not the rest of Mexico. By holding fast, Polk weakened both extremes in Congress. Polk used legislation to abrogate the conventions with England to achieve a similar purpose in the Oregon expansion. Debate over that legislation for five months kept the extremists in Congress at bay while Polk counted on his original compromise proposal, offered to the British in spring 1845, and events in Oregon, such as ongoing American settlements, to move the negotiations in his direction. He created new circumstances, which helped line up events with his goals.

On the other hand, leaders cannot just *will* events to move in the direction of their ideas. Not all traditions succeed in any given setting.[72] Jefferson tried in 1805 to acquire the Floridas using the same ideas that worked successfully in 1803 to acquire Louisiana. Those ideas called for a threatened alliance with England to persuade France and its ally Spain to sell the Floridas. But these ideas did not work in 1805 because circumstances had moved in directions unfavorable to Jefferson's ideas. France had become stronger and Great Britain weaker in Europe, and Jefferson had edged closer to a war with England over impressment of American sailors. Similarly, Reagan used SDI to frighten the Soviets into negotiations, but he never converted it into a credible deterrence strategy to eliminate offensive nuclear weapons. He not only failed to eliminate strategic weapons, he confused his supporters and weakened his legacy in the process.

Exogenous events also matter. Polk failed to get an agreement with Mexico in January 1846 because a hard-line government seized power in Mexico City. He succeeded in January 1848 because a more moderate government came to power. Gorbachev clearly facilitated Reagan's agenda. To some extent such events may be endogenous. Two years of war in the case of Mexico and U.S. military and economic ascendance in the case of Reagan softened America's rivals. But events are never entirely endogenous. Otherwise, human agency would be all that mattered.

Circumstances clearly adjudicate between ideas and outcomes, but ideas (traditions) identify which events can be changed or created and which cannot. Successful leaders must read the tea leaves (facts) accurately, but they must also brew the water—create the new events—that eventually dissolves the tea leaves and brings to fruition the goals they seek. Policy never errs by reading the tea leaves, but it is also superfluous if it does only that. If human agency matters, ideas create and push events around, while later events ultimately validate some ideas but not others.

My study finds that conservative internationalism has deep historical roots, just like nationalism, realism, and liberal internationalism. If realism takes inspiration from Alexander Hamilton and Teddy Roosevelt and liberal internationalism from Woodrow Wilson, conservative internationalism draws historical lessons from Jefferson, Polk, Truman, and Reagan. The latter presidents pursued similar strategies in different circumstances with equal success. If circumstances always determined ideas, their strategies would have been different. America was a very different nation in Jefferson's and Reagan's time, both in terms of relative power and in terms of institutional ties to the international system. Yet their ideas were quite similar across nearly two centuries, and their success equally impressive. Traditions obviously matter and reflect the way in which human agency influences world events. Because of these four American presidents, freedom now stands farther forward in the world than ever before and flourishes on the borders of tyranny in Russia, China, and the Islamic world, where today's struggles between democracy and despotism continue. Should America retreat in the wake of war fatigue, the fortunes of freedom may turn again. Much depends, therefore, on the debate among the traditions in the domestic political arena.

Domestic Politics: Normal Not Partisan

Traditions are debated in the context of partisan domestic politics. They contend to shape both policy in the public arena and the legacy of policy in the academic arena. Retrieved by Reagan, conservative internationalism is a latecomer to the contemporary political and academic arenas. Like all latecomers, it is unwelcome. The other traditions consciously or unconsciously try to marginalize it. Liberal internationalists fight to retain their exclusive turf as the one tradition that promotes democracy,[73] and realists seek to conflate conservative internationalism with neoconservatism and what they perceive as the imprudent ambitions of George W. Bush.[74]

Domestic and foreign policy views are closely intertwined. For that and other reasons, I pay attention in this study to the domestic ideas of presidents and how these ideas interacted with the goals and means of their foreign policy. Liberal internationalism is frequently associated with social democracy, Franklin Roosevelt's New Deal, and a commitment after World War II to what was called "embedded liberalism."[75] Conservative internationalism is associated with classical liberal or market democracy, Calvin Coolidge's and Ronald Reagan's policies to promote individual freedom, and economic entrepreneurship.[76] Domestic preferences clearly influence foreign policy views.[77] As I explore in later chapters, Jefferson's domestic ideas of limited government dictated many of his foreign policy differences with the Federalists. Polk's domestic views on slavery are believed by many historians to have guided his expansionist foreign policy. Truman was more sensitive to moral issues in world affairs because he had deeper roots in America's religious traditions. Reagan's strong anti-communist foreign policy views derived from his limited government commitments. Foreign policy debates always include alternative visions of domestic affairs. Should global governance be limited or activist? Should it pay more attention to political ideas (democracy) or welfare (aid) issues? Should expertise (bureaucracy) or the public square (direct elections of leaders) prevail in international institutions? Should legal institutions (UN Human Rights Council) be autonomous or accountable? Presidents carry these questions in their heads when they contemplate foreign policy decisions. They are not always consistent. Richard Nixon, the archconservative foreign policy realist, promoted liberal domestic programs—welfare, affirmative action, and price controls. Bill Clinton, the liberal internationalist, pronounced the conservative end of the era of big government. But some presidents, such as the ones investigated in this study, are consistent. They often have a greater impact because consistency of ideas over time is not the hobgoblin of little minds but the hinge by which great leaders may change the course of history.

Conservative internationalism is not only relatively new to the partisan foreign policy debate, it is a tougher sell to the public than realism or liberal internationalism. This is both because it is more ambitious and pursues freedom not just stability and because it is more risky and uses or threatens force earlier and more often. Forging a domestic political consensus to support such a foreign policy is challenging. External threats and difficult times help. Anti-communism helped fuse divisions under Reagan, and economic depression and war did the same under Franklin Roosevelt. But domestic divisions and politics also play a critical role.[78]

Realists often view domestic politics as unhelpful, preventing statesmen from managing the world as only they know how to do. Liberal internationalists often yield to public opinion, reluctant to act without a broad domestic and, often, international consensus. Conservative internationalism navigates between world constraints and public opinion. Like liberal internationalism, it considers public opinion as the final arbiter of "democratic" foreign policy. Like realism, on the other hand, it challenges and leads public opinion. The trick is not to circumvent or wait on public opinion but to lead it successfully toward a consensus on an armed diplomacy to spread freedom. If public opinion does not follow, no leadership can be considered legitimate even if it succeeds. In short, no American leader can justify a foreign policy undertaking purely on the basis of geopolitics (realist) or ideology (liberal internationalist), arguing that history will vindicate that undertaking even if the people don't support it. Authority in foreign affairs, as in domestic affairs, comes from the consent of the people, and the people render the ultimate verdict of history.

But leadership today, it is often argued, has become more difficult because foreign policy has become more polarized. From the early 1940s until the early 1970s, party politics stopped at the water's edge. Democrats (Roosevelt, Truman, Kennedy, and Johnson) and Republicans (Eisenhower and Nixon) supported a forward-based policy to defeat fascism and contain the Soviet Union. The underlying logic of containment was a combination of liberal internationalism (freedom) and realism (deterrence). But the Truman-inspired postwar consensus, while conservative compared to Roosevelt's liberal internationalism, ended in Vietnam. When Reagan forged a new foreign policy consensus in the early 1980s, he did so on a more explicitly conservative rather than liberal internationalist or realist basis.

The emergence of a conservative internationalist foreign policy tradition mirrored the growing strength of conservative forces in American domestic politics. For a half century, from 1933 to 1981, Democrats controlled both houses of Congress except for two years in each branch (1946–48 in the House and 1952–54 in the Senate). One-party control of Congress embedded liberal internationalist and realist thinking deep into the consciousness and infrastructure of American foreign policy.[79] Under Reagan, Republicans finally recaptured the Senate in 1981 (until 1986) and, under Newt Gingrich, took back the House of Representatives in 1994 after more than sixty years of Democratic control. The parties began to compete with one another more evenly, vying for the vital center of American politics and foreign policy. Since then, it can reasonably be argued, politics and foreign policy have returned to normal, not become more partisan or polarized.[80] Washington think tanks and cable media outlets are better balanced. There is a vital conservative foreign policy (and domestic policy) voice, not just a liberal one.

A more balanced contest for the center of American politics necessarily means more volatility in American foreign policy. Republicans and Democrats are not only normally partisan about foreign policy; they also hold different views about world affairs.[81] Normal partisanship is reflected in election data.[82] Since the early 1950s, when a Democrat sits in the White House, Republicans disapprove of American foreign policy more than Democrats; and when a Republican holds the presidency, Democrats disapprove of foreign policy more than Republicans. But there is also evidence, as in the readiness to use force (MI/CI index referred to earlier), that Democrats and Republicans hold different preferences about the goals and means of foreign policy.[83] When a Democrat occupies the White House, Republicans expect U.S. foreign policy to depend too much on diplomacy and international institutions and too little on force and counterbalancing, such that threats build up in the world and America's security suffers. Similarly, when a Republican holds the presidency, Democrats expect U.S. foreign policy to rely too much on force and too little on diplomacy, increasing terrorism and unilateralism and consequently causing America's standing in the world to fall.

Pendulum Swings

As a result, American foreign policy swings like a pendulum between different administrations and between realist phases of retrenchment and liberal internationalist phases of overreach. This debate, I hope to show, suffers from the empty box in Figure 1.2, the absence of a fourth tradition of conservative internationalism. This tradition offers a *logical* stopping point between realism and liberal internationalism and may under certain circumstances attract enough bipartisan support to offer a *political* stopping point to moderate cycling. With lots of fluctuation, this is essentially what happened during the "long peace" of the Cold War. As chapters 6 and 7 show, Presidents Truman and Reagan initiated and ended the Cold War by applying similar tenets of conservative internationalism.

After Reagan's more assertive or conservative internationalist use of American power, George H. W. Bush swung American policy decisively back toward realist goals (world order) and liberal internationalist means (the UN). In the first Persian Gulf War, he led the only universally authorized military operation in history, validating Wilson's concept of collective security.[84] Then, just as decisively, Bill Clinton pulled back from the UN. He abandoned assertive multilateralism, withdrew American forces from the UN intervention in Somalia, and stemmed violence in Bosnia and Kosovo through the realist mechanism of NATO not the liberal internationalist institution of the UN.

George W. Bush pushed the pendulum even further away from the UN and multilateralism. After 9/11, Bush eschewed both liberal international (UN) and realist (NATO) solutions and waged two wars in Afghanistan and Iraq, more or less on a nationalist basis. His desire before 9/11 for a more "humble" foreign policy, his quip after 9/11 to "bring them on," his overriding concern with weapons of mass destruction in Iraq, his preference for coalitions of the willing rather than alliances, and his disdain for nation-building all echoed nationalist and realist sentiments in American history. But then victory and the overthrow of central governments in Afghanistan and Iraq left him with the need to put domestic institutions in their place, and he pivoted to a liberal internationalist agenda to promote democracy and nation-building in the Middle East and south Asia.

In President Barack Obama's first term, U.S. foreign policy swung back again toward realism. Obama downplayed the promotion of democracy, called for a more pragmatic realist approach to security interests, and pledged to use force only after the United States is attacked (Bin Laden and Afghanistan), an international consensus exists (Libya), or nonmilitary sanctions fail (potentially Iran). Obama widened diplomatic initiatives, scaled back supporting military forces, cut defense budgets, and supervised a weak economic recovery. If he had priorities, they seemed to be domestic and social, the instincts of a *nationalist* rather than realist or liberal internationalist, albeit a *liberal* nationalist.

The most successful American presidents stopped the pendulum to achieve novel and lasting contributions to American security and ideals. Franklin Roosevelt ended American isolationism by committing the United States to the UN, a liberal internationalist project, with the Security Council great power veto, a realist instrument. And when the UN system failed, Truman forged the regional institutions of NATO, the U.S.-Japan Security Treaty, Bretton Woods, and the European Union (EU) by combining realist force with democratic institutions. Ronald Reagan then ended the Cold War by challenging the Soviet Union to a realist arms race while offering it a liberal internationalist future of arms reductions and globalization.

Plan of the Book

Will the pendulum swing again in 2013 and beyond? External events may be a factor. Another incident like 9/11 would refocus America's attention on security and military affairs. But it matters even then how presidents interpret external events. George W. Bush's conservative nationalism spiked his response to 9/11 with warlike sentiments and no doubt blinded him to nation-building aspects after the wars ended. Obama's liberal nationalism makes it hard for him to see the potential dangers that may be accumulating from American weakness abroad.[85] Hence it is worthwhile to study the interpretations of presidents who managed to stop the pendulum.

Chapter 2 defines the conventional traditions in American foreign policy and outlines the tenets of the neglected tradition of conservative internationalism. Chapter 3 uses the traditions to examine and compare the foreign policies of recent presidents. Chapters 4–7 apply the traditions to explore empirically the foreign policies of Jefferson, Polk, Truman, and Reagan. Finally, the conclusion distills the lessons of these historical cases and applies the tenets of the neglected tradition of conservative internationalism to a strategy for American foreign policy in the years ahead. I do not claim that conservative internationalism supplants the other traditions or offers a better approach to these traditions under all circumstances. But I do claim that this tradition deserves equal treatment and consideration in a foreign policy debate that otherwise cycles repetitively between realist restraint and liberal internationalist exuberance.

Chapter 2

America's Foreign Policy Traditions

U.S. FOREIGN POLICY TRADITIONS have been shaped by both events and intellectual ideas. There are four main traditions, as established in the previous chapter: nationalism, realism, conservative internationalism, and liberal internationalism.[1] Each tradition in turn has variations. Isolationism is a minimalist version of nationalism; imperialism is a maximalist version of realism. In addition, the isolationist, nationalist, and realist traditions have liberal and conservative variants, just like the internationalist tradition. There are pacifist (liberal) and nativist (conservative) isolationists, social (liberal) and militant (conservative) nationalists, and defensive (liberal) and offensive (conservative) realists.

As I explain in chapter 1, the four-part matrix of Figure 1.2 does not accommodate radical or revisionist critiques of American foreign policy. To the extent that these critiques indict American liberal values as baneful for American foreign policy, they reflect realist or nationalist sentiments and can be accommodated within those traditions.[2] To the extent that they chastise American society and capitalism as irredeemably evil, they fall outside the purview of my study.[3]

Each main tradition identifies with a particular historical period and reflects a coherent logic about the way the world works. Some studies label the traditions by the presidents they are associated with—Jeffersonian for isolationism, Jacksonian for nationalism, Hamiltonian for realism, and Wilsonian for liberal internationalism.[4] But then too much rests on how the analyst interprets a particular president. Was Jefferson a liberal internationalist, a liberal isolationist, or, as I argue, a conservative internationalist? Moreover, some traditions originate in time before the presidents with whom they are identified. The nineteenth-century missionary zeal to spread Christianity or Western civilization (later democracy) predates Woodrow Wilson, for example.

What is more enduring about these traditions is the underlying logic they employ. They represent a limited number of possible ways to think about American foreign policy. Hence I opt for analytical labels such as nationalism, realism, and internationalism and call them traditions to suggest their origins in both logic and history.[5]

The minimal nationalist or isolationist tradition derives from George Washington's famous farewell address and influenced the new republic's early relationships with Europe. The normal nationalist tradition emerges with Andrew Jackson and the relentless expansion of the new republic across the continent. The realist tradition picks up with Theodore Roosevelt and the eruption of the United States on the world scene as a global power. A later more defensive- or diplomacy-focused version appears under President Nixon. The liberal internationalist tradition identifies with Woodrow Wilson and Franklin Roosevelt and America's leadership to spread democracy through the development of universal international institutions. More recently, a conservative internationalist tradition emerged in the foreign policy of Ronald Reagan, which defends and spreads democracy through a diplomacy leveraged by military strength and alliances rather than by universal institutions. According to this study, Thomas Jefferson, James K. Polk, and Harry Truman also represent earlier examples of conservative internationalism.

The traditions differ intellectually as well as historically. They place different relative emphasis on three factors that cause or shape foreign policy and international outcomes: ideas, international institutions, and military power.[6]

Isolationists emphasize American "exceptionalism" and the causal role of ideas and example. They attribute less influence to activist diplomacy and the balance of power. Nationalists see America as "unique" or different but not exceptionalist with relevance for other nations. They place less emphasis on ideas and more on power, generally limited to defense and the western hemisphere.

Realists see America as "ordinary" (another culture or civilization) not exceptionalist (a superior civilization perhaps, as Teddy Roosevelt believed, but not applicable to other countries) and stress the need to manage the balance of power not only in the western but in other hemispheres as well (Europe and Asia). Ideas have less influence, and power matters more, including the aggregation of power through certain types of international institutions such as alliances. Offensive realists are imperialists always interested in more power. They pursue hegemony because more power, they believe, provides more security. Defensive realists are generally satisfied with equal power. They pursue equilibrium because more power, they believe, only produces counterbalancing and therefore less security.

Table 2.1
U.S. Foreign Policy Traditions: Ideas, Institutions, and Power

Foreign Policy Traditions	Variations	Historical Examples	Causal Emphasis on Ideas, Institutions, and Power by Each Tradition		
			Domestic Ideas/ Identity	International Institutions	Use of Force/Balance of Power
Nationalism	Minimalist (Isolationists)	George Washington, Alexander Hamilton	Exceptionalist by example only	Wary of alliances, non-entanglement	Commerce increasingly important factor
	Militant (Hemispheric)	Andrew Jackson	Unique but not exceptionalist	Selective alliances if controlled unilaterally	Vigorous use of force after attack but not for wider balance of power
Realism	Defensive (Equilibrium)	Richard Nixon	Different but not important in foreign policy	Institutions reflect underlying great power balance	Use of force for global balance of power
	Offensive (Hegemony)	Theodore Roosevelt	Superior culture and Western civilization	Imperialism	Dominance is best distribution of power
Liberal Internationalism		Woodrow Wilson, Franklin Roosevelt	Exceptionalist and important in foreign policy	Interdependence and universal institutions play causal role	Force is a last resort and eventually a past resort
Conservative Internationalism		Thomas Jefferson, James K. Polk, Harry S. Truman, Ronald Reagan	Exceptionalist and important in foreign policy	National sovereignty persists with cooperation mainly among sister democratic republics	Force and balance of power remain requirements of freedom

Note: The classification of presidents in this table reflects conventional wisdom, except for the presidents identified in this study with the conservative internationalism tradition. Jefferson is conventionally classified as a liberal isolationist or internationalist, Polk as an offensive realist (imperialist), Truman as a liberal internationalist, and Reagan as a realist or liberal internationalist.

Liberal internationalists consider America "exceptionalist," like isolationists, but place less emphasis on power and more on universal international institutions. They advocate collective security, pooling military power globally, and eventually substituting for the balance of power by settling disputes peacefully through "domestic-like" mechanisms of compromise and the rule of law. Conservative internationalists also consider America exceptionalist but place more emphasis on the use of force to defend and spread democracy because international institutions, which include nondemocracies, may have little interest in democracy or the rule of democratic law.

Table 2-1 summarizes the historical and intellectual differences of the various traditions. The rest of this chapter clearly differentiates among the mainstream traditions, something the literature muddles as traditions vie for supremacy, and then shows precisely how conservative internationalism compares to and differs from the more familiar traditions.

Nationalism

Nationalism comes in two forms: a minimalist neo-isolationism and a more common militant brand emphasizing border or hemispheric (neighborhood) defense.

Isolationism, some may argue, is no longer a relevant foreign policy tradition. Given America's preeminent power in the world today, the United States is unlikely to withdraw into isolationism. But isolationism was a factor, as late as the middle of the twentieth century, and neo-isolationism is evident today in the growing public fatigue with war and disillusionment with globalization.[7] This foreign policy tradition could easily reassert itself in the years ahead.

Isolationists focus overridingly on America's domestic political experiment. Liberal isolationists stress American values;[8] conservative isolationists stress American folk culture, robustness, and self-reliance.[9] Foreign involvement threatens this domestic experiment either by fostering a large military and industrial establishment (garrison state), as liberal isolationists fear, or by contaminating American culture, as conservative isolationists fear.

For liberal isolationists, an active foreign policy directly undermines "republican" domestic policies. It encourages large military forces and powerful multinational industrial corporations, both of which militate against individual liberty. Moreover, foreign involvement is unnecessary. The Old World is largely benign and nonthreatening, populated by diverse cultures that have a right to coexist and may even offer some desirable features that America could emulate. To engage actively in this world is imperialist because every country has something to contribute and a right to be left alone. Liberal isolationists are often pacifists, not out of a fear of war but out of a conviction that meddling abroad leads to war.

Conversely, conservative neo-isolationists see the Old World as alien and threatening, populated by despots that disdain the New World of liberty. To engage actively in this Old World risks making America more like the despots. It also opens up America to excessive immigration and baleful influences of foreign cultures.

Thus, for isolationists on the right and left, the world remains what it is, either benign or hostile, and there is little that America can or should do abroad that can make the world a better place. The best course is to stay home and nurture America's uniqueness, as conservative isolationists emphasize, and respect other nations, as liberal isolationists advocate. America inhabits a "delightful spot."[10] As George Washington intoned, "why forego the advantages of so peculiar a situation? Why quit our own to stand upon foreign ground?"[11] The United States enjoys "strategic immunity."[12] It is the only major power in history that is separated from other regions by two large oceans and does not confront another great power in its own region.[13]

Hence America defends itself best by simply reassuring other nations that it will not threaten them if they do not threaten America's core interests. Core interests constitute at a minimum the defense of American borders and at a maximum the defense of neighboring sea lanes in the Caribbean and western hemisphere. Security is strictly "homeland" security; beyond that the United States has no stake in world affairs. Private groups can engage in low-risk, limited interventions abroad to assist democracy and free trade, but the government has no strategic interests in these activities.

Isolationism developed its roots in the early American republic when foreign policy was mostly about domestic policy. Should the government be centralized or decentralized, aristocratic or republican? America's first political parties coalesced around these issues. Alexander Hamilton, the first treasury secretary under the new constitution, led the Federalist Party, which favored a strong central government that not only assumed debts of the old Confederation but also exercised executive authorities similar in some ways to the emerging constitutional monarchy in England. Thomas Jefferson, the first secretary of state and third president of the new republic, led the Republican Party, which feared a British-style monarchy in America and supported decentralized government rooted in local and populist sentiments, similar to the objectives but not the later outcomes of the French Revolution.

These domestic preferences dictated foreign policy views. Hamilton championed the Jay Treaty, which aligned the United States with Great Britain, while Jefferson supported the old Revolutionary War alliance with France. George Washington's famous warning in his farewell address "to steer clear of foreign alliances" was a message to both emerging parties not to let foreign interests intrude in the creation of the new American republic. It was less a warning against American involvement in the world, where America had already formed alliances with France during the Revolutionary War, than counsel against giving foreigners the opportunity to meddle in America's domestic affairs, disrupting the great American experiment of liberty. John Adams, the second president of the United States, referred to foreign influences as "one of the most baneful foes of Republican government."[14] For isolationists then, as for neo-isolationists today, American foreign policy is all about domestic politics, and American exceptionalism cannot be championed but only corrupted by foreign policy.

The second form of nationalism, militant nationalism, is less absorbed by domestic affairs and more focused on national defense and power. Militant nationalists believe that the world is unlikely to be influenced significantly by the American domestic experiment, either through example or coercion. America is neither "good, bad nor ugly."[15] If it is exceptionalist, its exceptionalism is unique and not particularly relevant to other countries and foreign affairs. Self-determination, which leaves other nations free to choose their own politics, trumps "self-government" or liberty, which some countries may choose not to adopt. But the United States is vulnerable, like all other nations. Thus the overriding imperative of foreign policy for all nations is defense. The United States must spare no effort to defend its independence. And because other countries will do the same, there is little need for the United States to help them by entering into alliances or foreign adventures.[16]

For nationalists, foreign conflicts are self-balancing. Nations in other regions are historically divided and will balance each other off long before foreign conflicts reach America's shores. Look at how the former Soviet Union almost singlehandedly defeated Nazi Germany in World War II. As militant nationalists argue, the United States benefited in that war by delaying the establishment of a second front and would have benefited even more if it had stayed out of the war altogether.[17] So, unlike realists (see the next section), nationalists see no need to balance power actively around the world in order to defend the United States at home.

On the other hand, if America is attacked, nationalists strike back fiercely and destroy the enemy. They carry the revolutionary banner "Don't Tread on Me." In war, national honor, not just national interest, is at stake. And there is only one possible outcome in war: victory. Once the enemy is defeated, however, nationalists are eager to return home. There is nothing more to do. Nation-building is not for Americans or any nation, except at home. As I discuss in chapter 3, George W. Bush reflected all of these sentiments after the 9/11 attacks.

Nationalists also reject an active foreign policy to engage the world economically. Conservative nationalists see trade as potentially entangling or directly detrimental to national welfare. Protectionism is preferable. American jobs are not for export.[18] Other conservative and more liberal nationalists embrace free trade but see no need to defend it by protecting sea lanes or allies. Countries trade because they benefit from it, and they will continue to do so as long as the benefits outweigh the costs. When they stop and decide to block free trade, they hurt themselves as much as others. No American foreign policy should try to rescue them from their own folly.

Alliances are admissible to defend the country, but they should not be considered permanent. And they remain acceptable only as long as the United States needs or dominates these institutions to advance its independent national interests.[19]

The nationalist grand strategy emerged in the course of the nineteenth century. The Monroe Doctrine in 1823 elevated the idea of being wary of foreign intervention in American affairs to a grand strategy embracing the entire hemisphere. The United States would accept no interference by European or Asian powers in the western hemisphere. It rejected any new colonies, transfer of colonies, or reversion of independent states to colonial status in the region. Foreign powers were put on notice that the United States would defend the status quo in the rest of the hemisphere.

At the same time, the United States was free to alter that status quo for its own purposes and expand the American republic across the continent "from sea to shining sea." The Monroe Doctrine proscribed foreign but not U.S. expansion in the hemisphere. America embraced expansionism with no explicit commitments to alliances or the spread of democracy. To be sure, the United States benefited from the implicit protection of the British navy. But before issuing the Monroe Doctrine, the United States rejected a British offer to act jointly. Unlike the realist tradition, the nationalist tradition shuns alliances unless they are absolutely necessary for survival.

Nationalist logic also eschews any special obligations of American foreign policy to export liberty. Unlike the liberal and conservative internationalist traditions, nationalists expand to defend security and promote development (the justification for seizing Indian lands) but never to spread democracy. Liberty may be desirable but culture is more determining. Nationalists are champions of assimilation and are charged at times with anti-immigration sentiments bordering on racism and xenophobia.

Andrew Jackson epitomized the nationalist tradition. He championed union rather than exceptionalism and feared secession more than he savored expansion.[20] Nevertheless, he seized Indian lands, and his successors, under the banner of manifest destiny, annexed the Texas, Mexican, and Oregon territories. And they did so without alliances; indeed, they expanded precisely to preempt the possibility of alliances that might have followed if European powers had colonized parts of the continent. For nationalists, foreign policy is not dangerous or irrelevant, as it is for neo-isolationists; it is essential to keep foreign interference at bay. But it is also not imperialist. Nationalists extol the exploitation of new frontiers, such as space and missile defense, but they aim to fulfill national needs, not to gain international advantage.

Lincoln and the Civil War resolved the legal contradiction in America's domestic identity that made the early republic so vulnerable and foreign intervention so dangerous. Freedom eclipsed slavery, and the country's domestic identity emerged stronger and became an increasing influence in American foreign policy. The "new birth of freedom" ignited a massive economic boom and hoisted the specter of America's commitment to support freedom abroad. The next three traditions bring these two elements of power and identity to the fore. Realism trumpets American power in world affairs, and liberal and conservative internationalism showcase American ideals.

Realism

Realists, like nationalists, consider American ideas to be no better or worse than those of other nations but, unlike nationalists, have less confidence in the automatic operation of the balance of power to defend national interests. Other countries may falter in their own defense, and global alliances may be necessary to head off power imbalances. International diplomacy, including some international institutions such as concerts of great powers, may be needed to ensure stability and peace.[21]

Realists differ on the configuration of power that best ensures peace. Offensive realists or primacists believe that hegemony stabilizes and that America, which is now a hegemon, should strive to maintain that status.[22] Defensive realists or power balancers believe that equilibrium stabilizes and urge the United States to anticipate and accommodate counterbalancing challenges, whether from democracies (e.g., Europe and Japan) or nondemocracies (China, Russia, Venezuela, Iran, etc.).[23]

Realists are skeptical about the role of values in international affairs. Classical or American realists, such as George Kennan, champion free societies at home, but they do not advocate the export of freedom, except by example and emulation. Even then, expanding freedom is not an explicit objective of foreign policy. Kennan foresaw already in 1948 that America's best defense against the Soviet Union was to strengthen its own free society. And although he advocated military containment (balancing) to deter the Soviet Union, he never expected that freedom would or should spread to the Soviet Union. He predicted instead that when communism mellowed, the Soviet Union would return to its Russian roots and authoritarian nationalist traditions. He opposed any injection of ideology in foreign policy and rejected every extension of containment against the Soviet Union (Korea, Vietnam, etc.) that went beyond the central defense perimeter of central Europe. He anticipated the end of the Cold War, which other realists like Henry Kissinger, who were more skeptical of domestic institutions, did not. But neither Kennan nor Kissinger expected a Boris Yeltsin to emerge and seek to liberalize Russia in the 1990s, albeit with limited success.

Realists support free trade and institutional cooperation among allies but not with adversaries.[24] Trade brings mutual benefits, as liberal nationalists believe, but it also distributes those benefits unequally. While it makes sense to strengthen allies under certain circumstances, it makes no sense to strengthen adversaries under any circumstances.[25] And while some cooperation is possible among great powers, relying too heavily on universal institutions undercuts American foreign policy. For example, the UN Security Council gives a veto to Russia and China. These countries are not current adversaries, but they may become such, and no American grand strategy can commit itself to work primarily or exclusively through international institutions that formally depend upon the goodwill of other powerful states.

Although realism was evident from the beginning of the republic (e.g., the Revolutionary War alliance with France), President Teddy Roosevelt first celebrated the assertive role of American military power. A Rough Rider in Cuba during the Spanish-American War, he savored the sacrifice as well as glory of the warrior. He understood that the United States was a rising power and deserved a place at the table of great powers. He sent the "Great White Fleet," the American navy, around the world and engineered the breakaway of Panama from Colombia to acquire and construct the Panama Canal. His intervention in the Russo-Japanese War heralded America's diplomatic debut. Altogether, he exuded the virility of the new American power.

The United States did not form any alliances immediately and resisted standing alliances until the end of World War II. Yet, informally, it forged a closer and closer association with the world power it was replacing, Great Britain. This alignment proved critical to allied victory in World War I. And after the war, Roosevelt and other realists, such as Henry Cabot Lodge, sought to maintain the Anglo-American alignment to defend Europe against a resurgent Germany.[26] They supported concrete alliance commitments and strongly opposed the League of Nations as a substitute for the balance of power.

During the Cold War, Richard Nixon and his national security sidekick, Henry Kissinger, personified the defensive realist tradition in relations with the Soviet Union. They threw a blanket of détente over containment to stabilize postwar superpower relations. Arms control agreements codified Soviet nuclear parity, while political agreements recognized two Germanys and established formal spheres of influence in central Europe. Defensive realism expected that coexistence would go on forever and that neither side would dominate externally or change significantly internally.[27]

But the Soviet Union did change internally, and the United States did dominate externally. Communism and the Soviet Union expired, and Western democracy spread its tentacles across Europe and much of the rest of the world. Now offensive realism seized the moment. It foresaw the potential for long-term stability on the basis of American preeminence, not a return to the balance of power. Pentagon officials, scholars, and commentators outlined the strategy of primacy and preemption to preserve American hegemony and secure lasting peace.[28]

Realism does not exclude values. Teddy Roosevelt promoted the values of Western civilization and embraced America's role as its standard-bearer in the Philippines.[29] Nixon and Kissinger pursued détente to secure Western values in the Cold War. And primacists such as Samuel Huntington and Charles Krauthammer advocated a "democratic" not a despotic realism.[30] But values for realists apply at home, not abroad. They are relative, not absolute. American realists may consider Western values superior, but they do not consider them universal.[31]

Liberal Internationalism

Unlike nationalists and realists, liberal internationalists give priority to ideas and institutions over power (Table 2-1). They see international institutions playing a key role to "domesticate" international politics and eventually to shift the international system from warlike military balances to domestic-like peaceful settlement of disputes enforced by police actions.[32] They envision the day when the liberal experiment prevails across the globe, but they believe the world gets to that point best not by relying on example or the balance of power but by including all nations whether democratic or not in universal international institutions that regularize procedures and the rule of law for resolving international disputes peacefully without the use of force.

Treating countries equally, whether free or not, through a process of open diplomacy and trade is the best way to encourage them over the long term to become free and democratic. Liberal internationalists do not eschew the use of force; they use it vigorously to defend America. Nevertheless, they insist that the use of force beyond America's borders can be done legitimately only by universal institutions. In contrast to realists, they see force not as a normal instrument of global diplomacy but as an instrument of "last" resort after diplomacy has failed. In the long run, they hope that the use of national military force becomes a "past" resort as war is "domesticated" through international institutions and transformed from military balances to police enforcement.

Woodrow Wilson is the author and lodestar of the liberal internationalist grand strategy. He designed the first permanent universal institution to manage the affairs of war and peace. The League of Nations relied on collective security and the common pooling of force rather than national security and the balance of power. Wilson was quite self-conscious about what he was doing. He was committing the United States to the security of the world, not just to the security of the United States.[33]

The League of Nations called upon all nations to consider threats anywhere to be threats everywhere and to act unanimously to deter such threats, first by automatic and collective economic sanctions and then if necessary by the combined military forces of the world. Peace was indivisible and therefore universal. But that did not mean war had to be universal. Because the world's combined military forces would overwhelm any recalcitrant country, it was unlikely these forces would have to be deployed. In fact, the world could promote disarmament and still marshal sufficient military forces to prevail against offending states. The League promised to do for international politics what national governments had done for domestic politics—reduce matters of war and peace to police actions.

The liberal internationalist grand strategy relies on the exercise of cooperation to instill the habit of cooperation. Nations working together daily in international institutions get used to one another and increasingly empathize, maybe even identify, with one another. Agreement among them becomes easier and easier. An unspoken expectation is that such cooperation will engender values of pluralism, tolerance, and eventually democracy. These values are not prerequisites of cooperation but consequences of cooperation over time. The best way to spread democracy, therefore, is to treat all states equally and cooperatively, whether they are initially democratic or not. Except in dire emergencies, such as direct attack, liberal internationalists are not only comfortable working with nondemocracies but eager to do so. Cooperation is sticky, and the hope is that nondemocracies will get stuck in the glue of democracy. A consolidation of democratic authority at the international level then ushers in the democratic peace.

The League went too far for American nationalists and realists. A combination of them, led by William Borah and Henry Cabot Lodge, defeated it. But the League idea did not fade away. It was resurrected after the war in the UN, this time with Roosevelt's realist twist. The UN Security Council operated on the principle of unanimity of great powers, not the unanimity of all powers, great and small. This feature improved the odds that the great powers would join the UN and, if they agreed, ensure its success. That hope was quickly eclipsed by the Cold War. But briefly when the Cold War ended in 1990–91, the UN functioned as it was envisioned by liberal internationalists. Wilson's idea was no longer utopian. The UN went to war to expel Iraq from its conquest of Kuwait. But with Kuwaiti sovereignty restored, the UN did not go to Baghdad to remove Saddam Hussein. Collective security served the status quo: to restore sovereignty, not to change regimes or spread democracy. Eventually disagreement over how to deal with Iraq almost destroyed the UN. Since 1991 it has never functioned again as a collective security institution.

Conservative Internationalism

Conservative internationalists consider America as an exceptionalist and indeed leading liberal society, and they advocate the defense and promotion of democracy in other countries. But they do so primarily by competitive means rather than international institutions. They anticipate a world in which nondemocracies persist and use force to oppress their own citizens and gain advantage against other nations. They doubt that these countries can be persuaded to disarm primarily by institutional processes. Hence opportunities must be sought to shift the balance of power against these countries, to make the international system less hospitable to despotism, and to tilt the balance of power toward freedom by, among other things, assisting internal regime change toward democracy.

Even as more countries become democratic, however, conservative internationalists do not see a centralized role for international government. Whether domestically or internationally, conservatives prefer smaller government. They fear too much international government and despotism (hierarchy) as much as liberal internationalists fear too little international government and war (anarchy).[34] And while conservative internationalists believe in free trade, they do not believe, as many liberal internationalists and isolationists do, that commerce and wealth eventually eliminate dangerous political differences. Even among democ-

Table 2.2
Main Features and Tenets of Conservative Internationalism

Three Main Features	*Eleven Tenets*
I. Pursue Disciplined Goal of Freedom	Tenet 1: spread freedom
	Tenet 2: focus first on material, not ideological, threats
	Tenet 3: tilt the balance of power toward freedom
	Tenet 4: prioritize promotion of freedom on borders of existing free countries
II. Integrate Force, Diplomacy, Sovereignty, and Markets	Tenet 5: arm diplomacy with force
	Tenet 6: discipline military force with diplomacy and compromise
	Tenet 7: connect force and diplomacy to democratic national, not universal international, institutions
	Tenet 8: open international markets and borders
III. Observe Constraints of Domestic Politics	Tenet 9: don't expect international markets to liberalize domestic politics
	Tenet 10: respect cultural and national diversity
	Tenet 11: always trust the people to decide

racies or within a world of all democracies, the threat of dominant and potentially oppressive power remains.[35] The best defenses against this threat are the strong advocacy of freedom, a decentralized world system, and the right to bear arms. Just as conservatives embrace the Second Amendment, conservative internationalists foresee a world in which even democratic states retain independent national defense forces as the ultimate protection against the potential tyranny of the majority.

We can summarize the conservative internationalist tradition in eleven tenets. To simplify I subsume them under the three main features: the disciplined goal of freedom (tenets 1–4); the means of integrating force and diplomacy (5–8); and the constraints of domestic politics and culture (tenets 9–11). Table 2-2 abbreviates this breakdown. Along the way, I clarify how conservative internationalism overlaps and differs from the other traditions as well as from neoconservatism.

Pursue Disciplined Goal of Freedom

TENET 1: THE GOAL OF AMERICAN FOREIGN POLICY IS
TO SPREAD FREEDOM, NAMELY REGIME CHANGE.

First, the goal of conservative internationalist foreign policy is to expand freedom and ultimately increase the number of democratic, constitutional, and republican governments in the world community. In this respect, conservative internationalism shares the same goal as liberal internationalism. American conservatives are classical liberals. They believe in individual liberty and do not defend authoritarian institutions as traditional or European conservatives did. Like Jefferson, they embrace John Locke and Adam Smith.[36] But they are not social liberals. Along with Friedrich Hayek and William F. Buckley, conservatives stand "athwart history yelling Stop . . ." when the ideas of economic and social equality threaten individual liberty.[37]

Thus conservative internationalists give priority to liberty over equality and work to free countries from tyranny *before* they recognize these countries as equal partners in international diplomacy. Jefferson and Polk were unequivocal about expanding liberty, even if it involved slavery and imperialism, because they believed that liberty would eventually expand and bring greater equality. By contrast, liberal internationalists give priority to equality over liberty and grant all nations equal status in international institutions, whether free or not, because they believe that treating countries equally will eventually bring them around to embrace the values of liberty. For conservative internationalists, legitimacy in foreign affairs derives from free countries making decisions independently or working together through decentralized institutions; for liberal internationalists, legitimacy derives from all countries, free or not, participating and voting equally in universal international organizations. For conservatives, the *character* of countries matters more, whether free or not; for liberals the *conditions* under which these countries operate matter more, whether they are weak or strong and participate or not.[38]

TENET 2: FOCUS INITIALLY ON MATERIAL,
GEOPOLITICAL THREATS, NOT IDEOLOGY.

Second, conservative internationalism focuses *initially* on material, not ideological, threats. In this respect, it shares much with realism. Both focus on immediate dangers and seek to avoid the pursuit of military might or "noble purpose" for its own sake. On this point, conservative internationalists are defensive, not offensive, realists (imperialists). They are also not liberal internationalists or neocons. Poverty (Somalia) or oppression (Iran) abroad is not enough to trigger intervention. There has to be a physical effect on the United States, as realists require, such as terrorist attacks or oil supply disruptions. In the absence of such significant material threats, most conservative internationalists do not see ambitious foreign agendas as necessary to bolster domestic morale.[39]

The difficulty today is that material threats to freedom are more difficult to perceive. Terrorism is an "immanent" rather than "imminent" threat. It is present potentially everywhere in sleeper cells and illegal arms networks, but it is not actually visible anywhere until it happens. Such a threat blurs conventional distinctions among threats: threats that are known and can be "contained"; threats that are emerging (e.g., gathering on the border) and can be "preempted"; and threats that are not yet visible (terrorist sleeper cells) but may arise in the future and can only be "prevented." Compared to Soviet missiles, the terrorist threat is more of an emerging and invisible than known threat. To cope with such a threat, conservative internationalists expect to have to take more preemptive or preventive actions, not as matters of choice but of necessity. Neither containment, which realists recommend, nor treating terrorism as crime, which liberal internationalists recommend, is likely to suffice. But neither is terrorism necessarily as big a threat as communism was.[40] Soviet Marxism embraced science and modernization; jihadist terrorism does not. It throttles science with religious dogma. As long as that is the case, terrorism engenders more fervor than might. But terrorism is clearly a more uncertain threat, which makes it more difficult to ascertain and hence more prone to exaggerate or underestimate.

TENET 3: SEIZE RELATED OPPORTUNITIES TO TILT THE BALANCE OF POWER TOWARD FREEDOM.

Third, while conservative internationalism starts with threat and geopolitics, it does not end there, as realism does. Conservative internationalism not only defends the status quo but also seizes related and incremental opportunities to expand freedom. It seeks, in short, to tilt the balance of power toward freedom. Force is useful not just to deter despots but also to weaken them. Liberal internationalists almost always consider the use of force as provocative and detrimental to diplomacy. Hence it is a last resort after diplomacy fails. Conservative internationalists see force as necessary before and during diplomacy, closing off alternatives to negotiations and thereby incentivizing opponents to negotiate seriously.

Jefferson, Polk, Truman, and Reagan all positioned forces to narrow their opponent's options and to tilt negotiations toward change that favored freedom. Perhaps the best example is Ronald Reagan's policy toward Eastern Europe. As I recount in chapter 7, Reagan established early on that his objective was not just to stabilize Eastern Europe, as containment and realists prescribed, but to revoke the Yalta compromise and set Eastern Europe free. This policy did not call for direct intervention to "roll back" communism. Rather, it called for a patient but armed diplomacy, which Reagan visualized already in the 1960s. The United States would challenge and outcompete the Soviet Union across a broad front of economic, military, and ideological capabilities. Had Reagan stopped with geopolitics and not raised the costs of competition, Gorbachev might have never climbed to the top of Russia's leadership scaffold. Russia needed him to meet Reagan's deeper challenge of technological change and domestic reform, not merely to stabilize Russia's military position in Eastern Europe.

TENET 4: PRIORITIZE OPPORTUNITIES TO SPREAD FREEDOM ON THE BORDERS OF EXISTING FREEDOM.

Fourth, although conservative internationalism is more ambitious than realism, it is prudent in picking its targets to expand freedom. *It sets priorities.* It perceives the incremental opportunities to push back tyranny primarily on the periphery or borders of existing free societies. The vast majority and certainly the most important and enduring cases of the spread of democracy in recent decades have occurred in proximity to existing free countries: Eastern Europe, Mexico, and South Korea/Taiwan. In these cases the costs are lower, and the presence of nearby democracies increases the chances of success. The pursuit of freedom everywhere at once is not only unrealistic; it is radical, not conservative.[41]

Truman succeeded ultimately because he gave priority to freedom in Western Europe where after World War II nearby democracies were strong (principally Britain, the Low Countries, and Scandinavia) but other countries were still fascist (Germany recently, and Spain, Portugal, and Greece at the time) or vulnerable to communism (France and Italy). He did not get distracted by Eastern Europe, Latin America, or the Middle East, where democratic influences were much weaker. The one exception, which cost him his popularity, was the Korean War. But that war was initiated because the United States did not take actions in Asia to deter Soviet aggression and Stalin backed North Korea's invasion of South Korea. Had Truman not created NATO, the same might have happened in Western Europe. Reagan also set clear priorities. He concentrated on freedom in Eastern Europe, bordered in the 1980s by a fully free and united Western Europe. He avoided costly military ventures in Lebanon and elsewhere, not because he was reluctant to use force, as some liberal internationalists argue who try to claim Reagan for their own, but because he wanted to keep his powder dry for the principal showdown in central Europe.[42]

Both Truman and Reagan accepted the reality that the United States might have to cooperate with nondemocratic governments in lower-priority areas to secure freedom in higher-priority areas. Both strongly supported alliances with authoritarian governments outside the European area (and in Truman's case inside Europe when fascist countries such as Spain and Portugal were included in NATO). Critics often attack such cooperation as hypocrisy or condescension, considering some countries less capable of democracy than others. But it is neither. It is setting priorities and recognizing the limitations of both resources and public will to support the end of tyranny everywhere at once. In theory, democracy is universal. But in practice, it succeeds best near where it currently exists. Conservative internationalism encourages an "inkblot" rather than "leapfrog" strategy to expand freedom, oozing freedom outward from existing free countries rather than leaping over despotic regions to build democracy in countries remote from free ones.[43]

Integrate Force, Diplomacy, Sovereignty, and Markets

TENET 5: ALWAYS ARM DIPLOMACY WITH FORCE, AND
EXPECT TO USE SMALLER FORCE EARLIER AND MORE OFTEN
RATHER THAN LARGER FORCE LATER AS A LAST RESORT.

Fifth, conservative internationalism expects to use more force to achieve its objectives than does realism or liberal internationalism. The reasons are simple. The objective of expanding freedom is more ambitious than preserving stability favored by realists, and the obstacle to expanding freedom is authoritarian and oppressive states that already use force against their own people and thus are more likely to use it against other countries. As Ronald Reagan once put it pointedly: "if [oppressive countries] treat their own people this way, why would they treat us any differently?" Rather than being willing to compromise with other nations in international institutions, as liberal internationalists expect, authoritarian countries are more likely to engage in a contest of strength to settle issues outside the arena of negotiations or tip those negotiations decisively in their favor.

For conservative internationalists, therefore, force is not a "last" resort that kicks in only after diplomacy and economic sanctions fail; it is a parallel resort that accompanies diplomacy at every step of the way—demonstrating resolve, creating policy options, narrowing the maneuvering room of authoritarian opponents outside negotiations, and providing bargaining chips to conclude favorable deals inside negotiations. Conservative internationalists remind us, for example, that in 2002 there was no diplomatic option of UN inspectors in Iraq searching for weapons of mass destruction. The use of force had both eliminated and then reinserted that option. Saddam Hussein kicked out UN inspectors in 1998, and U.S. policy at that time did nothing other than economic sanctions and random cruise missile attacks to put the inspectors back in. The assembly of massive U.S. forces in the Persian Gulf in fall 2002 to invade Iraq finally pressured Hussein to readmit UN inspectors. A forceful military action created a diplomatic option, and now it could be debated how long the inspectors should be given to find weapons of mass destruction before a UN-blessed military force invaded.[44]

By contrast, liberal internationalists aspire to domesticate world affairs and therefore play down the use of military force. They do not reject the use of force. Far from it—Wilson and Roosevelt, preeminent liberal internationalists, led America into war. But that was after the United States was attacked. Liberal internationalists are consistently more reluctant than conservative internationalists to use force to deter, preempt, or prevent the use of force *before* an attack. In the Cold War, they preferred détente, smaller defense budgets, arms control, and economic sanctions.[45] Their commitment to multilateralism, while laudable for other reasons, further limited the opportunities to use force. If everyone has to agree before force can be used, it is not likely to be used very often. Liberal internationalists seek over time to reduce the salience and use of military force in international affairs. As in Wilson's League, they hope to pool military power and then reduce reliance on it by disarmament and common diplomatic and economic sanctions. If some states still resist peaceful solutions, multilateral economic sanctions will isolate and bring them to heel. The use of traditional military force is a last resort and then only with the consent and thus legitimacy of the international community as a whole.

TENET 6: ALWAYS DISCIPLINE MILITARY FORCE
WITH DIPLOMACY AND COMPROMISE.

Sixth, as prevalent as force is in a conservative internationalist perspective, it does not substitute for diplomacy. The best force can do is win the war; it cannot win the peace. As Napoleon once quipped, "you can do anything with bayonets except sit on them." Defeated governments and countries have to be reconstructed. And that is a diplomatic task. In this regard conservative internationalism shares a lot with defensive realism. Don't start wars until you have figured out how to end them.[46] But defensive realists fight and end wars to preserve peace; conservative internationalists fight and end wars to spread democracy.

Conservative internationalists also stress the continuous interaction of force and diplomacy. They time diplomatic initiatives to coincide with maximum military strength, and they delay diplomatic initiatives until they have mobilized adequate military strength. As I show in chapter 7, Ronald Reagan did not change his strategy from his first term to the second. He used the arms buildup in the first term to enable the arms reductions in his second. Conservative internationalists also know when to cash in military gains to advance diplomatic ones, to take half a loaf today and come back for the rest tomorrow. They give adversaries a way to surmount disagreements, not just surrender. Reagan did that with Gorbachev and disappointed some neoconservatives. The best example, perhaps, as I will show, is President Polk. He was a master at marrying the use of force and diplomacy. And he accepted compromises even when they were negotiated by disaffected envoys.[47] By settling the Mexican War quickly on terms he outlined before the war, he outmaneuvered the extremists and avoided a long-term occupation or annexation of all of Mexico.

TENET 7: CONNECT FORCE AND DIPLOMACY TO DEMOCRATIC NATIONAL, NOT UNIVERSAL INTERNATIONAL, INSTITUTIONS.

Seventh, diplomacy for conservative internationalists does not mean primarily international institutions. Conservative internationalism is not enthusiastic about international institutions even if—or one might say especially if—these institutions are effective. Conservative internationalism is just that, conservative. It advocates a "small government" version of internationalism and thus does not favor, like liberal internationalism, the construction of an ever larger world community of centralized organizations and rules. Indeed, it seeks to reduce the size of government in world affairs both by democratizing national regimes that are authoritarian and by building up nongovernmental aspects of global civil society such as markets, religious institutions, and charitable associations. Nor is conservative internationalism indifferent to the big-government or garrison-state implications of foreign policies that stretch national resources beyond justifiable limits. Conservatives are patriots, not jingoists. They are naturally suspicious of governments and favor self-reliance and civil society institutions. They take their cue from Thomas Jefferson that the first and best government is self-government and that national and international governments should do only what local and national governments cannot do.

TENET 8: OPEN INTERNATIONAL MARKETS AND BORDERS.

Eighth, the best international tool for inching freedom forward not only in bordering but also in distant regions is economic engagement or the free movement of goods, capital, and people. Both conservative and liberal internationalists agree on freer trade. But liberal internationalists see a greater need to restrain private markets through international regulations and foreign aid. They worry that private greed and inequality may threaten public freedoms. Conservative internationalists have more confidence in markets and self-reliant individuals. They expect private actors to rely more on virtue, religion, and other moral foundations of civil society to exercise self-restraint and worry that government bureaucracies, because they operate in a less competitive environment, may become corrupt and unaccountable.[48] Conservatives see development not as a process of helping others, full stop, but of helping others help themselves. Free trade encourages self-help; aid creates dependency, not only among recipients but also among donors who become addicted to compassion and paternalism.

Observe Constraints of Domestic Politics

TENET 9: DON'T EXPECT INTERNATIONAL MARKETS TO LIBERALIZE DOMESTIC POLITICS; ALWAYS KEEP YOUR POWDER DRY.

Ninth, unlike liberal internationalists, conservative internationalists do not expect economic liberalization to lead automatically to political liberalization. Liberal internationalists believe that powerful historical forces, particularly the forces of modernization, abet the march of freedom. The world will eventually become free and force obsolete if prosperity spreads far enough and diplomacy is patient enough. Conservative internationalists are not so sure. They support modernization and globalization but worry that political freedom may not follow ineluctably from economic development. History has gone backward as well as forward and in all cases only with struggle.[49]

Ideologies shape human behavior more deeply than material forces, and cultures do not disappear with prosperity. Fascist regimes in Germany and Japan modernized but did not liberalize. And China today is modernizing but not democratizing. Hence it is essential to maintain the role of force in case modernization only produces stronger adversaries. What is more, modernization brings new challenges and conflicts. It secularizes and potentially weakens the spiritual and moral character of some societies, while it uproots traditions, especially religious traditions, and radicalizes the politics of other societies. Conservative internationalists see a continuing role for religion in modern life; liberal internationalists tend to see secularism prevailing.

TENET 10: RESPECT CULTURAL AND NATIONAL DIVERSITY.

Tenth, democracy for conservative internationalism is not only a local process; it is also a difficult one. Culture constrains democracy. It may

not make democracy permanently impossible in some countries, as nationalists and some realists argue, but it does make democratic development messier and more imperfect than liberal internationalists may wish.
Democracy has three key pillars: regular (not one-time) and fair elections
in which opposing parties compete and rotate in power; elected authorities that control the major bureaucracies, especially the military; and an
independent civil society that protects free speech, private property, and
impartial justice. Electoral democracies are often vulnerable and weak.
They are referred to as illiberal democracies.[50] Liberal democracies are
more durable and depend on the development of the other two pillars of
government: transparency and civil society. None of these pillars is easy
to construct.[51] Best then to target democracy where it is most likely to
succeed, namely on the border of existing democracies, and make compromises with authoritarian realities in other places as long as it advances
the cause of freedom in priority areas.

TENET 11: ALWAYS TRUST THE PEOPLE TO DETERMINE THE LIMITS OF BOTH FREEDOM AND FORCE.

Eleventh, and perhaps most important, conservative internationalism accepts the premise that public opinion in free societies is the final arbiter of America's foreign policy choices. It does not assume that foreign
policy elites know best, as some realists do, or that public opinion will
always accept a policy as long as it succeeds, as some nationalists or
neoconservatives may contend. But unlike liberal internationalism, it is
also not willing to wait for unanimous consent to act. No democracy requires unanimity to act domestically, and no community of democracies,
let alone institutions that include both democracies and nondemocracies,
should require unanimity to act internationally.

However, because conservative internationalism expects to use force
more aggressively than do either realists or liberal internationalists, it
faces a tougher sell with public opinion. In democracies, public support
for war is limited, especially if casualties persist or the threat is less visible, as in the case of terrorism. That reluctance, most would probably
agree, is a good thing. If the people decide against force, after hearing
all the arguments in the public square, elites should get out of the way,
even if the decision of the public proves to be wrong. In a democracy,
the majority has a right to be wrong, more so than individual leaders or
elites. The public debate, of course, goes on continuously. So elites may
try anew to persuade the public. But in the end, for better or worse, the
people decide. Hence, when faced with persisting public opposition either
at home or among democratic countries, conservative internationalism is
more willing to scale back or terminate interventions. It looks for part-

nerships with other democracies and finds it incongruous to persist in spreading freedom to new democracies if that policy is resisted by majority opinion in the old democracies.

Competing Traditions

All of America's grand strategy traditions remain in play today. Neo-isolationists and nationalists vigorously oppose America's wars in Iraq and Afghanistan. Liberal nationalists find wars wasteful and destructive of domestic freedom and harmony.[52] Conservative nationalists bristle at breaches of American borders by terrorists and illegal immigrants and call for a national security strategy that secures the borders and deploys national missile defenses rather than stationing forces abroad. Realists see the need to balance power in the Middle East and South Asia but prefer to do it by a counterterrorism strategy that deters adversaries by naval forces and offshore missile strikes to destroy terrorist camps after they attack the United States.[53]

Conservative internationalists advocate more aggressive strategies to counter terrorism. Some, especially neocons, support a counterinsurgency approach (COIN) that employs boots on the ground to defeat terrorism and vigorous nation-building to train local forces and governments.[54] Other conservative internationalists prefer to prioritize objectives, limit ambitions in remote areas, and retain the capacity to intervene in future situations with public support. Liberal internationalists decry the unilateralism and militarism of conservative internationalists and work to restore American standing and leadership in international institutions.[55] They prioritize international collaboration to curb nuclear proliferation, fight global warming, convert to green energy sources, and tame failed capitalist financial markets.

In the next chapter, we look at how the foreign policy traditions have influenced recent presidents. America may be moving incrementally toward a new kind of nationalism that it has not known since the interwar years. George W. Bush and Barack Obama, for all of their internationalist rhetoric, are arguably both nationalists at heart, more interested in a "humble" foreign policy and domestic reforms of "compassionate conservatism" and "hope and change." A globalized world may not let them have their preferences, as George W. Bush clearly experienced. But the nationalist drift could still mean a globalized world without a pilot, or with a very different pilot—perhaps China. This prospect sharpens our interest in the conservative internationalist tradition, which offers a logical resting spot between realism and internationalism and might moderate the political cycling toward a new nationalism.

Chapter 3

Recent Presidents
THE PENDULUM SWINGS

AMERICAN FOREIGN POLICY swings like a pendulum. It promotes realist goals of stability at one time, liberal internationalist goals of spreading democracy at another. And it rotates realist means of military power with liberal internationalist instruments of multilateralism. Often it swings between presidents. But sometimes it swings in the middle of the same presidency.[1]

George H. W. Bush pursued realist goals of stability with liberal internationalist means of multilateralism. He feared instability in the former Soviet Union more than he sought democratic change. But he made the instrument of UN collective security work for the first time in history—to restore Kuwaiti sovereignty (world order), however, not to promote regime change (democracy) in Iraq.

Bill Clinton reversed H. W.'s preferences. He pursued liberal internationalist goals of democratic enlargement and economic engagement, and after a brief flirtation with liberal internationalist means of "assertive multilateralism," revived realist means, NATO not the UN, to quell ethnic violence in Bosnia and Kosovo.

George W. Bush swung U.S. foreign policy back again toward realist if not nationalist goals and means. Unlike his father, he championed a more humble foreign policy and, when attacked on 9/11, reacted like a nationalist and rejected both UN and NATO help. Once he overthrew governments in Kabul and Baghdad, however, he invoked the goals of liberal internationalism, to spread democracy, but he never embraced the means, to build nations and strengthen international institutions. He ended his presidency with another nationalist military surge in Iraq.

Barack Obama reversed U.S. goals yet again. He backed off W.'s rhetoric to spread democracy and urged more realist and pragmatic goals.

He set about to end two wars in Iraq and Afghanistan and, like the early W., sought a more modest American role—as one aide put it, "leading from behind." But, unlike W., he employed mostly diplomatic or liberal internationalist means to restore American standing and credibility in the world.[2] Although he escalated force in specific areas—drone attacks, special operations, such as the one that killed Osama Bin Laden, and cyber warfare—he downplayed military means overall, cutting defense budgets, ending the two-war military defense guidance, and anticipating a relative decline in America's role in the world. Although the jury is still out, Obama, like Bush, may be more of a nationalist than a realist or internationalist. He wants to transform American society at home and expects, as a liberal nationalist, that as America steps back from world affairs, other countries will step forward to help sustain global peace and prosperity.

Notice that none of these presidents since Reagan combined the goals of liberal internationalism with the means of realism in an explicit strategy to advance freedom in the world. None was a conservative internationalist. Clinton came closest, but he led with liberal internationalist sentiments and adopted realist means only when the Balkan crisis forced him to. He exploited Reagan's legacy of enlarging freedom but never identified with military force, the way Reagan did. He navigated the American ship of state in a decade when American power unexpectedly predominated.

Pendulum Swings

The swings between administrations are in part a consequence of partisanship. Republicans and Democrats cycle in the presidency. Under partisan pressures, they pull U.S. foreign policy back and forth, distancing themselves from their predecessor. Bush's "Anything But Clinton" (ABC) and Obama's "Anything But Bush" (ABB) become election mantra. As Figure 3.1 shows, this pattern is well established going back to the Eisenhower years.[3] When a Democrat occupies the White House, Republicans disproportionately see U.S. foreign policy growing weaker. When a Republican sits in the White House, Democrats disproportionately see U.S. standing growing weaker. Apparently the pendulum swings because each party, for partisan reasons, rejects the foreign policy of the incumbent party and seeks to reverse that foreign policy when it comes into office.

But the swings also reflect something deeper than party partisanship: different domestic and foreign policy worldviews.[4] Americans react to world events not only out of partisan sentiments but also out of domestic

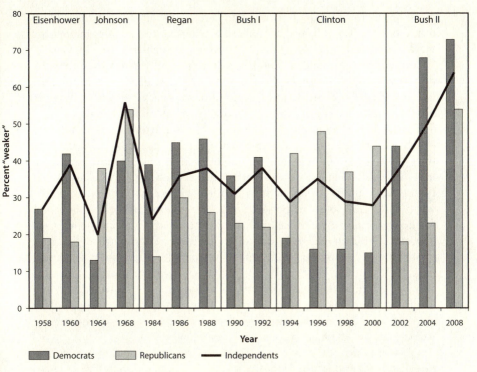

Figure 3.1. Believe U.S. position in the world has grown weaker in the past year.

ideological and foreign policy convictions. As I note in chapter 1, liberals and conservatives emphasize different aspects of America's domestic ideology, while nationalists, realists, and internationalists think differently about the goals and means of American foreign policy. Based on the MI/CI index (see chapter 1), conservatives are three times more likely than liberals to support the use of force in foreign affairs, while liberals are twice as likely as conservatives to support diplomatic means.[5] Similarly liberals are also more likely to favor internationalist goals, while conservatives prefer nationalist or realist ones. As Miroslav Nincic and Jennifer Ramos conclude, "where international affairs are concerned, conservatives are more likely to favor self-regarding ends and punitive means, with liberals more apt to endorse other-regarding objectives and policy means based on positive incentives."[6]

Parties compete with different foreign policy ideas. They represent alternative schools of thought, which assess American foreign policy from the standpoint of different logics and experiences. Democrats tend to be more liberal internationalist (Wilson, Carter) and defensive realist (Clinton, Obama); Republicans, too, may be defensive realist (Nixon, George H. W. Bush) but otherwise tend to be more nationalist (Hoover, George W. Bush), offensive realist (Teddy Roosevelt), and conservative internationalist (Reagan). At times the differences are minimal, for example, between George H. W. Bush and Clinton. But at other times the differences are greater, for example, between George W. Bush and Obama.

Thus, when a Democrat is in the White House, Republicans disapprove of that administration for domestic ideological reasons but also because they distrust the administration's judgment in foreign affairs, expecting it to depend too much on diplomacy and too little on force, such that threats build up in the world and America's reputation suffers. Similarly, when a Republican is in power, Democrats oppose the administration for domestic ideological reasons but also because in foreign policy they expect Republican leaders to use too much force and too little diplomacy, provoking terrorism, and anti-Americanism and consequently damaging America's standing abroad. If ideas drive American responses to foreign affairs, how presidents and their party supporters see the world may tell us more about the swings in American foreign policy than simple party identification. Indeed it suggests that partisanship has an intellectual as well as reactive dimension.

Presidents do not look at the world exclusively in either realist, nationalist, or liberal internationalist ways. They mix and match their views depending on circumstances and even shift their views within their own term in office. When that happens, it usually reflects the impact of events. Presidents move from one foreign policy strategy to another because events compel them. Clinton is a case in point. George W. Bush is perhaps another. In this instance, their ideas have less influence on outcomes. Circumstances drive events, not ideas. On the other hand, presidents that maintain a consistent strategy or approach to foreign policy throughout their presidency have a better chance to alter events and move them in their direction. Ronald Reagan did this with considerable success, moving U.S.-Soviet relations from arms competition to arms reductions. George W. Bush had less success, although he salvaged the situation in Iraq at the end of his presidency by a unilateralist military surge that was consistent with his initial nationalist instincts and went against all prevailing opinions and circumstances. In the intermediate time frame, it succeeded nonetheless.

Liberal internationalist presidents, like Obama, define objectives ambitiously but economize on means and hope that history is on their side. The more history helps, the less they have to do, sliding from liberal internationalist to liberal nationalist. They see the world primarily as a set of common problems, such as proliferation and climate change, which countries have to solve together. Because the problems are common, everyone must be included. And because interests are congruent, everyone benefits in the end. There are no winners and losers. No one is a troublemaker and everyone is satisfied once the problem is solved.

Realist and conservative nationalist presidents, like George W. Bush, define America's foreign policy goals more modestly, but they extol the means of national strength to pursue them and often, especially after being attacked, mobilize more force than is needed and less follow-up than is required. They see the world primarily as a competition for power in which players compete and seek to checkmate one another. Interests are not congruent, there are winners and losers, and outcomes are zero sum (what one gains, the other loses). Countries pursue different agendas and do not share a common vision of the kind of world they prefer.

All presidents, like all participants in world affairs, have a core preference. They don't just react to events. They are never pure pragmatists. Even if they claim to be, as Obama does, their pragmatism betrays an implicit worldview, a process-dominated world in which the need to respond to external events overrides conflicting ideologies and competitive intrigues. Pragmatists are reactive, not proactive. They respond to problems, not political agendas. No one causes the problems; no one is a troublemaker. And, by solving the problems, everyone expects to be satisfied.

Thus liberal internationalists or nationalists and some defensive realists are less prepared for a world in which more countries are troublemakers. They are more likely to minimize threats and miss cumulative shifts that alter the balance of material and moral competition among states. Conversely, conservative nationalists and offensive realists are less prepared for a world in which countries cooperate more than they compete. They are more likely to exaggerate threats and create a more troublesome world than may actually exist. They miss opportunities to solve common problems.

Recent presidents have all failed to stop the pendulum swings between liberalist internationalist and realist/nationalist approaches. They either cooperated too much or competed too vigorously. They found no happy equilibrium between the goals of foreign policy—how ambitious foreign policy should be—and the means—the match between ambitions and resources. A closer look at the experiences of George H. W. Bush, Bill Clinton, George W. Bush, and Barack Obama illustrates this proposition. These experiences suggest the American foreign policy debate may benefit from an intermediate approach, conservative internationalism, which combines the strengths of liberal internationalism, realism, and nationalism and might achieve under certain circumstances a better match of goals and capabilities.[7]

George H. W. Bush

George H. W. Bush was a realist in terms of foreign policy goals and a liberal internationalist in terms of means. He and his national security advisor, Brent Scowcroft, worried more about stability than change. They feared that the breakup of the Soviet Union might unleash violence in Eastern Europe far worse than the continued existence of a communist Soviet Union. Thus, when he came into office, Bush initiated a pause in U.S.-Soviet relations.[8] Reagan's push for democracy was going too fast, and Bush wanted more time to assess the implications of independence for Eastern Europe. He and his advisors saw the violence that was raging across the former Yugoslavia and feared the same might occur in Eastern Europe. When Bush visited Ukraine in summer 1991, he warned the protestors: "Americans will not support those who seek independence in order to replace a far-off tyranny with a local despotism."[9] Ironically, this trip took place just a few weeks before the attempted coup in Moscow that effectively unseated Mikhail Gorbachev and sealed the fate of the Soviet Union.

Not all members of his cabinet felt the same way. Defense Secretary Richard Cheney, for example, supported more ambitious goals. He saw the demise of the Soviet Union as an opportunity to increase American power. Even "if democracy fails" in the fifteen Soviet republics, Cheney argued, "we're better off if they're small."[10] Cheney was not a neocon tilting toward the spread of freedom. He was a more aggressive, offensive realist who seeks ever greater power because more power always means more security.[11] Offensive realists point out how much safer the United States is in the western hemisphere because it is hegemonic. By contrast, other states in other regions are less safe because they face rivals—Britain, France, and Russia in Europe and Japan and China in Asia.

While pursuing realist goals, the elder Bush nevertheless employed liberal internationalist means, organizing the first universal collective security operation in the history of international affairs. On August 2, 1990, Iraq invaded Kuwait. The UN immediately condemned the attack, and the United States, supported by all the great powers, mobilized a UN-flagged military force to eject Iraq from Kuwait. George H. W. Bush declared to Congress a "new world order . . . in which the rule of law supplants the rule of the jungle." He told the UN General Assembly: "This is a new and different world. Not since 1945 have we seen the real possibility of using the United Nations as it was designed: as a center for international collective security." For the moment, he was right. In contrast to Japan's invasion of Manchuria in 1931 or Hitler's annexation of the Sudetenland in 1938, international organizations responded in 1991 exactly the way they were supposed to under the liberal internationalist concept of collective security.

But the first Bush administration and the UN did not support liberal internationalist goals of spreading democracy. They did not authorize changing the regime in Baghdad. UN resolutions explicitly ruled out the invasion of Iraq. The mission was a realist one: to restore Kuwaiti sovereignty. Some in the Bush administration questioned this constraint.[12] But others, such as Cheney, did not.[13] He argued in 1991 against getting sucked into the "quagmire" of Iraq. Saddam Hussein was not only left in power, he was not even compelled to participate in the peace talks, which might have humiliated and weakened him at home. Instead Hussein emerged stronger from the debacle to wage war against the Kurds and Shia in his own country and to provoke another regional war in 2003. The winning powers respected the losing powers, regardless of their domestic policies. A realist world values the status quo, not regime change, and, by being prudent, sometimes misses opportunities to preempt or prevent later, more devastating wars. It shuns the short-term costs of regime change but incurs the long-term costs of continuing regime conflict.

Whether the first Bush administration, like the second Bush administration, would have acted against Iraq without UN approval is extremely doubtful. Its fundamental orientation was realist, and its ability to lead the first successful liberal internationalist collective security operation was more the consequence of a realist world, a weak Soviet Union, than of a Wilsonian internationalist vision.[14] There was a global consensus to defend sovereignty, not spread democracy. And as Bush himself recognized, "changes in the Soviet Union have been critical to the emergence of a stronger United Nations."[15] The Soviet Union was on the sideline and disintegrating. The United States was emerging as the world's sole superpower. The first collective security operation in history was possible because it was essentially a U.S. operation.

At the end of his administration, George H. W. Bush did authorize another U.S. intervention under UN auspices in Somalia. But this intervention was strictly humanitarian—to feed civilians—not to take sides in the domestic battle or engage in nation-building. It was an outgrowth, in part, of the momentum or euphoria surrounding the United Nations after the successful operation in Kuwait.[16] Although realists would not aggressively mobilize such interventions, they also would not necessarily oppose them. True, there was no vital U.S. national interest at stake, but the costs were minimal and the UN supported it. When the mission became costly and U.S. soldiers died, the United States withdrew. Had the realist George H. W. Bush still been in office when that occurred, it is doubtful that he would have done otherwise. His orientation was clearly to defend the status quo, not to pioneer regime change.

Bill Clinton

William Jefferson Clinton reversed America's dependence on liberal internationalist means even though he was the most liberal internationalist president in terms of foreign policy goals. He flirted briefly with the UN as the centerpiece of U.S. grand strategy. His ambassador to the United Nations and later secretary of state, Madeleine Albright, endorsed what she called "assertive multilateralism" or "multilateral engagement and U.S. leadership within collective bodies."[17] But when trouble erupted in Somalia and eighteen American servicemen died, memorialized by Hollywood in the movie *Black Hawk Down,* Clinton quickly withdrew American troops. During his first two years in office, Clinton downplayed the means of foreign policy, both liberal internationalist (diplomacy) and realist (force). He focused on domestic politics, deficit reduction and national health care reforms.[18] When genocide occurred in Rwanda in 1994, the United States did nothing, even though the stakes were higher than in Somalia. Clinton later apologized for this decision.[19] And when violence erupted in the former Yugoslavia, Clinton followed his predecessor's lead and looked initially to Europe, not NATO, to deal with the crisis in Bosnia.

From the outset, however, Clinton embraced liberal internationalist goals in foreign policy. Under the tutelage of his national security advisor, Tony Lake, Clinton crafted a strategy of "democratic enlargement" and "economic engagement." In his State of the Union message in 1994, he called "the advance of democracy elsewhere . . . the best strategy to ensure . . . [U.S.] security and to build a durable peace." He invoked the democratic peace explicitly, arguing that "democracies don't attack each other, [and] they make better trading partners and partners in diplomacy."[20] Under the banner of economic engagement, Clinton pushed through Congress both the North American Free Trade Agreement (NAFTA) and the Uruguay Round trade agreement, significant internationalist achievements negotiated by his predecessors. But the strategy of democratic enlargement employed mostly soft power—foreign aid and humanitarian relief—and led to criticism of Clinton's early foreign policy as Mother Teresa–type social work.[21]

Events eventually forced Clinton to harness realist means to his liberal internationalist goals. The European Community proved incapable of stopping the violence in Bosnia, and the NATO alliance was drifting aimlessly without an adversary. Realist logic offered no rationale to revive NATO once the Soviet Union was gone and there was no longer any external threat to Europe. If NATO were to survive, let alone expand, it would require liberal internationalist goals that focused more on building internal regimes and spreading democracy than resisting external aggression. That's exactly what happened. NATO not only intervened in summer 1995 to contain and then supervise ethnic conflict in Bosnia, it went on to expand in 1997 to include seven new members from the liberated region of Eastern Europe.

The objective in Eastern Europe was to reinforce nascent democratic regimes, not defend them against an external threat. The liberal internationalist logic was evident in the association of Russia with NATO. Russia became a partner in the alliance through the NATO-Russia Joint Permanent Council. By realist logic NATO was now an oxymoron, an alliance with a recent and potential enemy in its inner sanctum. Predictably, as realists would argue, Russia's partnership was not likely to be "permanent." The partnership collapsed when NATO intervened again in Kosovo to stop ethnic cleansing by Serbia. Nevertheless, it validated the Clinton administration's approach of channeling realist means to serve liberal internationalist goals.

By combining liberal goals and realist means, Clinton came as close to being a conservative internationalist as anyone since Ronald Reagan. In many ways, he validated the conservative polices of his predecessors, much the way Eisenhower, it is argued, validated the liberal policies of Franklin Roosevelt.[22] Clinton exploited Reagan's defense buildup both to deploy forces in Bosnia and Kosovo and to balance the budget, a conservative objective, through the peace dividend that the end of the Cold War brought. He also underwrote free trade policies of the Reagan and Bush era and did not endorse the Kyoto Protocol, which would have added costs to growth. Lastly, he endorsed a hard-line congressional resolution in 1998 to overthrow the Saddam Hussein regime in Baghdad and never endorsed the soft-line comprehensive test ban treaty at the UN.

Nevertheless, Clinton's instincts, like his early rhetoric, were liberal internationalist. He trusted in the goodwill of other countries—that they, too, were problem solvers, not troublemakers. He was disappointed. Russia not only opposed NATO's intervention in Kosovo, actually deploying forces at one point to stop NATO operations at the Pristina airport, but walked out of the Russia-NATO Council and under a new president, Vladimir Putin, reversed domestic democratic reforms.[23] Meanwhile, other troublemakers became active. A global terrorist menace percolated for eight years and then erupted after eight months under the next president, George W. Bush.

George W. Bush

Continuing the cycling, George W. Bush trimmed back both the liberal internationalist goals and the realist means of his predecessor. He took American foreign policy in a more conservative nationalist direction. He wanted a more "humble" foreign policy and expected to be left alone. But then, when attacked on 9/11, he reacted fiercely, like a good nationalist, to punish his adversaries. He preferred unilateralism and "coalitions of the willing" to multilateralism and standing alliances, which his more realist father touted. And after victory he celebrated the end of the mission, landing by fighter jet on an aircraft carrier emblazoned with the banner "mission accomplished." Although Bush did not request the banner, he also did not find it inappropriate.

Before taking office, Bush had no set foreign policy views. His instincts, however, were evident.[24] As a candidate in 2000, Bush led the attack against the "Mother Teresa" peacekeeping and nation-building policies of Bill Clinton. In debates with Al Gore, Bush said: "I'm worried about over committing our military around the world. I want to be judicious in its use. You mentioned Haiti. I wouldn't have sent troops to Haiti. I didn't think it was a mission worthwhile. It was a nation building mission. And it was not very successful. It cost us a couple billions of dollars and I'm not sure democracy is any better off in Haiti than it was before." He signaled early on that he did not see a connection between fighting wars and follow-up diplomacy after wars are won, a problem that bedeviled him later in Iraq: "Our military is meant to fight and win war . . . a civil force of some kind that comes in after the military, I don't think so. I think what we need to do is convince people who live in the lands they live in to build the nations." Bush urged holding back, doing less while clutching the arrows of military strength: "If we're a humble nation, but strong, they'll welcome us. And it's—our nation stands alone right now in the world in terms of power, and that's why we have to be humble. And yet project strength in a way that promotes freedom."[25] His starting point was clearly more nationalist than internationalist, certainly in comparison to Clinton and even to his father, who entertained a more expansive notion of realist diplomacy. Bush's secretary of defense, Donald Rumsfeld, worried that Bush's domestic priorities squeezed defense requirements.[26]

Other Bush advisors were more realist than the boss, and some were neocons. His national security advisor and later secretary of state, Condoleezza Rice, was a realist protégé of Brent Scowcroft and Bush's father. She saw the world primarily in terms of relations with great powers and called for a return to balance of power diplomacy that paid more attention to important states than to unstable developing countries.[27] This great power orientation caught Bush and his administration off guard when terrorists or nonstate actors from unstable less powerful states attacked the United States on September 11, 2001. The 9/11 Commission and Clinton aides accused the Bush team of looking for enemies in the wrong direction and neglecting intelligence reports that a terrorist attack was imminent.[28] If true, the Clinton administration looked in the wrong direction, too, and for a lot longer. It missed opportunities to take out Bin Laden.[29]

The events of 9/11 also led the Bush administration to claim that everything had changed, and in one sense it had. America had not been attacked directly on its home turf since the British sacked Washington in August 1814. (At the time of Pearl Harbor, Hawaii was a territory.) But in another sense the world had changed less than the administration assumed. Bush might have been better-off if he had embraced NATO and started early to craft a liberal internationalist design for postwar diplomacy in southwest Asia and the Middle East. Instead his nationalist impulses took over. He saw the world in fiercely competitive terms and declared countries to be "either for or against us." To the terrorists, he threw down the gauntlet. "Bring them on," he told the first responders at ground zero. His style was "right back at you" and his goal was revenge.[30]

Bush acted impatiently, by many appearances imperiously and unilaterally. He rejected NATO's offer to assist in Afghanistan. Under Article V, Europe for the first time declared an attack against the United States to be an attack against all alliance members, a commitment the United States often expressed toward Europe but Europe had never invoked on America's behalf. Why didn't Bush embrace this offer? One reason was fear that NATO required consensus.[31] Running a war by NATO committee had been tested in Kosovo and come up short.[32] Unwilling to repeat that experience, Bush mobilized ad hoc "coalitions of the willing" in place of NATO and insisted on victory without careful planning for the diplomacy that comes after victory. These are not the reactions of a liberal internationalist who spreads democracy by consensus or a conservative internationalist who closely integrates force and diplomacy.

In addition, Bush quickly widened the specter of threats, linking terrorist cells in unstable states with the potential acquisition of nuclear weapons from rogue states. He envisioned a potential nuclear attack on the United States. In October 2002, Bush said: "we cannot wait for the final proof, the smoking gun, that could come in the form of a mushroom cloud."[33] The administration then promptly preempted that threat by invading Iraq, without the consent of the UN or NATO. The evidence at the time made a plausible case that Iraq possessed weapons of mass destruction (WMD).[34] When no weapons were found, however, the war became a preventive not preemptive war, attacking a threatening country not because it has weapons of mass destruction now but because it may have them in the future. International support withered away.

Bush waged wars in Afghanistan and Iraq for solid nationalist reasons (to destroy terrorists and preempt WMD), not for realist aims (to promote world order like his father) or for liberal internationalist ends (to spread democracy). And, up to the point of victory in Kabul and Baghdad, his nationalist instincts served him well. The wars in Afghanistan and Iraq went better than anyone expected. And had WMD been found in Iraq, Bush would probably have had the last word on who had overstated or understated the threat.

But the failure to find WMD revealed the nationalist's failure to prepare for postwar diplomacy. Even if weapons had been found, the mission in Iraq was far from accomplished. After victory, the administration faced a bewildering array of postwar problems, including restoring governments in Kabul and Baghdad and promoting regional peace settlements in the Middle East and South Asia. Military power had done its job; now it was time for diplomacy to solve problems. But Bush missed or delayed multiple opportunities to rally international support for nation-building and to launch regional peace initiatives in the Middle East and southwest Asia. He dawdled for four years before undertaking an Arab-Israeli peace initiative (unlike his father, who did so in six months after the first Iraq War), and he "fiddled" with postwar reconstruction efforts in Afghanistan for six years and Iraq for four years until sectarian forces "burned" their way back into contention and U.S. troops had to be surged in both countries to quell them.[35]

Out of necessity, Bush turned to the democratic aims of liberal internationalism to replace defeated regimes in Kabul and Baghdad. Now, according to some accounts, he revealed his true neocon credentials or, perhaps because he had no foreign policy experience, the neocons hijacked his foreign policy.[36] Whatever the case, the administration proceeded to export democracy at the point of a gun. The argument is captivating and entertaining, which explains why it drew so much attention. But it is not plausible. The U.S. government is not that easily hijacked. And even if it were, the argument suggests that Bush was not a neocon to begin with. His instincts were nationalist. Moreover, the six people, who according to James Mann did the hijacking, differed too widely among themselves to engineer a neocon hijacking. They included defensive realists like Colin Powell, Condoleezza Rice, and Richard Armitage, offensive realists like Donald Rumsfeld and Dick Cheney, and only one confirmed neocon, Paul Wolfowitz. So if Bush's foreign policy is discredited, realists share as much blame as neocons.[37]

Though inexperienced, Bush was not a cipher; nor was he insincere about democracy. He believed that liberty was a promise for everyone.

But the decision to go into Iraq was made on solid realist grounds: to pre-empt the acquisition of weapons of mass destruction. The famous "axis of evil" was evil not because it was nondemocratic but because it aspired to nuclear weapons. And while Bush mentioned democracy already in his West Point speech in June 2002, he escalated the democracy rhetoric dramatically after the failure to find nuclear weapons.[38] By January 2005 in his second inaugural address, George W. Bush staked his foreign policy to the utopian mast of ending tyranny and promoting democracy everywhere: "it is the policy of the United States to seek and support the growth of democratic movements and institutions in every nation and culture, with the ultimate goal of ending tyranny in our world."[39] The goal was laudable—though certainly not humble—but neither realist nor liberal internationalist means were ever adequate to meet the goal. Under a light footprint strategy, military balances deteriorated in both Afghanistan and Iraq, and diplomatic initiatives languished. George W.'s anchor was still the nationalist game, and he left office ordering another military surge, again unilaterally, to check the terrorist threat in Iraq.

Barack Obama

Barack Obama pulled back sharply from Bush's liberal internationalist aims. As one widely read article concluded, "most of the foreign-policy issues that Obama emphasized in his first two years involved stepping away from idealism."[40] He declared himself to be a realist and focused U.S. policies on more limited security objectives. But he ignored realist means and turned for the most part to liberal internationalist diplomatic initiatives to address almost every hot spot in the world.[41] He expanded the objectives of American foreign policy even as he downsized the means, cutting defense missions and budgets and superintending the slowest economic recovery since the Great Depression. In the end, Obama may have the instincts of a liberal nationalist. He wants to focus on domestic affairs, expanding government at home, and expects that, because the world is not that threatening, other countries will step up and help take care of world problems.

Obama reset relations with Russia, touted a strategic partnership with China on economic recovery and climate change, wound down wars in Iraq and Afghanistan, expanded drone attacks in Pakistan, Yemen, and North Africa, tightened sanctions on Iran and North Korea, announced a new pivot to Asia, sought to regain Europe's trust, extended an open hand to the Muslim world, and tried to jump-start the Middle East peace process. He rarely indicated which problems were more important than others and bounced from topic to topic and region to region. As Niall Ferguson, the British historian, notes, "the defining characteristic of

Obama's foreign policy has been not just a failure to prioritize, but also a failure to recognize the need to do so."[42]

Obama is a self-declared pragmatist. He reacts to events rather than to an agenda. He has no clear priorities of his own, and he assumes others do not either. He does not ask where problems come from or who might have created them; he simply inherits them (domestic ones, too) and, as a pragmatist, fixes them once they appear. As he told a Republican congressional audience in January 2010, "I am not an ideologue."[43]

Yet his pragmatism, like all pragmatism, conceals an ideology. A pragmatist sees the world in mechanistic terms. Problems are systemic, not separate, and they can be fixed by bringing together different parts and participants because interests are shared and congruent, not sovereign and conflicting. Everyone has something to contribute, so everyone must be at the table. Multilateralism is the mantra of the pragmatist. And most important, the pragmatist uses force only as a last resort after the cooperative effort fails. During negotiations the use of force destroys trust and respect and breaks up the cooperative game.

At the UN, Obama declared: "It is my deeply held belief that in the year 2009—more than at any point in human history—the interests of nations and peoples are shared."[44] He defined "four pillars" of shared engagement: nonproliferation and disarmament; the promotion of peace and security; the preservation of our planet; and a global economy that advances opportunity for all people. He did not mention democracy. Earlier in Prague, he dismissed domestic differences among nations: "when nations and peoples allow themselves to be defined by their differences, the gulf between them widens."[45] He turned his back on the Green Revolution in Iran in 2009 because he wanted to negotiate with the oppressive government and was caught flatfooted and largely immobilized by the revolutions of the Arab Spring in Tunisia, Egypt, and Syria. The pragmatist tacks away from topics that divide nations—democracy and defense—toward topics that unite them—diplomacy and economic hopes.

So, as Thomas Carothers explains, while Obama has clear commitments to democracy, as all traditions do, he mixes "that outlook . . . with strong pragmatic instincts." These include "a wariness of overstatement, a disinclination to lead with ideology, and the desire to solve problems through building consensus rather than fostering confrontation."[46] And when the problem is solved, everyone is satisfied. The world is united. As Zbigniew Brzezinski concludes, "He [Obama] doesn't strategize, he sermonizes."[47] He preaches to the choir—to those who are already converted, apparently.

Obama has not eschewed the use of force. In fact, his increase in drone attacks, targeted raids to kill terrorists, and cyber warfare to disrupt Iranian nuclear programs surprised many commentators and angered some supporters.[48] In Oslo in December 2009, when he received the Nobel Prize, Obama addressed the use of force head-on:

> We must begin by acknowledging the hard truth: We will not eradicate violent conflict in our lifetimes. There will be times when nations—acting individually or in concert—will find the use of force not only necessary but morally justified . . . I face the world as it is, and cannot stand idle in the face of threats to the American people. For make no mistake: Evil does exist in the world. A non-violent movement could not have halted Hitler's armies. Negotiations cannot convince al Qaeda's leaders to lay down their arms. To say that force may sometimes be necessary is not a call to cynicism—it is a recognition of history; the imperfections of man and the limits of reason.[49]

Yet in the same speech Obama praised nonviolence. He paid tribute to Martin Luther King and acknowledged that his presidency was a direct consequence of King's belief that "violence never brings permanent peace . . . [and] solves no social problem: it merely creates new and more complicated ones." He said that the Prague Spring in Czechoslovakia in 1968 "shamed those who relied on the power of tanks and arms to put down the will of the people" and taught us the value of "peaceful protest"—that "moral leadership is more powerful than any weapon."[50] He acknowledged briefly the role of military might, "the strongest alliance that the world has ever known . . . that stood shoulder to shoulder—year after year, decade after decade—until an Iron Curtain was lifted, and freedom spread like flowing water." But then in Moscow, he said that the Cold War ended when the people of Russia and Eastern Europe "stood up and decided that its end would be peaceful."[51]

All of this is true. Violent power and nonviolent protest *both* serve to save and spread freedom. But, on balance, Obama seems to be influenced more by the limits of power than by its uses. That may be in part a function of his times. He arrived when defense budgets were already being cut and wars being wound down whoever might be president. But it's hard to imagine Obama identifying with military power, except in the extreme case that America is attacked once again. He cut defense spending in 2011 by $487 billion over ten years and did so again by roughly the same amount in 2013 when he let the so-called sequester take effect, a proposal he made and Republicans in Congress accepted in 2011 to slash defense spending across the board if no other solution could be found.[52] Even when Obama increased the use of force, as he did twice in Afghanistan, he did so without conviction, announcing in the same breath that those forces would be withdrawn by a specific date.[53] Not until January

2012 did Obama visit the Pentagon and "for the first time," as the *New York Times* reported, "put his own stamp on an all-encompassing American military policy," something that might have been done more sensibly before he announced sizable defense and troop cutbacks.[54] His new strategic military guidance issued on the same occasion ended the doctrine of fighting two wars simultaneously in separate regions and declared that U.S. capabilities would now be strong enough only to "defeat" an attack in one region and to "spoil" an attack in a second region. Then, on top of that, Obama announced a pivot of America's military forces to Asia to counter increasing Chinese belligerence and North Korean hostility. Given the new defense guidance, the additional forces for the Pacific will have to come from the Middle East, weakening America's capabilities in that region just as the United States draws nearer to a military showdown with Iran if economic sanctions fail.

Obama did not leave behind a residual force in Iraq, which might have helped deter Iranian influence in Iraq.[55] He could not persuade Baghdad to accept a Status of Forces Agreement (SOFA) that would protect American troops from local prosecution. The Iraqi leadership sided with local Shiite militia who, along with Iran, opposed a residual force. Baghdad seemed to bet on Tehran for its future rather than the United States. In Afghanistan, Obama progressively narrowed U.S. objectives to match its military retreat, from "defeat al Qaeda in Pakistan and Afghanistan" to "deny al Qaeda a safe haven . . . , reverse the Taliban's momentum and deny it the ability to overthrow the government" to negotiations "that reconcile the Afghan people, including the Taliban."[56] If the Taliban rejoin a weak Afghan government, the conditions that created al-Qaeda training camps and the 9/11 attacks in the first place may reemerge. Although Obama used force in Libya, he did so from "behind" in a situation that had mostly humanitarian, not strategic, implications.[57] And his bewildering response to the terrorist attacks on the American consulate in Benghazi raised further questions about the administration's readiness to use force. By contrast, in Syria, a situation of much greater strategic significance if Syria defeats the opposition rebels, Obama explicitly refused to use force, even though all of his foreign policy cabinet members recommended arming the rebels in 2012.[58]

Meanwhile, Obama ignored Russian arms and support for both Syria and Iran, and said that the United States and Russia are no longer antagonists because "the pursuit of power is no longer a zero-sum game."[59] But Russia knows it is still a *relative*-sum game. While the United States makes concessions to Russia on NATO missile defenses in Europe and signs a New START Treaty that cuts U.S. but not Russian warheads, Russia pursues a "sphere of privileged interests" in the former Soviet area.[60] It attacks and occupies Georgia, fuels separatists in Moldova, launches cyber attacks against Estonia, meddles in Ukrainian elections, protects naval bases in Syria, helps Iran avoid crippling oil sanctions, and looks ahead to replace U.S. influence in Central Asia as America withdraws from Afghanistan.

According to Walter Russell Mead, Obama is not yet a victim of the "The Carter Syndrome," afflicted by a weak defense.[61] But in a competitive world, Obama risks allowing the United States to be painted as a paper tiger. Speaking to reporters in Singapore in 2010, Secretary of Defense Robert Gates had to deny the charge: "I don't think anybody believes the United States is a paper tiger."[62] And in March 2012 Obama himself had to protest he was not bluffing when he said he would use force on behalf of Israel: "I think that the Israeli government recognizes that, as president of the United States, I don't bluff."[63] Vice President Joe Biden repeated again in March 2013 that the president was not bluffing.[64] When you have to deny something that often, it generally suggests the charge is beginning to stick.

Richard Holbrooke, Obama's late envoy to South Asia, once boasted that "diplomacy is like jazz—an improvisation on a theme."[65] But diplomacy is also percussion. And Obama's diplomacy may be too much melody and too little percussion. He may be putting too much faith in understanding, empathy, reaching out, and compromising and too little in building up forces, pushing back on the ground in regional disputes, narrowing an opponent's options away from the bargaining table, and standing up for one side or the other when conflicts break out.

Will the pendulum swing stop between too much force under Bush and too much diplomacy under Obama? If not, Obama may lose control of events. Circumstances, not ideas, will drive his policy. Obama seems to believe that if America does not use force, others will not either. But there's the problem. Other nations may see the world more in competitive than in cooperative terms. If the United States does not push back to stop nuclear proliferation in the Middle East and Asia, other countries will. Israel is close to that point already, and if North Korea continues to develop nuclear weapons, Japan may demand more extensive U.S. nuclear protection or decide to acquire nuclear weapons of its own. The use of force only when it is absolutely necessary does not minimize risks; it simply leads to much bigger risks later on.

Obama has been called a president for the post-American world, but he may actually be a president for the post-sovereign or postmodern world.[66] A postmodern world is not threatening, and America can relax and let other countries step up as the United States steps back. In France in 2009, Obama disowned the idea that America had a special role: "I believe in American exceptionalism, just as I suspect that the Brits believe in British exceptionalism and the Greeks believe in Greek exceptionalism."[67]

He is aware of America's contributions: "Whatever mistakes we have made, the plain fact is this: The United States of America has helped underwrite global security for more than six decades with the blood of our citizens and the strength of our arms."[68] And he likes to refer to America as "the indispensable nation," borrowing a phrase from Clinton's secretary of state, Madeleine Albright. But he is confident that other nations can contribute just as much. History is on our side, and there may be less for America to do in foreign affairs. America can focus on its domestic problems. All along, Obama may have harbored the core instincts of a liberal *nationalist* rather than a realist or liberal internationalist.

Domestic Politics of Foreign Policy

Under recent presidents, as discussed in chapter 1, the domestic politics of American foreign policy have become more contested. During World War II and the early years of the Cold War, Democratic presidents molded a consensus that married partnership (diplomacy) and power (force). Their approach was identified with liberal internationalism and Republican dissent with "liberal internationalism-lite" or realism.[69] This consensus broke down during the Vietnam War, it is argued, and foreign as well as domestic politics, poisoned by Watergate, became more "polarized." But this interpretation overlooks the Reagan era in which the Cold War was renewed and Reagan forged a different consensus between partnership and power. There are now two alternatives for an internationalist foreign policy, one liberal, one conservative.

The debate today is more complicated. Both internationalisms offer the majority of Americans what they are looking for in terms of foreign policy goals. Polls show that most Americans consider the country exceptional and expect it to defend and promote freedom in the world.[70] The question is at what cost. Experience shows that Americans have a limited appetite for protracted conflicts if casualties persist.

Liberal internationalism offers a low-cost version of foreign policy, one that suggests diplomacy can carry the lion's share of the foreign policy burden and force will be used only as a last resort and with the consent of international institutions. Given the number of countries in the UN today and the discord among them, this standard usually means force will not be used very often, if at all—at least in a timely fashion. The American public can have a foreign policy that doesn't cost very much but is also unlikely to deliver very much.

Realism offers a higher-cost version of foreign policy, more reliance on the use of force and less dependence on universal institutions, but it also offers the American people less satisfying objectives. Americans are asked to expend blood and treasure not to spread freedom but to balance power and preserve the status quo—in short, to tolerate and accommodate despotism in the world since peace offers the best hope for eventual freedom assuming history is on freedom's side.

Conservative internationalism offers the same goals as liberal internationalism but raises the stakes higher than either realism or liberal internationalism. It envisions the earlier and more frequent use of force to counter tyranny. America will have to lead more aggressively, sometimes even unilaterally, and depend more on makeshift alliances, such as coalitions of the willing, than on standing alliances and international institutions.

The tug-of-war among the different foreign policy approaches exhausts the American public. They may be persuaded to use force for realist reasons, as they were in 1991 to restore sovereignty in Kuwait. But the vote is usually very close, even with UN consent. Voting *after* the UN had already approved the use of force, the Senate barely passed the resolution for war, 52–47, with 42 Republicans and only 10 Democrats voting in favor. The House voted 250–183, with 164 Republicans and 86 Democrats in favor.[71] Moreover, the public shifts its focus quickly if the goal is simply realist, that is, to defend other countries or preserve access to resources such as oil that America may be able to replace. In presidential elections one year later, Democrats readily routed George H. W. Bush's realist foreign policy successes by arguing that he spent too much time and money on "world order" and neglected domestic goals, including the opportunity to achieve energy independence from Middle East oil.

The swing to liberal internationalist goals under Bill Clinton was no more satisfying. Now Americans discovered that supporting good causes like feeding civilians in Somalia or protecting ethnic groups in the former Yugoslavia also cost lives. More worthy goals like human rights and freedom inevitably require greater sacrifice than less worthy goals such as stability. Republicans stormed back into the White House in 2001 calling for America to pursue a more humble foreign policy.

One might have thought that the attacks of 9/11 would anchor the American public for the long term to pursue more ambitious goals of defense and freedom in world affairs. And it did for a short while. But, paradoxically, 9/11 also opened wide the door for American nationalism to reemerge. Dormant since the late 1940s, nationalism is the least ambitious and least costly version of American foreign policy—at least in the short run. It suggests that America can defend itself vigorously when attacked without being part of standing alliances—the Afghan and Iraq wars were fought without NATO—and return home quickly after war is won to avoid quagmires and focus on domestic problems. Conservative nationalists abandoned Bush when he spent more to defend Iraq and Afghanistan than to protect America's borders. And liberal nationalists criticized Barack Obama when he spent more money to pay for foreign wars than to restore American jobs. Nationalism, however, sets up the country to pay the highest price for foreign policy in the longer run. A nationalist era preceded World War II, and a much briefer flirtation with nationalism, during the campaign of 2000, preceded the attacks of 9/11. Nationalist sentiment is higher in 2012 than it has been since 1947; 38 percent of the American people say the United States should stay out of world affairs.[72]

The domestic politics of American foreign policy is clearly open to an alternative foreign policy tradition. Public opinion is looking for something to stop the cycling between liberal internationalist goals and realist/nationalist ones. Conservative internationalism is a long shot, but it is a possibility.

Conservative internationalism sets the highest goals for American foreign policy—expansion of freedom—and extracts the highest costs—a strong military and greater willingness to use force. In the short run, it imposes greater burdens on the American public. But over the longer run it saves American lives and money. It deters, preempts, and prevents wars so that they occur less often or are smaller when they do occur. It does so by being willing to use force early and continuously throughout negotiations rather than late and all at once after negotiations fail. And it intervenes for shorter durations, understanding that military force is only as good as the diplomatic goals that guide it. It compromises before the American public sours on war, as it does after three to four years, however worthy the cause.

Conservative internationalism has a record of success. Presidents who did the most to expand freedom also used force assertively and diplomacy integrally. They not only combined more ambitious liberal goals with stronger realist capabilities, they compromised military gains for acceptable diplomatic outcomes and persuaded the American people to stay onboard. In the end they saved money and lives. By expanding the country aggressively, Jefferson and Polk saved the country from interstate wars that might have followed if European powers had occupied North America and drawn it later into fratricidal wars. Truman started a Cold War in Europe but undoubtedly averted a hot war such as the one that broke out in Korea. And Reagan risked a frightening military buildup to end the Cold War without firing a shot. Worthy goals in the end may be worth warlike means. We take a closer look at each of these presidents in the chapters that follow.

Chapter 4

Thomas Jefferson
EMPIRE OF LIBERTY

JEFFERSON IS SUCH A PROTEAN and complex figure he belongs to every school of American government and foreign policy. Liberals and conservatives claim him, as do various foreign policy traditions. Walter Russell Mead sees Jefferson as a liberal nationalist or isolationalist.[1] He says Jefferson considered America as an exceptionalist, not just unique, country, unlike a conservative nationalist, but as an example, not an exporter, of liberty, unlike a liberal internationalist. Further, Jefferson focused American policy on economic, not security, concerns, unlike a realist. On the other hand, Robert W. Tucker and David C. Hendrickson consider Jefferson a liberal internationalist and associate him with Woodrow Wilson and the conviction that America "was acting for all mankind" by developing a new diplomacy that rejected the logic of European monarchies and embraced the republican idea that "relations among states ought to be based on the same spirit and principles that govern relations among individuals." Yet unlike a realist, Jefferson, they argue, avoided the military means that would have been needed to accomplish such ambitious ends. He concocted the fanciful notion of "peaceable coercion" that substituted economic sanctions for war.[2]

Such interpretations reflect the ongoing debate among America's foreign policy traditions. Realists are particularly critical of Jefferson. They resent his injection of moral purpose into foreign policy because such moralism is bound to fail and contrast his policies unfavorably with those of Alexander Hamilton and George Washington, who identified more easily with military power and the realpolitik traditions of Europe. Nationalists like the parsimony (minimalism) and elegance of Jefferson's foreign policies, and liberal internationalists appreciate the novelty of his focus on commerce, although they do not share and often ignore his commitment to limited and decentralized government.

This debate is unlikely to be resolved.[3] And adding one more interpretation presented here will not be wholly persuasive. Nevertheless, in today's terms, Jefferson is perhaps the most conservative of the founding fathers, if conservative means classical liberal devoted to widening liberty even in the absence of full equality. He had an almost libertarian commitment to limited government; and as a consequence of drafting the Declaration of Independence, he became fossilized in American revolutionary lore as the embodiment of individual liberty *in pursuit* of full equality. True, he was less bound by tradition, especially religion, than someone like John Adams, and liberals claim him because of his unflinching commitment to the rule of reason in politics. Nevertheless, Jefferson's emphasis on liberty and limited government, as opposed to authority and centralized government, makes him genuinely conservative rather than liberal. Based on distinctions discussed in chapter 1, Jefferson was a solidly majoritarian conservative committed to the public square, with libertarian leanings as well. If he was also internationalist, rather than nationalist, he is a candidate to be the first conservative internationalist American president.

First Conservative Internationalist

Existing interpretations ignore two aspects of Jefferson's diplomacy that stand out when viewed in the context of his times. Jefferson was a passionate expansionist compared to almost all of his contemporaries, and he used force at a time when America had no military force to speak of: a miniscule navy and a regular army of less than three thousand men. Nevertheless, he used all the force America did have, especially against the Barbary pirates. Given these circumstances, Jefferson combined ideological ambition and the use of military power in ways that one would not expect of a nationalist or realist.[4]

There is little doubt that, as defined in this study, Jefferson was an internationalist. He believed that the Old World system of anarchy and balance of power could be changed and that democracy could be spread to bring about a better world system.[5] In his second inaugural address, he made the point that principle was the source and purpose of power in foreign affairs: "with nations, as with individuals, our interests, soundly calculated, will ever be found inseparable from our moral duties; and history bears witness to the fact that a just nation is taken on its word when recourse is had to armaments and wars to bridle others." No realist or European diplomat at the time would have made such a statement. And the statement is not utopian. Principle is not a substitute for power; it is what makes a nation just and ensures that it will be taken at its word when it has recourse to power. Jefferson was no pacifist: "My hope of preserving peace for our country is not founded in the Quaker principle of non-resistance under every wrong, but in the belief that a just and friendly conduct on our part will procure justice and friendship from others."[6] Once again, principle, Jefferson understood, validates power, and no use of armaments and war was either credible or effective without it. Add to that Jefferson's expansionist zeal, his belief that freedom would eventually populate the western hemisphere and beyond, and Jefferson becomes a committed internationalist, someone dedicated to not only defending but spreading liberty.

Yet how did he see America's role in this process? Was it primarily as an example, which other nations would follow on their own, as liberal nationalists believe? Or was it more as an active exporter of liberty looking for opportunities to succor freedom in other countries, as liberal internationalists prefer? Jefferson indulged both ideas, partly because America had few capabilities at the time to promote liberty abroad. But if he had not leaned consistently toward the export of freedom, it is doubtful that he would have sat at the table with French revolutionaries in Paris to design a "charter of rights" that included habeas corpus and freedom of the press or maneuvered so patiently to acquire the Louisiana Territory, which doubled the domain of American freedom.[7] He defended America vigorously, perhaps too vigorously, against the Barbary pirates as we will see, but he also looked for opportunities within the interstices of the European balance of power to spread freedom in the Americas. He secured Louisiana where other founding fathers might have never ventured.

However, Jefferson was not an active interventionist on behalf of freedom. He was more of an opportunist.[8] He opposed intervention for what we would call today "regime change." He argued that the United States "cannot deny to any nation that right whereupon our own government is founded—that every one may govern itself according to whatever form it pleases . . . and may transact its business with foreign nations through whatever organization it thinks proper, whether king, convention, assembly, committee, president or anything else it may choose."[9] At the same time, Jefferson did not consider all such choices equally legitimate. A republic was more just than a monarchy. But a republic was also potentially more vulnerable. More than anything Jefferson feared the harmful consequences of foreign interventions on the republican form of government. Foreign affairs was the playground of despots, and international interventions too often a ruse to reinforce domestic tyranny. "Though I cordially wish well to the progress of liberty in all nations," he remarked, "they are not to be touched without contamination from their other bad principles."[10]

Nevertheless, if Jefferson opposed foreign interventions to *promote* freedom, he also opposed them to *crush* freedom. Intervention at the time meant mostly intervention by European monarchs to repress liberal revolutions, such as the French Revolution. If liberal revolutions were to survive, they needed outside help. When French revolutionaries issued decrees in 1792 that extended "fraternity and assistance to all peoples who shall wish to recover their liberty," Jefferson supported them and declared that "the liberty of the whole earth was depending on the issue of the contest" and that "rather than it should have failed, I would have seen half the earth desolated."[11] Washington and Hamilton opposed the revolutionary decrees.[12] For Jefferson, sovereignty protected both liberal and traditional regimes, but it drew its legitimacy ultimately from regime type. Conservative thinking ever since has championed an Old World, traditional sovereignty to defend liberty at home (conservative nationalism) and a New World, republican sovereignty to nurture liberty abroad (conservative internationalism).

In this commitment to liberty, Jefferson was neither Pollyannaish nor cynical. He knew that American liberty was flawed. In rough drafts of the Declaration, he railed against the slave trade as "execrable commerce" and "a cruel war against human nature itself."[13] And in his proposed constitution for Virginia, he sought to ban future slavery and later advocated resettling emancipated slaves in the Caribbean or Africa. Yet he owned slaves and never freed them. "For all of his enlightenment," as Merrill Peterson notes, "Jefferson suffered the color prejudice of Western man."[14] Still, in his time, he thought beyond his own limits and circumstances and looked ahead to a future when young men who had "sucked in the principles of liberty as it were with their mothers' milk" would right this wrong. A few decades later, one of these young men, Abraham Lincoln, used Jefferson's words to declare that the principle of equality in the Declaration must be "constantly looked to, constantly labored for, and even though never perfectly attained, constantly approximated and thereby constantly spreading and deepening its influence, and augmenting the happiness and value of life to all people of all colors everywhere."[15] For both Jefferson and the Jefferson-inspired Lincoln, the language is remarkable for their times, presaging by two hundred years the relentless spread of freedom to "all people of all colors everywhere."

Jefferson's commitment to liberty made him no more sympathetic to centralized authority abroad than to national government at home. He did not envision a world of centralized institutions, either national or international, as modern-day liberals and liberal internationalists do. He was skeptical, as we will see, even of alliances, especially standing ones, which were the principal form of international institutions at the time.

He anticipated instead a continent and eventually a world of decentralized democracies—"sister republics" living side by side "with a people speaking the same language, governed in similar forms, and by similar law."[16] Thus, while he foresaw a new world of democratic states, like Immanuel Kant and later Woodrow Wilson, he did not foresee a new world of centralized institutions. He was, in this sense, a "conservative" not a liberal internationalist.

Suspicious of international institutions, Jefferson did subscribe to the liberal internationalist's focus on economics. In this respect he embraced the new diplomacy of "sweet commerce," as Montesquieu called it, and the prospect that countries would need each other increasingly to profit from trade and would therefore go to war with one another less often than if they did not trade. He undoubtedly overestimated the value of U.S. trade, a flaw in his embargo policy toward England. But Jefferson's economic diplomacy did not distract him from realist or military means; it drew him toward the use of force to defend expanding trade rather than away from it in the hope that trade would substitute for war. The need to protect trade led to his war against the Barbary pirates. And economic sanctions against England, as history proved, constituted as much a step toward war as a substitute for war. His economic diplomacy was never abstract or isolated from a larger strategy. It was directed toward exploiting America's principal realist capability at the time: its expanding commercial trade upon which European powers increasingly depended.[17] Nor did he expect trade to trump power politics. He tracked shifts in power in Europe assiduously, recognizing that they affected trade as much as trade may have tempered them.[18] His skepticism toward alliances applied only to "entangling" or what we would call today "standing" alliances, not temporary alliances he threatened to form on several occasions to offset America's adversaries.

Was force then a last resort for Jefferson, after all economic means had been exhausted? Jefferson certainly temporized. In his own words, his strategy for the acquisition of Louisiana was "to palliate and endure."[19] He hated war and sought to conquer by peace, as his critics allege.[20] But the question is whether his economic diplomacy overall was one of temperament or strategy, an aversion to war or a strategy to postpone as well as prepare for war. His critics say it was one of temperament.[21] He never really intended to use force, and hence force was a "last" or perhaps even a "past" resort, as some contemporary visionaries might aver. Other evidence suggests, however, that his caution was one of strategy. He took into account the new "force" of commerce and integrated it with foreign and domestic considerations, something which realist logic, less focused on trade, was less likely to do at the time. As Merrill Peterson concludes, "he knew when to wave the sword and when to sheathe it."[22] If force is closely coupled with diplomacy and diplomacy succeeds, it often appears that the use of force was small or inconsequential.[23]

Jefferson saw threats to liberty from both internal and external sources. A strong central government disposing of a standing military force was the principal internal threat. He supported a strong navy and deployed it aggressively in the Barbary wars.[24] But he was more skeptical about land forces. Stationed within the society, they were more dangerous for democracy. He preferred state militia if possible. These views were not pacifist; they were practical given the tension between the new republicanism and war. Indeed his preferences were reflected in the Constitution itself, which required a national army to be reauthorized every two years but contained no such provisions for the navy.[25]

Jefferson had experienced firsthand the mobilization of national militia by the Federalist-led government to crush the Whiskey Rebellion in 1794 and again to prepare for war against France in 1798. He saw how war preparations stoked political passions and forged the Alien and Sedition Acts, under which several hundred journalists who supported him were imprisoned without the right of habeas corpus. These acts, not war, constituted the worst threat to civil liberties in the early days of the new republic. Thus Jefferson took the need for force in foreign affairs seriously, but he also measured its consequences against the liberal constitution of the new republic. Foreign policy was intended to defend, not dismantle, liberal republicanism.[26]

As a consequence, Jefferson always calculated the need to use force against the size and nature of external threats. He did not pursue foreign adventures for honor or glory, as European monarchs did, or even for principle, as French revolutionaries did. When threat was lower, as it was in 1800–1801 after France made peace with the United States and England, he scaled back the size of forces. When threat reemerged and war resumed in Europe, he built up forces once again. He tracked power struggles in Europe carefully and manipulated small U.S. forces and the possibilities of alliances with European powers deftly to achieve territorial and trade advantages. And, with his embargo policy, he put the country on a course to war, which he hoped to avert but from which he never shrank, supporting the war wholeheartedly when it finally came after he left office. In light of such evidence, it is hard to conclude that Jefferson was a pacifist or utopian.

Jefferson's domestic views are crucial for understanding his foreign policy. His domestic conservatism is closely linked to his foreign policy internationalism and distinguishes him clearly from liberal internationalists. He favored "a wise and frugal government, which shall restrain men from injuring one another, which shall leave them otherwise free to regulate their own pursuits of industry and improvement, and shall not take from the mouth of labor the bread it has earned." "This," he concluded in his first inaugural address, "is the sum of good government."[27] This conservative view of government is not static, either at home or abroad—just the opposite. It envisions "pursuits of industry and improvement," but these pursuits are by individuals, not governments, and the purpose of government is to empower civil society, not to replace it.

So Jefferson, more so than any other founding father, was sensitive to the domestic costs of defense and foreign policy. He tailored foreign policy to threats, prioritized opportunities to spread freedom, and kept the costs to an absolute minimum.[28] To argue that he was a nationalist who had no ambitions to change the international system or that he was an internationalist who did not use sufficient power seems incongruous. Jefferson combined liberal internationalist goals with realist military means, and he did so simultaneously and continuously. As Alexander DeConde concludes, "using a mixture of threat and restraint in diplomacy, he [Jefferson] never lost sight of his desired objective."[29] Altogether, his foreign policy strategy emphasized a strong role for both American ideas and American power and a minimal role for international institutions. Jefferson was indeed the first conservative internationalist president.

Let's examine more closely three cases of Jeffersonian diplomacy that bear out this interpretation: the dispatch of the U.S. Navy to the Mediterranean to pursue the Barbary pirates, Jefferson's military and diplomatic maneuvers to secure the purchase of Louisiana, and his embargo against England to redress attacks on American shipping.

In the first case, Jefferson used American military power to the hilt, belying the realist critique that he failed to back his ambitions with adequate resources. In the second, he deftly combined force and diplomacy, coupling modest military means, because that is all he had, with deft diplomatic maneuvers to put himself in a position to purchase Louisiana. The opportunity may have fallen into his lap, as Henry Adams later argued,[30] but his lap had to be positioned properly to catch it. In this instance, Jefferson demonstrated not only how force backs diplomacy but how diplomacy, through his proposed alliance with Great Britain, magnifies force. And in the third case Jefferson pursued an economic embargo not as a replacement for military power but as a maneuver to buy time to avert war if possible but prepare for it if necessary. In this instance, he may have missed a chance to conclude an agreement with Great Britain, which, though imperfect because it did not resolve the issue of impressment, might have avoided war. If so, he erred on the side of expecting too much from the use of force, not too little thinking the embargo would obviate the use of force. He failed to tailor the use of force to a feasible diplomatic outcome, more the failing of a nationalist who expects too much from force and too little from diplomacy than of a liberal internationalist who expects the reverse.

Barbary Pirates

Jefferson was familiar with the raids of Barbary pirates in the Mediterranean from his days as American ambassador to France in the 1780s. Four Barbary states—Morocco, Algiers, Tunis, and Tripoli—repeatedly seized European and American ships and demanded payments to desist from doing so. Once America became independent, England no longer protected American shipping. Thus, in 1785, when the dey of Algiers captured an American ship, Jefferson initiated an independent effort to negotiate with the Barbary states to protect American shipping.

He and John Adams met in March 1785 with Abd al-Rahman, Tripoli's ambassador in London. In an early "clash of civilizations," al-Rahman informed them that the justification of the raids "was written in the Koran, that all Nations who should not have acknowledged their authority were sinners, that it was their right and duty to make war upon whomever they could find and to make Slaves of all they could take as prisoners."[31] Provoked by such zeal, Jefferson wrote Adams four months later: "I acknoledge [sic] I very early thought it would be best to effect a peace thro' the medium of war."[32] And in a letter to James Monroe on August 18, 1786, Jefferson gave his unqualified support to building

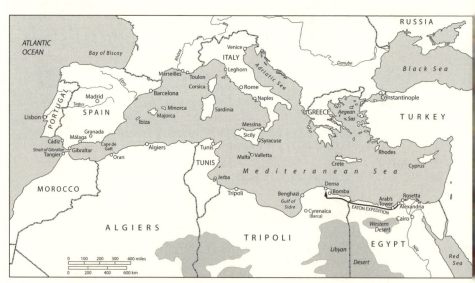

Map 4.1. The Mediterranean in 1800. Redrawn from Joseph Wheelan, *Jefferson's War.* Perseus Books Group, 2004.

a strong naval force, noting that a navy was much less threatening to a republic than an army:

> the [Barbary] states must see the rod. . . . Every national citizen must wish to see an effective national instrument of coercion, and should fear to see it on any other element than the water. A naval force can never endanger our liberties, nor occasion bloodshed; a land force would do both.[33]

In the same year, he also wrote Ezra Stiles, the president of Yale College, "it will be more easy to raise ships and money to fight these pirates into reason, than money to bribe them."[34] These comments, even before the new Constitution created and constrained national forces, showed Jefferson's firm commitment to "national" defense and his preference for naval over land forces.

Jefferson had better luck with the Moroccans, with whom the United States signed a treaty in 1786. But the other Barbary states continued to resist, and there was no U.S. Navy at the time to show them "the rod." So Jefferson threw himself into the task of organizing a coalition of countries to confront the Barbary states. He negotiated with Portugal, Naples, the two Sicilies, Venice, Malta, Denmark, and Sweden, but France and England were uninterested. They went their own way. Their naval forces were sufficient to deter the pirates, and they were not unhappy to see the Barbary states raid the weaker countries to preserve France's and Britain's monopoly of Mediterranean trade. Fortuitously, at the time, Portugal was at war with Algiers and blocked the Straits of Gibraltar, protecting American ships in the Atlantic. Thus, while Jefferson's first encounter with the Barbary states added little to the scales of power, he left that encounter, it might be argued, with a clear predisposition to go to war.[35]

In one of his first acts as secretary of state under the new Constitution, Jefferson sent a message to Congress in December 1790 advocating the use of force against Algiers and calling for the creation of a U.S. Navy.[36] Congress was uninterested. But in 1794, after making peace with Portugal, Algiers seized 11 U.S. ships and 119 sailors; and in 1795, the United States paid nearly $1 million in ransom for the sailors.[37] In direct response to these attacks, Congress authorized the first six battleships of the U.S. Navy and in 1797–98, in the shadow of the quasi-war with France, commissioned an additional 37 warships, including 12 battleships with up to 22 guns each. It also tripled the army to 10,000 men and created an additional reserve of 10,000 troops.[38] Jefferson as vice president supported the legislation, despite the fact that many in his own party opposed it and the war scare spawned the repugnant Alien and Sedition Acts, which imprisoned hundreds of Republican journalists.[39]

In the campaign of 1800, Jefferson called for a reduction of the army and navy. But the Federalists did, too. Jefferson inherited a defense budget that had already been cut by two-thirds from $6 million in 1799 to $1.9 million in 1801. Adams signed the bill just before leaving office, selling all but thirteen of some thirty frigates, six of which were to go into dry-dock.[40] The reason for the cuts was simple. The war scare with France, which had prompted the extraordinary increase in defense expenditures, was over. The United States and France signed the Treaty of Mortefontaine in October 1800, and France and Britain signed the Peace of Amiens in October 1801. The Tory government in London, which had waged the conflict against American shipping most aggressively, lost power in February 1801, and a more pliant Whig government took office. It was plausible to believe that the threat to neutral rights, which the war in Europe had created and which led to British seizures of American ships and impressment of American sailors, might now abate. Peace was breaking out. Jefferson calculated defense needs against actual threats, and threats were visibly receding. He did not fear peace just as he did not fear war. It is easy in retrospect to see that the "rash" of peace was short-lived. But that's hardly a basis for concluding that Jefferson was starry-eyed about it.

Equally important for Jefferson was the need to address the domestic distortions caused by defense mobilizations. Domestic debt had soared, federal taxes had been instituted, and citizens protested, including farmers in western Pennsylvania who refused to pay taxes on whiskey, which they made from leftover grain. The new national government crushed the Whiskey Rebellion and passed the Alien and Sedition Acts, which vitiated civil rights. A standing army in times of peace meant "recruiting officers lounging at every court-house and decoying the laborer from his plough."[41] Jefferson despised such intrusions on domestic liberties and considered himself the point man of what he called the second American Revolution, the confirmation of a democratic rather than oligarchic republic in which the people and Congress reigned supreme over aristocratic elites and executive power. In these circumstances, Jefferson saw the internal threat of debt and tyranny as just as great as the external threat of impressment and war.

Thus, when Jefferson became president, he had few military options. But he used the ones he did have almost immediately. Shortly after he took office on March 4, 1801, he acted to show "the rod" to the Barbary pirates. The pasha in Tripoli had just quadrupled demands for tribute. Jefferson responded without convening Congress or even waiting for his cabinet to assemble (which took some time in those days). He issued orders on March 23 to ready a squadron of warships to sail to the Mediterranean. In May 1801, after cabinet discussions, he dispatched three

American frigates plus an armed schooner under Commodore Richard Dale to defend American shipping. At the time, this contingent made up half of the newly founded U.S. Navy (six frigates and two schooners). Jefferson made the decision himself. There was no secretary of the navy. Jefferson's first four nominees refused the job, some not once but twice.[42] Robert Smith, the first secretary of the navy, did not take his post until July. America's first war in Europe was clearly Jefferson's war and not the policy of some war hawk in his cabinet or a restless military.[43]

But that still doesn't answer the question why he was so eager to deploy a diminished navy against distant and lesser threats. That had to do with his conception of national security. Jefferson assessed the Barbary threat not in territorial terms but in terms of his expansive view of the rights of nations to trade at sea. He believed all nations should be free to develop trade unless they were direct belligerents in war, and belligerents had no right to interfere with neutral country trade even if neutral ships picked up trade in wartime that was previously carried by belligerents in peacetime. His views in 1794 and later in the 1800s brought him in conflict with Great Britain, which claimed the right to intercept all commerce in war whether derived from wartime or peacetime trade.

Jefferson's ambitious (realists would say lofty or utopian) view of the right of free ships, those from countries not at war, to carry free goods led him to identify a threat where realists might find none. But Jefferson was not far off the mark. America's commercial strength was its principal "realist" asset at the time, and other countries might more readily covet American trade than they would American territory or friendship. More than 158 American merchant ships sailed to the Mediterranean in 1801 alone.[44] The Barbary states threatened that trade, and Jefferson set about to impress them that he would protect it.

This was not the action of a pacifist or realist since it implied a military action of choice not necessity, an early not a last resort to force; and it stretched American naval resources beyond anticipated limits. Indeed, it required a substantial increase in appropriations for the navy at the same time Congress was also contemplating huge sums for the purchase of the Louisiana Territory. In 1802–3 Congress approved the construction of four more sixteen-gun battleships and fifteen gunboats. Naval appropriations alone went up to almost $1 million in 1802 and nearly doubled again in 1803, when Jefferson overruled Albert Gallatin, his treasury secretary, who feared resulting deficits.[45] Jefferson committed everything he had to brandish the "rod."

Henry Adams (no fan of Jefferson's), writing later in the 1880s, put it all in perspective. He described the naval force in the Mediterranean in 1804 as "such a force as the United States never before or since sent in hostile array across the ocean." As Adams further noted, "with the exception of the frigates 'Chesapeake' and 'United States', hardly a sea-going vessel was left at home."[46] Jefferson's policy toward the Barbary pirates strongly suggests a strategy that included both expansive ideological aims and risky, critics might say even reckless, military actions.

What is more, Jefferson did it all unilaterally. Why didn't he tuck in behind the naval power of European states as he had tried to do through negotiations in the 1780s when the United States had no navy? There were multilateral options. The League of Armed Neutrality reemerged in 1801–2. It was a coalition of countries pulled together initially in 1780–83 by Russia to uphold the free ships/free goods principle against the English embargoes, or Orders in Council, as they were called. This League might have been the basis for collective action against both Barbary and English deprivations on the high seas. By this point, however, Jefferson had soured on the usefulness of alliances. Fresh from the battles of the 1790s over the Jay (England), Pinckney (Spain), and French treaties, he had formulated the injunction in his first inaugural address to "have peace, commerce and honest friendship with all nations but entangling alliances with none." His objective was to "avoid implicating ourselves with the powers of Europe, even in support of principles which we mean to pursue."[47]

Moreover, the threat from London, as we noted, was receding; and London, under a more cooperative Whig government, had opened the British ports of Gibraltar, Minorca, and Malta to the U.S. squadron in the Mediterranean for stationing and resupply. Finally, Jefferson caught wind just about this time of Spain's decision to cede Louisiana back to France. He set his priorities on acquiring that prize and later threatened to ally with Britain to deter France from reoccupying Louisiana. For Jefferson, acting unilaterally or multilaterally was not a matter of principle, as it might be for nationalists and liberal internationalists, respectively; it was a matter of priorities and tactics.

In seeing distant threats that had little to do with territorial claims, Jefferson clearly went beyond realist thinking at the time, and realists criticize him for being softheaded. But to argue that Jefferson's "empire was one of liberty and not of power" and "did not require 'an army, and a navy, and a number of things'" is not fully consistent with the facts.[48] Jefferson did not expect to achieve his ambitious liberal internationalist goals without force. As noted, he used almost every bit of power America had at the time, not only most of the available U.S. Navy but also an overland expeditionary force led by the American adventurer William Eaton that stormed Derna on the Tripoli coast. Jefferson did not authorize this expedition to threaten the domestic regime in Tripoli and was reportedly cool to the idea when Eaton presented it to him.[49] After all, Jefferson was not an interventionist seeking "to intermeddle in the domestic contests of other countries."[50] Nevertheless, he did not stand in the way of this early attempt at regime change, and Eaton's dramatic expedition across the Mediterranean coast from Egypt to Derna was a clear example of armed diplomacy to influence negotiations. In January 1805 Jefferson ordered Samuel Barron, commodore of the U.S. squadron in the Mediterranean, and Tobias Lear, U.S. counsel general in Malta, to ratchet up military force until America could dictate peace terms.[51] Eaton's raid did just that, inspiring the words of the "Marines' Hymn" "to the shores of Tripoli." Embattled, the pasha at Tripoli sued for peace and American frigates returned home, just in time to face a threat much closer to American shores: the blockade of New York harbor by British frigates.

Jefferson's Barbary wars thus came to an end. He committed almost the entire navy to a foreign conflict, which constituted more of an opportunity to expand American commerce than to defend American territory; and he did it unilaterally while focusing his attention on a bigger prize in Louisiana. From a fresh perspective, Jefferson's Barbary policy looks very much like a conservative internationalist strategy that stretched both American ideals and American power to the limit.[52]

Louisiana Purchase

The Louisiana Purchase was without question the crowning achievement of Jefferson's diplomacy. In bringing it off, he demonstrated how ideas do not just respond to circumstances but alter them. He saw the opportunity to expand freedom, he deployed the use of force and threat of alliance to influence France's perceptions of the balance of power in Europe, and he exercised patience to achieve a timely compromise, even when that compromise impinged on his strong commitment to constitutional restraint. If Jefferson's strategy in the Barbary wars seemed heavy on the use of force to achieve a relatively modest objective, namely expansion of free commerce, his strategy in the Louisiana Purchase was light on the use of force to achieve a much bigger objective, namely doubling the domain of liberal republicanism. In both cases, however, it was not the amount of force used but the careful tailoring of force to diplomatic goals and the timing of concessions that ensured success. A conservative internationalist strategy is not bellicose for the sake of reputation or power; it matches force with threat and then seizes related opportunities to expand freedom abroad at minimum cost to domestic republicanism.

Already in 1786, Jefferson had his eye on territory: "our confederacy must be viewed as the nest from which all America, North and South is to be peopled."[53] To Monroe in 1801 he wrote: "it is impossible not to look forward to distant times, when our rapid multiplication will expand itself beyond these limits, and cover the whole northern, if not the southern, continent."[54] He did not envision a single government of the Americas, but he did envision a common civil society. As Dumas Malone writes, for Jefferson, "the Union was always the means, not an end in itself."[55] A great believer in decentralization, Jefferson talked about parallel "sister republics" in the Louisiana territory and appealed dispassionately to "keep them in the union, if it be for their good, but separate them, if it be better."[56] And he embraced an early form of nation-building to develop a citizen-led civil society. Because he distrusted the autocratic Creole elites that governed New Orleans under French and Spanish rule, he appointed territorial governors that installed American-style courts and the English language. He counted on white Americans to settle Louisiana, reform the authoritarian institutions of Spanish and French rule, and prepare the territory for statehood. Property was the great molder of citizenship. To be sure, he could not "contemplate with satisfaction any blot or mixture on that surface," which excluded blacks; but he said to a group of Indians in 1808, "When once you have property, you will want laws and magistrates to protect your property and person. . . . . You will find that our laws are good for this purpose; you will wish to live under them, you will unite yourselves with us, join in our great councils, and form one people with us, and we shall all be Americans."[57]

For this early experiment in occupation and democracy building, Jefferson was severely criticized. John Quincy Adams condemned Jefferson's plan as "complete despotism." But Jefferson believed that liberty preceded equality, that union derived from free peoples associating voluntarily with one another, not from equal participation among diverse peoples— some of whom were free (American settlers) and some of whom were not (Creole class)—binding one another through ordinances and other "institutional" constraints. From today's vantage point, his views are racist and imperialist.[58] But at the time America was the leading democracy in the world. It offered the vote to a larger number of white people with property than Britain or any other country.[59] This commitment eventually extended to Indians (as Jefferson's comment above envisioned), slaves, women, and minorities and remains today the source of the continuing struggle against discrimination.

For conservative internationalists, liberty is the equalizer of cultures. Cultures that oppress are not equal to cultures that liberate. Cultural differences may be respected but they are not considered legitimate unless they incorporate the universal principles of individual rights and self-government. National or international union, therefore, is not the overriding goal, as nationalists or liberal internationalists might argue. Liberty comes first. Diverse peoples become equal by accepting the standards of freedom, not by merely exercising power or sovereignty, as realists believe, or by participating equally in institutions that decide collectively what is legitimate, as liberal internationalists advocate.

Would other founding fathers who did not have Jefferson's vision, like Alexander Hamilton or Aaron Burr, have positioned America as well to acquire Louisiana? Would Louisiana have fallen into their laps as easily as it did into Jefferson's lap? Perhaps. Hamilton plotted in the 1790s to use the big national army he promoted and commanded to seize Spanish territories in Florida and the southwest, and in 1803 he advocated war to seize the Floridas and New Orleans as an alternative to negotiations.[60] Burr pursued a bizarre conspiracy in the 1800s to sequester Louisiana and take it out of the Union.[61] But both efforts were fanciful, and it seems unlikely that anyone else at the time could have positioned America better to secure Louisiana peacefully than Thomas Jefferson.

Jefferson was delicately attuned to the political currents in the western territories, both the threats of war that Spanish, French, and British power posed on the western frontier and the independent spirit of the farmers and settlers on the frontier for whom expansion meant the opportunity for land and liberty.[62] Ever since the revolution, Spain had periodically suspended the rights of navigation in the lower Mississippi and the rights of deposit (export and import) in New Orleans, doing so again in October 1802. These actions angered western opinion and fueled plots of secession and foreign intervention. Already in the 1790s, Jefferson braced for the use of force to secure the Mississippi River frontier: "were we to give up half of our territory rather than engage in a just war to preserve it, we should not keep the other half long."[63]

The knock against Jefferson is that he never intended to use force to block a French attempt to occupy Louisiana.[64] It was all bluff and then dumb luck when Napoleon did not call the bluff because his invasion force was defeated by black rebels in Santo Domingo.[65] Nevertheless, Jefferson did apply leverage in the Louisiana negotiations. As Merrill Peterson explains, "the preparations went forward in silence: army recruitment was stepped up, arms, troops, and supplies concentrated at Fort Adams, Indian tribes on the left bank pressed to cede their lands, and the passage of western mail expedited."[66] Jefferson's ace in the hole was the dominance of American settlers and traders in the Mississippi River Valley. Settlers had seized Natchez in 1799, and New Orleans farther down the river was almost completely dependent on trade with American merchants. As Madison warned the French in December 1802, "there are now or in less than two years will be no less than 200,000 militia on the waters of the Mississippi, every man of which would march at a moment's warning to remove obstructions from that outlet to the sea." DeConde describes the impact of this reality on France: "the depth of the American resentment, the threats of war, and the whole issue of the

Mississippi gave France a taste of the kind of problem the possession of Louisiana could generate."[67] In October 1803, Jefferson gave orders to General James Wilkinson to prepare to take New Orleans by force if the Spanish refused to deliver the province to France as called for by agreement.[68]

Jefferson had committed the navy to the Mediterranean. Realists fault him for that whimsy, especially given the gathering French threat in the Caribbean; but this commitment was in response to an immediate threat to trade in Europe, which Jefferson saw as a new element of republican national security. In 1801 the port of New Orleans was still open and there was no immediate threat to trade. Once the Barbary wars ended in 1805, Jefferson immediately recalled the navy to assume its vigil along the American coast. In its absence, he compensated by the threatened alliance with Britain, which was all about bringing the British fleet into play on America's behalf.

So Jefferson acted consistent with his priorities and used as much force as he had. But because his diplomacy succeeded and America had little force, it seemed as though he used none at all. Jefferson's key means of force was the growing number of American settlers and British naval power. Britain was France's main rival. And here Jefferson succeeded in connecting in Napoleon's mind the possibility that if Napoleon went to war with England in Europe, he might have to fight England in Louisiana as well.

On October 1, 1800, Spain ceded Louisiana to France in the Treaty of San Ildefonso. Secret and conditional (on Spain getting a French-occupied duchy in Italy), the cession revived the prospects of French-British rivalry in North America. That rivalry had led to the French and Indian War of 1756–63 and the original loss of Louisiana by France to Spain (including portions east of the Mississippi that went to England). Jefferson now cleverly exploited this rivalry.

Learning of the secret treaty in May 1801, before France and England signed a temporary peace at Saint Amiens in October 1801, Jefferson initiated negotiations to purchase New Orleans and the Floridas and made his first allusion to an alliance with Great Britain. He instructed the American minister in Paris, Robert Livingston, to warn Paris that the cession of Louisiana "may turn the thoughts of our [U.S.] citizens to a closer connection with her [France's] rival and possibly produce a crisis in which a favorable part of her dominions would be exposed to the joint operation of a naval [England] and territorial [U.S.] power."[69]

Jefferson was acting before there was any real threat; he was preempting. Spain, which still controlled Louisiana, did not revoke the right of deposit in New Orleans again until November 1802. Thus, like an internationalist and unlike a nationalist, Jefferson was reacting to related opportunity rather than immediate threat, albeit within the context of previous threats of foreign intervention along the western frontier. In a subsequent letter to Livingston in April 1802, he reinforced the possibility of an alliance with England. The letter informed the French that should they repossess Louisiana, "from that moment we [the United States] must marry ourselves to the British fleet and nation."[70]

Jefferson knew that this threat would mean nothing in Paris unless France and England went to war again: "I did not expect that he [Napoleon] would yield till a war took place between France and England, and my hope was to palliate and endure . . . until that event . . . [and] I believed that event not very distant."[71] Jefferson offers this explanation in January 1804 after war between France and England had resumed in fall 1803, so we might be skeptical about his forecasting acumen. Nevertheless, he was a close student of European affairs, and he knew the French mind quite well. The Peace of Amiens proved to be brief (eighteen months), the only respite in over twenty years of continuous war between France and England. So it's not entirely implausible that Jefferson anticipated that war would resume, in foresight as well as hindsight.

Back at war with England, Napoleon had no desire to drive America into the arms of England and may have seen an opportunity to strengthen America at England's expense. Coupled with the defeat of his ill-fated naval expedition in Santo Domingo, Napoleon decided to sell not just New Orleans but the whole of Louisiana to the United States, even though the French treaty with Spain explicitly prohibited the "alienation" of Louisiana to another country.[72]

Was Jefferson's threat relevant? Adams says no: "fear of England was not . . . the cause of the sale."[73] Tucker and Hendrickson say, not really. They acknowledge that once war broke out in Europe, "Napoleon was at pains to see that the United States did not ally itself with Great Britain."[74] But Napoleon ceded Louisiana, among other reasons they argue, not to deter an American alliance with Britain but to build up "a power in the New World that might in time provide a serious challenge to the maritime power of England."[75] Henry Adams agrees: Napoleon "expected to check the power of England by giving Louisiana to the United States."[76]

The argument splits hairs. Whether to prevent an alliance with England or to promote a future rival to England, Napoleon weighed America's power in the balance between France and England and that is what Jefferson intended. Napoleon apparently believed that the United States might occupy New Orleans.[77] Alexander DeConde concludes, for example, "the American threat to regain the deposit by force—which, according to Monroe, the First Consul [Napoleon] knew the United States could accomplish—when followed by Jefferson's offer to purchase New Orleans, clinched the decision."[78] Intentions, of course, are hard to read.

As Henry Adams concedes, the "real reasons . . . remain hidden in the mysterious processes of his [Napoleon's] mind."[79]

The controversy hinges on whether Jefferson's threat of alliance with England was intended and effective. Tucker and Hendrickson argue that Jefferson never offered explicit alliance conditions that England could accept and therefore never intended such an alliance at all.[80] But Jefferson's coyness has another explanation. His objective was to prevent both French *and* English occupation of Louisiana. If he had to threaten alliance with Britain to prevent French occupation, he also had to avoid British occupation.[81] To that extent, indeed, he did not intend or want an alliance with Britain. But if no occupation of Louisiana by either country was his preferred outcome, alliance and possible occupation by Britain was still more acceptable than French reoccupation of Louisiana. He used British power, without ever embracing it until it was absolutely necessary, to ward off French power. And in the process he succeeded brilliantly in warding off both.

He asked his cabinet to consider the British alliance, offering three inducements to attract Britain: not to make a separate peace with France, letting England take Louisiana if necessary, and granting England commercial concessions.[82] The cabinet rejected the last two inducements but authorized alliance talks "as soon as . . . no arrangements can be made with France." So Jefferson did consider reasonable conditions to lure Britain into an alliance, and the alliance proposal, calling for territorial and commercial concessions to England, was carefully thought out and intentional even if ultimately rejected.[83] As Henry Adams writes, the alliance "contradicted every principle established by President Washington in power and professed by Jefferson in opposition."[84] If Adams is right, Jefferson would not have proposed such an alliance without serious intent.

What is more, Jefferson suppressed his constitutional scruples on both territorial acquisition and debt to carry off the Louisiana Purchase. The Constitution made no explicit provision for the federal government to expand the Union, and Article III of the Louisiana Purchase called for the inhabitants of Louisiana to be incorporated in the United States. Technically, one could argue, a constitutional amendment was necessary to provide such explicit powers. Jefferson himself thought so and discussed it with his colleagues. But warned that the French might back out of the agreement if it was delayed, he went ahead without the amendment. Congress did have authority to ratify treaties, and it subsequently passed the Louisiana agreement by a wide majority. So public opinion was satisfied, which is the ultimate check on executive power. Jefferson commanded large majorities of popular support, right through to the end of his presidency. Thus it is hard to argue, even in his own terms, that he seriously damaged the "limited power" fabric of the new constitutional republic.

Perhaps as big a concern for Jefferson was the cost of the Louisiana Purchase. Considered today the best deal in history, the $11.5 million purchase price at the time (or $15 million if you include the private claims against France that the United States assumed) was three times larger (or nearly five times larger) than the entire annual federal budget (equivalent today of about $10 trillion, three times annual federal spending of around $3.5 trillion). What is more, the federal government already had a large national debt ($71 million in 1791), which Jefferson and his party of limited government were determined to pay down. Jefferson is belittled by his critics for opposing debt while then increasing it, another indication, they say, along with his abandonment of his constitutional scruples, of blatant hypocrisy.

But think about it. Jefferson's reasoning in both cases was consistent. He opposed expanding executive powers in the late 1790s when it meant war with France and the infringement of civil liberties under the repulsive Alien and Sedition Acts. In 1803 he supported expanding executive powers because the purchase of Louisiana preempted war and expanded the domain of civil liberties to potential "sister republics." For Jefferson as for most conservatives, it matters toward what ends and in what proportion to civil society federal power expands, not whether federal power expands at all.[85]

Limited government conservatives, of whom Jefferson was certainly one, do not oppose expanding government per se; they oppose expanding government disproportionately and for the wrong reasons. Crowding out private capital (civil society) and infringing on civil liberties are the wrong reasons. Thus, while increasing the national debt, Jefferson also paid it down even more. From a total of $83 million in 1801, the debt was slashed by one-third to $57 million by 1809, despite the unusual costs of the Barbary wars and the Louisiana Purchase.[86]

Jefferson had principles, to be sure, and those principles guided the general purposes for which he thought government should be responsible. But he was no ideologue, standing on procedural principles—executive powers or use of force—when the higher cause was the substantive opportunity to preserve and expand freedom. The great issues of the republic were resolved in the public square not by institutional mandate.[87] He knew how to prioritize and integrate principle and practice and played a masterful hand in the Louisiana episode, both at home in the personalized politics of the new republic and abroad in the perilous politics of world affairs.

In the end, of course, Jefferson's diplomacy would not have succeeded without the help of unrelated circumstances (much as Reagan's diplomacy would not have succeeded without Gorbachev [see chapter 7]). As Tucker and Hendrickson astutely point out, the "mark of an effective, and even a great, statecraft is not that it is unattended by fortunate circumstances . . . [but its] ability to adapt to, and make use of, such circumstances when they arise."[88] War in Europe, as Jefferson anticipated, was a prerequisite to effect the sale of Louisiana. But war alone was not sufficient. War raged in Europe again in summer 1805 when Jefferson tried briefly a similar diplomacy of threatening alliance with England to pressure France to persuade its ally Spain to sell the Floridas to the United States. But this time France was in a stronger position than in 1803, and Jefferson's ploy did not work.[89]

From 1804 to 1808 Napoleon's fortunes in Europe steadily improved. France had less reason to fear British power, let alone a British-American alliance. Indeed in this period France made plans to invade England.[90] In addition, U.S.-British relations became more troubled as Britain stepped up impressments of U.S. seamen, perhaps because England was now weaker in the European balance and desperately needed to tighten the blockade against France. Thus in the earlier period, when France's position was more precarious and better U.S.-British relations prevailed, it is not improbable that Jefferson's threat of alliance with Britain was a significant, if not decisive, consideration affecting Napoleon's calculations.

Embargo against England

If there was any doubt about Jefferson's willingness to use military force, it should have been dispelled by his ill-fated decision in 1807 to impose an embargo against all American trade with England, an embargo he knew would most probably lead to war unless some significant event occurred in Europe. In fact the embargo did eventually lead to war. But Jefferson's critics interpret this decision as evidence of his determination not to use military force and of his utopian design to replace the use of military force with the sanctions and benefits of commerce. In their mind the embargo confirms both Jefferson's internationalist bent to transform international politics by commerce in place of war and his isolationist bent to withdraw whenever international conflict threatens. The embargo, in effect, called American ships into port and removed the targets from the possibility of British aggression.

The criticism is well-taken. After all, this time America was attacked, and instead of going to war, as nationalists such as Andrew Jackson advocated at the time, Jefferson withdrew.[91] In July 1807 a British warship, the *Leopard*, fired upon an American frigate, the *Chesapeake*, killing three and wounding eighteen Americans. This was the first time Britain attacked a U.S. government vessel as opposed to privateers or private vessels harassing British shipping. Jefferson himself called the attack "this enormity" that "was not only without provocation or justifiable cause; but was committed with the avowed purpose of taking by force from a ship of war of the U.S. a part of her crew" who "were native citizens of the U.S."[92] Yet Jefferson dithered for six months until France and Britain announced in November even more stringent restrictions on neutral trade. Then he imposed the embargo that quickly did more harm to American merchants than did British aggressors.

Isn't this proof that Jefferson was anything but a conservative internationalist who uses military power assertively to expand freedom? Under direct attack, he eschewed military retaliation and responded with a self-defeating embargo. Well, maybe. It depends on whether Jefferson intended the embargo as a final or as an interim measure, and whether he knew that war was likely to follow but wanted to buy time either to allow Congress to take the initiative as he believed the Constitution required or to see if events in Europe might lessen the prospect of war.

Considerable evidence suggests that Jefferson saw the embargo not as an alternative but as a prelude to military force. The threat from England had risen visibly by the middle of the decade. The Pitt government had returned to power in May 1804 and resumed the aggressive campaign against American shipping. Jefferson believed Britain had seized as many as five hundred ships.[93] British frigates blockaded New York and in one encounter with American ships killed an American boat captain, John Pierce, stirring reprisal fever among the American public. A British judge further inflamed American opinion when he pronounced the famous Essex judgment that justified seizures of American ships under the hated Order in Council Laws of 1756.[94]

In addition, conflict with England and Spain on the western frontier was intensifying. Spain conducted raids in the southwest, and General Wilkinson, Jefferson's appointment as governor of the Louisiana Territory, conspired with Aaron Burr, Jefferson's first-term vice president, to encourage the secession of western territories from the United States. In this adventure, Wilkinson and Burr solicited money and assistance from both England and Spain. But for the death of William Pitt in early 1806, England may well have participated.[95] And Spain had been dabbling in such adventures for decades.

Jefferson's messages and budgets to Congress at the beginning of 1806 and 1807 addressed the heightened threats. He called for a rapid acceleration of military spending. Referring in the 1806 message to conflicts with Britain, he said: "some of these conflicts may perhaps admit a peaceful remedy. Where that is competent it is always the most desirable. But some of them are of a nature to be met by force only, and all of them may lead to it."[96] To back up word with deed, Jefferson proposed a comprehensive system of national defense, including the fortification of seaports, organization of a national militia, construction of new battleships and gunboats, and prohibition of exports of arms and ammunition. He emphasized that materials for building ships of the line were already on hand, although he suggested (again) that some vessels be dry-docked in peacetime to save money.[97] Congress approved fifty new gunboats although not the six new battleships Jefferson requested.[98] Robert Smith, Jefferson's secretary of war, supported the buildup, but Madison, his secretary of state, and Gallatin, his secretary of the treasury, had doubts. John Randolph, Jefferson's principal rival in the Republican Party, opposed it outright. Randolph felt that Jefferson had betrayed the philosophy of limited government by advocating a bigger navy and other national projects (including roads to facilitate land defense).

Jefferson's critics say again that he did not really mean the show of force. In a private message, he talked about peace.[99] But, as before, Jefferson was steering between the Scylla of foreign policy and the Charybdis of domestic policy. His announcement at the beginning of his second term that he would not run for a third term (something that was not banned at the time) sparked a furious battle for his succession. Jefferson favored Madison but Randolph favored Monroe. In the political maelstrom that followed, Madison struggled not to become too closely identified with Jefferson.

Nevertheless, Jefferson persisted to boost defense outlays, and the fact that he did so against so much domestic opposition, even from his closest friends (such as Madison), suggests that he understood the need to back up sanctions with the use of force. After the *Chesapeake* incident in July 1807, as even his critics acknowledge, Jefferson "gave considerable thought to the prospect of war with England" and "[a]t various moments in the late summer and fall of 1807 . . . appeared to consider it, on balance, a path superior to a trial at economic coercion."[100]

Thus it is hard to conclude that Jefferson thought of economic sanctions or "peaceable coercion" as an alternative totally distinct from war. More likely, as other accounts suggest, he faced three options in response to the *Chesapeake* incident: do nothing, impose an embargo, or go to war.[101] He chose embargo as an intermediate response that might have to be followed by war. He told his son-in-law in fall 1807 that the embargo would likely end in war, and in January 1808 he wrote: "The alternative was that [embargo] or war. For a certain length of time I think the embargo is a lesser evil than war, but after a certain time it will not be so. If peace should not take place in Europe & if both France and England should refuse to exempt us from their decrees & orders, . . . it will remain for Congress . . . to say at what moment it will become preferable for us to meet war."[102] Again in March 1808 he said the time would likely come "when our interests will render war preferable to a continuance of the embargo."[103]

Without doubt Jefferson believed, falsely as it turned out, that the costs of cutting commerce would hurt England more than it actually did. But he had reason to believe so. The U.S. share of trade on the high seas increased enormously from 1801 to 1805.[104] U.S. shipping *was* vital to England. Why not give this growing form of power a chance to work before plunging the country into war? After all, war with England was different than war with the Barbary pirates or with France through alliance with Britain. War with England would require a maximum domestic effort and raise all the dangers for the U.S. constitutional system that Jefferson feared. Why not step into such a war one toe at a time and in the meantime hope that events beyond one's control—notice the allusion in the quote above to peace between England and France—might reduce the likelihood of war? Nevertheless, Jefferson did contemplate war and in the end it followed, not on Jefferson's watch but under his protégé James Madison. And when it came, Jefferson supported it unhesitatingly.

The knock that Jefferson could not bring himself to use military force in foreign affairs does not hold up. By imposing the embargo, he used a new form of economic coercion, albeit initially peaceful (nonmilitary), to buy time and perhaps avoid the subsequent use of military force. But he did not believe that economic coercion was somehow not coercion or that it alone might suffice to bring about peace. He knew, from his experience with the Barbary pirates, that trade invited the use of force and needed to be protected. So too might sanctions invite the use of force and would have to be backed up at some point with military measures.[105] He used force less than a nationalist might have, who declares all-out war when America is attacked, but also more than an isolationist would, who considers trade as a positive benefit only. And he defied realist logic by employing means that went well beyond his aims (rather than what realists usually fear, namely, that resources will fall short of ambitious aims). The embargo, it could be argued, cost as much if not more than war, and it had much less chance of achieving what Jefferson was after, namely, stopping British impressment. In this case in the end, Jefferson acted more like a liberal than conservative internationalist. He did not use military force early and in smaller amounts but gave sanctions as much time as possible and saw war primarily as a last resort. But he was not a more extreme liberal internationalist who believed that the new diplomacy of sanctions could substitute for war.

What then, short of war, did the embargo hope to achieve? A more telling critique of Jefferson's embargo policy has to do with his diplomatic aims and his assessment of the balance of power in Europe, not his belief that the embargo could substitute for war. He came to see Great Britain as a bigger threat to the United States than France or Spain, when at the time Spain was a bigger threat in the Floridas, and the United

States needed Britain to pressure Spain and its stronger ally, France, to sell the Floridas.[106] As noted above, by 1807 France was much stronger in Europe and, through its alliance with Spain concluded in 1805, posed a bigger threat in the Floridas than did England. Meanwhile, England had become much weaker, one reason no doubt Britain stepped up its efforts to interfere with neutral trade. England's belligerence was a sign of weakness, not strength, particularly after the Whigs came back into power when Pitt died in early 1806. Yet Jefferson rejected a treaty with England in 1806 that, though silent on impressments, might have arrested the deterioration in U.S.-British relations. In a side note, Britain promised to exercise "the greatest caution in the impressing of British seamen."[107] Might this treaty have prevented the *Chesapeake* incident and the ill-fated embargo experiment? Perhaps, but not if the British position vis-à-vis France had continued to deteriorate. That would have made Britain more desperate to stop neutral trade.

Nevertheless, Jefferson might have done better to tilt toward Britain in this period. Britain was weak and offered a concession on impressment that moved toward America's objectives. But Jefferson felt British weakness provided the occasion to settle the impressment issue once and for all. He pressed to exploit British weakness and wanted an explicit commitment on impressment before he risked alienating France, whose support he needed to persuade Spain to sell the Floridas.[108] In the end he got satisfaction on neither impressment nor Florida and weakened America's position in the process.

His error, however, lay not in shying away from the use of force, as his realist critics contend, but in expecting too much from its use, as liberal internationalist critics might argue. Force is only as good as the diplomacy that accompanies it. And Jefferson did not fail to use enough force to achieve his objectives; he failed to trim his objectives to what he could achieve without having to use more force. He did not take the half loaf Britain offered and come back another day for the rest. He held out for the full loaf, and that eventually required war. That seems a more credible criticism of his policy than that he was blinded by his utopian vision of economic power as a substitute for war or that constitutional scruples against war interfered with his prosecution of foreign policy.

The fact that he missed an opportunity to cash in on the embargo for partial objectives suggests that his perception of the embargo as a prelude to war was stronger than any of his critics recognize. If he had been as afraid of war as they suggest, he would have gladly accepted the British offer, especially after his closest associates, Madison and Monroe, negotiated it. Furthermore, Jefferson sacrificed his strict constructionist interpretation of the Constitution on multiple occasions—sending the navy to fight the Barbary pirates, acquiring Louisiana, increasing debt, and enforcing the embargo. He cannot be accused of multiple instances of both hypocrisy *and* strict ideological views. Either he had no principles, which seems unlikely even to his critics, or he had principles that were not as irreconcilable, as his critics allege.

More surprising is why Jefferson did not feel a closer affinity for Britain based on its democratic evolution, as he had with France during the early years of the French Revolution. Britain, whatever its monarchic features that repelled Jefferson, was now much closer to Jefferson's democratic ideals than was the despotic dictator in Paris. Jefferson had long ago soured on the French regime. Napoleon represented for him precisely the militarized state he feared. But by this point, Jefferson apparently made few distinctions among autocrats in Europe. Democratic regime change was possible only by revolution, as in the United States and France. Britain's constitutional advance was taking place more subtly and was therefore, apparently, much less visible to Jefferson.

Jefferson and Domestic Politics

Jefferson's faith in democracy and the common man is one of the great mysteries and marvels of the early American republic. He was an aristocrat, not a commoner or an upwardly mobile man like Hamilton. As Claude Bowers writes, "It is easier to understand the Hamiltonian distrust of democracy than to comprehend the faith of Jefferson—a faith of tremendous significance in history."[109] Jefferson not only believed in democracy; he practiced it. He was the first political organizer of grassroots politics in America. In fall 1791, Jefferson encouraged the formation of a national newspaper, *The National Gazette*, to counter the newspaper that Hamilton started two years earlier, *The Gazette of the United States*. In that same year, competing pamphlets by the European conservative, Edward Burke, and the American revolutionary, Thomas Paine, stoked divisions between more traditionally oriented Americans, who favored an oligarchic republic along the lines of England's constitutional monarchy, and more grassroots revolutionary-minded Americans, who favored a democratic republic with all power vested in the legislature.

Jefferson, against all expectations of background, education, and lifestyle, sided with the revolutionaries.[110] After he left office in 1794, as Bowers chronicles, "he set out to arouse the masses, mobilize, drill, and lead them." "Quite as remarkable as his faith," Bowers observes, "was the ability of Jefferson to mobilize, organize, and discipline the great individualistic mass of the town, the remote farms along the Savannah, the unbroken wilds of the Western wilderness."[111] For the 1796 elections, he had lieutenants in every state, and his supporters had organized Democratic-Republican Clubs all over the country. Jefferson may have initiated the first "tea party" movement in America, if that phrase refers to a grassroots movement vigorously opposed to big government and eager to participate in self-government. He was literally the founder of modern American party politics.

Jefferson believed in "absolute acquiescence in the decisions of the majority—the vital principle of republics." From this principle, he argued, "there is no appeal but to force, the vital principle and immediate parent of despotism."[112] For Jefferson, the critical distinction between republics and autocracies hinged on the use of force in domestic politics. In autocracies force was the arbiter of politics, in republics reason was. "He who would do his country the most good he can," observed Jefferson, "must go quietly with the prejudices of the majority until he can lead them into reason."[113] And, as Jefferson said in his famous line from his first inaugural, reason tolerated even treason as long as it was open: "If there be any among us who would wish to dissolve this Union or to change its republican form, let them stand undisturbed as monuments of the safety with which error of opinion may be tolerated where reason is left free to combat it."[114]

Again, Jefferson not only believed it, he practiced it. His contemporaries were dismayed at his long-suffering patience during the events surrounding the conspiracy of Aaron Burr. He met personally with Burr at the time despite Burr's attacks on his presidency. He repeatedly refused to place either Burr or Wilkinson under surveillance let alone arrest them. Critics chalk it up to Jefferson's naïveté, but a more favorable interpretation might contrast Jefferson's tolerance of such dissent with that of the Federalist-run government when it tried to squash dissent through the Alien and Sedition Acts.

Jefferson was the "classical liberal" republican of his day. He accepted both the rule of reason over tradition and religion and the rule of majoritarianism over pure libertarian views represented by Randolph. He fit squarely in the top right-hand box of Figure 1.1. He did not reject tradition or religion. In his *Notes on Virginia* published in 1787, he asked: "can the liberties of a nation be thought secure when we have removed their only firm basis, a conviction in the minds of the people that these liberties are the gift of God?"[115] But he rejected specific religions and any special social status derived from tradition. And he clearly favored less central government than did his Federalist rivals. He was a bottom-up democrat. In 1816 he wrote Samuel Kercheval: "The article nearest my heart is the division of counties into wards. These will be pure and elementary republics, the sum of all which, taken together, composes the State, and will make of the whole a true democracy as to the business of the wards, which is that of the nearest and daily concern."[116] Jefferson cut taxes and debt and preferred civil society institutions, such as education and media, over government, even when some of those institutions were stacked against him. Jefferson thought little of the press of his day and once commented that "when I read the newspapers and see what a mass of falsehood and what an atom of truth they contain, I am mortified . . . that 99/100th of mankind pass through life imagining they have known what was going forward when they would have been nearer the truth had they heard nothing."[117] Yet with the Federalists accounting for three-quarters of the national press, Jefferson nevertheless asserted: "If left to me to decide whether we should have a government without newspapers or newspapers without a government, I should not hesitate for a moment to prefer the latter."[118]

In retrospect, the differences among Americans at the time were probably not as great as they are today. Most Americans were classical liberals; social liberals and social democracy did not appear until the end of the nineteenth century. As Merrill Peterson points out, "'reason' for him [Jefferson], in the final analysis, was perhaps not very different from that of most Federalists, but he preferred to find it in the majority opinion of the community rather than in the conceits of self-styled guardians of the public interest [experts]."[119] Jefferson himself once defined the difference as follows: "The one [party] desires to preserve an entire independence of the executive and legislative branches on each other and the dependence of both on the same source—the free election of the people. The other party wishes to lessen the dependence of the Executive and one branch of the Legislature on the people, . . . so as to reduce the elective franchise to its minimum."[120]

Jefferson was also exceedingly gentle in how he practiced these differences. He visited Adams in the brand-new President's House (as the White House was originally called) shortly after he defeated Adams in the closest (a tie in the Electoral College and 36 ballots in the House of Representatives) and perhaps most bitter election in American history. Adams began tartly, "you have turned me out"; Jefferson responded:

> I have not turned you out, Mr. Adams; and I am glad to avail myself of this occasion to show that I have not and to explain my views. In consequence of a division of opinion existing among our fellow-citizens, as to the proper constitution of our political institutions, and of the wisdom and propriety of certain measures . . . that portion of our citizens that approved and advocated one class of these opinions and measures selected you as their candidate . . . and their opponents selected me. If you and myself had been inexistent, or for any cause had not been selected, other persons would have been selected in our places; and thus the contest would have been carried on, and with the same result,

except that the party which supported you would have been defeated by a greater majority, as it was known that, but for you, your party would have carried their unpopular measures much further than they did.[121]

The statement depersonalizes partisan politics yet enthrones partisan public opinions as the arbiter of American politics. It provides a timeless lesson for contemporary American politics. Jefferson embraced partisanship as the only way to safeguard the truth, which no one monopolizes. On the other hand, he understood that partisanship is not warfare. As he said in his first inaugural, "Every difference of opinion is not a difference of principle."

Jefferson accepted majoritarian decisions even when he believed they contravened the Constitution. He did not challenge the constitutionality of the Alien and Sedition Acts, even though both acts passed the House by slim majorities (46–40 and 44–41, respectively). The bills expired on his watch, and Jefferson never proposed legislation to rescind them, although he pardoned those prosecuted and imprisoned under the acts. As his comment to Adams suggests, he trusted more in the decisions of the public square (e.g., the 1800 elections) than in the rulings of courts. By contrast, Jefferson backed legislation, the Judicial Act of 1801, to rescind the "midnight" appointments of judges used by Federalists to stack the federal courts before leaving office. For him the arbiter was always the people and the legislature, not the courts and executive power. He was content to let the people decide and rejected the idea, popular among Federalists and activist government enthusiasts thereafter, that bureaucratic precedents should play a large role in fleshing out the implied powers of the executive branch.

Jefferson saw the purpose of the new Constitution to lie primarily in the area of foreign policy: "to make the States one in everything connected with foreign nations, and several as to everything purely domestic."[122] Nevertheless, as he experienced, divisions played out in foreign policy no less than in domestic policy. Such divisions also had to be tempered by the rule of reason. When divisions spawned by the Genet affair became too intense—the French envoy who stirred up Americans to defy the neutrality policy of the Federalist administration—Jefferson backed the recall of Genet. When Jefferson acted to purchase Louisiana without explicit powers, he left it up to the Senate to ratify the treaty. And when he contemplated war, he was ever mindful that the people paid the ultimate costs: "It is for the benefit of mankind to mitigate the horrors of war as much as possible." The final arbiter of all decisions was public opinion. In this sense, as Peterson further notes, "popularity was a positive value;

had he not possessed it, Jefferson would have deemed his presidency a failure."[123]

Jefferson's passion for peace in foreign affairs was not a function of utopianism; it was a consequence of his republican views of government. Any foreign policy action had to meet the approval of the people, immediately or within a reasonable period of time prescribed by elections. With that as an ultimate constraint, Jefferson ventured far more in foreign policy than would a realist, who often finds public opinion to be a nuisance, and he challenged public opinion far more than would a liberal internationalist, who is often content to follow rather than lead public opinion, especially on matters of the optional use of force. He desired peace and non-entanglement for his country but not at the expense of foregoing opportunities to spread freedom abroad, something nationalists and neo-isolationists never consider. The conservative internationalist undertakes ambitious objectives that demand more in terms of the use of force but never breaches the discipline of majoritarian public opinion that ultimately legitimates an armed diplomacy for freedom.

For all of these reasons—spreading freedom, arming diplomacy, advocating small government, promoting education and civil society, and challenging but ultimately yielding to the will of the people—Jefferson was more of a conservative internationalist than a realist, nationalist (isolationist) or liberal internationalist.

Chapter 5

James K. Polk
MANIFEST DESTINY

JAMES POLK WAS WITHOUT question one of the most ambitious and successful presidents in American history. In four short years, he expanded American territory to incorporate Texas, the southwest territories of New Mexico and California, and the northwest territories of Oregon. Remarkably, he announced all of these goals beforehand. And he accomplished them as a lame-duck president facing a cabinet and Congress of presidential wannabes because he promised upon his unexpected nomination in 1844 to serve only one term. Historians generally rank Polk quite high, consistently around the top ten.[1] As Paul Bergeron writes: "Polk's achievements in diplomacy were among the most remarkable in American history."[2] "In the nineteenth century," John Seigenthaler adds, "only Thomas Jefferson, Andrew Jackson, and Abraham Lincoln would wield the power of the office of chief magistrate as effectively."[3]

But Polk is also at the epicenter of unparalleled controversy among historians. He did not succeed without war with Mexico and without contributing to the passions of the slavery question that led a decade and a half later to the Civil War. For these reasons, Polk's star has been diminished by many historians.[4] The main charges are threefold: (1) Polk was a "sectionalist," if not racist, slave master who expanded the country to promote slavery, hastening the onset of the Civil War; (2) Polk was an aggressive "continentalist" or imperialist who used force unnecessarily and excessively to expand the country when diplomacy might have sufficed; and (3) Polk was a mendacious, unprincipled individual who lacked human empathy and manipulated colleagues and adversaries to serve his own ambitions.

Interpretations of Polk reflect the debate among America's foreign policy traditions. Polk's most severe critics are liberal internationalists, in his day the opposition Whig Party. Led by Henry Clay in the Senate and John Quincy Adams in the House, Whigs championed activist government projects such as national roads and central banks and "opposed the use of force to achieve [expansionist] ends, believing that contiguous lands would voluntarily join the Union" or "ripen like fruit and fall into the lap of the United States."[5] William Seward of New York, a leading Whig at the time and later Lincoln's secretary of state, explained the liberal internationalist logic: "open borders and increasing commerce coupled with respect for local autonomy would draw the foreign [territories] inescapably into the most advanced form of Western civilization and hence also serve to elevate [them]."[6] Whigs favored negotiation by consent of all parties concerned (multilateralism) and resort to force only if negotiations failed. They opposed annexing Texas without Mexican consent and accused Polk of waging an unnecessary and illegitimate war against Mexico. In time, they believed, American settlers would have populated and incorporated these territories peacefully into the United States, either as independent republics or as states annexed to the United States.

From this point of view, the war was immoral and unnecessary. By going to war, Polk threatened to saddle America with multiple "Irelands"— conquered territories that would bleed the United States dry and, more important, gut its model of a peaceful democratic republic, as Ireland had done to the English Westminster model for a century after its violent conquest.[7] Finally, abolitionist Whigs accused Polk of exporting racism not freedom and doing it in the most arrogant and unilateral fashion imaginable, "insensitive to the ideals and convictions of others" with no "ability to appreciate a foreign people's hopes, fears and driving impulses and to see America and himself through their eyes."[8]

The realist tradition considers Polk too aggressive. He exaggerated the threats facing the United States and addressed too many of them at once. He almost involved the country in simultaneous wars with Mexico over California and New Mexico and Great Britain over Oregon. John C. Calhoun, the senator and secretary of state under Polk's predecessor, President John Tyler, repeatedly advised Polk on realist grounds to avoid war with both Great Britain and Mexico, although he embraced the annexation of Texas to expand slavery. Unlike the model realist, however, Polk did not see the world primarily in terms of good relations among the great powers. He resisted personal diplomacy and "could not bypass the restricted official channels through friendly private discussion, for he usually viewed foreign representatives with suspicion and treated them with stiff propriety"[9] As Charles Sellers writes, "he scorned the ordinary considerations of prudence in his dealings with other nations," prudence being the hallmark of the consummate realist statesman.[10]

Nationalists offer the most sympathetic interpretation. After all, Polk was a protégé of Andrew Jackson, the lodestar of American nationalism. According to David Pletcher, he "epitomized the self-centered, aggressive nationalism prevalent in the Mississippi Valley during much of the nineteenth century."[11] "[T]o Polk," Walter Borneman writes, "the issue of national expansion was imperative to the nation as a whole and distinctly separate from the advancement of a slave-based economic system."[12] Sean Wilentz, another historian, concurs: "Polk emphatically did not seek California to spread slavery and enlarge the slaveholders' political power. . . . Rather, he expected the efforts to acquire new territory would unite men of good will in a national endeavor."[13] Nor, for nationalists who assess Polk favorably, was such expansion imperialism; it was the spread of restless and energetic self-government. As Polk explained in his inaugural message, "our people . . . have filled the eastern valley of the Mississippi, adventurously ascended the Missouri to its headsprings, and are already engaged in establishing the blessings of self-government in valleys of which the rivers flow to the Pacific." To those who argued that the annexation of Texas was incompatible with liberty because of local institutions condoning slavery, Polk responded: "Upon the same principle that they would refuse to form a perpetual union with Texas because of her local institutions our forefathers would have been prevented from forming our present Union."[14]

Even for some nationalists, however, Polk went too far. He was too eager to expand and promote self-government. He went beyond what his mentor Jackson did. In 1836, Jackson faced an *existing* war between Texas and Mexico and, as Borneman writes, "even Andrew Jackson—the very embodiment of what would soon be called manifest destiny—failed to annex Texas."[15] Jackson's commitment was to union, not expansion of union.[16] Polk, by contrast, some critics argue, *created* a war to annex Texas and expand. Nationalists preserve the status quo; they don't disrupt it. And they don't interfere with national autonomy. Polk and other Americans before him meddled mischievously in Mexican affairs and denigrated Mexican culture.[17] From this critical nationalist perspective, Polk was both too radical and too imperialist. He turned the defensive intent of the Monroe Doctrine to forestall European intervention in the western hemisphere into an offensive strategy to facilitate American intervention across the continent.[18]

Polk defies easy categorization by the familiar traditions. Whether he exported self-government or slavery, he cared about changing the status quo, not preserving it. For him, it was not just about material power, as nationalists and realists sometimes insist. And although he used force to the fullest, he always used it in close association with diplomatic aims, which liberal internationalists value. In fact, as I show in this chapter, he coupled force and diplomacy so adroitly that his approach remains a model for contemporary statesmanship. He took military risks to achieve ambitious objectives but was always flexible with a diplomatic plan to compromise military gains for peace at any time. Finally, it is true that he was a consummate politician. He often kept his actual purposes hidden and opened himself to charges of duplicity, mendacity, and lack of scruples. But what good statesman doesn't exhibit these traits at times? And, as Bergeron writes, "he was, after all, engaged in a game of high-stakes diplomacy with the powerful rival Great Britain during a time of intense nationalistic feelings in America."[19] In this supercharged environment, he might be forgiven if he did not always behave like an altar boy. He still practiced one of the most open forms of cabinet government in the young republic's history.

A Conservative Internationalist Interpretation

Polk exemplified the three main attributes of conservative internationalism. He went beyond the status quo to spread democratic self-government but disciplined this quest by setting clear priorities. He used force to arm his diplomacy but never to replace it. And he respected the right of Congress and public opinion to pass final judgment on his foreign policy. He was not wiser than the people, as some realist statesmen think themselves to be; nor was he constrained to act only with foreign consent, especially the consent of despots, as liberal internationalists prefer.

In his day, it can be argued, Polk fought for freedom not just for nation, race, or land. To be sure, he supported slavery where it existed, Lincoln's position until 1862. And unlike Lincoln, he also supported the Missouri Compromise to permit slavery in new territories to the south. Moreover, he owned slaves and expanded his slaveholdings during his presidency.[20] Still he believed that slavery "would probably never be . . . practical . . . if we acquired New Mexico & California, because there would be but a narrow ribbon of territory South of the Missouri compromise line of 36° 30', and in it slavery would probably never exist."[21] If slavery had been his primary objective, he would have wanted more of Mexico than this "narrow ribbon," from the beginning; yet his bottom line never included territory below the thirty-second parallel, which would have incorporated today's northern provinces of Mexico. Moreover, he was just as enthusiastic about expansion in Oregon where slavery was never a possibility.

Like the founding fathers, who were also slave masters, Polk did not envision self-government for manacled slaves, dispossessed Indians, and subjugated women; but he did promote it for an ever larger number of white male farmers who were often uneducated and rebellious. Polk believed, as Jefferson did, that these rowdy settlers had the right to govern themselves or they would never be able to govern others. Already in the 1770s, the average electorate of the American colonies was four times as large as that in Britain, and after 1789 the executive and both houses of Congress were elected whereas the executive and upper house in Britain were appointed by the crown.[22] By 1840, 78 percent of adult white males were eligible to vote in the United States, a higher percentage than any other Western country at the time.[23] Expansion was central to widening this franchise because the frontier was all about land, independence, *and* liberty for white settlers.[24] In his first message to Congress Polk explained: "It is the true purpose of the Government to afford facilities to its citizens to become the owners of small portions of our vast public domain at low and moderate rates."[25] The government facilitates opportunity, and an ever larger number of people possess and dominate the land—an early version of the limited government, entrepreneurial democracy championed by many conservative Americans today.

In hindsight Polk is unquestionably a racist, if not worse when one considers the genocide that decimated native Americans and their lands. But in foresight, it can be argued, he represented and articulated the expansive vision of a young and struggling republic that granted more liberty to more white people *then*, and went on to secure more liberty for more peoples of all colors *later*, than any other country that might have settled and governed the western territories after 1848. The Declaration of Independence haunted Polk, just as it did Washington and Jefferson.[26] All of these men, along with Andrew Jackson, promoted a mass electorate, limited at the time to yeoman farmers of their own race but pregnant with possibilities for eventual emancipation of all races.[27] The surging republic that Jefferson and Polk expanded, then half slave and half free, was the same country that went on to end slavery, emancipate women, redress Indians, and welcome people of every color and gender. Henry David Thoreau, the radical advocate of American individualism, protested the Mexican War and spent time in jail because of it; and Abraham Lincoln, the great emancipator and a young congressman at the time, denounced the war on the House floor and voted against it. The country was not yet whole, or indeed has never been, but it was moving in the right direction, arguably faster than others.

The real question is whether emancipation for blacks and others would have come sooner if the course of history had moved in a different direction. What if Mexico had retained jurisdiction of New Mexico and California? Mexico abolished slavery in 1828, but Mexican farmers, nominally free Indians, lived in virtual serfdom and the aristocracy and church monopolized the best lands and official positions.[28] Elites in Mexico, unlike those in the United States, did not advocate widening ownership of land and citizenship for Mexican farmers, and Mexico had as much unused land as the United States. What if European nations had colonized the western territories instead of the United States? England abolished slavery in 1833 and expanded the franchise in 1832 (still not as widely as in the United States). Both Mexico and England favored abolishing slavery in Texas. France, Spain, and Russia also competed for the western territories, and each at the time was experiencing liberalizing influences to one extent or another. What if independent or "sister republics" had spread across the continent, as Jefferson envisioned and Texas initially represented? This is the most intriguing possibility, since it might have led to a more equitable and diverse American continent. But the expectation of an early "democratic peace" across the American continent seems a bit of a stretch. And if we consider how the other possible outcomes later fared, it seems far-fetched. For, over the next century, Mexico stagnated in warlordism and poverty; colonial powers such as Spain and Russia succumbed to fascism and communism; and the balance of power in Europe, which foreign colonization would have brought to the American continent, devoured liberal and despotic prospects alike in two horrific world wars. Moral judgments about history are never easy, but that holds for a confident condemnation of Polk no less than for a cautious vindication. On balance, given the imponderables of history, it is not unreasonable to conclude that, over the next hundred years, expansion of the American republic in the 1840s served the cause of freedom for natives and settlers alike better than any of the alternatives would have.[29]

Could expansion have occurred without war? This is a more telling critique. Polk's use of force was aggressive. To critics, it amounted to salami tactics—the application of military force, then a diplomatic offer that the adversary could not accept, and then more military force.[30] But what if the use of force was not intended to displace diplomacy but to empower it? Polk armed his diplomacy to move negotiations toward freedom, not to win wars without negotiations. David Pletcher, who has written one of the most detailed histories of the annexations of the 1840s, calls the approach "aggressive negotiations." He describes it this way:

> Polk . . . set forth on a foreign policy of strong stands, overstated arguments, and menacing publications, not because he wanted war but because he felt that this was the only language which his foreign adversaries would understand. . . . . Impelled by his conviction that successful diplomacy could rest only on a threat of force, he made his way, step by step, down the path of war. Then, viewing the war as a mere extension of his diplomatic stance,

he proceeded as confidently as a sleepwalker through a maze
of obstacles and hazards to the peace settlement he had calmly
intended from the beginning.[31]

Polk was unique among expansionists in believing that he could acquire
the western territories by purchase, not by force.[32] But to do so, he had to
persuade Mexico that there were no better options outside the negotiating process. If Mexico believed it could hold the land militarily, it would
have no incentive to sell. Polk's combination of force and diplomacy was
risky, to be sure, and unnecessary if one did not share his territorial goals.
But given his goals the threat of force was necessary to conclude negotiations without war; and, once war occurred, Polk's use of force involved
lower cost outcomes than other alternatives would have, such as the conquest and occupation of all of Mexico. Moreover, Polk's diplomacy was
not the sole reason for war. If Mexico had been sufficiently united during
this period to make decisions, it might have settled the Texas issue sooner
and made a better deal for the rest of the southwest territories than the
one that eventually resulted. Certainly it would have made a deal before
the Americans occupied Mexico City. But as Pletcher concludes, "Mexico
could neither defend the region effectively nor sell it honorably."[33] It decided by default as much as by logic to seek a better deal by force of arms.
The decision proved fatal.

Did Polk's policies cause the Civil War? This argument is least persuasive. Expansion, it is claimed, abetted secessionist tendencies, provoked
congressional legislation containing the Wilmot Proviso that banned
slavery in the southwest territories, and directly caused the Civil War.[34]
But the congressional votes that ratified expansion crossed party and regional lines and at least for the moment overcame rather than exacerbated sectional differences.[35] To be sure, expansion shattered the Missouri
Compromise of 1820 and spawned the controversial concept of popular
sovereignty—new states deciding on their own whether they wanted to
be free or slave. But slavery would have almost certainly provoked war at
some point with or without expansion. The Kansas-Nebraska conflict in
1854 was a more direct antecedent to the Civil War, and it had nothing
to do with the expansion of the country in the 1840s. It was a product
of an earlier expansion, the Louisiana Purchase, and was an issue both
before and during the Mexican War. In August 1847 James Buchanan,
Polk's secretary of state, proposed extending the Missouri Compromise
to accommodate the Mexican territories, and in the next month Polk's
vice president, George Dallas, came up with the idea of letting the people
of each territory determine whether they wanted slavery.[36] These ideas
eventually became the epicenter of civil conflict in Kansas and Nebraska,
suggesting that civil war was coming whether or not the country ex-

panded in the 1840s.[37] Expansion, therefore, cannot be blamed for the Civil War (unless you want to blame the Louisiana Purchase). That conflict was deeply embedded in the young republic since its birth. "It would be safer to argue," as Pletcher does, "that Texas, Oregon, and the Mexican War hastened and intensified trends that might have led to the same results eventually."[38]

Expansion in the 1840s, on the other hand, may have affected the outcome of the Civil War in a positive way. In 1840 borders were in dispute everywhere in North America—not only in the southwest and northwest but also in the northeast where the United States and Great Britain did not settle the Maine border until 1842. Expanding the country before the Civil War preempted border threats from foreign neighbors that might have weakened the Union during the Civil War. Mexico, Britain, France, and Spain all plotted to exploit America's divisions between North and South. As it was, France intervened in Mexico, Spain briefly reannexed Santo Domingo, and Great Britain flirted with recognition of the Confederacy. Had European powers been able to carry out these interventions from borders that existed in 1844 rather than ones that existed in 1861, they might have been more successful. In that sense, the Mexican War preempted the potential dismemberment of the American republic. As Pletcher writes, "European efforts against American expansion did not entirely cease after 1848, but never again did their agents act so boldly and so close to American borders as did Captain Charles Elliot, the British consul in Texas [who promoted a British-Mexican proposal to guarantee Texas independence without annexation]."[39] Finally, earlier rather than later annexation helped the Union prepare for war. Immigrants poured into northern states in the 1850s to take advantage of the opening up of western lands. These immigrants ensured northern superiority in numbers when war ultimately came, a crucial advantage given the unprecedented carnage of that conflict.

What about the charge that Polk was duplicitous and mendacious? There is little doubt that Polk was strong-willed and self-confident. Sam Haynes writes, "the president was a complete stranger to self-doubt and was rarely dissuaded once he made up his mind."[40] Arthur Schlesinger Jr., too, concludes: "Polk has been excelled by few presidents in his ability to concentrate the energies of his administration toward the attainment of given ends."[41] And Stephen Skowronek adds: "Once in office, Polk threw himself into his task with a single-minded passion. . . . He rushed headlong to complete one agenda item after another in as uncompromising a fashion as possible."[42] So Polk knew how to set priorities and stalk his prey. He combined the intellectual acumen of Jefferson with the military instincts of Jackson and forged a strategy of diplomacy and power that rivaled any in American history.

But did he lie and deceive? Some critics see in his personality the poisons of paranoia and conspiracy. Dusinberre says he had a lifelong need to prove himself, perhaps because of a traumatic operation at age seventeen to remove gall bladder stones in an age before anesthesia, which left him sterile.[43] More historians argue that he deceived a group of senators about the acquisition of Texas and, on many occasions, was less than forthright with foreign interlocutors as well as congressional colleagues. But in fact Polk ran a more open government than any president up to that point.[44] All major decisions he aired not once but repeatedly in cabinet meetings, and his schedule of consultations with Congress was unprecedented. Did he say some things to one group and other things to another group? Yes, as almost all successful politicians have done. But as a strict constructionist and former Speaker of the House, Polk respected the role of Congress; and as a Jeffersonian Democrat, he had a keener sense of the public mood, especially for western expansion, than his Whig opponents and some in his own party. As we will see, he tolerated insubordination from military commanders as well as cabinet officers yet maintained a steady hand on his goals. In the end he satisfied both domestic public opinion bent on western expansion and foreign rivals who contested but then accepted American expansion.

Let's look more closely at Polk's foreign policy accomplishments: the annexation of Texas, the acquisition of the southwest territories and war with Mexico, and the settlement of the Oregon issue.

Annexation of Texas

Texas was the issue, it could be said, that made Polk president. The issue had festered since the mid-1830s when Texas defeated Mexico and declared its independence. Thereafter Texas and Mexico continued to fight over the western border of Texas between the Nueces and the Rio Grande rivers (including a salient going north to include Sante Fe and the eastern part of New Mexico). And Texas flirted both with annexation to the United States and with independence under a guarantee from Mexico and Great Britain if Texas foreswore annexation with the United States. The issue came to a head in April 1844 when President John Tyler signed an annexation agreement with Texas in which the United States committed to defend Texas's disputed borders, sending for the first time an army force to Fort Jessup on the Louisiana border of Texas near the Sabine River and a naval force to the Gulf of Mexico to patrol the southern border of Texas, including the mouth of the Rio Grande.

Long before Polk became president, John C. Calhoun made slavery a central issue in the annexation debate. As secretary of state in spring 1844, he responded to a British dispatch, which affirmed Britain's desire to abolish slavery in Texas but also stated its intention not to intervene to

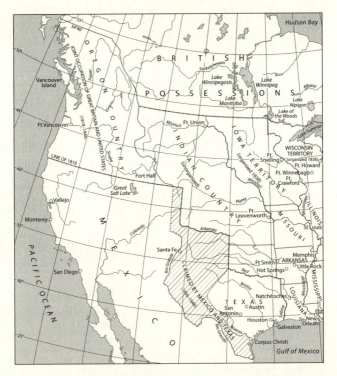

Map 5.1. The contested areas in the Texas, Mexican, and Oregon expansions. Redrawn from Albert Bushnell Hart, LL. D., *The American Nation, Vol. 16*. New York, NY: Harper and Brothers, 1906. Courtesy of Maps ETC.

that effect, by extolling the virtues of slavery and declaring that slavery was essential to the safety, peace, and prosperity of the South. By implication he made slavery the rationale for annexing Texas. Abolitionists wasted no time taking up the fight, and the agreement to annex Texas failed Senate ratification in June 1844 by a significant margin, 35–16.[45] Thus if the issue of expansion became sectionalist, it did so in summer 1844, well before Polk became president. Rather than exacerbating sectionalism, Polk may have actually tempered it, securing annexation one year later without splitting either his party or the country along sectional lines.

Texas now became the key issue in the 1844 presidential race. All candidates were canvassed about their views on Texas. Polk, even before hearing what other candidates had said, declared unequivocally for "reannexation" of Texas, using the term that implied Texas had belonged to the United States under the Louisiana Purchase.[46] Martin Van Buren, the former president and front-runner for the 1844 Democratic nomination, opposed Tyler's Texas treaty, fearing it would split the Democratic Party. Unhappy with Van Buren's decision, Andrew Jackson and other expansionist-oriented Democrats looked immediately for another candidate. Polk had been running for vice president as a "stealth horse"; now he seized the nomination for president as a "dark horse," displaying some of the political finesse that characterized his diplomacy.[47] To appease better-known rivals, Polk pledged immediately to serve only one term and got Jackson to persuade Tyler not to run as an independent candidate on the Texas issue. He also softened Jackson's distemper over Van Buren's defection on Texas. He needed Van Buren and the northern Democrats to win the election. As it was, he won New York, Van Buren's state, by a mere 5,107 votes out of 485,000 cast (the abolitionist third party, the Liberty Party, drew away 15,812 votes), clinching the Electoral College in a razor-thin popular vote.[48]

Polk's election confirmed public sentiment for annexation. Immediately after the election, Tyler resubmitted the Texas agreement to a lameduck Congress as a joint resolution, circumventing the Senate's jurisdiction over foreign treaties. He aggressively pressed the House to pass the resolution, which it did in January 1845. The bill admitted Texas as a state (which the Constitution explicitly authorized [Article IV, Section 3]) rather than as a territory (as in the earlier submission, for which there was no explicit constitutional authority). The Senate, reflecting liberal internationalist sentiments and led by Thomas Hart Benson from Missouri, favored renegotiating the agreement to secure Mexican consent. Robert J. Walker, senator from Mississippi and subsequently Polk's secretary of treasury, proposed a compromise, apparently suggested by Polk.[49] It gave the president the option to proceed under the House plan (annexation) or the Senate plan (renegotiation). The compromise passed the Senate by two votes, and the House then approved the Senate version. At this point Polk is accused of mendacity. According to accounts drawn up three years later in the midst of the 1848 election campaign, Polk assured Benson and other senators that he would choose the Senate plan. Reportedly, according to one of the senators involved, John Dix, Polk said "if he had any discretion placed in his hands, he would exercise it in such a matter as to satisfy us."[50]

Perhaps to reduce that discretion, Polk did nothing when Tyler instructed Andrew Jackson Donelson, Jackson's nephew and the American negotiator in Texas, to proceed with annexation. Informed of Tyler's action by Calhoun the day before he took office on March 4, 1845, Polk "declined to express any opinion or to make any suggestion in reference to the subject."[51] Once in office, however, he implemented Tyler's policy. Following a cabinet meeting on March 10, he instructed Donelson to proceed with annexation without delay. He later refused to show these instructions to Benson.[52] So, as Pletcher concludes, "Polk probably welcomed Tyler's impetuous action as a release from his own commitment to the Benton clique."[53] Was it duplicitous? Maybe, as Sellers concludes, the best answer is ambiguous: "Clearly Polk deceived . . . [but] his deception was partly unconscious, neither altogether intentional nor altogether inadvertent."[54]

Is there any chance that Mexico might have consented to the peaceful annexation of Texas by renegotiation? The answer is a resounding no. On March 6, 1845, the Mexican ambassador in Washington, Juan N. Almonte, condemned the congressional actions of late February as "an act of aggression, the most unjust which can be found recorded in the annals of modern history, namely—that of despoiling a friendly nation like Mexico, of a considerable portion of her territory." Mexico, Almonte added, would continue "by every means which may be in her power . . . to recover the above mentioned province of Texas."[55] Mexico broke ties, as it had promised to do in the case of annexation already in August 1843, and the two countries headed toward war in March 1945 if Texas agreed to annexation.[56]

The alternative to annexation was a British-Mexican proposal, negotiated by Charles Elliot, the British minister in Texas, to recognize Texas independence if Texas agreed never to annex itself to another country.[57] Mexico approved this proposal on May 19, 1845, and on June 4 Anson Jones, the president of Texas who had succeeded Sam Houston in September 1844, formally announced the agreement with Mexico and proclaimed an end to the Texas-Mexican war. He also called for a general convention of the Texas legislature to consider both the Mexican agreement and U.S. annexation. A major issue was defense of the Texas border on the Rio Grande. The British-Mexican agreement was also ambiguous on this border.[58] Polk's emissaries in Texas reassured Jones that the United States would defend the Rio Grande border, and Houston, seen as the power behind Jones, went to visit Andrew Jackson to secure further assurances (arriving a few days after Jackson died).

In early June, Polk wrote Houston that after annexation "we will maintain all your rights of territory." In a letter to Donelson on June 15, he ordered U.S. troops under Zachary Taylor to move from Ft. Jessup in Louisiana, where they had been posted in spring 1844, to encamp along "the [south] western frontier of Texas . . . on or near the Rio Grande del Norte, such a site as will consist with the health of the troops, and will be best adapted to repel invasion, and to protect what, in the event of annexation, will be our [south] western border." He also sent an additional squadron under Commodore Robert F. Stockton to reinforce U.S. naval forces patrolling along the Gulf coast.[59] Polk's letter to Donelson did not specify the exact location of the troops but gave Donelson discretion to position them as needed in the case of invasion. Polk did say: "I would maintain the Texan title to the extent which she claims it to be and not permit an invading enemy a foot of the soil East of the Rio Grande."[60] On

June 28, fearing an overthrow of the Jones government by swelling annexation sentiment and a Mexican attack on the Rio Grande, Donelson directed Taylor to take up positions at San Antonio and Matagordo Bay, east of the Nueces River, and at Corpus Christi, just barely west of the mouth of the Nueces.[61] Thus, as the Texas ratification conference met on July 4, U.S. forces were en route to positions next to but not yet directly in the disputed region between the Nueces and Rio Grande rivers. The Texas conference, comprised almost entirely of American settlers, opted nearly unanimously for annexation with the United States. U.S. troops arrived in San Antonio and Corpus Christi one week later to defend what was now arguably the new border of the United States.[62]

Did Polk deliberately seek a war to compel the annexation of Texas? Later Commodore Stockton, who along with other Polk emissaries such as William S. Parrott, Alexander Yell, and Charles A. Wickliffe pressured and perhaps bribed Texas legislators to pass annexation, alleged that Polk tried to get Jones to "manufacture" a war with Mexico to bring about annexation. Based on a narrative written five years later by Jones, most historians doubt the charge.[63] As Pletcher writes, "while Stockton may have plotted with Texan expansionists for an invasion of northern Mexico, there is no conclusive evidence that he did more than encourage the Texans to defend themselves against a Mexican crossing of the Rio Grande. If the commodore had aggressive intentions, it is certain that these did not receive the slightest support from Donelson," who "cautioned the commodore against aggressive action."[64] "Polk," Pletcher concludes, "was not trying to provoke a Mexican attack during the spring of 1845."[65] It is more likely, as Sam Haynes argues, that by early summer "Washington aimed to send a clear and unequivocal message to Mexico and Great Britain that it would brook no interference in its plans to annex Texas."[66]

Had Polk wanted or expected an attack in Mexico, his actions at the same time in the Oregon conflict are inexplicable. In late August, Polk withdrew his compromise offer to settle the Oregon issue with the British, intensifying that conflict, a step he was unlikely to have taken if he was looking toward an imminent war with Mexico.[67] And Polk did not explicitly authorize troops to occupy the disputed Texas territory until January 1846 after he made a serious effort in fall 1845 to settle the southwest territories issue peacefully for cash and without California if necessary. Polk sought to use force to arm his diplomacy, not diplomacy to rationalize the use of force. Pletcher once again summarizes best Polk's conservative internationalist instincts:

> Polk's every action in foreign affairs, beginning with his inaugural address, indicates that he preferred to negotiate from a position of strength, real or apparent. This being the case, it was

logical for him to send Parrott to inquire about the possibilities
of negotiation and, hearing rumors of Mexican attack, to occupy
at least part of the territory he intended to gain. From March
through July all evidence suggests that no one expected Mexico
to attack. Gerolt's [Prussian ambassador in Washington] confidential information [that Mexico was sending troops to reinforce the border] caused a brief flurry of genuine surprise and
hasty preparations that were entirely defensive. Instead of ordering Taylor to advance, Marcy instructed him to wait until the
Mexicans crossed the Rio Grande.[68]

The argument does not end there, however. Polk's critics point out that he
sought a greater prize. If war was not necessary to acquire Texas, it was
necessary to acquire New Mexico and California. We now turn to Polk's
diplomacy to acquire the southwest territories.

Acquisition of New Mexico and California

As Paul Bergeron writes, "the annexation of Texas set in motion an almost irrepressible movement to stretch the nation's boundaries."[69] This
was the era of manifest destiny, and whether Polk shaped or simply reacted to it, he staked out expansionist aims he never doubted.[70] Polk's
aim was not just to annex Texas and defend its disputed border with
Mexico on the Rio Grande but to acquire the entire southwest region.
Sellers writes: "in his vision of an American California he was ahead of
all but a handful of dreamers among his countrymen."[71]

But Polk wanted to acquire New Mexico and California by purchase,
not by conquest. His efforts involved four distinct strategic forays that
tightly linked the dispatch of diplomatic envoys with the incremental escalation of force. The first was the Slidell mission of fall 1845 to purchase
the territories, followed by the gradual forward positioning of American
forces in the Rio Grande Valley and eventually the invasion of northern Mexico. The second was the Mackenzie mission of summer 1846 to
assist Santa Anna, then exiled in Cuba, to return to power in Mexico,
followed by the opening of a second front to seize the Mexican port of
Veracruz on the Gulf of Mexico. The third was the Beach and Atocha
missions of winter 1846–47 to negotiate simultaneously with different
factions of the Mexican government, followed by the decision to attack
the capital of Mexico City, captured in September 1847. And the fourth
was the Trist mission of 1847–48 that ultimately ended in a peace settlement in February 1848, the Treaty of Guadalupe Hidalgo. In each case,
diplomacy led armed by force. When force was escalated, it was always
accompanied by a renewed effort at diplomacy.

Polk launched his first foray in September 1845 immediately after the annexation of Texas. He sent Congressman John Slidell of Louisiana to Mexico City with what he called "one great object of the Mission": to purchase the territories of New Mexico and California.[72] Before dispatching Slidell, however, Polk armed his diplomacy. He wanted Mexico to know that the longer it delayed or refused a sale, the more likely war was. And once war broke out, territorial demands might escalate.

In late July and August, Polk reinforced Taylor's forces on the Nueces, anticipating reports that Jose Joaquin Herrera, president of Mexico, had ordered General Mariano Paredes y Arrillaga, one of his rivals, to move his forces, some seven thousand men, north to join Mexican troops already stationed on the Rio Grande (an order Paredes never implemented). The policy was still defensive. In a July 28 dispatch, Polk told Taylor: "you will approach as near the boundary line, the Rio Grande, as prudence will dictate."[73] Later that month he told his vice president, George Dallas, "I intended to be understood as meaning, that we would not commence the war."[74] But if Mexican troops crossed the Rio Grande, there would be war, and the United States would take the offensive. In October, Polk tightened the instructions even further, telling Taylor to move as close to the disputed Rio Grande border, not "as prudence will dictate" but "as circumstances would permit." Taylor, a Whig who "before leaving Fort Jessup . . . had repeatedly denounced the annexation of Texas," nevertheless stayed put in Corpus Christi.[75] Rather than being provocative, Taylor refused Jones's request in mid-August to defend outlying settlements of San Antonio, which were located across the Nueces in disputed territory. Polk did not explicitly order Taylor to move into disputed territory until January 1846, and Taylor did not actually move his troops until early March, well after the Slidell mission had failed.

Polk's military moves supported his peaceful diplomacy; they did not undermine it. Polk's navy and war secretaries explicitly informed U.S. commanders: "while the annexation of Texas extends our boundary to the [Rio Grande] del Norte, the President reserves the vindication of our boundary, if possible, to methods of peace." U.S. forces were "to commit no act of aggression . . . [not to] employ force to dislodge Mexican troops from any post east of the Del Norte, which was in the actual possession of the Mexicans at the time of annexation." In short, Polk accepted Mexican intrusions into the disputed territory, if they existed at the time of annexation, while not explicitly ordering U.S. troops to intrude. As Sellers concludes, "the deployment of the nation's military and naval might along the Mexican borders and coasts was designed to reinforce the sword-and-olive-branch diplomacy which Polk had long since set in motion and which he hoped might gain all he wanted from Mexico without resort to actual hostilities."[76]

Polk also took steps to strengthen U.S. military forces in California. He alerted Commodore John D. Sloat, commander of the Pacific Squadron, to keep his forces ready and to seize San Francisco and blockade other California ports if war broke out with Mexico. He instructed the American consul in Monterey, Thomas O. Larkin (an early American trader who arrived in California in 1832), to watch for intervention of foreign powers, read principally Great Britain, and invited two aggressive individuals to join the effort to forestall British intervention in California: he sent Commodore Robert F. Stockton, a loose cannon in the annexation of Texas, from the Gulf Coast to California and told John C. Fremont, an adventurer and troublemaker in the Oregon Territory, to move south to California. He also dispatched a marine messenger, Lieutenant Alexander H. Gillespie, with secret instructions for Larkin and Fremont. Whether Polk was seeking to foment a rebellion of settlers in California, which broke out in 1846, is much disputed. He may have intended to preempt a British protectorate in California or to take a first step to acquire California by military means if the purchase route should fail. Either way, Polk's military actions suggested a strategy to cut off possibilities outside the negotiations that might tempt Mexico to resist the purchase offer Polk was making inside the negotiations.

What territory would the United States then seize if it came to war? Polk made clear from the earliest stages of his administration that the acquisition of New Mexico and California was his bottom line. Once war broke out, seizing territory was a means to that end, and the longer the war lasted the more territory the United States might seize. Whether Polk ever favored the conquest of all of Mexico, as the All Mexico Movement in Congress advocated, is doubtful. He gives us the clearest indications of his intentions in a diary comment in May 1846. Polk records the following entry on May 30, 1846, after a critical cabinet meeting:

> I stated that if the war should be protracted for any considerable time, it would be in my judgment very important that the U.S. should hold military possession of California at the time peace was made, and I declared my purpose to be to acquire for the U.S. California, New Mexico, and *perhaps* [emphasis added] some others of the Northern Provinces of Mexico whenever a peace was made. In Mr. Slidell's Secret instructions last autumn, these objects were included. Now that we were at War the prospect of acquiring them was much better, and to secure that object military possession should with as little delay as possible be taken of all these provinces. In these views the Cabinet concurred.[77]

Though this comment was made after the war broke out in April and therefore may be considered hindsight, it squares completely with his secret instructions to Slidell in October 1845. In October 1845, after Mexico indicated its willingness to receive a U.S. negotiator, Polk dispatched Slidell to Mexico with intentions to purchase New Mexico and, if possible, California, warning that if Mexico failed to cooperate, he would ask Congress for "appropriate remedies," implying the use of force. The U.S. offer involved Mexico's acceptance of the Rio Grande border including the cession of the eastern half of New Mexico, U.S. assumption of all Mexican debts to Americans estimated at $5–6 million, another $5 million if Mexico added the western half of New Mexico, $20 million for the addition of northern California including San Francisco, and $25 million for both Monterey and San Francisco.[78] According to instructions from Buchanan, which followed in November, Slidell did not have to insist on the cession of California.[79] Whether this meant that Polk was relying on alternative plans to acquire California (his secret instructions to Larkin and Fremont) is one possibility.[80] But it also suggests that at this stage in the negotiations with Mexico he was not set on acquiring California, let alone the northern provinces of present-day Mexico between the twenty-sixth and thirty-second parallels. In fact, even after the war started, Polk suggested a willingness to forego the southern part of present-day California. He told Buchanan on July 7, 1846, that "if he could do no better," he would accept a boundary line just south of Monterey (around the thirty-sixth parallel), which excluded San Diego and which Buchanan at that time favored.[81] He obviously hoped to do better, but he was flexible on California both before and after the war began. With respect to Mexico's northern provinces, Polk's diary comments in May 1846 and subsequently (August 10) always prefaced the potential acquisition of these territories with the word "perhaps," suggesting they might be taken in a contingency but were not essential and served primarily as bargaining chips.[82]

Polk was particularly concerned about preempting foreign interventions in California. In summer 1845, both France and Britain had declared their intentions to preserve the balance of power in North America, meaning to prevent if possible the expansion of the United States.[83] The British had the means to contest such an expansion. Its fleet on the Pacific coast matched the U.S. fleet, and its commander, Sir George Seymour, was a war hawk who counseled London to pursue a hard line against the United States in California (and Oregon). Polk asked Slidell to ascertain if Mexico had any plans to cede California to Britain or France, which the United States "would vigorously impose to prevent." He inserted a warning in his message to Congress in December 1845 employing for the first time since 1823 the language of the Monroe Doctrine. In summer 1844 Britain and France had concluded the so-called Diplomatic Act to guarantee Texas independence if Mexico accepted Texas independence, and Mexico approached Great Britain in mid-September 1845 about a possible British protectorate in California, hoping to avoid further loss of territory if Mexico should go to war with the United States. But frictions between France and Britain precluded implementation of the Diplomatic Act. And without support from France, Britain dropped the proposal.[84]

The Slidell mission was the best opportunity to resolve the southwest territorial issue without war. Polk, the evidence suggests, was sincere in his desire both to limit the acquisition and to pay for it. In early December, after he learned that the British threat in California was not as imminent as he thought, he instructed Slidell through Buchanan that if the attempt to gain California would endanger his chances of getting the Rio Grande or New Mexico boundary, "you are not to sacrifice these in the pursuit of what is unattainable."[85] He wanted an attainable agreement on the Rio Grande and New Mexico, not a potentially unattainable agreement on California. He also omitted any mention of California in his December message to Congress. In a private letter to Slidell on December 17 he even authorized a higher maximum, up to $40 million, to facilitate the deal.

But at this crucial juncture, the United States lacked a negotiating partner. Slidell arrived in Mexico City on December 6 just as the Herrera government, which had deposed Santa Anna in December 1844, was itself being deposed by Paredes, the general who refused Herrera's order in July to reinforce Mexican troops on the Rio Grande frontier. Mexico in this period was a carousel of revolving governments.[86] A weak Herrera government had agreed in October to receive Slidell even though Mexico had no diplomatic relations with the United States. Polk asked Mexico to "receive an Envoy from the United States, entrusted with full power to adjust all the questions in dispute." From the U.S. point of view, the annexation of Texas was not in dispute; it was a done deal. But Mexico replied it would receive a commissioner only to settle the "present dispute," meaning Texas annexation. Mexico expected a U.S. emissary to renegotiate the Texas treaty, as the Senate plan in February called for, while Polk had already annexed Texas under the House plan and wanted to move on to the purchase of New Mexico and California. Polk hoped Mexico was weak enough to accept the American position, but in truth the Herrera government was too weak to accept it.[87] Although Herrera was open to negotiations, and Manuel de la Pena y Pena, his foreign minister, did not reject Slidell's credentials but asked that they be clarified, Mexico had not budged from its position of August 1843 that Texas annexation was casus belli. Now, under pressure from Paredes, Herrera had little room to maneuver.[88] When in early December 1845 Herrera ordered Paredes a second time to move his Mexican forces to the Rio Grande, Paredes revolted. He had been plotting for some time with the Spanish minister in

Mexico City, Salvador Bermudez de Castro, to establish a monarchy. On January 2 he marched into Mexico City and took over the Mexican government.[89] Slidell was left "standing at the altar."[90] He retreated to Jalapa and then Veracruz and tried until March to begin talks but to no avail.[91]

Now Polk sharpened his sword. Taylor was ordered on January 13, 1846, to move from Corpus Christi on the Nueces to the Rio Grande and occupy positions at Port Isabel and Laredo. This message was the first explicit instructions from Polk to enter disputed territory. Taylor was told not to navigate the river or to treat Mexico as an enemy. However, if attacked, his orders read: "you will not act merely on the defensive."[92] Taylor, who repeatedly questioned Polk's orders, again delayed and did not set out for the Rio Grande until early March.

In the interim, Polk kept negotiations open. He met in Washington with Alexander Atocha, an envoy from Santa Anna, who was exiled in Cuba. Santa Anna was looking for a way to get back in the game in Mexico and urged Polk to take a hard line toward Paredes. Polk agreed and made clear that if Paredes ultimately refused, "the cup of forbearance will then have been exhausted." "Nothing can remain," Polk clarified, "but to take the redress of the injuries to our citizens and the insults to our Government in our own hands."

"Once again," as Pletcher notes, "Polk had chosen to negotiate from a position of strength."[93] The early and aggressive use of force empowered Polk's diplomacy to resolve the matter short of war, but at some point it also risked peace. Was it reasonable to demand the purchase of a significant chunk of another country's territory and then threaten war if that country did not agree? In theory, no; but in practice it was better for Mexico to accept payment for the territory than for foreigners to take the territory by force without compensation, as the Texans had already done in 1836. Polk genuinely believed the Mexicans would see the logic of their choices. As Gene Brack points out, however, Mexico "did not respond logically, but patriotically."[94] Honor, a deep-seated nationalist sentiment, is sometimes more important than the realist impulse of rational calculations based on power.

Slidell made one more démarche in March. The Paredes government refused again, and Slidell left Veracruz on March 31. Paredes now finally sent reinforcements north under the command of General Pedro Ampudia. Mexican troops arrived on the Rio Grande a few days after Taylor, and both sides dug in. Paredes, under pressure from even stronger hard-liners (such as Juan N. Almonte, a strong pro-monarchist, who had resigned earlier as minister of war under Paredes), issued orders on April 23 to defend Mexican territory—"from this day defensive war begins."[95] The inevitable clash came on April 25. Mexican forces crossed the Rio

Grande and ambushed American forces on the eastern (disputed) side of the river. The conflict was under way.

His diplomacy at a dead end, Polk drew the sword. After Slidell returned to Washington in early May 1846, Polk asked Congress to declare war. Congress obliged by a wide margin, and Polk ordered deployment of U.S. forces in three directions. First, Taylor was ordered "to march a competent force into the Northern provinces and seize and hold them until peace was made."[96] Taylor's early successes at Palo Alto and Resaca de la Palma in late May probably diminished Mexico's chances to raise funds in Britain. Paredes had offered California as security for a British loan. But the British government, weakened by a political crisis and perhaps concerned more about Oregon, did not bite.[97] Second, Colonel Stephen W. Kearny was directed to lead an expedition toward Santa Fe, New Mexico,"to protect our traders" and subsequently to the coast of California to meet up with U.S. naval forces. And third, Sloat was instructed to blockade the California coast and seize ports as possible, not just San Francisco, Monterey, Los Angeles, and San Diego but also Mazatlán and Guaymas in Lower California or as far south as the twenty-sixth parallel. Polk signaled that he was flexible on the eventual border with Mexico as long as New Mexico and Upper California became part of the United States.[98]

But the sword always served the olive branch. Polk simultaneously launched his second strategic foray to win the peace. He had conferred already in February in Washington with Atocha, the representative of Santa Anna. Now, in July, he sent navy commander Alexander Slidell Mackenzie, the nephew of John Slidell, to consult directly with Santa Anna in Havana.[99] Santa Anna had converted to federalism and was urging the northern Mexican provinces, friendly toward federalism, to revolt against Paredes. Polk, although he later denied it (Mackenzie had no written instructions), now resorted to regime change.[100] Frustrated by Paredes and the hard-line central government or monarchist group, he decided to gamble on Santa Anna. Mackenzie expressed support for Santa Anna to return to power, reiterated Polk's Rio Grande and Upper California demands and willingness to pay for them, and told Santa Anna that the commodore in charge of the U.S. fleet in the Gulf had been instructed to let Santa Anna pass through the U.S. blockade of the Mexican coast should he decide to return to Mexico.[101] In the first half of August, Santa Anna transited U.S. naval forces in the Gulf and reclaimed power in Mexico at the invitation of General Jose Mariano Salas, who had arrested Paredes. On July 27, anticipating Santa Anna's takeover, Polk had renewed his negotiating offer to Paredes and even asked Congress to make an advanced appropriation so Mexico could be paid immediately.

This was the legislation that provoked the famous Wilmot Proviso linking slavery and abolition to the Mexico question.

But Polk, as he had learned in the Slidell mission, was playing in troubled waters. Mexico, once again, was too weak and divided to make a decision. Back in Mexico, Santa Anna turned against the United States and deferred a response to Polk's offer until the Mexican Congress met in December. Recognizing that this meant rejection, Polk declared an end to his second diplomatic offensive.[102]

Following diplomatic failure, in typical sequence, Polk ordered new military measures. Plans were drawn up to occupy Tampico, a port on the coast of Mexico between the mouth of the Rio Grande and Veracruz, and to launch a supporting army campaign in the neighboring province of Tamaulipas. Sloat was now in charge of California ports, and Kearny had seized Santa Fe and was on his way to California. Word arrived in September that Taylor's forces had taken Monterey. But then, against Polk's wishes, Taylor declared a truce for eight weeks. Polk still hoped for a limited war and a quickly negotiated peace. The key was to keep steady pressure on Mexico.[103] Frustrated by Taylor's truce, which gave Ampudia's army a chance to withdraw and regroup, Polk made the decision to open a second front to seize Veracruz, an even more important port farther south on a direct land route to Mexico City. In a rebuke to Taylor, he assigned General Winfield Scott, another potential Whig presidential candidate, to lead the Veracruz assault. Although Polk had quarreled with Scott from the outset of the war, he displayed once again his uncanny ability to work with insubordinate commanders.[104]

Never abandoning diplomacy, Polk conducted his third foray for peace. He continued to press Congress for money to pay Mexico and finally got a bill in February 1847 without the "mischievous" (as Polk saw it) Wilmot Proviso. His envoys in this third strategic foray were perhaps the most chimerical. They operated without instructions and, as events unfolded, perhaps even at cross-purposes. One was Moses Y. Beach, a journalist with the New York *Sun* newspaper and an ardent expansionist with close ties to the Catholic Church in Mexico. In November 1846, Buchanan met several times with Beach and wrote an official letter appointing him "special agent" to gather information and presumably open negotiations.[105] Polk met Beach briefly but later wrote that Beach "was not clothed with any Diplomatic powers" and that Beach's November visit made "so little impression" on him that he made no note of it in his diary.[106] Nevertheless, Beach arrived in Veracruz in January 1847 and began talks with a monarchist, pro-clerical group disaffected with the Santa Anna government. The pro-Church elements in Mexico were smarting under an expropriation decree issued on January 10 by Valentin Gomez Farias, Santa Anna's vice president. Farias was hoping to make the Church pay for more of the war expenses. While Santa Anna led the army in the north, successfully in a standoff against U.S. forces at Buena Vista in February, Farias waged political war in Mexico City against the pro-Church group as well as his own boss, Santa Anna.

Beach almost got a deal with the pro-Church group. It involved a boundary line at the twenty-sixth parallel (which includes today's northern provinces of Mexico), a transit strip across the Isthmus of Tehuantepec in central Mexico, and assumption of all U.S. claims against Mexico plus an additional sum, perhaps $3 million. Beach wrote to Buchanan on March 17 that the deal was ready. Informed of Beach's letter on April 14, Polk treated it dismissively without any great expectations: "It is clearly to be inferred from his [Beach's] letter that he will make a Treaty with them if he can. Should he do so, and it is a good one, I will waive his authority to make it, and submit it to the Senate for ratification. It will be a good joke if he should assume the authority and take the whole country by surprise & make a Treaty. Mr. Buchanan's strong impression is that he may do so."[107]

Polk was clearly not relying on Beach. In the same period he took advantage of a second emissary. While Beach negotiated in Mexico, Santa Anna's agent, Atocha, the same agent who visited Washington in February 1846, came to Washington again in January 1847. Atocha met with Buchanan and Benton but not Polk. The United States was now negotiating with all sides in the internal disputes inside Mexico—Santa Anna and the federalists through Atocha, the monarchists and pro-Church group through Beach, and the Farias government, nominally on Santa Anna's side but jockeying for power between Santa Anna and the monarchists. Santa Anna, Atocha reported, was ready to neutralize the Rio Grande strip and sell California but not New Mexico. Buchanan told him a neutral Rio Grande strip was not negotiable and that New Mexico had to be included. Atocha apparently did not balk at these demands.[108] He took a sealed message back to Mexico City that the United States was ready to send peace commissioners to settle all issues as soon as Mexico City was ready. By the time Atocha reached Mexico City, however, Farias had seized control from Santa Anna. He placed Atocha under house arrest and then, to embarrass his pro-Church rivals, distorted and published Atocha's peace offer, which included Beach's provision that the United States was demanding the twenty-sixth parallel.[109] By the time Santa Anna returned to Mexico City in March to depose Farias, the Atocha proposal was discredited and Beach had slipped quietly out of town.[110] Atocha delivered Santa Anna's rejection to Washington on March 20, and Polk's third strategic foray came a cropper. According to Bergeron, "Atocha's message of rejection greatly disappointed the president and his cabinet, so much so that it prompted the decision to send Scott's army all the way to Mexico City."[111] As Polk expressed it: "No alternative was now left but the most energetic crushing movement of our arms upon Mexico."[112]

Scott took Veracruz in late March 1847. But even before that event, on March 20, the same day Polk got the bad news from Atocha, Polk ordered Scott to march overland from Veracruz to capture Mexico City. With diplomacy stalled, it was time again to brandish the sword. Scott moved deliberately, defeating Santa Anna's forces at Cerro Gordo on April 18–19 and then moving on to Puebla by mid-May, a stronghold of pro-clericalism. There he halted for three months. He did not storm Mexico City until September.

As always with Polk, however, the sword never worked without the olive branch. Right on rhythm, Polk launched his fourth and what would be final strategic foray to achieve peace.[113] In April Polk sent Nicholas P. Trist to Mexico City. Trist was chief clerk to Secretary of State Buchanan. Buchanan had, on repeated occasions, showed less enthusiasm for territorial acquisitions than Polk, arguing at the cabinet meeting in May 1846 right after the war broke out that the United States should have no territorial objectives south of the thirty-second parallel.[114] And Trist, as he later disclosed, was a bitter opponent of the war from the very beginning.[115] Although Polk did not know that at the time, by sending Trist he clearly signaled that his aims were not maximalist. In fact, his instructions to Trist were crafted as carefully as those to Slidell in Polk's first diplomatic foray and were strikingly consistent with his aims even before the war began. He told Trist that the United States would pay up to $25 million for the territory from "the Rio Grande from its mouth to the point where it intersects the Southern border of New Mexico, the whole of the Provinces of New Mexico & Upper and Lower California to be ceded to the United States." "If Lower California [between the twenty-sixth and thirty-second parallels] could not be obtained," Polk continued, "then the maximum sum to be paid for the Rio Grande as a boundary & the cession of New Mexico & Upper California should not exceed $20 million." And if the Isthmus of Tehuantepec were included, along with New Mexico and Upper and Lower California, Trist could pay up to $30 million. Polk explicitly stated that "the free passage across the istmus [sic] of Tehuantepec should not be a *sine qua non* to the making of a Treaty."[116] And his willingness to forgo Lower California affirmed once again that he was not a proponent of maximalist demands, as his harshest critics insist.[117]

In July, with Mexico still refusing to enter negotiations, Polk raised his demands, specifying a reduction of the maximum sum from $30 million to $15 million and a southern boundary proposed by Buchanan (now suddenly becoming more expansionist) around "the parallel of thirty-one degrees or thirty-one degrees thirty minutes of North Latitude from the Rio Grande to the Gulf of California, instead of the parallel of 32 degrees which Mr. Trist had been authorized to accept." Polk also declared himself "in favor of acquiring the cession of the Department of Tamaulipas, if it should be found practical to do so."[118] As always, Polk had a bottom line but was willing to acquire more territory if circumstances allowed. Nevertheless, in July, as a sign of their lack of priority, he did not convert these increased demands into new instructions, awaiting news of Scott's progress.

Trist arrived in Veracruz on May 6. He and Scott initially feuded but then, aided by British officials, opened negotiations with Santa Anna. At one point in August or September Santa Anna, crippled by a divided Congress, actually urged Scott through the British ambassador in Mexico to advance on Mexico City to strengthen his hand with the opponents of peace. Then later he negotiated with Scott to stop the battle for Mexico City short of full invasion.[119] As always, the scene inside Mexico was chaotic if not bizarre. Santa Anna proposed a peace agreement, which conceded Upper California roughly along the thirty-second parallel (Polk's bottom line) but refused to sell New Mexico and demanded the Nueces River boundary for Texas. Trist now egregiously exceeded his instructions, showing a willingness to forego parts of New Mexico and agreeing to transmit the Nueces demand to Washington, even though that demand had never been negotiable.[120] But his freelancing did no good. The war hawks in Santa Anna's cabinet prevailed and Mexico refused the offer on September 5, demanding all of New Mexico and California up to the thirty-seventh parallel (which included Monterey). Scott attacked Chapultepec on September 13 and captured Mexico City a day later. Santa Anna counterattacked at Puebla but then fled the country (only to return again five years later). Pena, a moderate, became president. Farias and other irreconcilables refused to recognize Pena.

When Polk learned of Trist's concessions on October 2, he recalled Trist and suspended negotiations (even before learning of Scott's capture of Mexico City). Nevertheless, if Trist had a treaty already in hand, Polk added, he should bring it with him.[121] Trist received notice of his recall on November 16 but at the urging of British officials stayed on to negotiate with the reassembled Mexican government in Querétaro. Trist's dispatches not only rebuked Polk's instructions but disparaged the president personally. As Bergeron notes, "the entire cabinet shared Polk's sense of outrage."[122] Polk came to believe that the two men, Trist and Scott, were conspiring against him.[123] When he learned late in December that Scott among other things had court-martialed Polk's friend and political confidant Gideon Pillow (serving in Scott's army), Polk replaced Scott and ordered the arrest of Trist. Polk was about to end the fourth strategic foray by putting his own emissary in chains.

Such was the state of play when another government shuffle in Mexico put a moderate leadership in place. This development more than anything else saved Polk's diplomacy, just as a shuffle to a hard-line leadership (from Herrera to Paredes) had scuttled Polk's diplomacy two years earlier. Mexican leaders suddenly decided to accept the realities and sue for peace. Pena, a moderate who was Herrera's foreign minister in 1845 during the Slidell foray, became president in January 1848. He instructed his negotiators to accept greater territorial concessions. The last sticking point was San Diego. When Mexico balked, Trist threatened to break off negotiations as Polk had instructed him to do three months earlier, and Scott threatened to attack the Mexican government at Querétaro. On February 2, literally under the gun, Mexico finally capitulated. Trist signed the agreement in the small northern suburb of Mexico City known as Guadalupe Hidalgo, chosen because it was outside the range of American cannons. The Treaty of Guadalupe Hidalgo met all of Polk's conditions. It included the Rio Grande border, Upper California and New Mexico roughly along the thirty-second parallel, excluded the Tehuantepec transit strip, and paid the Mexicans a total of only $15 million.

Trist's agreement reached Washington on February 19. Pletcher calls Trist's performance "courageous insubordination."[124] Polk had every reason to reject it.[125] In February 1848 the All Mexico Movement in the U.S. Congress, which demanded the annexation of all of Mexico, was at its peak.[126] Polk might have marched to the head of this parade and demanded further concessions. Presidential aspirants, such as Buchanan, who had previously opposed broad claims, now did just that. But Polk's leadership was not about politics or personalities; it was about policy. If the treaty was a "good" one, as he had said in the case of other recalcitrant emissaries, he would accept it. Like all great negotiators, Polk also had an exquisite sense of timing. The Democratic Party had lost the House elections of fall 1847. The American people were growing weary of war. He knew a long occupation of Mexico would be costly. Moreover, the presidential campaign of 1848 had started. Scott, Taylor, Buchanan, and other prominent players were tossing their hats into the presidential ring.

So Polk was not misled. Rather than rejecting the treaty out of personal pique, he submitted it immediately it to Congress to undercut the All Mexico Movement. He then threw himself unsparingly into the process of confirming the treaty, and the Senate approved it in record time on March 10 by a very healthy margin, 38–14 with 4 abstentions. What is more, the vote crossed party and regional lines and at least for the moment overcame rather than exacerbated sectional differences. Ten Whigs and eight Democrats voted against the treaty or abstained, while seven northerners, five southerners, and six westerners did the same. Sectionalism was not evident in the final vote. In May the Mexican Congress also comfortably passed the agreement—51–35 in the Chamber and 33–4 in the Senate. The moderate, Herrera, became the first postwar president of Mexico, and U.S. troops were out of Mexico City by the end of June and Veracruz by the end of July. What is more, the peace stood on its own, as Europe, caught up in the revolutions of 1848, refused to act as guarantor of the peace.[127]

A conflict that had stirred so much passion ended with a whimper and left a legacy of permanent borders between Mexico and the United States, albeit amid seething resentment in Mexico that lingers to the present day. Polk had successfully navigated the treacherous shoals of multiple rip tides: the competition of international politics from European powers, the insubordinate character of American politics with defections by cabinet officers, generals, and peace negotiators, and, perhaps most important, the obscurity of Mexican politics. He used America's material dominance to prevail. About that there can be no doubt. Mexico had its back to the wall before it relented, and that speaks well of its courage as well as ultimately its politics as an independent nation, younger at the time than the United States. But Polk's diplomacy and timely willingness to compromise also spared the two countries a brutalizing conquest and long occupation—the Ireland nightmare that critics feared. And Mexico's leadership or lack thereof also shared blame for the war. Time and again, revolving Mexican leaders were unable to unite the country to face the stark reality that Mexico could not settle and hold the western territories in competition with U.S. settlers. In the end, therefore, it was the freedom and explosiveness of the American republican system that, with all its flaws at the time, carried the day. And it is possible to argue that the benefits for freedom for everyone were greater in the long run than they would have been under any alternative scenario.

Oregon Territory

As if Texas and New Mexico/California were not enough, Polk also took aim in his one-term presidency at the Oregon Territory. Like Texas, the Oregon issue had been on the table for some time. The terms of a possible agreement were less the problem than diplomatic face and domestic politics. In 1843–44, Tyler's secretary of state, Abel Upshur, and Lord Aberdeen, the British foreign minister, "had come close to agreement on terms almost identical with those of the final treaty in 1846."[128] The agreement involved a compromise on the forty-ninth parallel, roughly

halfway between the maximalist U.S. demand at the parallel of 54° 40'
(which includes western provinces of present-day Canada) and the maximalist British demand at the forty-second parallel, the northernmost line
of Spanish territory ceded to the United States in the Adams-Onis Treaty
of 1819 (which includes present-day U.S. states of Washington, Oregon,
and Idaho and portions of Montana and Wyoming). Pending final agreement, the two countries shared jurisdiction over the region under two ac-
cords negotiated in 1817 and 1827. Each country could withdraw from
this joint occupation arrangement by giving notice of one year that it
intended to abrogate.

Before the issue could be settled, however, "Polk took the country to
the brink of war with Great Britain."[129] Like Mexico, Britain had both
territory and face at stake. But British leaders had recognized since the
1820s that American settlers held the upper hand in the region owing
to their fecundity.[130] British interests were largely commercial, the Hudson Bay Company and fur trade. Nevertheless, imperial competition in
Europe was at its peak, and Britain could not appear to be cowed by an
upstart America. France, its principal rival, might misjudge such concessions. American leaders had domestic politics and a presidential election
to contend with. While the diplomats continued to converge (Secretary of
State Calhoun conducted intensive negotiations with the British minister
in Washington in August and September 1844), President Tyler, seeking
reelection in 1844, sent a message to Congress in December 1843 that
advocated the maximalist 54° 40' line.[131] The Democratic Party platform
in June 1844 echoed the same demand.

Polk, as we have learned, was no piker when it came to expansion.
He took up the stanchion for 54° 40', and his election confirmed public
sentiment to expand. The lame duck House of Representatives passed a
bill in January 1845 by a 3–1 margin that called for the United States
to establish a territorial government in all of Oregon as well as a string
of forts and land allotment programs, essentially abrogating the joint
occupation agreements and engaging in what British officials called a
"flagrant encroachment."[132] In his inaugural address in March 1845 Polk
declared that the U.S. claim to the Oregon Territory was "clear and unquestionable," without specifying exactly what border he was talking
about. London took offense. Sir Robert Peel, the Tory prime minister,
and his foreign minister, Aberdeen, retorted in Parliament: "We too, my
lords, have rights which are 'clear and unquestionable.' "[133] Thus, as Polk
assumed office, the diplomacy of settling the Oregon issue was clearly
running afoul of the domestic politics needed to do so.

Nevertheless, Polk soon revealed his true colors, which were more
moderate. In April the British renewed their offer, made earlier in 1844, to
submit the dispute to arbitration. This diplomatic nicety enabled Britain

to make concessions to third parties without appearing to bend to American demands. Americans, on the other hand, did not trust neutral arbitrators. Faced with the Texas and larger Mexican issues, Polk set priorities and looked for a quick way to resolve the Oregon question. While rejecting arbitration, Polk used the British offer to propose a compromise based on the forty-ninth parallel. The offer drawn up in April also contained contingency instructions that gave U.S. negotiators the authority, if the British insisted, to cede the entire island of Vancouver, the southern end of which would have been hived off by the forty-ninth parallel. In addition, it allowed, if necessary, the right of navigation on the Columbia River for seven to ten years to the Hudson Bay Company to operate a string of fur-trading posts on the river.[134] By all measures, the proposal was fair and flexible, foreseeing a settlement almost identical to what was ultimately accepted a year later. And it was timed for July to coincide with the arrival of Polk's new envoy to Great Britain, Louis McLane, who opposed the 54° 40' line.[135] It's hard to argue that Polk's offer was not sincere.

But the British minister in Washington, Lord Pakenham, assigned from Mexico to Washington specifically to negotiate the Oregon issue, abruptly rejected the proposal without even referring it to London, despite the fact that Aberdeen had instructed him earlier that London would be "favorably inclined to support such a proposal."[136] Why did Pakenham do this? Pletcher blames Polk's "awkwardness in diplomacy and Pakenham's lack of perception."[137] Buchanan's compromise offer, under Polk's instructions, contained a long and tedious replay of America's legal claims to the Oregon Territory. Perhaps, as Pletcher believes, Pakenham was offended by Buchanan's legal case. But Pakenham was a seasoned diplomat. He would have recognized Polk's need, especially in light of the conciliatory offer of the forty-ninth parallel, to genuflect to domestic expansionist opinion. There may have been other reasons. Pakenham may have hoped the United States would begin a process of negotiating with itself, that the novice president would quickly make another, perhaps even better offer, and that London could stand by while the president under pressure from Congress progressively modified the American proposal in London's favor. Whatever the reason, the moment passed, and a whole year would be spent trying to regroup the two countries' positions.

Given the apparent confusion on the British side, Buchanan and others favored resubmitting the U.S. offer. But Polk displayed once again an uncanny instinct for timing—when not to negotiate as well as when to close negotiations. He decided to be patient, and he looked for leverage to motivate the British. He waited until late August, after the scare of war with Mexico subsided (to avoid prospects of conflict on two fronts), and then withdrew the offer. In a "blunt and curt" notice, he also reasserted U.S. maximalist claims to the border at 54° 40'.[138] Polk realized that his plate in Congress was full with Texas and the evolving New Mexico and California issues. If he negotiated too hastily, the British might accomplish exactly what Pakenham may have intended, namely draw the Americans into a negotiation with themselves. Congress was divided on the issue and pressed Polk incessantly in different directions. Polk needed some leverage both to demonstrate that he, not Congress, controlled the issue and to compel the British eventually to make the next offer. He guessed correctly that the forces outside the negotiating process were working in his favor. American settlers were flooding into Oregon; London seemed to regard California as a more urgent issue than Oregon; and the Tory government in London was weak, falling temporarily from power in December and reconstituting the government only after the Whig opposition proved even less capable of unifying their ranks. He could afford delay better than the British could.

He developed the leverage he needed by submitting legislation to Congress in December 1845, which gave notice that the United States would withdraw from the two agreements with Britain and abrogate the joint occupation of the Oregon Territory in one year. Drawing from the House bill passed in January, the legislation also provided for land grants to settlers, the establishment of Oregon courts, and the construction of military forts. Polk was exploiting the advantage the United States held outside the negotiating process, warning the British in effect that the longer they delayed in submitting the next proposal the more the territory would slip into U.S. hands (the same advantage he exploited in negotiations with Mexico). About the same time, Britain renewed its proposal for arbitration; some historians believe Polk now made the same mistake that Pakenham made earlier: he missed a good opportunity to settle.[139] But the arbitration proposal was not new, London was in the midst of a government crisis, and Polk wanted a direct British offer, which, if it contained a compromise on the forty-ninth parallel, he said he would submit for consultation to the Senate, signaling once again what his bottom line was. Polk judged correctly that the United States could afford to wait.

In January, Polk backed his diplomacy with some military bluster and force. Meeting with Congressman James A. Black on January 4, he made his famous comment about England using the cartoon epithet of John Bull: "the only way to deal with John Bull was to look him straight in the eye . . . I considered a bold & firm course on our part the pacific one; that if Congress faultered [sic] or hesitated in their course, John Bull would immediately become arrogant and more grasping in his demands."[140] Pulling Congress together through the abrogation legislation was clearly critical for his plan. In addition, he asked Congress to increase army and navy appropriations, the navy by $6.625 million or 22 percent of the preceding year's expenditures.[141] There were rumors that Britain was engaged in extensive naval and military preparations, and in early February, McLane notified Washington that a large flotilla of British warships had just left England for North America. War clouds made Polk's advisors nervous, and they urged him to consider navigation rights for the British on the Columbia River. But Polk, applying admirable common sense, noted already in his December message to Congress that he could never concede the right to navigate a river through the heart of American territory.[142]

The request to Congress for abrogation legislation was a brilliant political move by Polk. It kept Congress busy and out of the direct negotiations with London, while Polk refused to make another offer before the British did. The congressional hard-liners, led by David Atchison of Missouri and John Quincy Adams of Massachusetts in the House and Lewis Cass of Michigan, a perennial presidential candidate, and William Allen of Ohio, chairman of the powerful Foreign Relations Committee, in the Senate, badgered Polk to stick with the 54° 40' claim. The Whigs in the Senate, under Daniel Webster of Massachusetts, and some southern Democrats, under John C. Calhoun of South Carolina, argued for compromise. "Exactly what motivated the South Carolina Senator," as Bergeron muses, "to embrace a cautious, moderate course on Oregon, after having stirred bellicose sentiments on the matter of Texas annexation, is not easily comprehended or explained."[143] But as a later incident with Buchanan confirmed, Polk had no doubts about what was going on. His colleagues were all potential presidential rivals. "Each leader," Polk observed, "looks to his own advancement more than he does to the success of my measures." In this environment, Polk may have muffled his real intentions from time to time. Responding to senators demanding to know what his plans were, Polk said: "I would answer to no man what I would do in the future . . . wait until I act and then approve or condemn what I may do."[144] The man knew how to negotiate, with Congress as well as with foreign powers.

The House passed legislation on February 9 granting the notice to abrogate the joint occupation convention but adding that this legislation should not impede the prospects of negotiations.[145] The Senate deliberated for another two months. Calhoun eventually accepted the abrogation notice when he became convinced it would not mean war with England, but the hard-liner Allen never did and resigned as head of the Foreign Relations Committee when the legislation finally passed. Throughout Polk pressed the Senate for further legislation to transform and defend the Oregon Territory once the convention was abrogated. Finally, on April 23, nearly five months after submitting the legislation, Polk got what he wanted. A final Senate-House conference gave him authority to abrogate the joint occupation convention.

The British apparently took note. Despite the outbreak of war with Mexico, Polk still insisted that Britain make the next move. In June, John Bull finally relented. The British offer, worked out with McLane beforehand, was for all practical purposes the same proposal the British had rejected one year earlier. But now the British were taking ownership of it. The forty-ninth parallel became the final border, bent around Vancouver Island to give the British full control. The Hudson Bay Company and British subjects trading with the company gained temporary navigation rights on the Columbia River for ten years. Ownership of the San Juan Islands was left ambiguous but awarded to the United States in a later treaty in 1872. Otherwise, the deal showed little effect from an entire year of diplomatic jousting.

Why did the British suddenly do what they had refused to do for more than two years, namely make an offer rather than insist on arbitration and a conciliatory one at that, not just "accepting" but "proposing" the compromise line of the forty-ninth parallel? One possibility is that they took stock of their negotiating partner and realized that Polk, now armed with the abrogation legislation and the backing of Congress, held the upper hand outside the negotiating process and could change the status quo in the Oregon Territory if they did not make a deal quickly. If so, the outcome confirms the importance in Polk's diplomacy, and in diplomacy in general, of both patience and leverage. Polk took the issue away from Congress and made the British deal with him seriously inside the negotiating process. A second possibility is that the longstanding Tory government in London was coming to an end and it wanted to clear this issue from its desk before it left office.[146] The Peel government fell in June 1846, shortly after repealing the historic Corn Laws, and the Whigs under Lord Russell and his foreign minister, Lord Palmerston, were thought to be more unpredictable on the Oregon issue. But a weak government is often in no position to make concessions—think of Mexico in the U.S.-Mexican war—and it is unlikely that the Peel government would have made a conciliatory proposal, especially if it was weak, without some sense that the Whigs would also support it, as they ultimately did.

Still a third possibility is that the British were preoccupied with the Mexican situation. War between Mexico and the United States had broken out in May 1846. This was the moment, it will be recalled, when Mexico was foraging for war funds in London and asking the British to assume a protectorate in California to forestall further loss of Mexican territory. If Britain helped Mexico, which it considered for a moment, it might not want war with the United States over Oregon as well. Sellers notes, for example, that "Polk's aggressive Oregon diplomacy had affected Britain's attitude toward the Mexican problem precisely as Armstrong [U.S. consul in Liverpool] hoped it would, causing the British to restrain rather than to encourage Mexican aggressiveness."[147] So the argument that the United States was constrained by the desire to avoid two wars at the same time may have also applied to the British. And it may have been more telling for the British because the United States had no need to declare war on Great Britain. It held the advantage in the Oregon Territory and could tolerate the evolving status quo while Britain was under pressure to do something before it lost its foothold in Oregon.[148] Aberdeen did not change his instructions to Pakenham after he learned of the Mexican war, so the argument here is circumstantial at best.[149] Nevertheless, the inverse argument—that the United States made the key concessions to avoid war—is even less circumstantial because the terms of the U.S. negotiating positions in May 1845 and May 1846 were almost identical.[150]

There was one more trial for Polk before the Oregon agreement became law. And it constitutes one of the most unusual instances of insubordination to the president of the United States one can imagine. Polk endured many such episodes of impudence, from Scott, Trist, Buchanan, and others, but this one from Buchanan probably tops them all. It says volumes about the political obstacles Polk had to overcome and the extraordinary personal qualities that enabled him to do so.

On June 6, Polk assembled his cabinet to discuss the British proposal. The sticking point was when the temporary British navigation rights on the Columbia were due to expire. Buchanan took the floor and seemed to reopen the boundary issue, protesting, according to Polk's diary entry, that "the fifty-four forty men were the true friends of the administration and he wished no backing out on the subject."[151] Ignoring him, Polk asked Buchanan to draft a message to the Senate saying the administration would reject the British proposal if a majority of the Senate disapproved. Buchanan declined, saying he would merely comment on Polk's draft. Two days later in a private conversation, Polk asked Buchanan again for help. Buchanan declined a second time and said to the president: "Well! When you have done your message I will then prepare such an one as I think ought to be sent in." This time Polk lost his temper: "For what purpose will you prepare a message? You have twice refused, though it is a subject relating to your Department, to give me any aid in preparing my message; do you wish after I have done, to draw up a paper of your own to make an issue with me?" "The conversation," Polk noted, "became a very painful and unpleasant one."[152] But that was not the end of it. At a cabinet meeting on June 9, Polk read his message to the Senate and all present approved it except Buchanan. Buchanan asked if he could take the president's message into another room and draw up a draft such as he could approve. With the patience of an angel, Polk said yes. Buchanan went away for more than an hour. The draft he finally produced was unacceptable, but to get cabinet unity Polk excised "a large part" of his own draft, stripping it down to a mere request for the Senate's advice and his willingness to abide by it. Buchanan finally concurred.

Polk now threw himself into an intensive lobbying effort on the Hill to convince the Senate to accept the compromise proposal. He knew what the game was—politics and presidential aspirations—and that game could only be won among the representatives of the people. He succeeded, and the Senate approved the president's message on June 12 by a comfortable margin 37–12 and ratified the treaty on June 15 by an even wider margin 41–14.

One measure of a successful agreement is the consensus it ultimately generates. Conservative internationalist leadership does not wait on consensus, as liberal internationalists might, but it brings consensus along, which realists might regard as unnecessary. The Oregon vote moderated congressional divisions. Even ardent 54° 40' men, such as John Quincy Adams and Lewis Cass, eventually accepted the Oregon agreement. Negotiating partners, too, were complimentary. Lord Palmerston commented: "it would have been strange if the Americans had not been pleased with the arrangement which gives them everything which they ever really wanted."[153] Buchanan and McLane later conceded that Polk's December decision to seek abrogation authority may have been the key factor rousing the British to grasp the necessity of a speedy settlement. As Sellers concludes, "by a remarkable combination of nerve, judgment, and disingenuous manipulation of men, Polk had completed the first two phases of his continentalist program, Texas and Oregon, and [in summer 1846] began his third," the acquisition of California and New Mexico."[154]

Sellers's charge of "disingenuous manipulation of men" invites one further comment. It is premised on his view that Polk was bluffing with his threat to abrogate the joint occupation agreement.[155] That is frequently the charge made against statesmen who use force or the threat of force to negotiate more aggressively than critics think is necessary. As we shall see in chapter 7, Ronald Reagan was criticized for his defense buildup, especially the strategic defense initiative (SDI). Detractors assume that if these men succeed without having to use the force they muster, they must not have been serious about that force in the first place. They were just bluffing and had to be manipulative to conceal it. But a good case can be made that these men are not bluffing. They are arming their diplomacy with force and accepting the risks, if diplomacy fails, of using that force. If bluffing were mostly a matter of clever deception and often successful, it would be done a lot more, and the world would become an even more dangerous place than it already is. So it is also dangerous to write off successful uses of force as bluff, unless it can be shown that no actions were taken to implement the bluff. In Polk's case the evidence is quite the contrary. He pressed military preparations throughout the winter, and his willingness to use force against Mexico had to be noticed in London. Had Britain not offered a proposal, Polk was clearly ready to implement the abrogation option and take the risk, calculated correctly as low, that Britain might go to war over it.

Domestic Politics

Polk's domestic credentials as a conservative are impeccable. He was an "orthodox Jeffersonian" who believed in limited central government and states' rights. That included, as it did for most Americans at the time, a strong suspicion of foreign governments, alliances, and international treaties and a Jacksonian commitment to national sovereignty. He also believed in economic entrepreneurship and competition, though he thought of economic activity like Jefferson largely in terms of the development of land and agriculture rather than industry. On foreign policy, he took Congress and the people into account more than any previous president. International activity was not the predominant domain of the executive branch or crown, as European realists at the time such as Lord Palmerston believed. Nor did it require the consent of foreign governments to be legitimate, as liberal internationalists preferred in seeking the consent of Mexico for the annexation of Texas.

Polk was wedded to a strict construction of the Constitution. "The Government of the United States is one of delegated and limited powers," he said in his inaugural address, "and it is by a strict adherence to the clearly granted powers and by abstaining from the exercise of doubtful or unauthorized implied powers that we have the only sure guaranty against the recurrence of those unfortunate collisions between the Federal and State authorities which have occasionally so much disturbed the harmony of our system and even threatened the perpetuity of our glorious Union."[156] This did not mean that states dominated any more than the general government did: "While the General Government should abstain from the exercise of authority not clearly delegated to it, the States should be equally careful that in the maintenance of their rights they do not overstep the limits of powers reserved to them." The balance between the rights of Union and states was delicate and, for Jeffersonian conservatives (classical liberals), lay at the core of the American republic.

That's how Polk viewed the slavery issue. There were two red lines in the Constitution. One was the attempt to abolish slavery without the consent of states where it existed; the other was to secede from the Union. Echoing Jackson, he said:

> Our Federal Union—it must be preserved. To preserve it the
> compromises which alone enabled our fathers to form a com-
> mon constitution for the government and protection of so many
> States and distinct communities, of such diversified habits, inter-
> ests, and domestic institutions, must be sacredly and religiously
> observed.

Going on to echo Jefferson, Polk added: "Nothing human can be perfect . . . [but] if . . . error and wrong are committed in the administration
of the Government, . . . remember . . . that under no other system of government revealed by Heaven or devised by man has reason been allowed
so free and broad a scope to combat error."

To use the terms in the introduction to this volume, Polk was a libertarian and majoritarian conservative, more so than a religious conservative or government reformer.[157] On the one hand, the American people
had the right "collectively and individually to seek their own happiness
in their own way," a libertarian appeal. On the other, the people could
change their government only on the basis of the contract by which they
had entered into it, namely a majoritarian decision. The Constitution
protected minorities, but it also protected majorities. When it came to
union, minorities had but one right and that was to convert itself into
a majority, peacefully and legally.[158] Polk, who is often associated with
Calhoun on the slavery question, was never the moralist that Calhoun
was. Slavery for Polk was neither a virtue nor a sin until the people made
it so, peacefully by majority opinion. Nor, of course, was Polk the government reformer that Lincoln eventually became. Lincoln believed that the
central government, even if it does not represent a majority, has to take
sides at some point to create the moral majority.[159] For Polk, the national
government should always stay out of the substance of the issue.

Polk was a fiscal conservative and the first president to exercise personal control over the bureaucracy and budget process.[160] As Pletcher
writes, Polk "mastered the routine and details of every executive department, delegated power with great reluctance, and called for frequent and
full accountings." He once bet Buchanan a bottle of champagne that Buchanan had made a mistake in drawing up a diplomatic document. Polk
won the bet.[161]

Polk's two domestic priorities were to enact an independent treasury
bill doing away with a national bank and to lower the tariff rates under
an 1842 bill. Both priorities were conservative sacred cows and represented embittered national disputes. The bank issue dogged Jackson for
his entire eight years in office, and the tariff issue provoked the threat of
secession in the Abomination Tariff of 1832. Yet both issues were resolved
by Polk within fifteen months. Polk was an absolute master at being both

principled and pragmatic. He succeeded through a combination of stub-bornness and suppleness. He finessed the tariff issue, which might have cost him the state of Pennsylvania and the election, by supporting tariffs for revenue rather than protection of industry. It passed the Senate by only one vote, a tiebreaker from his vice president, George Dallas.

In a way, Polk was the first modern president. He "skillfully utilized all the tactics for executive leadership of Congress that were eventually to become standard operating techniques of the presidency. All were based on the Jacksonian premise that the people's will must prevail, and that the president was uniquely qualified to appeal to and represent the will of the whole people."[162] He "tried to associate Congress in some way with every important decision he made."[163]

The people's will, of course, was divided. Democrats split between Free Soilers in the North, such as Silas Wright, governor of New York, and slavery advocates in the South, such as Calhoun. Whigs split between conscience Whigs in the North, such as Martin Van Buren and Daniel Webster, and cotton Whigs in the South, such as Henry Clay. Further fault lines existed over expansion. Cass of Michigan led the extremists, Benson of Missouri the moderates. Calhoun was extremist on Texas an-nexation, moderate on southwestern expansion, and mostly opposed on northwestern expansion.

How Polk navigated these crosscurrents is best told by the fate of his rivals who shipwrecked on the rocks of political intrigue. Cass won the Democratic nomination in 1848 but lost the election to Taylor, who trumped him as the expansionist hero of the Mexican war. Benson came out more decisively against slavery and lost his Senate seat as well as a governor's race. Scott lost the presidency in 1852 to a more accommodat-ing Franklin Pierce. And Buchanan, although he won the presidency in 1856, had trimmed his sails so many times by that point that he ranks as one of the weakest and worst presidents in American history. As Sellers writes, "where Polk gave the impression of a master planner, his fingers on every issue, Buchanan often resembled a finicky, cautious old maid."[164] Whether Polk might have won and fared as well in a second term we'll never know. He died a few months after leaving office. That he saw the need to limit his efforts to one term may have been another sign of his political genius. Although other presidents, such as Jackson and William Henry Harrison, had promised the same, Polk kept his promise even though his record of accomplishment clearly put him in a position to win a second term if he had wanted it.[165]

Polk was a consummate politician as well as a visionary statesman and imperialist. Critics contend that he managed all of these diverse interests only by logrolling them to wage an unnecessary war. But then the war should have controlled him, not the other way around. In fact, his ability to carve out a principled but proportionate position between isolationists and opportunists on the one hand and expansionists and racists on the other enabled him to gain his monumental goals with minimal lasting losses. He ended America's first war of choice in a relatively short period of time and in a way that damaged U.S.-Mexican relations, to be sure, but did not result in a much more damaging, long-term occupation or annexation of Mexico.

In the end, Polk was neither a calculating realist settling for a European-style balance of power in the western territories, nor a complaisant liberal internationalist expecting the territories to succumb on their own to the fruits of common consent and commerce, nor an irrepressible nationalist intent on taking all of Mexico or all of Oregon. He was in fact a conservative internationalist, committed to widening self-government, aware that force was a steady and necessary handmaiden of an ambitious diplomacy, and ready to compromise when he sensed the limits of the people to shoulder the costs of armed diplomacy.

Chapter 6

Harry S. Truman
LIBERTY IN WESTERN EUROPE

HARRY TRUMAN IS MOST frequently classified as a liberal internationalist. He was committed to the spread of freedom and the development of
international institutions. But if Truman was a liberal internationalist,
he was a different one from Woodrow Wilson or Franklin Roosevelt.
Wilson was a liberal internationalist first class. He invented the League
of Nations and believed collective security would replace the balance of
power and make the world safe for democracy. Franklin Roosevelt was
a liberal internationalist second class. He added a realist component to
Wilson's League, the United Nations Security Council (UNSC), giving
great powers veto rights, not all powers great and small equal rights.
Still, on balance, he believed that diplomacy within the UNSC, especially
personal diplomacy with Stalin, could manage relations with the Soviet
Union peacefully. Truman was a liberal internationalist third class. He
saw himself following in the footsteps of Wilson and Roosevelt: "We are
trying heroically to implement the program which was started by Woodrow Wilson, was carried forward by Franklin Roosevelt, and was finally
consummated at San Francisco."[1] But unlike Wilson and Roosevelt, Truman believed, on balance, that diplomacy required a more assertive use
of force to contain the Soviet Union and an ideological campaign to promote liberty and stop the spread of communism in Western Europe. By
co-opting both force and ideology, Truman pursued a more conservative
form of internationalism and distinguished himself from realists and liberal internationalists.

In the end, had Roosevelt lived and faced the same contingencies, he
might have taken the same positions as Truman. We will never know. But
if that had been the case, Truman's (and Roosevelt's) approach might be
better called conservative rather than liberal internationalism because it

tilted toward free countries that founded NATO rather than all countries that made up the United Nations, deployed American power for the first time in peace not war to defend and promote liberty abroad, and drew more from the morality and common sense of populist America than the rationalism of elitist expertise.[2]

If Truman was not a liberal internationalist, he was also not a classical realist like George Kennan.[3] Kennan believed that communism and ideology in general were aberrations in foreign policy, not the lodestar around which one contained and defeated the Soviet Union.[4] For Kennan, the source of Russian aggression was historical and cultural, not ideological. Centuries of insecurity made Russia paranoid. After the war, Moscow was programmed to carve out a sphere of influence in Europe. The United States should have accepted this division and paid less attention to the UN. The real danger was economic and psychological unrest in the West. Kennan helped design and supported the Marshall Plan and backed a military alliance to defend Western Europe but not to challenge communism in Eastern Europe or elsewhere. Counter any Soviet expansion in Europe, he believed, and the Soviet Union would gradually mellow and return to its Russian roots.

Truman alienated Kennan and defensive realists on three crucial points. He broke off U.S.-Soviet talks in the late 1940s, militarized and globalized containment, and promoted American exceptionalism. Kennan, like Roosevelt, was an inveterate believer in diplomacy, albeit outside the UN. For the next two decades, he deplored the absence of détente with the Soviet Union. He also opposed the Korean War and the Indochina conflict that followed. Most of all, he opposed the intrusion of ideology in foreign affairs. He argued in the Long Telegram of 1946 that "never since the termination of the civil war [1921] have [sic] the mass of Soviet people been emotionally farther removed from the doctrines of the Communist Party than they are today." And he accused Truman of responding to a Russian psychosis of insecurity with an American psychosis of exceptionalism and anti-communism. American freedom was special, but so was Russian culture. America might learn from "certain elements [of communism] which I think are probably the ideas of the future."[5] Kennan was an early believer in convergence. But Western values would never prevail over the Soviet Union. Realists like Kennan never envisioned the collapse of the Soviet Union or the democratic revolution in Russia under Yeltsin. Realism targets stability not transformation of the international system, whether through institutions (UN) or ideology (democratic peace).[6]

Of the presidents studied in this volume, Truman was the most liberal domestically. He believed in activist government. In 1948 he proposed compulsory national health care and repeatedly called for taxing the rich to help the poor. But Truman's values were rooted in the Midwest, in religion, and in other institutions of civil society. He drew deepest from a moral sense of right and wrong rather than from a secularist attachment to reason and expertise. The role of government was to strengthen moral values and civil society, not to displace them. In that sense, he qualifies as a reform conservative (see chapter 1). Compared to Roosevelt, his foreign policy had moral not just practical roots. As we will see, he perceived the UN Charter as an aspiring version of the U.S. Constitution.

Three postwar developments reveal Truman's conservative internationalism and its distinctiveness from either liberal internationalism or realism: the tilt from 1945 to 1947 toward a more ideological rather than geopolitical interpretation of the conflict with the Soviet Union reflected in the Truman Doctrine; the decisions during 1947–49 to deploy American military power in Europe for the first time in peace rather than war through NATO; and the shift after 1949 away from negotiations with the Soviet Union in the UN toward the containment of Soviet power in Europe and elsewhere around the world through alliances, not the UN.

Truman Doctrine

Roosevelt was not naïve about the domestic character of the Soviet regime. He told Joseph Davies, his close pro-Soviet advisor, "I can't take communism nor can you, but to cross this bridge I would hold hands with the Devil."[7] The bridge Roosevelt wanted to cross was managing postwar diplomacy with the Soviet Union peacefully. Truman wanted to cross the same bridge.[8] For both, diplomacy had to trump ideology. But Truman and Roosevelt differed precisely on the question of how diplomacy and ideology interacted. At Yalta, Roosevelt let ideological differences pass. When Roosevelt insisted that Polish elections must be as pure as Caesar's wife, Stalin responded that Caesar's wife was known to have her sins. Roosevelt politely agreed. For him, ideology only complicated diplomacy. At Potsdam, when Churchill complained that the Soviet Union blocked access to the Balkan countries and Stalin replied that it was "all fairy tales," Truman jumped to Churchill's side and rebuked Stalin. For Truman, ideology clarified diplomacy. Churchill told aides later that evening, "if only this had happened at Yalta."[9]

Truman's notes from Potsdam reveal his sharper edges.[10] On July 25, he wrote to his wife, Bess: "There are some things we can't agree to. Russia and Poland have gobbled up a big hunk of Germany and want Britain and us to agree. I have flatly refused. We have unalterably opposed the recognition of police governments in the Germany Axis countries. I told Stalin that until we have free access to those countries and our nationals had their property rights restored, so far as we were concerned there'd never be recognition. He seems to like it when I hit him with a hammer."

On July 29, he called the negotiations "a brawl" and commented slyly, "Stalin is 'stallin'." On the other hand, like Roosevelt, Truman instinctively liked Stalin, once comparing him to his mentor and political boss in Missouri, Tom Pendergast: "I like Stalin. He is straightforward. Knows what he wants and will compromise when he can't get it. His foreign minister isn't so forthright."[11]

But Truman did not confuse the personal with the political.[12] "The bitterest debate" at Potsdam, Truman describes, concerned the recognition of Soviet puppet governments in Rumania, Bulgaria, Hungary, and Finland. When Stalin compared Eastern European countries to Italy, Churchill and Truman pointed out that the Soviets had access in Italy. By contrast, Churchill complained of "an iron fence"—according to the British minutes, "an iron curtain," a term he had used in a cable to Truman in May—that had come down around the British mission in Bucharest.[13] Averill Harriman, the U.S. ambassador in Moscow, called the Soviet advance toward Berlin a "barbarian invasion of Europe" and told Truman in April 1945 that "Soviet control over any foreign country meant not only that their influence would be paramount in that country's foreign relations but also that the Soviet system with its secret police and its extinction of freedom of speech would prevail."[14]

This characterization resonated with Truman's instinctive distrust of totalitarian systems. In June 1941, even before the United States entered the war, Truman revealed his gut feelings about fascism and communism: "If we see that Germany is winning we ought to help Russia and if Russia is winning we ought to help Germany and that way let them kill as many as possible, although I don't want to see Hitler victorious under any circumstances. Neither of them think [sic] anything of their pledged word."[15] Once the United States entered the war, Truman understood that alliances with dictators were ephemeral. In April 1942, he wrote his wife, Bess: "we must take this [war] to its conclusion and *dictate* peace terms from Berlin and Tokyo. Then we'll have Russia and China to settle afterwards."[16] In longhand notes throughout the spring and summer 1945, Truman anticipated troubles with democracy's foes: "I've no faith in any Totalitarian State be it Russian, German, Spanish, Argentinian, Dago, or Japanese . . . all start with a wrong premise—that lies are justified and that the old disproven Jesuit formula—the end justifies the means is right and necessary to maintain the power of government."[17] In October 1945, before a Navy Day audience in New York, Truman juxtaposed good and evil: "we shall firmly adhere to what we believe to be right; and we shall not give our approval to any compromises with evil."[18]

Roosevelt was equally suspicious of totalitarianism. But he dealt with it differently. In September 1944, he wrote Churchill that the United States and USSR should get along "by adjusting our differences through compromise by all the parties concerned and this ought to tide things over for a few years until the child learns how to toddle."[19] Roosevelt believed the Soviets could be mentored; Truman was decidedly more skeptical.

Two events in 1946 confirmed Truman's tilt toward ideology as a decisive impediment to diplomacy. In February 1946 Truman invited Churchill to speak at Westminster College in Fulton, Missouri. He not only accompanied Churchill to Fulton by train (discussing the presidential seal) and introduced him but read Churchill's speech beforehand. According to Churchill, Truman said the speech was "admirable and would do nothing but good, though it would make a stir."[20] Churchill's "iron curtain" speech was, as many historians see it, the opening shot of the Cold War: "From Stettin in the Baltic to Trieste in the Adriatic, an Iron Curtain has descended across the Continent."[21] It shocked the press, and Truman afterward tried to muffle his support of the speech. He argued deceptively that he did not know what Churchill was going to say. But George Elsey, Truman's close aide at the time, confirms that Truman read Churchill's speech beforehand.[22] Later in notes recorded by Jonathan Daniels, Truman not only acknowledged that Churchill "said what I wanted him to say—glad he said what he did" but went on to regret that he did not follow Churchill's advice in spring 1945 "not to withdraw troops from Prague, etc. and to go ahead and take Berlin." At the time Truman felt that agreements with Russia bound the United States not to do that. "But if I had known then what I know now," Truman continued, "I would have gon [sic] to the eastern boundaries of Russia."[23]

In early 1946, Truman was clearly ahead of public sentiment. Liberals in the administration, including Eleanor Roosevelt and Secretary of Commerce Henry Wallace, whom Mrs. Roosevelt had supported over Truman for the vice-presidential slot in 1944, sharply criticized Churchill's speech. But public sentiment was changing. In late 1945, 30 percent of the public disapproved of the Soviet Union's foreign policy; by mid-March 1946, 71 percent did.[24] This shift in public opinion one year before Truman announced the Truman Doctrine casts some doubt on the argument that Truman hyped the Soviet threat to gain the support of the American people.

The second event in 1946 involved Truman's secretary of commerce. On September 12, Henry Wallace, the "most insistent liberal in [Roosevelt's] administration," gave a speech denouncing what he perceived to be a shift in U.S. policy toward a hard-line, "get tough with Russia" policy.[25] In a letter to Truman in July, released only after his speech in September, Wallace laid out the liberal internationalist view of U.S.-Soviet relations: "We should ascertain . . . what Russia believes to be essential to her own security . . . judge her requirements against the background of what we ourselves and the British have insisted upon as essential to our respective security . . . [and] be prepared, even at the expense of risking epithets of appeasement, to agree to reasonable Russian guarantees of security."²⁶ Wallace opposed all military programs because they provoked rather than deterred aggression. He subscribed to the liberal internationalist view that conflict originated in reciprocal interactions, not ideology: "The tougher we get, the tougher the Russians will get."²⁷ By the same token, cooperation begat cooperation. He favored economic and trade cooperation with the Soviets and believed in convergence: "Under friendly peaceful competition the Russian world and the American world will gradually become more alike. The Russians will be forced to grant more and more of the personal freedoms; and we shall become more and more absorbed with the problems of social-economic justice."²⁸

For public relations reasons, Truman equivocated after Wallace's speech, as he had after Churchill's. But along with other developments at the time such as the report by close aides Clark Clifford and George Elsey, which documented Soviet treaty violations, there was little doubt where Truman was heading. Truman met with Wallace and told him "to give no more speeches on foreign affairs." When Wallace leaked the content of the meeting, Truman fired him. In his diary, Truman vented: "I believe he's a real Commy and a dangerous man." Charlie Ross, his press secretary, complimented Truman, saying that he had demonstrated that he'd rather be right than president. Truman replied jokingly: "I'd rather be anything than President."²⁹

Thus, by the end of 1946, Churchill's hard line was in and Roosevelt's soft line was out. Truman was clearly on Churchill's team. Later Churchill paid tribute to Truman. Acknowledging that he held Truman in low regard in summer 1945, he said to Truman in 1952: "you, more than any other man, have saved Western Civilization."³⁰

Truman never gave up on diplomacy. As he explained later in his memoirs: "I had hoped that the Russians would return favor for favor, but almost from the time I became president I found them acting . . . in direct violation of the obligations they had assumed at Yalta."³¹ And it is fair to say that in the early going he gave the Russians the benefit of the doubt. "During 1945 and 1946," as Anne Pierce concludes, "Truman and his administration were largely apathetic and silent about political oppression in Bulgaria and throughout the Balkans."³² Truman saw, however, that there were ideological as well as interactive sources of diplomacy. States did not just act on the basis of other states' actions; they also acted on the basis of ideological convictions. Sometimes ideology created unbridgeable gaps, however patient and persistent diplomacy might be. Truman ultimately "rejected Roosevelt's belief that cooperating with the Soviet Union would lead them to cooperate with us."³³

Might Roosevelt have responded to unfolding events in 1946 in the same way? Perhaps, but Roosevelt would have never allowed Churchill to put him into a box vis-à-vis the Soviet Union. Roosevelt often joked that the British "were perfectly willing for the United States to have a war with the Soviet Union at any time," and Eleanor Roosevelt once commented that her husband "always thought that when peace came he would be able to get along better with Stalin than with Churchill."[34] Roosevelt reflected the liberal internationalist view that patient diplomacy usually surmounts ideological differences. And while Roosevelt dumped Wallace for Truman on the presidential ticket in 1944 (largely for domestic reasons), Wallace's views about the Soviet Union were certainly closer to Roosevelt's views and those of his closest pro-Soviet advisors, such as Harry Hopkins and Joseph Davies, than they were to Truman's.[35]

Therefore, by the time, the British announced in February 1947 that they were pulling forces out of Greece and Turkey, Truman was primed to identify regime type or ideology as the root cause of the failure of postwar liberal internationalist diplomacy. He declared in March to a joint session of Congress: "this [policy to help free peoples to maintain free institutions] is no more than a frank recognition that totalitarian regimes imposed on free peoples, by direct or indirect aggression, undermine the foundations of international peace and hence the security of the United States."[36] He appealed to every nation to choose between two alternative ways of life, one democratic, the other oppression:

> One way of life is based upon the will of the majority, and is distinguished by free institutions, representative government, free elections, guarantees of individual liberty, freedom of speech and religion, and freedom from political oppression.
> The second way of life is based upon the will of a minority forcibly imposed upon the majority. It relies upon terror and oppression, a controlled press and radio, fixed elections, and the suppression of personal freedoms.

The speech appalled George Kennan.[37] From this point on, Truman took leave of his realist advisors. In his message to Congress in December 1947 he stressed American exceptionalism: "our moral strength, resulting from our faith in human rights, is the inspiration of free men everywhere."[38] At a joint session of Congress on March 17, 1948, Truman deplored the loss of freedom in Europe: "Since the close of hostilities, the Soviet Union and its agents have destroyed the independence and democratic character of a whole series of nations in Eastern and Central Europe."[39] On the same day in a St. Patrick's Day speech in New York, he described communism as tyranny: "It denies that man is master of his fate and consequently denies man's right to govern himself." "Even worse," he added, "communism denies the very existence of God."[40] His inaugural address in 1949 drew repeated contrasts between liberty and communism.[41] In April 1949, he told NATO foreign ministers: "We should appreciate that Soviet nationalism is dynamic; it must expand, and the only way to defeat it is not merely to contain it but to carry the ideological war to the Soviet sphere itself."[42] And in October 1949 he dismissed the liberal internationalist idea of a settlement with the Soviet Union. He told reporters that someone had advised him to settle with the Soviet Union by giving them what they wanted; after all, isn't settlement what you want, his interlocutor queried? Truman replied: "Oh no, that is not what we want at all. That's what they want."[43]

The full shift from Kennan's realism, which focused on geopolitics, to Truman's conservative internationalism, which focused on domestic ideologies, came in winter 1949–50. The National Security Council document, NSC-68, that defined America's Cold War policy for the next forty years, rebutted Kennan's argument about Russian insecurities: "The Soviet Union, unlike previous aspirants to hegemony, is animated by a new fanatical faith, antithetical to our own, and seeks to impose its absolute authority over the rest of the world." Contrasting freedom with communist slavery, the document globalized the conflict with the Soviet Union well before the Korean War in June 1950: "The assault on free institutions is world-wide now, and in the context of the present polarization of power defeat of free institutions anywhere is a defeat everywhere." And it made clear that this global conflict would be won not just by containment but by the commitment to "foster a fundamental change in the nature of the Soviet system. . . . The idea of slavery can only be overcome by the timely and persistent demonstration of the superiority of the idea of freedom." NSC-68 called for a policy "to check and roll back the Kremlin drive for world domination." "The only sure victory," it added, "lies in the frustration of the Kremlin design by the speedy development of the moral and material strength of the free world and its projection into the Soviet world in such a way as to bring about an internal change in the Soviet system."[44]

Did Truman hype the ideological threat? What's worse, did he do it for cynical political reasons to win congressional approval and reelection? Quite a few historians, reflecting realist and liberal internationalist sentiments, think so.[45] They believe Truman discounted too readily genuine Soviet security needs and prospects for Soviet cooperation. Henry Wallace called the Marshall Plan the "Martial Plan" and a "declaration of war."[46] In his view the Berlin Blockade was a response to the Marshall Plan, and Stalin did not extend but restrained Soviet policy in 1945–46

when the Soviet Union might have taken advantage of Western demobilization and expanded its military control into the Balkans and central
Europe.

But, as noted earlier, public opinion did not need to be hyped. By February 1946 most Americans already saw the Soviet Union as a troublemaker. Were they and Truman wrong? Was the Soviet Union just another
great power hiding behind the guise of Marxist ideology, as Kennan
thought? Was diplomacy up to the task of coexistence between ideological as opposed to geopolitical adversaries, as Roosevelt believed? Truman linked the cause of freedom closely to threat, and he distinguished
between the threat to Greece and Turkey on the borders of free Europe
and the threat to China in remote Asia.[47] His approach was neither utopian nor cynical. Roosevelt believed in 1943 that Stalin "doesn't want
anything but security for his country and I think that if I give him everything I possibly can and ask nothing in return, noblesse oblige, he won't
try to annex anything and will work with me for a world of democracy
and peace."[48] At the very least, had he lived, Roosevelt would have been
slower to conclude that communist ideology mattered. Charles Bohlen,
who worked closely with Roosevelt and Hopkins on Soviet policy, once
said: "I do not think Roosevelt had any real comprehension of the great
gulf that separated the thinking of a Bolshevik from a non-Bolshevik, and
particularly from an American. He felt that Stalin viewed the world somewhat in the same light as he did."[49] After an exhaustive study of the differences between Roosevelt and Truman, Wilson Miscamble agrees: Roosevelt "either downplayed or simply failed to appreciate the ideological
chasm that divided the democracies from Stalin's totalitarian regime."[50]

By 1947, Stalin also saw the relationship more in ideological than geopolitical terms.[51] In Finland, on the periphery of Eastern Europe, Stalin
tolerated a non-communist government as long as Finland was a foreign
policy ally. In Eastern European countries, however, Stalin decided that
the governments had to be communist, not just geopolitical allies. That
made the confrontation ideological. As Thomas Risse argues, "had Stalin
'Finlandized' rather than 'Sovietized' Eastern Europe, the Cold War could
have been avoided."[52] But Stalin's ideological commitments ran too deep
to separate domestic ideological aims from geopolitical foreign policy
concerns. Liberal governments in Eastern Europe, whatever their foreign
policies, threatened communism in Moscow, no less than communist
governments in Western Europe threatened liberalism in Paris and Rome.
That's why Stalin vetoed Eastern European participation in the Marshall
Plan and Soviet agents murdered the democratic leader of Czechoslovakia in a communist coup in February 1948. As a result, "Soviet power became threatening as a tool to expand the Soviet domestic order."[53] Thus
ideological divergence preceded and precluded a more moderate "spheres

of influence" or "UN institutional" solution to superpower relations in Europe.[54] Ideas gave meaning to and drove power balances and negotiations rather than the other way around. The ideological division of Korea, which also took effect in 1948, provided further evidence that at the time ideological factors overrode geopolitical ones.

Ideological conflict does not necessarily equal military conflict. What it does mean, however, is the need to balance power because, given the gap in self-definition, neither side can feel safe unless it is able to defend itself. Balancing power in turn entails risks of war. Nevertheless, differences, if recognized, can be managed—most safely by mutual attention to balancing competitive military and economic capabilities and, since force and diplomacy always work together, by careful and delicate diplomacy to identify sufficient or overlapping interests, especially in a nuclear age. Hence power balances and diplomacy are not irrelevant. But they take their cue from ideological divergence.[55]

By this logic, Truman did not ignore either geopolitics or diplomacy. He simply made a calculation that the moral content of any diplomatic settlement mattered as much as the settlement itself. After 1945–46, he could not envision a settlement that would not weaken or even eviscerate the cause of freedom in Europe. And that was too high a moral price to pay for diplomatic business as usual. A settlement was not off the table, but it would have to wait for the balancing of Soviet power and the demonstration that freedom was the future of Europe, not communism. He understood, as ultimately the Congress and the public did as well, that an *expansion* of Soviet ideology, which was at stake for the first time in Greece and Turkey, was a different kettle of fish than a *consolidation* of Soviet ideology in territories already occupied by the Soviet Union at the end of World War II (such as Poland). Public opinion solidified quickly once the Marshall Plan made it clear that it was Western not Eastern Europe that was at stake.

NATO and Military Force

If Truman parted company with realists over ideology, he parted company with liberal internationalists in believing that the use of force has to accompany if not at times precede negotiations if those negotiations are to result in a morally acceptable outcome. As Anne Pierce concludes, "Truman came to believe that sheer physical might was essential for stopping Soviet aggression."[56]

From 1943 to 1947, neither Roosevelt nor Truman saw force and the balance of power as an intimate instrument of national diplomacy. Instead, true to liberal internationalist instincts, they backed Roosevelt's idea of a muscular Security Council in the United Nations charged under

Chapter VII of the Charter to use collective military power to enforce the peace. National military force would defer to international military force. Roosevelt pledged to Stalin at Tehran in November 1943 that the United States would remove all forces from Europe within two years after the end of the war. He told Elsey in October 1944 that he hoped "Russia would get lots of Germany. Stalin already had a million German prisoners. He makes Napoleon look like a piker." [57] Roosevelt repeated the pledge to demobilize at Yalta, even as Soviet forces were rumbling toward Berlin. To be sure, after the Soviet Union moved in late February and early March 1945 to install a communist government in Poland, Roosevelt cabled Churchill in early April, shortly before he died, that "our armies will in a very few days be in a position that will permit us to become tougher" and the two leaders may have "to consider most carefully the implications of Stalin's attitude and what is to be our next step." [58] As Robert Ferrell notes, Roosevelt's "last days had been marked by almost open disagreement with the Russians." [59] Still, the record of Roosevelt's last days is quite mixed. On March 24, Roosevelt blurted out: "Averell is right; we can't do business with Stalin. He has broken every one of his promises he made at Yalta." Yet on April 11, one day before he died, Roosevelt cabled Churchill that they "minimize the general Soviet problem as much as possible because the problems, in one form or another, seem to arise every day and most of them straighten out." [60] In any case, it did not matter. In substance for the next two years, Truman's actions did not deviate from Roosevelt's liberal internationalist preference for collective diplomacy over selective force.

However, from the beginning, Truman's style and approach differed in important ways from Roosevelt's. As Elizabeth Spalding writes, "Truman believed in the goal of liberal internationalism, but he did not agree with the established approaches of Wilson and FDR." [61] He sought to expand freedom but by methods that were less conventional and more aggressive. [62] He spoke bluntly to Soviet foreign minister Molotov at their first meeting in April 1945. Truman told Molotov to tell Stalin that failure on the Polish agreement, which troubled Roosevelt just before his death, would "seriously shake confidence." At the end of the meeting, Molotov, according to Truman, said: "I have never been talked to like that in my life." Truman responded: "Carry out your agreements and you won't get talked to like that." [63]

Moreover, Truman, a front-line army captain in World War I, was not uncomfortable with the use of military force. In May and June 1945 he ordered Eisenhower to deploy U.S. forces to bloc Tito, the leader of communist partisans in Yugoslavia, from taking the port of Trieste. And on taking office, he was briefed on the atomic bomb and understood instinctively its significance. He called the bomb "his ace in the hole" [64] and, under the urging of Secretary of War Henry Stimson, who called the bomb "a royal straight flush,"[65] may have hoped that the A-bomb would give the United States an advantage in negotiations with the Soviets. Truman did not favor sharing the bomb's secret with the Kremlin and was skeptical of disarmament: "We should not under any circumstances throw away our gun until we are sure the rest of the world won't arm against us."[66] Truman not only used the bomb against Japan but later decided without hesitation to develop an even bigger, hydrogen bomb. While Roosevelt may have done the same, Truman never had any regrets.[67]

On the ground in Europe, however, Truman confirmed his reluctance to use force to arm his diplomacy. There the balance of power was shifting daily toward the Soviet Union; yet Truman did nothing to counter it for fear of damaging the prospects of cooperation with Russia. Although he had talked tough to Molotov about Poland, he had rejected Churchill's suggestion a few days earlier that western forces, which had moved about 150 miles beyond the agreed occupation zone into Germany and Czechoslovakia, remain in place as leverage to negotiate with Stalin over Poland and other issues. General Eisenhower opposed Churchill's idea. He saw it as injecting the political into the military. Berlin was not that important militarily, and the overriding priority at the time was to maintain political cooperation with Moscow. By siding with Eisenhower, Truman rejected the link between force and diplomacy. He acknowledged that "The Russians were in a strong position, and they knew it." But he countered their military strength with little more than moral example: "if [the Soviets] were firm in their way, we should be firm in ours. And our way was to stick to our agreements and keep insisting that they do the same."[68]

Churchill fretted throughout this period about U.S. troop withdrawals. According to Truman's aide Joseph Davies, who met with Churchill on May 26–29, Churchill reflected that "it would be a 'terrible thing' if the American army were vacated from Europe. Europe would be prostrate and at the mercy of the Red Army and of communism."[69] Using the phrase "iron curtain" for the first time, Churchill viewed "with profound misgivings the retreat of the American army to our line of occupation in the Central Sector, thus bringing Soviet power into the heart of Western Europe and the descent of an iron curtain between us and everything to the eastward."[70] Nevertheless, Truman informed Churchill and then Stalin that U.S. troops would be withdrawn starting June 21. In a slight twist of irony, Stalin requested a delay until July 1 so that Soviet generals could participate in a parade in Moscow.[71]

Truman later regretted this withdrawal decision: "perhaps they [agreements made in the war to keep Russia fighting] should not have been adhered to so quickly."[72] At the very least, he might have used the troop issue to clarify the terms of Allied access to Berlin. That matter had not been resolved at Yalta and was left to the generals in the field to negotiate in June 1945.[73] The matter returned to haunt the Allies in the Berlin Blockade of 1948.

In a way, Truman's reluctance to use force to influence negotiations worked against his own instincts. In October 1945 he sent Congress legislation calling for a thorough reorganization of the American military, including compulsory universal military training. "If we were to maintain leadership among other nations," Truman said, "we must continue to be strong in a military way." He had been distressed to learn that 30 percent of the men recruited during World War II had been rejected for physical reasons. He called for one year of training for all eighteen-year-olds "with no exemptions except for total physical disqualification." These men would become members of the General Reserve for six years and subsequently serve in a secondary reserve status. Truman later said: "I am morally certain that if Congress had enacted this program in 1945, . . . we would have had a pool of basically trained men, which would have caused the Soviets to hesitate and perhaps not bring on the Berlin crisis or the Korean aggression."[74]

Like Churchill, Truman fretted about the demobilization of Allied forces in Europe. In an Army Day address in April 1946, Truman said: "We cannot on one day proclaim our intention to prevent unjust oppression and tyranny in the world, and on the next day call for the immediate scrapping of our military might."[75] And in a press conference that same month, he called it the "most remarkable demobilization in the history of the world, or 'disintegration' if you want to call it that."[76] In fall 1945 U.S. servicemen were being discharged at a rate of 650 per hour. Yet Truman understood the domestic circumstances that drove demobilization: "In 1945–46 the American people chose to scuttle their military might. I was against hasty and excessive demobilization at the time and stated publicly that I was."[77] Over the next three years, Truman proposed a new Selective Service Act, the unification of the armed forces under a single defense department, the creation of Central Intelligence Agency (CIA), and the establishment of the National Security Council system. His instincts told him "good deeds are not enough."

Meanwhile, Stalin showed no hesitancy to use national force as a bargaining tool. He conditioned Soviet military participation in Asia on Yalta agreements to give the Soviets ports in Manchuria and control of Sakhalin Island, and he told Molotov not to worry about the Yalta clauses on free elections in Poland because the Soviet Union would be in a stronger military position later: "work it out. We can deal with it in our own way later."[78] As the war ended, Stalin's instincts were captured perfectly by his comment to Milovan Djilas, the Yugoslav communist: "whoever occupies a territory also imposes on it his own social system. Everyone imposes his own system as far as his army can reach."[79]

Truman's turn toward the more assertive use of U.S. force began in fall and winter 1945 and culminated in the study, drafted in summer 1946 by his advisors Clark Clifford and George Elsey, which became the blueprint for the Truman Doctrine, Marshall Plan, and NATO. In November and December 1945, Truman learned that Russia was adding to forces in northern Iran and had set up a revolutionary government in Azerbaijan.[80] Molotov refused to discuss the issue at the foreign ministers meeting in December. Russia was also pressuring Turkey to sign an exclusive agreement on the Dardanelles. In this setting, Truman drafted his famous unsent letter, dated January 5, 1946, to Secretary of State James Byrnes expressing his dissatisfaction with coddling the Soviets. The letter, which Truman claims he read to Byrnes but Byrnes denies, said in part:

> Russia intends an invasion of Turkey and seizure of the Black Sea Straits to the Mediterranean. . . . Unless Russia is faced with an iron fist and strong language another war is in the making. Only one language does the Soviet Union understand—"How many divisions have you" . . . I do not think we should compromise any longer. We should refuse to recognize Rumania and Bulgaria until they comply with our requirements; we should let our position on Iran be known in no uncertain terms and we should continue to insist on the internationalization of the Kiel Canal, the Rhine-Danube waterway and the Black Sea Straits and we should maintain complete control of Japan and the Pacific. We should rehabilitate China and create a strong central government there. We should do the same for Korea. Then we should insist on the return of our ships from Russia and force a settlement of the Lend-Lease debt of Russia. I'm tired of babying the Soviets.[81]

Soviet forces, although withdrawn from Iran by the end of May, maneuvered menacingly in the Balkans in August and September 1946. Twenty-five divisions massed on the southern border of the Caucasus to pressure Turkey and Iran. On August 7, the Soviets demanded a new regime governing the strait under joint Russian-Turkish control.[82] Now Truman took his first steps toward strengthening U.S. forces in Europe as an instrument of U.S. diplomacy. He increased significantly U.S. naval forces in the Mediterranean, sending the battleship USS *Missouri* from the Mediterranean to the Sea of Marmara (just south of the straits at Istanbul) and a larger aircraft carrier task force with the newly commissioned supercarrier, *Franklin D. Roosevelt*, to the eastern Mediterranean.[83] Through Byrnes, he told a German audience that summer that U.S. forces would not leave Europe unprotected, and Truman initiated joint war planning by U.S. and British military staffs.[84] In this context, Truman also ordered a report in mid-July from his hard-line advisors Clark Clifford and George Elsey to document Soviet treaty violations.[85]

The top secret Clifford-Elsey report, a hundred-thousand-word document, was submitted in September. It accused the Soviet Union of "conducting . . . a course of aggrandizement designed to lead to eventual world domination" and being "blinded by its adherence to Marxist doctrine" rather than pursuing legitimate security needs.[86] It concluded that the only way to avert war with the Soviet Union was to convince them that "we are too strong to be beaten and too determined to be frightened."[87] The report, like Churchill's iron curtain speech, was a bit premature. Once the Soviets pulled back in Turkey and realizing the stir the report might cause, Truman confiscated it. "It is very valuable to me," Truman told Clifford, "but if it leaked it would blow the roof off the White House, it would blow the roof off the Kremlin."[88] Worried about congressional elections, he was not quite ready to confront Soviet power with U.S. power. He still hoped the UN would succeed.

There is no doubt, however, that the Clifford-Elsey report reflected Truman's frame of mind as he launched the Truman Doctrine and Marshall Plan of 1947. As Clark Clifford later mused, "there was really nothing to impede Soviet forces, if they chose to, from just marching straight west to the English Channel."[89] By spring 1948, less than half a dozen American, British, and French divisions remained in the western half of Germany, while according to some estimates 175 to 200 divisions of the Soviet Union or its satellites occupied the eastern side of the country.[90] True, the United States had the A-bomb, but probably not enough of them, according to Secretary of Defense James Forrestal, to knock the Soviets out of a conventional war. In any event, who wanted to have the A-bomb as the only available military option?[91] The days of downplaying or misreading the conventional balance of power in Europe in order to make cooperation work were coming to an end.

In April 1947, after announcing the Truman Doctrine to Congress, Truman told a Jefferson Day Dinner: "It is no longer enough merely to say, 'We don't want a war.' We must act in time—ahead of time—to stamp out the smoldering beginnings of any conflict that may threaten to spread over the world."[92] In the same speech, he added: "We are a people who not only cherish freedom and defend it, if need be with our lives, but we also recognize the right of other men and other nations to share it." And on September 30, 1947, Truman wrote to Bess: "Suppose, for instance, that Italy should fold up and that Tito would then march into the Po Valley. All the Mediterranean coast of France then is open to Russian occupation and the iron curtain comes to Bordeaux, Calais, Antwerp and the Hague. We withdraw from Greece and Turkey and *prepare for war.* It just must not happen."[93]

The Truman Doctrine and Marshall Plan were economic and political, not military. But they clearly implied that military defense was coming. The Brussels Pact, an alliance of Western European states, was formed at the same time as the Marshall Plan, and NATO followed ineluctably. As Marshall told his Harvard audience, the initiative was not "directed against any country or doctrine but against hunger, poverty, desperation and chaos," but "its purpose should be the revival of a working economy in the world so as to permit the emergence of political and social conditions in which free institutions can exist."[94] In a message to Congress in December 1947, Truman said the Marshall Plan was "proof that free men can effectively join together to defend their free institutions against totalitarian pressures."[95]

The military point of no return came with the Berlin Blockade in 1948. The chickens of trusting Stalin at Yalta came home to roost. Left to the generals in the field, the terms of Allied access to Berlin had never been clarified, and the Soviets began tinkering with Allied entry even before the Marshall Plan took effect.[96] They had a decided geopolitical advantage in Berlin, and Stalin used it to arm Soviet diplomacy (as subsequent Soviet leaders did for the next twenty years). The only way to save West Berlin now was by military action. As Truman mused in his *Memoirs,* "The Marshall Plan had brought some relief, but the constant threat of unpredictable Soviet moves resulted in an atmosphere of insecurity and fear among the peoples of western Europe. Something more needed to be done to counteract the fear of the peoples of Europe that their countries would be overrun by the Soviet army before effective help could arrive."[97] A few advisors called for a showdown sending an armored train through the Soviet zone to the city.[98] But if the Soviets fought back, the United States would be outmatched. The majority therefore counseled Truman to give up the U.S. position in Berlin. But Truman cut off the discussion: "we are going to stay period."[99] He ordered the famous airlift. Truman was the first to grasp that "Berlin had become the symbol of America's— and the West's—dedication to the cause of freedom."[100]

However hesitantly Truman got there, his decision to erect Berlin as the outpost of Western freedom was monumental. It extended the Monroe Doctrine for the first time beyond the western hemisphere to Western Europe (no extraregional, meaning Russian, interference in Western Europe) and placed American forces at risk to defend the "disputed" borders of freedom in Europe, much as Polk had placed U.S. forces at risk to defend the "disputed" borders of Texas. It was a preeminent example of the preemptive use of force to deter aggression. Yes, it involved risks and prospects of Soviet retaliation. Thus realist and liberal internationalist critics of the use of force to leverage diplomacy immediately argued that Truman's actions "provoked" the Cold War.[101] Remember, they point out, the Soviet Union had attacked no one's territory; Moscow was simply defending its own occupied zone.

Yet one does not have to believe that the Soviet Union would have used force to invade Western Europe if the West had not rearmed; it is enough to believe that it was unwise to leave that option open while negotiating with the Soviet Union. NSC-68 rejected the argument that being defenseless was the best way to get cooperation: "No people in history have preserved their freedom who thought that by not being strong enough to defend themselves they might prove inoffensive to their enemies."[102] As Truman records, Ernest Bevin, Britain's foreign minister, pointed out the alternatives: "The principal risk involved, Bevin said, was that the Russians might be so provoked by the formation of a defense organization that they would resort to rash measures and plunge the world into war. . . . On the other hand, if a collective security system could be built up effectively, it is more than likely that the Russians might restudy the situation and become more co-operative."[103] Indeed if the United States had been better armed, it might have negotiated more confidently and sooner. Instead the need to rebuild Western strength in the face of overwhelming Soviet conventional forces in Europe stalled negotiations for the next twenty years.[104]

Sidelining the United Nations

For Roosevelt the realist element of the United Nations was never primary. Great power cooperation in the Security Council served the liberal internationalist purpose of collective security. There was no turning back to selective alliances and the old balance-of-power game. Returning from Yalta, Roosevelt sounded exactly like Woodrow Wilson returning from Paris twenty-five years earlier. He called for "the end of the system of unilateral action, exclusive alliances, and spheres of influence, and balances of power and all the other expedients which have been tried for centuries and failed."[105]

Perhaps such pronouncements were for domestic consumption only. But Roosevelt repeatedly resisted Churchill's urging for more selective U.S.-British cooperation to bargain with Stalin. For FDR, "Churchill represented the old order," and Churchill's "willingness to cut classic spheres of influence deals revealed him in Roosevelt's eyes to be at heart just another European politician."[106] Roosevelt bet the farm that he could win Stalin's trust, and it seems doubtful that had he lived he would have invited Churchill to Fulton less than a year later to call for a union of

Western democracies as an alternative to the United Nations.[107] Stalin agreed with Churchill. According to Truman at Potsdam, "[Stalin's] viewpoint was that Russia, Britain, and the United States would settle world affairs and that it was nobody else's business." Truman put himself on the side of FDR: "I felt very strongly that participation of all nations, small and large, was just as important to world peace as that of the Big Three. It was my policy and purpose to make the United Nations a going and vital organization."[108]

Thus, make no mistake; Truman was no less committed to the United Nations than Roosevelt. He carried in his pocket since 1910, he said, Tennyson's Locksley Hall poem, which rhapsodized about "the parliament of man":[109]

> Till the war-drum throbb'd no longer, and the battle flags were furl'd
>   In the Parliament of Man, the Federation of the World.
> There the common sense of most shall hold a fretful realm in awe,
>   And the kindly earth shall slumber, lapt in universal law.

In his speech at the UN in June 1945, he compared the UN Charter to the U.S. Constitution: "The Constitution of my own country came from a Convention which—like this one—was made up of delegates with many different views. When it was adopted, no one regarded it as a perfect document. But it grew and developed and expanded. And upon it there was built a bigger, a better, a more perfect union."[110] He saw agreement among diverse nations as the essence of democracy: "It was proof that nations, like men, can state their differences, can face them, and then find common ground on which to stand. That is the essence of democracy."[111] Truman was not being idealistic. He knew it would take years to develop international organizations and, along the way, "it would try the soul of many a statesman." "But," as Truman mischievously added, "I always considered statesmen to be more expendable than soldiers."[112] After all, this was the prize for which the United States had fought the war: "The forces of reaction and tyranny all over the world will try to keep the United Nations from remaining united."[113] "All I am interested in," Truman said in 1947, "is . . . to make the United Nations work—in the same manner in which the Colonies made the Federal Government work."[114]

But Truman had a substantive as well as practical view of the UN. At San Francisco, he said: "With this Charter the world can begin to look forward to the time when all worthy human beings may be permitted to live decently as free people." And he closed with these ringing words: "Let us not fail to grasp this supreme chance to establish a world-wide rule of reason—to create an enduring peace under the guidance of God."[115]

"Worthy humans beings" living "decently as free people" in peace "under the guidance of God"—mind you, he was talking to Joseph Stalin and the communist countries of the world who were committed to the almighty state, not worthy human beings, Marxism not freedom, and atheism not God's guidance. Which moral world would the UN serve? What kind of peace would it superintend? One in which freedom or communism advanced? Truman's dilemma with the UN may have also been Roosevelt's. But it's doubtful that Roosevelt would have been so up front about "the guidance of God." Truman drew more deeply from conservative religious roots, Roosevelt from liberal rationalist ones.

Nevertheless, despite these inherent tensions, Truman backed the UN at almost every point from 1945 to 1947, including proposing the far-reaching Baruch Plan to deposit all nuclear capabilities in a UN Atomic Energy Agency.[116] By early 1948, however, he began to see that the UN would not work, at least not without some help from free countries: As Elizabeth Spalding documents, "while never abandoning his hope for peace of a permanent nature under the United Nations, [Truman] now realized that 'free peoples'—those peoples that collectively came to be called the 'Western alliance'—superseded the international organization, a conclusion that informed all of his liberal internationalism along with containment."[117] He understood that freedom trumped both order and organization and "rejected the realist preference for order above all and the Wilsonian confidence in peace through a single universal organization."[118] He would reconstruct the UN through alliances rather than expect it to replace alliances.

In spring 1948 Truman took sides at the UN between freedom and consensus. He backed Britain and Israel, one old and one new democracy, to promptly recognize the new state of Israel. He took this position against the wishes of the United Nations and most of his advisors, even his own secretary of state, George Marshall, who told Truman he would vote against Truman in the next election if Truman recognized the Jewish state.[119] In his inaugural address in 1949, Truman still backed the UN with strong rhetoric, and in Korea he insisted that the United States work through the UN to resist aggression. He told an aide, referring to the decision to resist aggression in Korea, "I did this for the United Nations . . . in this first big test we just couldn't let them down."[120] But the circumstances (Soviet absence from the Security Council) that allowed the United States to act in Korea through the General Assembly would not be repeated again. The UN was a dead letter, and the United States and its allies moved into a decade of rearmament and selective alliance building that all but precluded negotiations with the Soviet Union.

Subsequently both liberal internationalists and realists strongly criticized the abandonment of significant negotiations with the Soviet Union after 1949.[121] Later crises in Berlin and Cuba, they believed, were direct outgrowths of the lack of negotiations.[122] But conservative internationalists, like Truman, saw it differently. When the Soviet Union exploded its own A-bomb in September 1949, the calculus of deterrence changed. With nuclear advantage equalized, the Soviet Union's advantage in conventional arms now loomed large in central Europe. Ignoring this advantage and negotiating from weakness, Truman understood, only invited appeasement or, at worst, Soviet aggression. Stalin's decision to authorize the invasion of Korea, which was suspected at the time and later confirmed, demonstrated what might have happened in Europe if the West had not rearmed.[123] Thus negotiations had to take a back seat to rearmament, and the buildup of countervailing conventional alliances in Europe and elsewhere was necessary to create the self-confidence both sides needed to negotiate.

As conservative internationalists see it, negotiations with the Soviet Union in the late 1940s and early 1950s, which both liberal internationalists and realists urged, would have risked the defense of central Europe. The western half of Germany was politically divided at this time between Christian Democrats, who put individual freedom and Western integration ahead of reunification (elected by one vote in 1949 to govern the new Federal Republic of Germany), and Social Democrats, who put social equality and reunification with East Germany ahead of Western integration. France was unreconciled to both NATO and the rearmament of West Germany. In 1952 Stalin proposed German reunification on the basis of neutrality.[124] It is not only possible but highly likely that if the United States had taken up that offer seriously, it would have tipped the political balance in Germany toward the Social Democrats and reunification and given France and other Western European countries decisive excuses not to arm NATO. Germany would have been reunited as a left-leaning neutral country with Soviet armies massed on its eastern borders and, as Clark Clifford later mused, nothing between Berlin and the English Channel to stop them if they decided to march.

Conservative internationalism does not oppose negotiations, but it conducts them with a vigilant eye on what is going on outside negotiations. If a country's position outside negotiations is weak, the stronger side will either dictate the outcome of negotiations or have little interest in negotiations. Thus advocating strength and boosting armaments in situations of weakness are not provocative but helpful to serious negotiations. Negotiations are not always desirable, though keeping open lines of communications is. What is always necessary, which pure hard-liners sometimes forget, is a vision of how the world might work once armaments are balanced and serious negotiations can take place without fear and intimidation. Realists envision coexistence, stability, and peace, with the struggle between freedom and tyranny unresolved and probably irresolvable. Liberal internationalists see universal world institutions and the rule of law, which is why they find it hard to get there by ever breaking off or resisting negotiations. Conservative internationalists imagine a world of independent free nations perennially resisting the temptation of tyranny through some common free world institutions but mostly through decentralized, competitive, and self-reliant, self-renewing civil societies.

In his farewell address in January 1953, Truman firmly set in place the initial bookend of a conservative internationalist view of the Cold War. He anticipated that the Soviet Union, not America, would change direction: "As the free world grows stronger, more united, more attractive to men on both sides of the Iron Curtain—and as Soviet hopes or easy expansion are blocked—then there will have to come a time of change in the Soviet world."[125] For Truman freedom produced strength, which blocked Soviet expansion and eventually brought about "a time of change in the Soviet world." Forty years later, his ideological soul mate, Ronald Reagan, adopted exactly the same point of view and, with the help of "men on both sides of the Iron Curtain," especially Mikhail Gorbachev, brought about the domestic change in Moscow that set in place the terminal bookend of the conservative internationalist view of the Cold War.[126]

Domestic Politics

Truman was not a conventional conservative. He did not believe in limited government, although he was a fiscal conservative. He was the first president to submit legislation to Congress for compulsory universal health care, and he ranted repeatedly against the wealthy and their special interest lobbies. He was a progressive Democrat. Among Republicans, he identified with Teddy Roosevelt, calling him "one outstanding Republican President . . . [who] contributed to the perpetuation of progressivism in American life."[127] Nevertheless, unlike Teddy or Franklin Roosevelt, as well as Wilson, Truman was folksy and not elitist.[128] He identified with the common man and complained of not having "a bigger bump of ego or something to give me an idea that there can be a No. 1 man in the world," as *Time* magazine designated him in 1945.[129] He wrote touchingly from Potsdam that he missed his wife's letters: "I've had only one letter from you since I left home" and "I look carefully through every pouch that comes—but so far not much luck."[130] He bucked both business and labor, emphasizing a "Fair Deal," and confounded his liberal colleagues by appointing a conservative, "perhaps his best friend," John Snyder, as head of the Office of War Mobilization and Reconversion and later treasury secretary.[131] George Elsey, an aide who knew him well, said: "I sensed in these candid moments that he was essentially a

conservative with little or no sympathy with organized labor and its leaders."[132] Another longtime acquaintance, Roy Roberts, said the same: he
possessed "the innate, instinctive conservatism, in action, of the Missouri-
bred countryman."[133]

Truman identified himself as a classical liberal: "I classify myself as a
Jeffersonian Democrat living in modern times."[134] Jefferson, according to
Truman, swept big-government types out of office and "restored liberalism in government after his election." Liberals feared that Truman would
reverse the New Deal. But he didn't. In fact some opponents, such as
Strom Thurmond, thought he was more New Deal than Roosevelt. "Truman really *means* it," Thurmond quipped. On civil rights, Thurmond
knew what he was talking about. Truman led the charge that culminated
twenty years later in Martin Luther King and the civil rights movement:
"What kept me going in 1945 was my belief that there is far more good
than evil in men and that it is the business of government to make the
good prevail." In this sense, Truman was a reform conservative, very
much in the mold of Abraham Lincoln.

Truman was like Lincoln in another way: he was very religious. He
saw human nature as flawed by sin, not perfectible by reason. And he
thought religion offered the way to redemption, to a direct, personal relationship to God: "the way was not through Caiaphas the High Priest
or Augustus the Emperor, the way is direct and straight, Any man can tell
the Almighty . . . his troubles and directly ask for guidance. *He will get
it.*"[135] Morality provided a standard for both individual and international
behavior. "Human freedom is born of the belief that man is created equal
in the image of God and therefore capable of governing himself," he said
at Arlington Cemetery in 1949.[136] Communism was most repugnant because it "attacks our main basic values, our belief in God, our belief in
the dignity of man and the value of human life, our belief in justice and
freedom."[137] Our task "is to preserve a world civilization in which man's
belief in God can survive."[138] "Stalin and his crowd," Truman believed,
"had no intellectual honesty and no moral code . . . [and] had broken 30
to 40 treaties they'd made with us and the free world."[139]

On the other hand, Truman was not pious or showy. He had little
use for the doctrinal squabbles among religions and denominations: "A
lot of the world's troubles have been caused by the interpretation of the
Gospels and the controversies between sects and creeds. It is all so silly
and comes of the prima donna complex again."[140] He tried unsuccessfully
several times to grant full recognition and appoint U.S. ambassadors to
the Vatican.

Like Polk, Truman was an unexpected president.[141] And like Polk and
Lincoln, he contended with egocentric presidential rivals, cabinets, and
generals who "got it into their heads that they, not the President, were the

policy-makers."[142] Henry Wallace, who became secretary of commerce, was Truman's predecessor as vice president. After Roosevelt sent Wallace off to China in 1944 to get him out of the way and replace him, Wallace stampeded the Democratic convention in July to try to retain his position, unsuccessfully as it turned out. James Byrnes, who became secretary of state, also pressed hard for the nomination. He even asked Truman to nominate him, hoping thereby to eliminate Truman as a rival. Roosevelt told Byrnes his advisors would make the decision based on who would cost him the least votes, and Roosevelt never asked Truman directly to serve.[143] Truman was eventually chosen on a second ballot and then cast the deciding vote in the Senate to confirm Wallace as secretary of commerce. Wallace went on to run against Truman in 1948 as a third-party candidate. In April 1951, Truman fired General Douglas MacArthur, the American commander in Korea and another presidential wannabe, "because he wouldn't respect the authority of the President."[144] He told Elsey later that "he had dug into the history books to refresh his memory of Abraham Lincoln's problems with General McClellan and Polk's with General Winfield Scott during the Mexican War."[145]

Unlike Woodrow Wilson, Truman was not a big fan of executive power. He "explicitly rejected what he saw as Roosevelt's unwarranted personal expansion of presidential powers." Roosevelt, Truman believed, "wanted to be in a position where he could say yes or no to everything without anyone's arguing with him or questioning him, and of course you can't do that in our system of checks and balances."[146] By contrast, Truman, like Polk, liked cabinet meetings in which "honest men can honestly disagree, and a frank and open argument of this kind is the best form of free expression in which a President can get all points of view needed to make decisions."[147] He delegated and in the early months relied heavily on Roosevelt's staff—Leahy, the chief of staff, and especially Russian advisors.[148] This may have accounted for the fact that it took him a while to hit his own stride on Soviet policy. Truman made sure that Byrnes was fully briefed even before his appointment was announced—delayed until the UN San Francisco conference was over. And he resented most the fact that Byrnes often failed to brief him as fully in return. This frustration no doubt influenced the real or imagined (depending on whether he read the letter to Byrnes) dressing-down he delivered to Byrnes already in January 1946.

Truman, again like Polk, was a product of the Congress and liked the Congress as an institution better than the presidency. Of the White House, which he once called "the great white sepulcher of ambitions and reputations," he said: "I hate the God-damned place. It's terrible. I want to be back in the Senate."[149] He felt the Congress was closer to the people and more likely to reflect their will: "Our government is by the consent of the people and you have to convince a majority of the people that you are trying to do what is right and in their interest. If you are not a politician, you cannot do it."[150] Or, again: "I have always believed that the vast majority of people want to do what is right and that if the President is right and can get through to the people he can always persuade them."[151] He considered the populist William Jennings Bryan, whose nomination convention he attended in 1900 with his father, "one of my heroes."[152]

Nevertheless, Truman exercised unprecedented presidential leadership. He shaped the consensus that launched the Cold War in 1947–48, even after the Democrats lost control of both houses of Congress in 1946.[153] And he left office with that consensus intact even though his approval ratings were the lowest ever and the Republicans recaptured the Congress and won the presidency in 1952. In between, of course, he and his party in Congress won decisive and unexpected victories in 1948.[154] He did all this with a combination of modesty and savvy from his days on the Hill. He let the recovery program become known as the Marshall Plan because he knew that a Republican Congress could support it more easily if it were not called the Truman Plan, and he forged an historic partnership with Senator Arthur Vandenberg, Republican from Michigan, to shepherd the Marshall Plan and NATO through Congress and end over a hundred years of American isolationism. Thereafter, as Donovan notes, "differences might arise on details, but on the main questions of a dominant American role, moral leadership, support of capitalist interests, and stopping Soviet expansion Truman stood at the heart of a broad and powerful consensus."[155] He disproved Kennan's realist thesis that "the diplomacy of a democracy can never be as effective as that of an authoritarian state," although he left office before the American people and history vindicated him.[156] To say the least, Truman's relationship to the people was both troubled and extraordinary.

Chapter 7

Ronald Reagan
LIBERTY IN EASTERN EUROPE

RONALD REAGAN RAN FOR the presidency against the realist policies of Richard Nixon and Henry Kissinger. He felt that their doctrine of peaceful coexistence muffled the ideological differences between the United States and Soviet Union. At the same time he rejected the liberal internationalist prescriptions of Jimmy Carter—détente, disarmament, and multilateralism. Reagan was obviously neither a realist nor a liberal internationalist.[1]

What was he then? Reagan was in fact the quintessential conservative internationalist. His strategy reflected the three principal features of conservative internationalism. He ardently advocated the expansion of freedom, not just coexistence with the Soviet Union, and denied moral equivalence to countries like the Soviet Union, which were not yet free. He assertively pursued the buildup of economic and military power to accompany and leverage his diplomacy. And he preferred to work through ad hoc and informal negotiating mechanisms that preserved national sovereignty rather than formal arms control treaties and universal organizations such as the United Nations that replaced it.

Reagan's view of government was also conservative. He championed limited government and trusted in civil society, especially families, churches, and markets. He was more majoritarian than reformist (see chapter 1), believing like Thomas Jefferson that the people acting in the public square and firms competing in open markets would make better decisions than experts or bureaucracies. Government should get out of the way; the people, not the government, were sovereign. For that reason, Reagan cared deeply about his image with the people. Popularity was important to him, for political rather than personal validation. And while he was religious and stressed moral roots in both individual and international life, he did not press religious values through public institutions.

Religion inspired individuals in civil society, as it did his own life; it did not dictate policy decisions in the public arena.

These emphases are evident in his policies to promote democracy, challenge the Soviet Union, reform international institutions, and trust the American people. I take up each of these initiatives in the sections that follow.

Westminster Initiative

Reagan's conservative internationalist view of the world unfolded in four parts: (1) the world works through a competition of ideas more so than a balance of power, as realists believe, or institutional rules and practices, as liberal internationalists believe; (2) there is no moral equivalence or "peaceful coexistence" among ideas, as realists accept; freedom trumps totalitarianism, and America is an exceptionalist nation because its freedom is most accessible; (3) the competition of ideas drives the balance of power, which does not hinder negotiations as liberal internationalists believe but is the only basis for successful negotiations in a morally contested world; and (4) the goal of foreign policy is to tilt the balance of power toward freedom and spread democracy, not to preserve the status quo, as realists prefer, or replace national sovereignty by centralized international institutions, as liberal internationalists foresee.

For Reagan, the bedrock force in international affairs was ideas—differing cultural, social, religious, moral, and ideological orientations—which defined the identities of nations and motivated the way they behaved in international institutions and what they did with their power. He said to a graduating class at William Woods College in Fulton, Missouri (where Churchill delivered his famous iron curtain speech), on June 2, 1952 (yes, that's 1952): "America is less a place than an idea . . . the idea of the dignity of man, the idea that deep within the heart of each one of us is something so God-like and precious that no individual or group has a right to impose his or its will upon the people."[2] Reagan was self-conscious about his orientation. As he told Peggy Noonan, a former speechwriter, "there is no question that I am an idealist, which is another way of saying I am an American."[3] Reagan clearly accepted a creedal definition of America; the idea and the nation were the same. National identities set the parameters of international affairs, not geopolitical circumstances (realism) or diplomatic and personal interrelationships (liberalism). As national identities crystallized, differed, and shifted, they established the degree of convergence or divergence between nations. The distance between ideologies in turn bracketed the basic conditions under which the balance of power and institutional institutions operated, enabling and limiting what these factors could achieve. When identities converged, trust and communications became easier. When they diverged, misperceptions and misunderstandings multiplied. Reagan saw the world in terms of a moral struggle that did not displace material and institutional progress but gave meaning to them.[4]

Reagan laid out his worldview in early conversations with Mikhail Gorbachev. At their first meeting in Geneva in November 1985, Reagan told Gorbachev: "Countries do not mistrust each other because of arms, but rather countries build up their arms because of the mistrust between them. I hope that in our meetings both of us can get at the source of the suspicions that exist."[5] And again at the Reykjavik summit: "We arm because we don't trust each other. So we must get at the human rights problems and regional disputes that are the sources of distrust."[6] For Reagan, the root causes of international disagreements were political and ideological, not military or diplomatic. The nature of the political system or type of regime a nation championed mattered more than personalities or relationships. Queried about the new leader of the Soviet Union, Mikhail Gorbachev, in June 1985, Reagan echoed Truman's comment about Stalin: "Well, I don't think there's any evidence that he is less dominated by their system and their philosophy than any of the others."[7] And political systems that mistreated their own citizens could not be trusted in international affairs. After the inconclusive summit at Reykjavik, Reagan told the American people: "For a government that will break faith with its own people cannot be trusted to keep faith with foreign powers. . . . When it comes to judging Soviet intentions, we're all from Missouri— you got to show us."[8] Again in Berlin in June 1987: "It is difficult to imagine that a government that continues to repress freedom in its own country, breaking faith with its own people, can be trusted to keep agreements with others."[9]

One of Reagan's most controversial steps was to call the Soviet Union an "evil empire." He did so deliberately: "I made the 'Evil Empire' speech and others like it with malice aforethought."[10] At his very first press conference in January 1981, Reagan shocked the press corps: "the only morality they [the Soviets] recognize is what will further their cause, meaning they reserve unto themselves the right to commit any crime, to lie, to cheat, in order to attain [that cause]." There was good and evil in the world, and Reagan meant to identify the Soviet government, and totalitarian governments in general, with evil. On March 8, 1983, before the National Association of Evangelicals, he emphatically rejected moral equivalence: "I urge you to beware the temptation of pride—the temptation of blithely declaring yourself above it all and label both sides as equally at fault, to ignore the facts of history and the aggressive impulses of an evil empire, to simply call the arms race a giant misunderstanding and thereby remove yourself from the struggle between right and wrong and good and evil.”[11] Referring to the Soviets, he added pointedly: “they are the focus of evil in the modern world.” He had changed the wording in earlier drafts from “surely historians will see there the focus of evil” to “*they are* the focus of evil [italics added].”[12]

Some historians dismiss these flourishes as mere rhetoric.[13] And, to be sure, Reagan was a commander not a captive of language. Tony Dolan, the aide who worked with him on the evil empire speech, wrote in one draft: “Now and forever, the Soviet Union is an evil empire.” Reagan crossed out the words “now and forever.”[14] Already by the end of 1983, when asked about the word “evil,” he told *Time* magazine: “No, I would not say things like that again, even after some of the things that have been done recently,” referring to the Soviets’ shooting down the Korean airliner in September 1983 and storming out of arms control talks after the deployment of NATO missiles in November 1983.[15] And five years later in Red Square, he consigned the evil empire phrase to the ash heap of history: “No, I was talking about another time in another era.”[16] Nevertheless, in April 1988, just a few weeks before going to Moscow, Reagan said to an audience in Springfield, Massachusetts:

> We spoke plainly and bluntly. . . . We said freedom was better than totalitarianism. We said communism was bad . . . experts said this kind of candor was dangerous. . . . But far to the contrary, this candor made clear to the Soviets . . . that the differences that separated us and the Soviets were deeper and wider than just missile counts and number of warheads.[17]

Even at this late date, the message stung in Moscow. Gorbachev threw a “tantrum” over Reagan’s remarks when he met with Shultz the next day.[18] Natan Sharansky, the Soviet dissident who spent years in the gulag before his release in 1986, testified most credibly to the power of Reagan’s rhetoric: “I think the most important step in the Cold War and the defeat of the Soviet empire was his words and actions at the beginning of his Presidency.”[19]

Here was vintage Reagan, persistently pointing out that ideas drive arms races, not the reverse, and that in the competition of ideas all ideas are not morally equivalent. History involves moral struggle, and some ideas win while others lose. In early January 1977, Reagan told Richard Allen, who became his first national security advisor: “Some people think I’m simplistic but there’s a difference between being simplistic and being simple. My theory about the Cold War is that we win and they lose. What do you think about that?” When Allen asked if he meant that, Reagan responded: “Of course, I mean it. I just said it.”[20] In Westminster Hall in June 1982, Reagan called for “a crusade for freedom that will engage the faith and fortitude of the next generation. For the sake of peace and justice, let us move toward a world in which all people are at last free to determine their own destiny."[21]

The United States led the crusade. As Lou Cannon points out, "Reagan held an innocent and unshakable belief in the myth of American exceptionalism."[22] Notice Cannon calls it a "myth," but for Reagan it was truth: "I've always believed that individuals should take priority over the state. History has taught me that that is what sets America apart—not to remake the world in our own image, but to inspire people everywhere with a sense of their boundless possibilities."[23] "If we lose freedom here [in America]," Reagan told the 1964 Republican convention, "there is no place to escape to."[24]

The moral struggle informed the military struggle. Right made might, not might makes right as the realist dictum goes. The balance of power was needed for safety in a world in which ideological divisions created distrust. But the balance of power was also needed for winning, not in a conventional military sense but in a contest of political resolve and commitment. In his now famous initiative at Westminster in June 1982, Reagan told the British Parliament: "the ultimate determinant in the struggle that's now going on in the world will not be bombs and rockets, but a test of wills and ideas, a trial of spiritual resolve, the values we hold, the beliefs we cherish, the ideals to which we are dedicated."[25] Already in 1963 (yes, again, that's 1963), Reagan laid out his prescription for how political competition would decide the final outcome: "The only sure way to avoid war is to surrender without fighting . . . the other way is based on the belief that in an all out race our system is stronger, and eventually the enemy gives up the race as a hopeless cause. Then a noble nation believing in peace extends the hand of friendship and says there is room in the world for both of us."[26]

An arms race was part of the "all out race" and it bore risks. But it was necessary to make diplomacy effective. Here Reagan displayed his conservative internationalist belief that arms leveraged, not impeded, diplomacy. By closing off options outside the negotiating process, an arms contest made serious negotiations possible. On the campaign trail in 1980, he told *Washington Post* editors that a rapid arms buildup would be good because it would bring the Soviet Union to the bargaining table.[27] And at an NSC meeting in April 1982, he said: "A vigorous defense build-up will also be a great help at arms control talks. The Soviets do not believe they can keep up with us."[28] Once negotiations were under way, an arms race also ensured a negotiating posture from strength and bargaining chips for trade-offs (e.g., SDI and INF).

Finally, the purpose of negotiations was not just to preserve the status quo but to win the moral contest *and* to win it peacefully. At Westminster, he said: "what we have to consider here today while time remains is the permanent prevention of war and the establishment of the conditions of freedom and democracy as rapidly as possible in all countries."[29] He wanted to rid the world of nuclear weapons and end communism, all at the same time. This was a tall order. Reagan's vision was anything but simplistic. How could he do both if aggressively challenging communism increased the risks of nuclear war and the desire to eliminate nuclear weapons removed a bulwark of deterrence while communism still existed? This is a puzzle that still baffles Reagan's supporters and opponents.[30]

Reagan's desire to end communism was well-known. He stated it often. At the University of Notre Dame in May 1981, he declared: "The West won't contain communism; it will transcend communism . . . it will dismiss it as some bizarre chapter in human history whose last pages are even now being written."[31] In a press conference in June 1981, he said in reference to the crisis developing in Poland: "communism is an aberration. It's not a normal way of living for human beings, and I think we are seeing the first, the beginning cracks, the beginning of the end."[32] And at Westminster Hall in 1982, he buried communism in the "ash heap of history": "What I am describing now is a plan and a hope for the long term—the march of freedom and democracy that will leave Marxist-Leninism on the ash heap of history as it has left other tyrannies, which stifle the freedom and muzzle the self-expression of the people."[33]

There is no doubt here that Reagan aimed to spread democracy and to spread it "as rapidly as possible to all countries" and "all people." "The objective I propose," Reagan went on, "is quite simple to state: to foster the infrastructure of democracy, the system of a free press, unions, political parties, universities, which allows a people to choose their own way to develop their own culture, to reconcile their own differences through peaceful means."[34] In the same year, Reagan sent legislation to Congress to create the National Endowment for Democracy (NED) and its affiliated institutes. He launched the era of democracy promotion that dominated world affairs over the next three decades.[35]

Reagan was talking about regime change from the bottom up: allowing different cultures to develop specific democratic institutions. His target was first and foremost the Soviet Union. In May 1982, before going to Europe, he approved NSDD-32, the first comprehensive study of U.S. policy toward the Soviet Union.[36] As Paul Lettow describes, "that document introduced and formalized the notion that the United States should seek not simply to contain the spread of Soviet influence but to reverse it as well, and to pressure the internal Soviet system so as to encourage change."[37] This guidance was reissued in January 1983 as NSDD-75, which read: "to contain and over time reverse Soviet expansionism by competing effectively on a sustained basis with the Soviet Union in all international arenas—particularly in the overall military balance and in geopolitical regions of priority concern to the United States . . . [and] to promote, within the narrow limits available to us, the process of change in the Soviet Union toward a more pluralistic political and economic system."[38]

Reagan never accepted a divided Europe as legitimate. He advocated knocking down the Berlin Wall as early as 1967. In a debate with Robert F. Kennedy, he explained: "We don't want the Berlin Wall knocked down so that it's easier to get at the throats of the East Germans. We just think that a wall that is put up to confine people and keep them within their own country instead of allowing them the freedom of world travel, has to be somehow wrong."[39] He seized on the Polish crisis in 1981 not as another challenge to preserve stability in Europe but as "the last chance in our lifetime to see a change in the Soviet empire's colonial policy."[40] And he told the reporter Laurence Barrett on December 29, 1981: "there is reason for optimism because I think there must be an awful lot of people in the Iron Curtain countries that feel the same way [as the Poles]. . . . Our job now is to do everything we can to see that it [the reform movement] doesn't die aborning. We may never get another chance like this in our lifetime."[41]

When Reagan visited the wall in June 1982, he called it "as ugly as the idea behind it." Asked at the time if Berlin would ever reunite, he replied simply, "Yes."[42] On the fortieth anniversary of Yalta in 1985, he reiterated this expectation: "there is one boundary that can never be made legitimate, and that is the dividing line between freedom and repression. I do not hesitate to say we wish to undo this boundary. . . . Our forty-year pledge is to the goal of a restored community of free European nations."[43] And in 1987 he challenged Gorbachev brashly to "tear down this wall." Reagan had a fixed moral compass, and it excluded communism.

Freedom was not only natural in Europe; it was destined for China and the Soviet Union as well. In 1984 Reagan told the Chinese: "We believe in the dignity of each man, woman and child. Our entire system is founded on the appreciation of the special genius of each individual, and of his special right to make his own decisions and lead his own life."[44] The Chinese government censored his quote from Lincoln: "No man is good enough to govern another without that other's consent." So Reagan repeated it in Shanghai where it was reported.[45] In Moscow in 1988, Reagan explained how freedom would sprout in the Soviet Union: "We hope that one freedom will lead to another; that the Soviet government will understand that it is the individual who is always the source of economic creativity, the inquiring mind that produces a technical breakthrough, the imagination that conceives of new products and markets; and that in order for the individual to create, he must have a sense of just that—his own individuality, his own self-worth. He must sense that others respect him and, yes, that his nation respects him—respects him enough to grant him all his human rights."[46]

Reagan's desire to eliminate nuclear weapons was less well-known, even though he repeated it just as often. He was preoccupied with the specter of nuclear war at the Republican convention in 1976 when he talked impromptu about a time capsule that would tell the world whether nuclear weapons had been used or not.[47] In meetings with papal emissaries in December 1981 he called nuclear conflict "the last epidemic of mankind." And he mentioned the elimination of nuclear weapons publicly for the first time in an interview with *New York Post* reporters on March 23, 1982.[48] Over the next seven years, as Martin Anderson and Annelise Anderson report, he "referred again and again—over 150 times—to the necessity of wiping out nuclear weapons."[49] But no one took him seriously. Apparently the press, not Reagan, was "sleepwalking through history."[50] When he announced the SDI in March 1983, critics argued it would only add to the proliferation of nuclear weapons. Reagan predicted confidently that it would "pave the way for arms control measures to eliminate the weapons themselves."[51] From the very beginning, he saw a non-nuclear SDI system as a means to eliminate offensive nuclear weapons and provide deterrence through beefed-up defensive systems rather than retaliatory offensive systems.

How do you square Reagan's desire to defeat communism with his desire to eliminate nuclear weapons? The answer lies in the tight connection Reagan drew between arms and diplomacy. He was just as fixed on setting diplomatic goals as he was in building up military and economic strength. In an NSC meeting on April 16, 1982, in which he called for "a vigorous defense build-up," Reagan also cautioned that the Soviets "will not engage us if they feel threatened. What we need is presence so that if they come in, they will have to confront the US. Can we use our presence in Europe to obtain that effect?"[52] Presence is an interesting term for deterrence. It's an actor's concept. It implies an impregnable profile, not pugnacity. At Westminster he said: "we must be cautious about forcing the pace of change, [but] we must not hesitate to declare our ultimate objectives and to take concrete actions to move toward them."[53] Arms acted as leverage to close off avenues of advance by which the Soviets might achieve their goals outside negotiations and to prod them toward compromise inside negotiations. Once at the table, the United States offered the Soviets an attractive alternative they could not resist: relief from an arms race that they could not win and access to a global economy that they needed to modernize.

Reagan's view of the way the world works was so visionary few shared it at the time. One person who did was Daniel Patrick Moynihan. In a commencement address at New York University in 1984, he said: "The truth is that the Soviet idea is spent . . . it is as if the whole Marxist-Leninist ethos is hurtling off into a black hole in the universe."[54] But Seweryn Bialer, a Russian expert at Columbia University, wrote around the same time in *Foreign Affairs*: "The Soviet Union is not now nor will it be during the next decade in the throes of a true economic crisis."[55] The vast majority of experts agreed with Bialer.[56] As biographer Lou Cannon notes, "hardly anyone in the West believed at the time of the Westminster speech that the Soviet Union was on its last legs."[57]

Even Reagan's own staff did not share his full vision. In the instant history of the time, Reagan was often viewed as a puppet of his staff.[58] But in truth, Reagan went through staff like water—six national security advisors, four chiefs of staff, and fourteen speechwriters. Although he needed them all, he did not need any one of them in particular. He took his most significant initiatives against the advice of staff—SDI, evil empire speech, zero nukes, and tear-the-wall-down speech.[59] The soft-liners opposed the harsh rhetoric and arms buildup, especially SDI. The hard-liners opposed all negotiations until the Soviet Union collapsed, and they were aghast at Reagan's desire to eliminate nuclear weapons. Only Reagan, like Polk, brought the arrows and the olive branch together. As early as May 1983, he described the synthesis: "some of the N.S.C. staff are too hard line and don't think any approach should be made to the Soviets. I think I'm hard-line and will never appease but I do want to try and let them see there is a better world if they show by deed they want to get along with the free world."[60] He combined, in an uncanny brew, the clarion call of principles, the use of force as leverage both inside and outside negotiations, and the articulation of alternatives that offered opponents a way out of confrontation rather than running over them.

Economic and Military Buildup

In his mastery of armed diplomacy, Reagan deployed three types of leverage. He launched a massive defense and economic buildup that afforded *background or strategic leverage* to negotiate from an undeniable position of strength. He deployed INF missiles in Europe and encouraged freedom fighters elsewhere around the globe to push back against the Soviet Union through *leverage on the ground* or tactical leverage. And he brought *bargaining leverage* to the negotiating table, building up arms in order to reduce them by trade-offs.

Two paradoxes follow for understanding Reagan's diplomacy. While he talked a lot about force and built it up massively, he never used much. Did he really mean to use it? Some interpretations of the Reagan record say he did not. Lou Cannon believes, for example, that "Reagan did not really believe in the Reagan Doctrine, except in Nicaragua and perhaps in Angola."[61] John Patrick Diggins says Reagan "was never quite comfortable with power politics except as a last resort."[62] So was Reagan bluffing? That's one interpretation. Reagan once said that international politics was more like a poker game than a chess match, and the two games differ precisely because capabilities are less visible in poker and bluff plays a more significant role. But if his buildup of force was a bluff, it was "the mother of all bluffs," so huge and so consequential that it seems implausible. Maybe Reagan meant to use force but eventually scared himself to death, especially during the troubled fall and winter of 1983. That's another interpretation. Reagan reversed course from his first to his second terms.[63] If it is true, the military and economic buildup was not only dangerous but pointless. Why, then, did the Cold War end? Maybe it was just dumb luck. Exogenous factors intervened on Reagan's behalf, especially the arrival of Gorbachev. Perhaps, but luck is a cop-out not an explanation. Finally, of course, the Cold War may have ended because leverage worked. Reagan's first-term military and economic buildup effectively bankrupted the Soviet Union and compelled it to sue for peace in the second term.[64] Reagan anticipated as much when he said in 1963 that the Soviets could not keep up in an all-out race and therefore would give up. If this last interpretation holds, Reagan's gamble may be the greatest example of "peaceful" preventive war in history, greater even than that of Truman because Truman *started* a Cold War without a hot war while Reagan *ended* a Cold War without firing a shot.

But a second paradox emerges. If SDI was mere bargaining leverage, why didn't Reagan at some point give it up? More recent interpretations of Reagan hold that he was at heart a pacifist and utopian.[65] He wanted to rid the world of nuclear weapons. Many of his most ardent supporters were aghast at this idea, first among them Margaret Thatcher. Some still are.[66] But if getting rid of nuclear weapons were more important for Reagan than deterrence in a world where evil persisted, he would have given up SDI at Reykjavik. He did not because SDI was a potential basis for future deterrence, not a bargaining chip to be traded off for zero nukes. The only way Reagan could accept the elimination of nuclear weapons was if shared missile defense systems based on non-nuclear systems subsequently provided a safeguard against the reemergence of offensive nuclear weapons. As the record shows, he conditioned the reduction of offensive missiles every step of the way on the development and deployment of SDI. As he told a National Security Planning Group

(NSPG) meeting in December 1984, "SDI is important in dealing with the problem of verification."[67] Without SDI there was no way to safeguard a world of zero nukes. If SDI didn't work, Reagan wanted no part of zero nukes. That's the real story of Reykjavik.[68]

Let's look at the Reagan record with respect to his use of the three types of leverage.

Background or Strategic Leverage

Reagan had a realist's commitment to a policy of "peace through strength." Nothing was more important when he entered office than restoring the economic and military might of the United States.[69] Achieving that in his first term was the foundation of his diplomacy in the second term. Soviet officials provide the best evidence for this conclusion. According to Alexei Arbatov, a hard-line Soviet official at the time, "Reagan's course in the early 1980s sent a clear signal to Gorbachev and his associates of the dangerous and counterproductive nature of the Soviet Union's further expansion, which was overstretching its resources, aggravating tensions, and provoking hostile reactions across the globe."[70] Alexander Bessmert-nykh, a foreign minister under Gorbachev, agreed: "The atmosphere in Moscow was very tense for the first few years of the Reagan administration especially because of the SDI program: it frightened us very much."[71] Hence long before Gorbachev arrived on the scene Soviet officials had taken note of America's newfound strength. Indeed, when Gorbachev came into office, hard-liners briefed him that the U.S. position was significantly stronger than the Soviet position.[72] In response, Gorbachev told the Politburo in October 1985, only six months after taking office, that the Soviet Union could never win an arms race against the United States and its allies:

> Our goal is to prevent the next round of the arms race. If we do not accomplish it, the threat to us will only grow. We will be pulled into another round of the arms race that is beyond our capabilities, and we will lose, because we are already at the limits of our capabilities. . . . If the new round begins, the pressure on our economy will be unbelievable.[73]

These facts make it hard to dismiss Reagan's arms buildup as inconsequential.

Early on, Reagan noted the diplomatic cost of being weak. In his diary on July 14, 1981, he wrote: "Can we afford to let Poland collapse? But in the state of our present economy can we afford to help in any meaningful way?"[74] Caspar Weinberger, then secretary of defense, told Reagan that "we don't have the ability to project our power that far and we could not, without very substantial help, successfully come to the aid of the Poles if they were invaded." The president responded: "Yes, I know that Cap. But we must never again be in this position."[75] Military and economic power was the indispensable prerequisite for all diplomacy. Shultz relates an incident in 1985 that corroborates Reagan's grasp of the importance of background leverage. Shultz gave Reagan an article "that stressed that negotiations for a solution mattered less than the environment in which they were conducted: if you surround a situation with force, that can work wonders for negotiations. The president told me that the article had made the biggest impression on him of anything he had read in a long time."[76]

What is certain is that Reagan was not encountering this idea for the first time. He had launched an unprecedented military and economic recovery from day one to empower not enfeeble negotiations. He acted, as Shultz later described, to "structure the bargaining environment to our advantage by modernizing our defenses, assisting our friends, and showing we are willing to defend our interests."[77] The strategy began to bear fruit in fall 1984 as the Soviet Union became convinced that Reagan had brought off the arms buildup politically both within the Western alliance and by reelection at home.

Leverage on the Ground or Tactical Leverage

The most significant step that Reagan took to push back against Soviet arms on the ground was the deployment of INF missiles in Europe. The division of Europe was his priority, and nothing had higher priority in his first term than INF deployment.[78] In the late 1970s the Soviet Union deployed intermediate range missiles, SS-20s, in Eastern Europe. By 1981 some 225 SS-20s existed with three warheads each. According to the nuclear calculus of the time, these weapons intimidated Western Europe. If war broke out, SS-20s gave Moscow the capability to threaten Paris without threatening New York, potentially creating doubt that the United States would retaliate against an attack on Paris because the Soviets might then respond with an attack on New York using intercontinental missiles (ICBMs). Such a scenario did not need to happen to affect psychology and weaken the Western alliance. And that was the Soviet objective.[79] Western Europeans, not the United States, sounded the first alarm. In 1977, Helmut Schmidt, the German chancellor, called upon NATO to deploy counterbalancing INF missiles in *Western* Europe. Now, in the war of psychological expectations, Europe, if attacked, would have its own means to threaten Soviet territory without widening the conflict immediately to an intercontinental level. That might mean a nuclear war

confined to Europe, something Reagan acknowledged in fall 1981, causing a big stir in Europe.[80] But this risk while undesirable existed anyway
if the Soviets had an intermediate range capability and an intercontinental response from the United States was to be doubted—unless, of course,
Western Europe just surrendered. NATO decided in 1979 to deploy such
weapons—consisting of Pershing II missiles, which fly fast to their targets,
and Tomahawk cruise missiles, which fly much slower—while pursuing
simultaneous negotiations to eliminate the Soviet SS-20s, the so-called
two-track approach.

Reagan understood that the Soviet Union was unlikely to give up a
deployed system for a Western system that in 1981 existed only on paper.
Nevertheless, he proposed abandoning NATO deployments if the Soviet
Union got rid of its SS-20s. The so-called zero option was immediately
lambasted by the media and critics as non-negotiable. Why would the
Soviets give up a missile in the hand for one in the bush? But while critics
simply accepted Soviet missiles, Reagan was determined to counter them.
He declared immediately his willingness to settle for any equal number
of U.S. and Soviet INF weapons, from zero to then Soviet levels. Here is
what he said at a top secret NSC meeting on November 12, 1981:

> Negotiating history and my experience tell me that we should be
> choosing something between these two options. We should not
> be saying zero or nothing, and we should not be proposing two
> positions at once. We should, instead, simply go in and say that
> we are negotiating in good faith for the removal of these systems
> on both sides. We should ask the Soviet Union to share in this
> effort. We should not say this is what we would like to have, but
> we will settle for less. One should ask for the moon, and when
> the other fellow offers green cheese, one can settle for something
> in between. . . . This is not an all or nothing approach.[81]

This is a remarkable revelation, especially since practically everyone at
the time accused Reagan of proposing the zero option to avoid, not facilitate, "negotiating in good faith." In fact, negotiations began two weeks
later and immediately intensified. In July 1982 Paul Nitze, Reagan's negotiator on INF, reached tentative agreement with his Soviet counterpart
in the famous "walk in the woods" negotiations. The Soviet Union would
retain 75 SS-20s (each with three missiles—a two-thirds reduction from
the already deployed levels) and agree to U.S. deployment of the same
number of Tomahawk launchers (each with four missiles), the slower and
lower-flying missiles. But the United States would have to forego the deployment of Pershing II missiles, the most direct military equivalent of the
SS-20s. Arms control experts and a good number of Reagan's advisors

blessed the deal as the best that could be achieved.[82] But Reagan was not persuaded. He refused the offer and told Nitze: "You just tell them you're working for one tough son of a bitch."[83] He believed that foregoing the Pershings left the Soviets with the upper hand and wondered if the deployment of the Pershings was now more necessary than ever to get the Soviets to give up the SS-20s. He was right because Soviet leaders, independently of U.S. deliberations, also rejected the "walk in the woods" formula. Why should they give up any SS-20s when the United States had nothing on the other side? In February 1983 at another top secret NSC meeting Reagan said: "We can say that we will start with a lower deployment of missiles and make it enough so that they will still face Pershings targeted at Russia . . . we are all agreed that we want equality, Zero-Zero, and at some point talk about reduced numbers as an interim step." Then he added insightfully, "the date to start is when we deploy." Reagan knew that the Soviets would not get serious until the West deployed its own INF weapons. He closed the meeting with a typical quip: "I have gotten so interested in the negotiating position perhaps I should trade jobs with Nitze."[84] The quip was both an indication of Reagan's comfort with the details, contrary to what his many detractors believed, and a subtle reminder to his staff that he, not Nitze, was in charge.

Reagan now devoted his attention to INF deployment. It wasn't easy; fall 1983 witnessed an uncanny cacophony of crises. Street protests in Europe mounted as the deployment date of November 1983 approached. In September 1983 the Soviet Union shot down a South Korean commercial airliner, killing 269 people including 61 American citizens, and Soviet intelligence picked up radar signals created by sunlight reflecting off the clouds above Colorado and almost interpreted them as the launch of five U.S. ICBMs toward Moscow. Then in October 1983, terrorists bombed the marine barracks in Lebanon, killing 241 American soldiers. In early November, Able Archer, an annual NATO nuclear exercise, created in the minds of some Soviet leaders the impression that the United States was about to launch a nuclear war under the cover of routine exercises (which Soviet war plans themselves envisioned).[85] The news media played up the hysteria with an apocalyptic film of nuclear winter, The Day After. Through it all, Reagan held the alliance together. The German Bundestag took a final vote in favor of deployment on November 22, and NATO installed its first Pershing missiles on November 23.

The short-term Soviet reaction was to abandon all arms control talks. U.S.-Soviet relations went into a tailspin, and according to advocates of the reversal theory Reagan himself became frightened and changed course. His speech in January 1984 offered the Soviet Union an olive branch. But the facts are more complicated: there was no panic; no policies were reversed; and INF deployments proceeded. In his diary on December 8, 1983, Reagan noted calmly, "they [the Soviets] didn't say they wouldn't be back."[86] By the end of 1983, Reagan's military and economic programs were bearing fruit, and the alliance was revitalized. Reagan was now armed for negotiations, the only basis on which the Soviets would negotiate seriously. In May 1983 he had told Helen Thomas that the prospects for a summit in 1983 were "dim" but "likely" in 1984.[87] Reagan was operating on his own long-established timetable. In March 1984 he proposed a summit meeting with Konstantin Chernenko.[88] But the Soviets said no. They wanted to wait out the elections. Maybe Reagan would still succumb to the peace protests.

Bargaining Leverage

But Reagan did not succumb. He was reelected in a landslide, forty-nine states to one. By September the Soviets knew they had to deal with Reagan for another four years. Andrei Gromyko visited the White House, and as Anatoly Dobrynin, the Soviet ambassador to the United States, reports, they agreed on frequent meetings between the two countries and the overall goal of eliminating nuclear weapons.[89] This means that the basic outlines of negotiations for the next four years were set *before* Gorbachev came into office. On December 5, 1984, Reagan said at an NSC meeting: "We and the Soviet Union may be coming together more than many people realize."[90] In his second inaugural address in January 1985, Reagan said: "We seek the total elimination one day of nuclear weapons from the face of the earth." One month later, Chernenko stated in Moscow: "Our ultimate goal is the complete elimination of nuclear weapons everywhere on this planet, the complete removal of the threat of nuclear war."[91] And on March 4, seven days before Chernenko died, Reagan wrote in his diary after meeting that day with the NSC: "Since they [the Soviets] have publicly stated that they want to see nuclear weapons eliminated entirely, I told our people to open by saying we would accept their goal."[92] In characteristic fashion, Reagan was ready to let the Soviets take the credit for a goal he had conceived and championed long before they did.

This evidence of rapid and radical rapprochement between the United States and the Soviet Union in winter 1984–85 raises the counterfactual and totally unexplored question (because the conventional wisdom is that Gorbachev changed everything) whether things would have turned out much differently if Chernenko had recovered or if someone other than Gorbachev had succeeded Chernenko. Gromyko played a key role in selecting Gorbachev.[93] So how likely is it that Gorbachev's ideas were all that different from the way Soviet policy was tending already? Of course, individual leaders matter, and Gorbachev made a difference. But the circumstances that produced him may have had as much to do with what followed as Gorbachev himself. And those circumstances were created in considerable part by Reagan's ideas and the revival of Western power. The Soviet economic crisis might not have meant the end of communism if capitalism had also sunk into terminal decline.

Thus, even before Gorbachev, negotiations were coming. And almost immediately SDI took center stage in the negotiations. SDI is another unresolved puzzle of the Reagan strategy. As already noted, almost everyone considered it to be mere negotiating leverage, a giant bluff to bring the Soviet Union to the table and trade away for complete nuclear disarmament.[94] But that was never the case for Ronald Reagan. For him, SDI was the basis of a future deterrence system that would end the appalling and inhumane strategy of mutual assured destruction (MAD). MAD, enshrined by the Strategic Arms Limitation Agreements (SALT treaties), kept peace by threatening to annihilate hundreds of millions of people on both sides, while the related Anti-Ballistic Missile (ABM) Treaty prevented countries from defending the people by developing defensive missile systems. Reagan objected to this MAD-ness long before he became president. He visited the Lawrence Livermore Laboratory in 1967 and NORAD in 1979 and expressed bewilderment that so much money was spent to destroy rather than protect people. Martin Anderson, an advisor, prepared an initial study to explore the prospects of defensive systems. The idea was embraced by the Republican platform of 1980 but for political reasons deemphasized in the campaign itself.

Once Reagan was in office, Anderson pursued the idea further. He convened informal groups on September 14 and October 12, 1981, including Ed Meese, counselor to the president, Richard Allen, the president's national security advisor, George (Jay) Keyworth, the president's science advisor, and three outside experts: Edward Teller, the renowned nuclear physicist; Karl Bendetson, retired CEO of Champion International; and General Daniel Graham, the leading proponent of space defenses or "high frontier" as he called it. On January 8, 1982, the group met with Reagan, Judge William Clark having replaced Allen as Reagan's new national security advisor. Three Reagan fund-raisers also joined the group: Jacqueline Hume, William Wilson, and Joseph Coors. The idea percolated, and in December 1982 Reagan met with the chairman and joint chiefs of the military services. He asked for their opinion about the idea. On February 11, 1983, they reported back that missile defenses were feasible, and on March 23, Reagan announced, to the surprise of almost everyone including his secretaries of state and defense, that the United States would pursue SDI.[95]

Reagan's interest in SDI stemmed from his longstanding desire to eliminate nuclear weapons. In announcing SDI, he linked it directly to arms reductions: "to give us the means of rendering these nuclear weapons impotent and obsolete . . . [and] to achieve our ultimate goal of eliminating the threat posed by strategic nuclear missiles."[96] If that possibility could ever be realized, what would protect the United States and the world against cheating by aggressive or rogue states? For Reagan the answer was deterrence based on mutual assured protection (MAP) rather than mutual assured destruction. As offensive weapon systems were reduced, defensive weapon systems would be built up. Eventually defensive systems would become effective enough to ensure the destruction of any offensive missiles that might remain or be reacquired. MAP (based on big defense and small or no offense) would replace MAD (based on big offense and small or no defense). As far as Reagan was concerned, MAP was no more infeasible or costly than MAD and unquestionably more credible and humane in an actual crisis. But it constituted a frontal assault on the entire détente-era arms control approach based on the SALT and ABM treaties and stirred furious controversy.

Reagan realized from the outset that the prospect of acquiring defensive systems while offensive systems remained in place raised the specter of a first-strike capability. If the United States or the Soviet Union developed effective missile defenses first, it might launch a first-strike attack, confident that its defensive system could destroy any missiles that might survive a first strike and be launched in retaliation (so-called second-strike capabilities). In an NSC meeting in November 1983, Reagan mused: "To take an optimistic view, if the U.S. is first to have both offense and defense, we could put the genie back into the bottle by volunteering to eliminate offensive weapons. The pessimistic view is . . . if the Soviets get new defenses first, we can expect nuclear blackmail."[97] His answer to this problem was as far-sighted—some would say illusory—as SDI. The day after announcing SDI he proposed to share it with the Soviet Union.

This proposal led Reagan into a thicket of issues about international control of strategic arms, which horrified advocates of national sovereignty. He told a NSPG meeting in December 1984: "SDI could be put in international hands to protect the whole world."[98] Was this the Baruch Plan all over again? Reagan had referred approvingly to that plan in a speech at the UN in June 1982. In a way sharing SDI was the same idea, although this time international control did not involve nuclear weapons. Reagan stressed that SDI should be a non-nuclear system: "we need to explain that it [SDI] is not a nuclear system."[99] At a press conference later on January 9, 1985, he said: "We're searching for a weapon that might destroy nuclear weapons, not be nuclear itself."[100] But international control raised all the same issues as the Baruch Plan. Stalin then and Gorbachev now questioned who would control and monitor the technology, and how the country behind, in both cases the Soviet Union, could ever

188 • Chapter 7

be sure it would gain full access to the technology. At Reykjavik, Gorbachev told Reagan: "Excuse me, Mr. President, but I do not take your idea of sharing SDI seriously."[101]

With all of these aspects of SDI unprecedented and unknown, the program nevertheless dominated subsequent summits. Eleven days after Reagan's reelection, the Soviets returned to arms control talks. Reagan had been right; they did come back. And now in December 1984, with uncanny insight, he predicted how the negotiations would go over the next two years. At an NSPG meeting on December 17, he interrupted his national security advisor, Robert (Bud) McFarlane, to say: "SDI is the main target of the Soviet Union in Geneva. They are coming to the table to get SDI."[102] Then, foreseeing exactly what would happen at Reykjavik two years later, he wrote in his diary on December 18: "More and more I'm thinking the Soviets are preparing to walk out of the talks if we won't give up research on the strategic defense system. I hope I'm wrong."[103] He wasn't. Although the Soviet Union and many of his own advisors saw SDI as a bargaining chip, Reagan did not. At the NSPG meeting on December 17, he said: "I emphasize that there is no price for SDI."[104] Again, at the same meeting: "Whatever we do, we must be resolved among ourselves that SDI is not the price for reductions."[105] Reagan could not have made it any clearer, but once again many of his advisors and Soviet leaders did not hear him.

The bargains almost struck at Reykjavik demonstrated the close link between SDI and offensive arms reductions. The last-minute proposal to bridge the gap called for elimination over ten years not just of all offensive or strategic ballistic missiles (land, sea, and air) but all nuclear explosive devices (short-range missiles and other forms of atomic weaponry) whether strategic or tactical. During that ten-year period, both sides would not withdraw from the ABM Treaty, which would continue to restrict SDI to research, development, and testing in the confines of the laboratory. After ten years, when there would no longer be any nuclear weapons, Reagan insisted that each side would have the right to deploy defensive systems as long as they shared it and developed other measures to deal with non-nuclear weapons in space.[106] For Reagan, as he later explained to the American public, "SDI was an insurance policy to guarantee that the Soviets kept the commitments Gorbachev and I were making at Reykjavik." For Gorbachev, SDI was the beginning of another arms race in space, more deadly if indeed nuclear weapons were eliminated beforehand. Gorbachev did not believe the Soviet Union could develop its own SDI or get it from the United States, although at the time Moscow had larger defensive systems than the United States, which the United States felt violated the ABM Treaty.[107] If the United States deployed SDI first, the Soviet Union would have to rely on offensive missiles to overwhelm the

SDI system. "I can't understand," Gorbachev told Reagan, "how you can ask the USSR to grant the U.S. the right . . . to test a space ABM system in space . . . at the same time we were destroying our offensive nuclear potential."[108] At the end, insisting that SDI be permanently restricted to the laboratory, Gorbachev blurted out, "it's laboratory or good-bye."[109] Realizing that his prediction that the Soviets would walkout over SDI had come true, Reagan picked up his papers and said good-bye.[110]

After Reykjavik, Soviet leaders decoupled INF reductions from SDI and the broader strategic package. "They blinked," as Reagan noted in his diary.[111] In October 1986, Gromyko told the Politburo in a stunning confession: "the deployment of the SS-20 was a major error in our European policy."[112] And in December 1987 Reagan and Gorbachev signed the INF Treaty, eliminating for the first time a whole category of nuclear weapons. The final result was the zero option that Reagan had proposed in 1981, and it represented a resounding triumph for Reagan's strategy that you had to build up arms in order to build them down.[113]

The two leaders failed to get an agreement on strategic weapons, and some Western leaders and specialists breathed a sigh of relief. What if Reagan and Gorbachev had abolished all nuclear weapons at Reykjavik? What would have provided deterrence, especially in Europe where the Soviet Union always had an advantage in conventional forces? Francois Mitterrand, the French president and a stalwart supporter of NATO's INF deployments, called Reykjavik a "nuclear Munich."[114] Margaret Thatcher was on the phone immediately urging Reagan to back off such ideas in the future. Jay Winik believes Reagan understood that elimination of all weapons meant reliance on conventional deterrence and accepted that.[115] SDI, as Reagan envisioned it, decoupled nuclear from conventional deterrence. The United States would no longer have the option, even if it reacquired the capability, to threaten to use nuclear weapons first to stop a Soviet conventional advance because the Soviets would now presumably have a defensive capability to neutralize that threat.

So was Reagan ever really serious about deterrence? He clearly thought about it, initially asking a series of questions in the first discussions of the zero option in October 1981: "do we really want a 'zero option' for the battlefield? Don't we need these nuclear systems? Wouldn't it be bad for us to give them up since we need them to handle Soviet conventional superiority? . . . How will we verify an agreement?"[116] Later he asked about "launch under warning," a posture for retaliating to a Soviet ICBM attack automatically once there was confirmation of a Soviet launch that in effect took any discretion out of the decision to retaliate. It's not clear exactly when he was briefed on the full nuclear retaliation plan, called Single Integrated Operation Plan (SIOP), but it seems hard to believe, given the risks he took in the early years, that he was not aware of or willing to use nuclear weapons to deter the Soviet Union.[117] With nuclear weapons out of the picture, what deterred Soviet armies in Europe? Reagan's thinking about deterrence in a world of no nukes with or without SDI invites much deeper research.

The Art of Negotiations: Leading the Allies and UN

Reagan was accused by both realists and liberal internationalists of abandoning negotiations in his first term. But he did nothing of the sort. Rather he understood as a conservative internationalist that diplomacy could accomplish very little unless the underlying balance of forces supported it. As Reagan explained to Walter Cronkite in March 1981, you need something to trade before "you sit with the fellow who's got all the arms"; and he told the NSC in April 1981: "we need positive momentum on modernization before we go into negotiations."[118] So, as Jack Matlock, Reagan's later ambassador to Moscow, records, "Reagan was not eager to take up serious negotiations with the Soviet Union the moment he took office."[119] But the intent to negotiate was the purpose of the buildup and delay. In a campaign speech in August 1980 to the Veterans of Foreign Wars, Reagan said he was "building up our defense capability pending an agreement by both sides to limit various kinds of weapons."[120] The defense buildup took place "*pending*" arms control agreements.

Thus from the beginning, Reagan, like Polk, coupled every military move with a diplomatic one. The defense buildup came with an appeal to Brezhnev to negotiate. INF deployments came with the zero option to eliminate them. SDI came with an offer to share it. As he launched his defense program in early 1981, Reagan contemplated a letter to Leonid Brezhnev and was unhappy with the draft proposed by the State Department. In April, recovering from the assassination attempt, he composed his own letter and, after his advisors objected, sent both the official letter *and* his personal one. The personal letter shocked the hard-liners. They called it "maudlin," "mawkish," and "sentimental."[121] In it, Reagan appealed to Brezhnev to consider the responsibility they bore to protect the people they served, and he lifted the grain embargo, which Jimmy Carter had imposed on the Soviet Union when it invaded Afghanistan in 1979. But the Soviet Union was in no mood to negotiate. Thirty-five Soviet divisions encircled Poland, and Moscow imposed military leadership and then martial law on Poland. Now, in December 1981, Reagan wrote a different letter, telling Brezhnev that Washington held Moscow, not Warsaw, accountable for what was transpiring in that country.

Also in December 1981, as Reagan's defense and economic programs were signed into law, Reagan met with emissaries from the pope. Pope John Paul II was Polish and had made a dramatic visit to his homeland in June 1979. Reagan told his papal visitors about his plans for an arms race, INF deployments, and the eventual elimination of nuclear weapons:

> currently the only way to deter nuclear war is to arm as strongly as the potential opponent. However, that is not good enough. There could be miscalculations and accidents. It is necessary to reduce the number of forces on both sides. The United States has made a start in Geneva, offering to dismantle one type of missile. It was hoped that this start can be turned into wider moves toward arms reductions.

Later in the conversation, Reagan made clear that weapons could be built down only by initially building them up: "There was no miracle weapon available with which to deal with the Soviets, but we could threaten the Soviets with our ability to outbuild them, which the Soviets know we can do if we choose. Once we had established this, we could invite the Soviets to join us in lowering the level of weapons on both sides."[122]

Reagan and Pope John, both having survived assassination attempts in the spring, bonded. They met in June 1982 for over an hour privately, and the pope's support for Reagan's first-term arms buildup and missile deployments in Europe proved crucial in swaying public opinion, especially in Europe.[123]

If Reagan was easily influenced by adverse circumstances, he should have reversed polices in fall and winter 1982–83, not winter 1983–84 when reversal theory advocates claim he abandoned hard-line and adopted soft-line policies.[124] In 1982 Reagan's policies appeared to be going nowhere, and his fortunes had plummeted both in congressional elections, where the Republicans lost twenty-six House seats, and in public opinion, where Reagan's approval rating dipped to 35 percent in January 1983. The U.S. and world economies remained in the doldrums, and economic issues—Soviet gas pipeline and high interest rates—divided the Western alliance. Meanwhile, the Soviet Union massed tanks in Eastern Europe, cheered on (and funded) the chorus of anti-INF peace protestors in Western Europe, exploited instability in Lebanon and elsewhere in the Middle East, occupied Afghanistan, and supported local communists in Central America, southern Africa, and Southeast Asia.

But Reagan did not flinch from his hard line. In August 1982, he warned his new secretary of state, George Shultz, not to be "overly anxious" to negotiate the Soviet gas pipeline controversy, and he resisted efforts by Shultz to get him to attend Brezhnev's funeral in November 1982 and to propose summit talks in 1983.[125] As Reagan said to Helen Thomas, prospects for summits in 1983 were still "dim." By the end of 1983, however, the U.S. and free-world economies were on their way back, the reelections of Thatcher in Britain and Kohl in Germany had confirmed conservative leadership in the alliance, and NATO had begun to deploy INF missiles. Yet when the Soviet Union abandoned arms control talks in December 1983, Reagan did not panic. Like Polk, he was patient. Reagan told the NSC in March 1984: "We can't go on negotiating with ourselves . . . I do not intend to make unilateral concessions to get them back to the table."[126]

When the time came to negotiate, it was Reagan not his staff who led the way. He wrote in his diary on March 1, 1984, that a visit from Suzanne Massie, an outside advisor who is often credited with bringing about Reagan's reversal in this period, "reinforced my gut feeling that it's time for me to meet personally with Chernenko." The next day, he repeated: "I'm convinced the time has come for me to meet Chernenko along about July."[127] Notice Massie "reinforced" Reagan's instincts and affected only their timing; she did not create or convert those instincts. Only the instant history view of Reagan as a puppet of his staff could imagine that she was the decisive influence. Shultz had been urging Reagan to negotiate since 1982 and Reagan himself had been preparing for this moment for four years, maybe twenty years since his comment in 1963. On March 7, Reagan penned a personal postscript in an otherwise pro forma State Department letter to Chernenko. He affirmed that he had no offensive intentions against the Soviet Union and expressed his desire for a summit meeting in July. Reagan was finally ready to negotiate. But the Soviets were not; they said no.[128] After Chernenko died, Reagan quipped: "I'm trying to negotiate with the Soviets but they keep dying on me."[129]

Negotiations with Gorbachev therefore are not hard to explain, at least from Reagan's end. They were baked in the cake from the beginning. And they did not go smoothly at first. The initial summit in Geneva accomplished nothing more than an agreement to have another summit. And after Geneva Reagan became the supplicant. He wrote Gorbachev four times before he got a response. Gorbachev may have been playing Reagan's first-term card, giving his domestic bureaucratic and economic reforms, perestroika, time to take effect. But in April 1986 a nuclear reactor at Chernobyl exploded. The performance of the Soviet bureaucracy in causing and covering up the accident exposed the deep-seated rot in the Soviet system. A collapse in oil prices further devastated the Soviet economy.

To regain political advantage, Gorbachev resumed the negotiating minuet with the United States. Agreement to meet at Reykjavik in October 1986, however, was not reached until three weeks before the meeting. Was the meeting poorly planned? It's doubtful. As noted above, many of the proposals at Reykjavik were developed in correspondence during the summer. Did Gorbachev set a trap for SDI? Perhaps. But Reagan was at the top of his game just before the Iran-Contra affair. He was well prepared and performed superbly.[130] By contrast, Soviet weakness was painfully apparent. Then Iran-Contra hit. Now Reagan, too, was weakened. Both leaders needed an international success. Once Gorbachev gave up the link with SDI, the INF Treaty followed inexorably. The summit in December 1987 was the culminating occasion.

Throughout the negotiations, Reagan's instincts were unerring. He did not change his mind about the Soviet Union in 1983–84; he did so only after the Soviet Union began to liberalize politically in 1988.[131] From 1985 to 1987 Gorbachev sought to reform the Soviet economy without liberalizing the political system.[132] During those early years, Gorbachev continued to increase Moscow's defense budget and production of nuclear weapons as well as its military outlays in Afghanistan and Nicaragua.[133] Within the first few months in office, Gorbachev did decide *privately* to withdraw Soviet forces from Eastern Europe. But that withdrawal did not start nor did the Soviet Union announce it *publicly* until 1989. Until 1988 Gorbachev was looking for a way to revive Soviet power without changing Soviet ideology. In 1988, however, at the Communist Party Congress, Gorbachev rolled out significant political reforms: glasnost. At that point, Reagan concluded that the ideological gap had narrowed enough to allow for greater trust between the superpowers. Reagan, again, was right. Eventually glasnost unseated Gorbachev and installed national leaders in the separate Soviet republics, the most important being Yeltsin in Russia. Democracy burst out across Eastern Europe and flickered for a decade even in Russia.

Reagan did not act alone. He acknowledged the need for allies, especially given American weakness in 1981. "The plain truth is," he wrote in his diary on January 30, 1982, "we can't—alone—hurt the Soviets that much."[134] But he was determined to lead the alliance, not accept consensus based on the lowest common denominator. He antagonized the allies with the Soviet pipeline sanctions, even as he rallied them to deploy NATO INF missiles in Europe. He formed a core alliance with Margaret Thatcher on both economic and military matters. When Thatcher visited Washington in February 1981, Reagan declared: "There is one element that goes without question: Britain and America will stand side by side."[135] He then aligned with the new conservative government in Germany in winter 1982 to nudge France toward disinflationary economic policies, and tapped France in summer 1983 to nudge a protest-torn Germany to deploy NATO missiles. He upgraded the U.S.-Japan alliance and in November 1983 gave the first speech by an American president to the Japanese Diet where he pledged to the only nation to endure atomic bombs to rid the world of nuclear weapons.[136] Gorbachev took note of

Reagan's success in establishing alliance solidarity when he told his Politburo colleagues in October 1985 that in any arms race "we can expect that Japan and FRG [West Germany] could very soon join the American potential."[137]

Reagan's diplomacy, as a conservative internationalist, did not depend heavily on multilateralism and international institutions. He derided the UN General Assembly although he defended and sought to reform the specialized agencies such as the World Bank and IMF. In September after the Korean airline incident, Charles Lichtenstein, deputy U.S. ambassador to the UN, said the UN could leave New York if it was unhappy with U.S. hosting: "We will be at the dockside, bidding you a fond farewell as you set off into the sunset." At a subsequent press conference, Reagan subtly backed Lichtenstein's comment with a statement of his own: "I think the gentleman who spoke the other day had the hearty approval of most people in America in his suggestion that we weren't asking anyone to leave, but if they chose to leave, goodbye. . . . Maybe all those delegates should have six months in the United Nations meetings in Moscow and then six months in New York, and it would give them the opportunity to see two ways of life [echoing Truman's contrast between the two systems in March 1947]."[138] As a place to get things done, he considered the United Nations "impotent," a "can of worms," and a "miserable place."[139]

On the economic front, Reagan was skeptical of summit diplomacy that fueled inflation, advocated oil and other resource cartels, and touted "global negotiations" to create a "new international economic order." At Cancun and G-7 economic summits he sought to revitalize not replace the Bretton Woods institutions.[140] He preferred spontaneous over scripted communiqués and converted summits into strategic not just economic affairs. He included Japan, which as Yasuhiro Nakasone reminded Mitterrand in 1985 had no peer group of democracies in its own region.[141] At Cancun in October 1981, Reagan recognized for the first time the rise of the emerging nations such as Mexico, and what was later dubbed the BRIC countries—China, India, Brazil, and Russia after the end of communism. And Reagan's farsighted appeal for a "North American Economic Accord" and the Uruguay Round of multilateral trade negotiations, the first named after a developing country, set in motion the forces that a decade or so later produced the North American Free Trade Agreement (NAFTA) and the World Trade Organization (WTO).

Given this record, it is hard to agree that Reagan made "meager contributions to the private economic summit and NATO meetings."[142] In fact, Reagan gave multilateral institutions new life and significance. By accelerating the end of the Cold War, he put the United Nations in a position to reclaim its original role as a concert of great powers to provide collective security. The UN Security Council decision in 1991 to expel Iraq from Kuwait was a classic example of collective security, the only one thus far in history. However, for Reagan, international institutions were the caboose not the engine of global change. The engine was free nations led by the United States and its allies.

Reagan's diplomacy and use of force were not always properly calibrated. He erred too much on the side of economic coercion when he bullied allies with high interest rates and volatile exchange rates and then failed to follow up with a framework of cooperation to consolidate his "domesticist" or decentralized, conservative approach to global economic relations.[143] And he erred too much on the side of diplomacy when he conducted ill-fated negotiations to trade arms for hostages in Iran. Perhaps his greatest failing was not to articulate fully how a nonnuclear SDI contributed to deterrence and how it might be shared by international agreement if it succeeded. He refused to give up SDI, which suggests that it was key to his thinking about continued deterrence in a world of zero offensive nukes. But the idea of eliminating all nuclear weapons was so revolutionary, it deserved vast amounts of study and deliberation. Yet Reagan never appointed a single commission for that purpose. The opponents of SDI did no better. They simply ridiculed the idea, giving it the "Star Wars" moniker. In any event, Reagan's mistakes left some supporters wondering if he wasn't a liberal internationalist after all, bent on eliminating nuclear arms and turning over deterrence strategy to international institutions.

When Reagan left office, freedom had sprouted everywhere. In Latin America in 1981, 50 percent of the people lived in freedom; by 1988, 96 percent did.[144] The real payoff came with the end of the Cold War in Europe and elsewhere. As Margaret Thatcher put it: "From the strong fortress of his convictions, he set out to enlarge freedom the world over at a time when freedom was in retreat—and he succeeded."[145]

In summary, as Henry Kissinger concedes, Reagan's diplomatic accomplishments were nothing short of "astonishing."[146] John Lewis Gaddis offers one of the more penetrating assessments:

> What one can say now is that Reagan saw Soviet weaknesses sooner than most of his contemporaries did; that he understood the extent to which détente was perpetuating the Cold War rather than hastening its end; that his hard line strained the Soviet system at the moment of its maximum weakness; that his shift toward conciliation preceded Gorbachev; that he combined reassurance, persuasion, and pressure in dealing with the new Soviet leader; and that he maintained the support of the American people and of American allies. Quite apart from whatever results this strategy produced, it was an impressive accomplishment simply to have devised and sustained it: Reagan's role here was critical.[147]

The last sentence is a throwaway line. If the strategy produced no significant results, it clearly wasn't "an impressive accomplishment." Maybe the
most confident and credible assessment of Reagan's significance comes
from his negotiating partner. Gorbachev met Shultz after he talked with
President George H. W. Bush in June 1990. Shultz remarked that he understood the talks had gone well; Gorbachev replied: "Yes, but Reagan
was there when times were really tough."[148] And in a later interview,
Gorbachev reflected: "He [Reagan] was an authentic person and a great
person. If someone else had been in his place, I don't know if what happened would have happened."[149] For Gorbachev, at least, Reagan made
the difference.

Domestic Politics

Reagan's domestic politics was conservative in four ways: (1) he always
gave preference to the individual not government; (2) he believed that religion was the source of human freedom; (3) he was self-confident about
his conservative philosophy even though it was questioned if not opposed by most of official Washington including some conservatives; and
(4) he was a paragon of character more than of puffed-up intelligence
even though the record shows that he was pretty smart as well.

At the end of his presidency, Reagan startled George Will and Bill
Buckley at a White House dinner with the following remark: "Well, you
know, is it possible that we conservatives are the real liberals and the
liberals are the real conservatives?" Buckley absorbed the comment af-
fably, but Will took offense, calling the remark "banal" and retorting to
the president: "I knew you were a liberal all along."[150] What did Reagan
mean? If he meant that American conservatives are classical liberals, his
remark is fully intelligible. American conservatives are liberal democrats
(small d) who believe in individual freedom and the capability of individuals to govern their own lives through the institutions of civil society,
especially family, religion, and entrepreneurship, and limited government.
American liberals, on the other hand, are social democrats who see the
community and state as the protector of individuals and the provider of
political order and moral authority. Much less content with civil society, especially religious institutions, liberals advocate secular standards
and state leadership in civil rights, education, health, environment, and
industry.

In a way, Reagan was claiming liberalism for conservatism, as in "all
Americans are conservative," just as liberals claim conservatism for liberalism, as in "all Americans are liberal."[151] He was right to do so. From
the time of Jefferson, American conservatism has stood for limited government and opposed an oppressive state. Reagan was unusually fond

of Jefferson. He quoted often Jefferson's famous inaugural lines: "Sometimes it is said that man cannot be trusted to govern himself. Can he then be trusted with the government of others?"[152] He paraphrased it in his own inaugural address and in his letter to Brezhnev in April 1981: "If they [the people of the world] are incapable of self-government, as some would have us believe, then where in the world do we find people who are capable of governing others."[153] Like Jefferson, he believed the people could make better decisions than the aristocrats or experts. "I've always believed," he told Peggy Noonan, "that individuals should take priority over the state."[154] "My attitude," he said, "had always been—let the people flourish."[155] People *could* "make the world over again," as Thomas Paine proclaimed, even if at the outset many were uneducated and excluded. Self-government meant they decided, not some self-selected group above them. "We the people" was now the authoritative "institution," and how the people organized their private lives in civil society was the only guarantee there could be of their freedoms. He elaborated in Moscow: "political leadership in a democracy requires . . . embracing the vast diversity of humanity and doing it with humility, listening as best you can not just to those with high positions but to the cacophonous voices of ordinary people and trusting those millions of people, keeping out of their way. . . . And the word we have for that is freedom."[156] In this sense, Reagan was majoritarian, not reformist. People's rights did not derive from government and did not need to be protected by government. Some post-Enlightenment conservatives, especially in Europe, never accepted this unbounded faith in individuals.

The reason the people could be trusted is because they were creatures of God. Reagan, like Lincoln, believed devoutly in a higher being.[157] He wrote to Sister Mary Ignatius in 1984: "Abe Lincoln once said that he would be the most stupid human on this footstool called Earth if he thought for one minute he could fulfill the obligations of the office without help from one who was wiser and stronger than all others. I understand what he meant completely."[158] Religion explains Reagan's bond with the pope, his repeated references to Armageddon, which he associated with nuclear weapons, and his comment after the assassination attempt: "Whatever happens now, I owe my life to God, and will try to serve him in every way I can."[159] In Chicago on May 4, 1988, before going to Moscow, he said: "Ultimately, our view of human rights derives from our Judeo-Christian heritage and the view that each individual life is sacred."[160] Then, in Moscow, the capital of atheist communism, he proclaimed his "hope for a new age of religious freedom in the Soviet Union." One Muscovite responded: "I'm not religious but I was delighted to hear him end his speeches by saying 'God bless you.' We never heard it said before on television."[161] For Reagan, religion was not prescriptive but inspirational. Contrary to his popular image, he loved work and saw it as a form of worship. His attitude was as Peter Robinson describes: "Pray as if everything depended upon God; work as if everything depended on you."[162]

On the eve of his election, Reagan told a radio reporter who asked what the American people saw in him: "Would you laugh if I told you that I think, maybe, they see themselves and that I'm one of them? I've never been able to detach myself or think that I, somehow, am apart from them."[163] He said as much in the title of his memoirs, *An American Life*. Reagan cared deeply about "his feeling of oneness" with the people, which is probably one reason why he could never believe he betrayed them in the Iran-Contra affair.[164]

Reagan did not disrespect government; he just respected civil society more. He once observed that if churches cared for ten poor families each, "we could eliminate all government welfare in this country" and "the actual help would be greater because it would come from the heart."[165] He respected Congress more than the executive branch. In his first one hundred days in office, he met with 467 members of Congress in sixty-nine separate meetings.[166] His budget passed the House in June 1981 by only six votes. Reagan passed the policies that ended the Cold War (1980–88) with a House that Democrats controlled, just as Truman passed the policies that initiated the Cold War (1947–48) with a Congress that Republicans controlled. He knew that Congress represented the people and he paid attention to it. On the other hand, if he disagreed with Congress, as George Shultz observed, "he would take his case to the American people and argue it flat out."[167] At an NSC meeting in January 1983 on his defense program, Reagan told the cabinet: "With regard to Congress, it is not necessary to have them see the light, only to make them feel the heat."[168] The people themselves, not institutions, were always the final arbiter.

Reagan treated the executive branch of government and his staff with similar measures of respect and circumvention. Unlike Congress, they were dispensable. They did not represent the people except through him. And Reagan went through cabinet officers and top staff with considerable abandon. For a man allegedly dependent on cue cards, Reagan was "warmly ruthless" with his staff.[169] The staff, in turn, often felt undervalued and marveled that "he [Reagan] knows so little and accomplishes so much."[170] The reason, they concluded, must be because of them.[171] Almost all of Reagan's associates fashioned themselves as his tutors.[172] They "treated Reagan as if he were a child monarch in need of constant protection. They paid homage to him but gave him no respect."[173] Members of Congress were no different. Democratic Speaker of the House Speaker Tip O'Neill told Reagan upon his arrival in Washington that he could not compete in the major leagues of Washington politics. Reagan shrugged it off and forged a happy albeit hard-hitting relationship with O'Neill.[174]

The most interesting question is why Reagan permitted this condescension. He seemed to cultivate underestimation. Indeed, on more than one occasion, he contributed to it: "I can't tell until somebody tells me. I never know where I'm going."[175] Or, again: "I know hard work never killed anyone but why take a chance?" For someone who scored high grades as a youth, had a photographic memory, was serenely self-confident in his unorthodox if not radical views about domestic and foreign policy, and, as we now know, spoke often with knowledge and details in top secret meetings, the reason for such self-deprecation is not obvious. Even if it helped him politically, it seems almost inhuman. Only once (that I have been able to find so far) did he address the matter. Asked in an interview in January 1985 what influence Nancy had on his policies, he responded in the following way:

> May I voice a frustration? It's not only my wife, it's everyone— this picture that is being created that I sit at a desk and wait to see who's going to grab this arm and pull me this way or grab this one and pull me that way. You know something? I'm too old and stubborn to put up with that. I make up my own mind. I do listen to counsel and advice. I want to get expertise from people that are expert in various fields. But I haven't changed my views since I've been here. And with Nancy, yes, . . . we talk and of course she has opinions. And I listen to her opinions. And sometimes we argue about them, and I don't listen. . . . Like any other human being, we don't always see eye to eye on something.[176]

The response is revealing. Reagan was enormously comfortable in his own skin. He let others claim credit and had a sign on his desk that read: "There is no limit to what a man can do or where he can go if he doesn't mind who gets the credit." He felt that when others advised or endorsed him they were adopting his ideas; he was not adopting theirs.[177] Hence he had no urgency to defend himself or quarrel. In the several dozen meetings I experienced with him, I never once heard him say: "Fellows I get it. Let's move on to the next topic." And many of the stories about his lapses that aides told were self-serving to put it mildly. One in particular always bothered me. A top aide claimed that Reagan received his thick briefing book for the Williamsburg summit in May 1983 only the night before the summit and then never opened it.[178] The implication was that Reagan was not prepared for the summit. I was with Reagan the night before the Williamsburg summit; when he left to go upstairs in the restored colonial home where he was staying, he had just completed a two-hour briefing in the dining room. At the bottom of the stairs, Bill Clark, the national security advisor, asked him if he wanted to take the briefing book with him upstairs. Reagan good-naturedly responded, "No thanks, Bill, I think I'll spend the evening with Julie Andrews." That evening he watched *The Sound of Music*, for probably the umpteenth time. What the top aide did not tell the reporter is that Reagan had been participating in regular in-depth briefings on summit issues for the previous three months. He was amply prepared for the Williamsburg summit, and the summit was a resounding success. It confirmed allied resolve to deploy INF missiles in the fall and provided in the communiqué and its annex the outline of Reagan's economic policies—low inflation, deregulation, and free trade—that dominated the global economy for the next two and a half decades.[179] Reagan often spoke in jokes and parables. But as Shultz observed, "that doesn't mean it didn't have a heavy element to it."[180] The declassified record and voluminous writings by Reagan reveal a very different Ronald Reagan than the one portrayed by many of his own top staff.[181]

Conclusion
FREEDOM AND FORCE

FORCE AND DIPLOMACY are two sides of the same coin. They cannot be separated or used in sequence. Nationalists limit force to defense and disdain diplomacy. Realists use both. Like Churchill's eagle head, they swivel back and forth but only for the purpose of preserving the regime status quo, not advancing freedom. Liberal internationalists revere diplomacy and use force only as a last resort after diplomacy fails. They hope that others also use force only as a last resort and that persistent diplomacy transforms the world and builds common institutions, which eventually convert military power to police force and solve disputes by the peaceful rule of democratically determined law.

American foreign policy suffers from the neglect of a tradition that uses force and diplomacy continuously to spread democracy and build a world of limited government and robust civil societies. That tradition is *conservative* internationalism, a foreign policy approach dedicated to both the spread of democracy *and* the preservation of national sovereignty. Conservative internationalism envisions a world of "sister republics," diverse in culture and geography but similar in republican ideology and democratic politics. Such a world is not defined by centralized institutions that monopolize force and is therefore never permanently free of the use of military force. If liberty is the goal, force cannot be ruled out. Even after democracy and union, force lurks in the shadows of peace. It did so after the American union, reemerging during the Civil War, and it did so again after the euphoric days of the early 1990s, reemerging in the terrorist attacks of 9/11. The problem of constructing a democratic republic in the world at large is the same as the problem of constructing a democratic republic in any specific country. Both republics must be compound, strong enough to resist anarchy and war yet weak enough not to threaten liberty and diversity.[1]

For a long time to come, nations will retain the right to bear arms. And it is doubtful that they will ever agree to a rule of law or set of common institutions that subjects the use of force to global constitutional constraints. Even then, as in the case of the Second Amendment of the U.S. Constitution, free nations like free individuals will insist on the right to bear arms. True, they may have no right to use those arms for insurrection against democratic sister republics. But they will use them, as the states of the union did in the Civil War, if they fear that their liberty (the South) or their union (the North) is threatened. Thus how nations (and individuals) interpret institutions and the military force those institutions control remains as powerful a factor in world affairs as the institutions and military force themselves. As long as these interpretations are genuinely free and competitive, the use of force in world affairs will always be with us.

Don't misunderstand: the world has made notable progress in disciplining the use of force, especially in the last seventy years. The world of today, as I will elaborate, is a far cry better than the world of yesterday. World wars and nuclear Armageddon have been avoided, and interstate violence has decreased substantially.[2] But that world has depended uniquely on the interpretations of force and institutions provided by the free countries of the West led by the United States. After the end of the Cold War, democracy metastasized; the world became ideologically more unipolar than ever before. Let this constellation of interpretations or ideologies change and the incidence of violence will also change.[3] After all, intrastate and domestic violence continue despite the decline of interstate violence, because nondemocratic ideologies persist at the domestic level—racist, fascist, Marxist, fundamentalist, and other radical movements. Some scholars believe that technology, especially nuclear weapons, slowly disciplines the use of force.[4] And they are certainly right, up to a point. Deterrence is the art of showing that the costs of war vastly outweigh the benefits of war. But deterrence also requires credibility, and if credibly threatening war is the only way to stop war, large conventional and even nuclear force may still be used. So, why would we ever want to stop thinking about the use of force and how to prevent both war and the loss of freedom? Deterrence, preemption, and prevention of war do not go away, except in our imagination. The issue of force in human affairs is not a problem to be eliminated but a dilemma to be managed—for the better if we pay attention to ideologies that set the ground rules for the use of force.

Ideology, Arms, and Peace

Conservative internationalism interprets the world more from the standpoint of domestic regimes and ideologies than international institutions or the balance of power. Authoritarian regimes use force arbitrarily in the world because they use it daily to sustain their rule at home. And even in democracies, especially weak ones, the use of force by some groups remains a possibility—for example, the one-vote, onetime radical groups (Jacobins).[5] As long as that is the case, force to defend freedom will be a pervasive component of diplomacy in world affairs, not because some groups in the United States or other democracies want it to be that way but because no groups in the United States or elsewhere can rule it out. It is part of the complexity of a world that remains beset by ideological foes of freedom.

The inseparable link between freedom and force is the alternative outlook that conservative internationalism brings to the foreign policy debate. Freedom cannot be ensured without the availability of force to defend it, and force cannot be used without posing a threat to freedom. Liberal internationalism in its zeal to eliminate the use of force underestimates the first possibility; realism in its commitment to stability and moral equivalence underestimates the second possibility. Conservative internationalism accepts the contradiction between force and freedom. It integrates force and diplomacy *before* a free nation is attacked because unfree nations do so as a matter of course. It does not consider force always appropriate any more than liberal internationalism considers it never appropriate. It is just more likely to advocate the use of smaller force earlier. Its counsel may be right in certain circumstances and wrong in others. But it is a mistake to exclude its counsel from the discussion, let alone to demonize it as militarist because it advocates a more assertive use of force. There are ideologies alive and well in the world that use force all the time and often brutally to suppress human rights and freedom. Unless democracies take this reality into account, they cannot deal effectively with the use of force in world affairs or with the art of diplomacy that may eventually narrow the use of force by means of a community of sister democratic republics.

This situation means that democracies have to do something abroad that runs counter to their daily behavior at home; they have to use force to arm their international diplomacy and counterbalance the tendency of nondemocracies to use force pervasively both at home and abroad. This is not easy and accounts for the fact that democratic public opinion is often resistant to the use of force in international affairs if it entails persisting casualties, unless a democracy is directly attacked. Conservative internationalism therefore has a particularly high hurdle to clear in the domestic discourse on foreign policy. It has to persuade a reluctant public, chary of central institutions using force, to arm its diplomacy.[6]

Three steps are important in making the case to a skeptical domestic audience that the continuous use of force in diplomacy is necessary. First, be prudent in defining threats. Here conservative internationalism takes a page from realism. Hyping threat to rally the public to use force in international affairs is counterproductive. It may work once but not twice; and if practiced regularly, it inures the public to the use of force, even when the need is more apparent. Foreign ventures are not needed to succor the spirit of freedom. Second, conservative internationalism needs to make the case to the public that, when justified by threat, the early use of force *before* an attack through deterrence, preemption, or prevention saves lives compared to the later use of force *after* an attack. As John Gaddis has noted, the public is generally unaware of the historical cases when the early use of force worked.[7] Indeed, scholars seldom do counterfactual research to explore these cases and demonstrate the worse outcomes that might have followed if force had not been used early or the bad outcomes that did follow because early force was not used effectively. The world never came closer to nuclear Armageddon than in the Cuban Missile Crisis of October 1962. But few scholars make the point that there would have been no Cuban Missile Crisis if the early use of force, the CIA-supported Bay of Pigs invasion in March 1961, had succeeded in overthrowing Fidel Castro. Instead, most scholars remain strongly critical of this intervention.[8] Third, conservative internationalism has to live by its own creed. If force is always a part of diplomacy, diplomacy is always a part of force. Having a clear *diplomatic* objective and recognizing that military victory is not the end of the matter are equally important. Timely compromise, knowing when to cash in military power to advance ideological goals, is the key to moving a world of ideological division toward a world of tolerance based on democratic community. Regime change is the ultimate goal because regime types determine the nature of international institutions and the operation of the balance of power. But regime change cannot be achieved in one fell swoop, particularly in parts of the world, such as the Middle East, that are devoid of democratic models and experience. The publics of free republics will never accept the costs of ending tyranny or spreading democracy in all parts of the world simultaneously.

These three steps constitute the main tenets of conservative internationalism: pursuing freedom disciplined by threat, integrating force and diplomacy, and respecting domestic constraints. Let's look further at each step in turn.

Threats and Opportunities

Conservative internationalists are often accused by liberal international-ists and realists of hyping threat. And sometimes they do. But the frequent criticism itself confirms the different propensities of the three traditions to support the use of force. If liberal internationalists tend to underesti-mate threats, conservative internationalists may overestimate them. Real-ists are the most hardnosed perhaps, looking to geopolitics rather than regime type or international diplomatic intentions to assess threats. Con-servative internationalism starts there. But realism relies on balancing power early and often to counterbalance threats anywhere in the world and doing so primarily to preserve the status quo. The American public is skeptical of such an expansive foreign policy for such limited purposes. Conservative internationalism applies the same realist methods for more worthy internationalist purposes.

While conservative internationalism starts with realist objectivity, it does not end there. It works at the interstices of threat and power to promote regime change and spread freedom. Deal with the world initially to counter geopolitical threats. If threats are less serious than before, as they were after the end of the Cold War and probably still are today even after 9/11, don't hype threat. If, on the other hand, these threats are more serious, as Truman believed in 1947, don't sugarcoat them. Trust the people to judge whether or not you are underestimating or overesti-mating the threat. There is no need to rally a skeptical public, as realists believe, who doubt that democracies can conduct an effective foreign policy. Conservative internationalists, like their liberal internationalist counterparts, have greater faith in the capacity of ordinary people, in-formed by a diverse debate and responsible press, to make sound judg-ments. And *conservative* internationalists have an even greater trust in judgments affected by morality and religion as well as by reason. There is less tendency to credit one group, the experts, with greater wisdom or to discredit another group, the evangelicals, with malevolent motives.

So if the American people cannot be persuaded to identify threats and counter them, conservative internationalists, even more so than realists, should be willing to accept that outcome. There is no higher law than the Constitution, which protects Jefferson's public square and the right of the people to hear all points of view, liberal and conservative, deploy-ing different proportions of reason and morality (see chapter 1), vying equally for the affection of public opinion. The people rule—for better or worse. What experts or scholars can add to the mix is to ensure that all points of view are vigorously represented in the public square. That is why this book is being written. The debate lacks a more explicit foreign policy tradition that spreads freedom by integrating force and diplomacy continuously to build a world of decentralized democratic republics.

Did Jefferson, Polk, Truman, and Reagan hype the threat that the American republic faced in their day? Liberal internationalists and realists think they did. But the accounts in this study suggest they did not.

Jefferson had an instinctive understanding that Britain was the principal threat to early American freedom. And by most objective standards, he was right. He defined that threat in commercial terms because American commerce was, arguably, more valuable in his day than American territory. He defended that commerce vigorously in the all-out war against the Barbary pirates and in the never-ending war against British trade restrictions. But he resisted the paranoia that gripped America during the phony war with France, and he repudiated emphatically the Alien and Sedition Acts. These acts constituted without doubt the greatest assault on American freedoms where they already existed, namely among propertied white males, until the time of the Civil War, which addressed these freedoms where they never existed before, namely among black American slaves.

Polk was, to be sure, a prisoner of his times, as all leaders are to one extent or another. But he was not a prisoner of slavery, any more than Jefferson, Washington, Madison, or Monroe was; and he completed and thereby strengthened, not weakened, the continental union before it met its most severe test of freedom in the Civil War. He saw that threats to America's freedom from outside its borders were just as great as threats to America's freedom from inside its borders. It wasn't the prospect of Mexican aggression that loomed as threat; in that sense, Polk's policy was never purely defensive.[9] It was rather the threat of competition and war with European powers—Britain, Spain, France, and Russia—on America's borders that might have constricted the new republic and conceivably sapped its dynamism and eventual survival. Polk was so far ahead of the thinking of his times that no one else in the country envisioned as he did the completion of continental union in a mere four years. And it was that vision that allowed him to navigate successfully the interstices of threat and opportunity to wedge open the doors of freedom for parts, not all, of Mexican territory long before it might have occurred under Mexican or other foreign rule.

Truman was the first American president to link threat and freedom beyond the American continent and hemisphere. Teddy Roosevelt came before, to be sure, but he was quite content to engage threat and competition for its own sake, or at most for the sake of demonstrating the superiority of Western culture and civilization. Woodrow Wilson championed freedom largely in the absence of threat, which in the run-up to World War I never really reached America's shores. He demonstrated the futility of pursuing freedom beyond the limits of actual threat and lost his quest for the League of Nations because it addressed all threats without confronting any specific ones and alienated the American public. Franklin Roosevelt harnessed the United States to the four-spanner plow—the four policemen—of the UN Security Council (enlarged to five with the later addition of France), but the UN never merited the moniker of freedom, dependent as it was, if it was going to work at all, on cooperation with the despotic Soviet Union. Only Truman made the crucial connection between threat and freedom. He saw that the Soviet Union was not a threat because of its power, which might be harnessed by the UN Security Council, but because of its ideology, which divided east and west whatever the UN might do or however separate spheres of influence might be arranged. And he countered the threat with the priority of enlarging freedom first in Western Europe, where all of the countries in 1947 were not free, not in all of Europe or in the entire world as Woodrow Wilson did. He thereby persuaded the American people for the first time that an expansive foreign policy, extended beyond the western hemisphere, was worth the costs of foreign entanglement.

Ronald Reagan revisited the ideological roots of threat first identified by Truman and then set his sights on pursuing opportunities for freedom on the borders of existing freedom in central Europe. Reagan, like Polk, thought way ahead of his times and already in December 1981 saw the Polish crisis not as another episode in preserving stability but as "the last chance in our lifetime," as he put it, to press for freedom in the Soviet empire. He never wavered from that goal, waging an arms race and political competition with the Soviet Union across the board while avoiding diversion of resources to peripheral conflicts in the Middle East or Latin America. The payoff came with the collapse of the Soviet Union and the greatest expansion of freedom the world has ever seen. In the 1990s alone, sixty-three countries became free that were not free. Some like Russia eventually lapsed back into despotism, but the ones that mattered most on the borders where freedom already existed became lastingly free. Europe was now, as George H. W. Bush declared, "whole and free," and Japan was joined in Asia by robust democracies in South Korea and Taiwan, along with budding democracies in Indonesia, the Philippines, and Thailand.

Presidents after Reagan lost the link between threat and opportunity to spread freedom. George H. W. Bush deftly harvested the fruits of freedom in Europe ripened by Reagan's exertions but then mobilized force in an unprecedented collective security operation in the Persian Gulf merely to preserve "world order." That objective quickly lost the support of the American people and gave Saddam Hussein another decade to wreak havoc in the region. Bill Clinton, with no foreign policy experience at all, sent the first Bush packing, arguably one of the most experienced foreign policy presidents in American history. But then Clinton, acting like the novice he was, dithered while ethnic threats built up in the Balkans, humanitarian threats haunted Rwanda, Bin Laden established training camps in Afghanistan, and terrorist threats pockmarked the decade, exploding in 9/11 only eight months after Clinton left office.

If Clinton was late to identify threats and prioritize opportunities for freedom, George W. Bush after 9/11 was arguably too quick to do so. He declared another global war against America's adversaries, like Truman's and Reagan's Cold War, and waved the banner of freedom all over the planet, like Woodrow Wilson's League. He prioritized freedom in the most unlikely places, Afghanistan and Iraq, far from the borders of existing freedom, and, like Wilson again, inevitably lost public support. Obama, taking most of his cues by doing the opposite of Bush, pulled back from both Iraq and Afghanistan and seemed less disturbed by a decline in U.S. influence. Acknowledging that other countries were exceptionalist no less than the United States, he seemed confident that other countries would step forward, as the United States hung back, to thwart threats and sponsor opportunities to spread freedom in the world.

Force and Diplomacy: Siamese Twins

As important as getting the goals right is the combination of force and diplomacy that successful presidents used to implement their goals. In some cases they got it wrong and learned; circumstances can be harsh teachers. But in other cases they got it right and their strategies altered circumstances to meet their goals.

The presidents studied in this volume understood the three roles military force plays in peaceful negotiations: as *background leverage* that establishes positions of strength or weakness and sets agendas before negotiations start; as *ground leverage* once negotiations get under way to ensure that adversaries cannot achieve their objectives by forceful means outside negotiations; and as *bargaining leverage* inside negotiations providing the arms and other material leverage to secure acceptable compromises.

Truman, for example, regretted the time he failed to back his diplomacy with force. In May 1945 American forces were moving eastward across Czechoslovakia.[10] Eisenhower sent a message to Moscow expressing his intention to station American forces beyond the capital of Prague on the west bank of the Vltava River. This position encroached on the Soviet zone agreed at Yalta. Stalin had no illusion that postwar diplomacy would be conducted without the use of force; he objected. Eisenhower backed down, thinking as a military man that the use of force ended with military victory. Churchill tried desperately to get Truman to overrule Eisenhower. But Truman was either too new to the job or not yet in touch with his deeper instincts; he refused. Soviet forces rolled into Prague on May 9, and American forces pulled out of Czechoslovakia altogether by the end of June. Soviet forces had commandeered Czechoslovakia and other eastern European countries even before postwar diplomacy commenced at Potsdam in July 1945. Now it was just a matter of time before domestic politics would follow Soviet tanks. Poland quickly slipped behind the Iron Curtain, and Czechoslovakia fell to a communist coup in 1948, becoming one of the incendiary events that sparked the Cold War.

Truman was influenced by the liberal internationalist view that the use of military force always makes diplomacy more difficult. If the United States exploited its military advantages, the Soviets would do the same. And what, then, would happen to the atmosphere of postwar diplomatic deliberations within the United Nations? The view is plausible as long as the other side, in this case the Soviet Union, thinks the same way. But what if it doesn't? What if nondemocracies are more inclined to use force to leverage their diplomacy? Stalin intended to use his military advantages and no doubt expected the United States to do the same. He would have objected to Eisenhower's proposition in any case, because if he could intimidate the other side to forego its advantage so much the better. But he probably would have been more impressed than offended if America had kept its forces beyond the agreed lines and then bargained for better terms in Berlin and Poland. What is more, he might have taken postwar negotiations more seriously. As it was, he told Molotov not to pay any attention to Yalta clauses on elections in Poland and instructed his generals not to agree to any details for American and Western access to Berlin. That matter was left unresolved by field commanders in June 1945 and never taken up in subsequent negotiations. Access to Berlin became another incendiary event that later sparked the Cold War: the Berlin Blockade.

Once Truman found his legs, however, he mobilized NATO and pulled off one of the most successful preemptive uses of military force in human history. It is always hard to confirm preemption because if it works whatever was preempted does not happen. In this case the Soviet Union did not seize West Berlin or invade Western Europe. Ergo, according to some historians, it never intended to do so, and Truman hyped threat and preemption by NATO was unnecessary. But we get a clue of what might have happened in Europe, if Truman had not drawn the line of containment, by what happened in Asia. Stalin was cautious but also aggressive. He probed for weaknesses. He wanted to know how committed the United States was to its interests in Europe and Asia. In Asia he pressed the point. And when Secretary of State Dean Acheson led him to believe that South Korea lay outside the perimeter of Western security interests, Stalin pounced and approved a plan by North Korea to storm and seize the southern half of the peninsula. The Korean War broke out. Now imagine if Truman had responded to the Berlin Blockade by retreating from Berlin. Most of his advisors recommended exactly that at the time. Is there any doubt that the Soviet Union would have moved into West Berlin and set its sights next on the western half of Germany? Truman's preemptive strike prevented war in Europe. Without the Marshall Plan and NATO in winter 1948–49, there is a high probability, albeit no certainty, that Stalin would have found a way to use force to advance his position in Europe, as he did in Asia. Containment did not plunge the world into a Cold War; it more likely saved the world from a hot war.

Jefferson worked with the least military power as background leverage, but he made the most of it both outside and inside negotiations. There is no explanation for his war on the Barbary pirates except his view, solidified in Paris in the 1780s, that military power impressed the Barbary pirates as well as the states of Europe and made serious negotiations with them more not less likely. In classic conservative internationalist fashion, Jefferson ordered the U.S. Navy, through Secretary of State James Madison and Navy Secretary Robert Smith, "to apply military force until America could dictate peace terms," "holding out the olive Branch in one hand & displaying in the other the means of offensive operations."[11] Despite doubts, he supported Eaton's risky filibuster to overthrow the regime in Tripoli, a maneuver that finally pushed the pasha in Tripoli to sue for peace.

Jefferson was also a better student of the balance of power in Europe than his Federalist rivals. They preferred an alliance with Great Britain, the one country with an unparalleled navy that could have done serious harm to the new republic—and did so by invading it in 1814. Jefferson understood that it was better to lean against that power than to be swallowed up by it. At the same time, he knew Britain was the only rival that France feared as well and therefore feinted three times to form an alliance with Great Britain against France—twice while in office to secure the Louisiana Purchase and then unsuccessfully to acquire the Floridas, and once while out of office to implement the Monroe Doctrine in 1823 (rejected by Monroe, who proceeded unilaterally). Jefferson was no James K. Polk or Ronald Reagan; he did not identify with military might or exemplify the martial spirit as they did. The republic was young, and Jefferson feared the costs of a large military establishment, especially a land army, for America's fragile freedoms. After the Alien and Sedition Acts, he had good reason for such fears. But he understood that the tyranny he feared at home was even more alive and well abroad and could be countered in international diplomacy only by military power. What else explains his self-defeating embargo of British shipping and then his embrace of war with London when war finally came under his successor?

Polk was the master of integrating force and diplomacy. On his first strategic foray to secure the southwest territories, he sincerely aimed to purchase them. Slidell had detailed instructions and flexibility to make a deal, excluding California if necessary. But Mexico was in disarray, and Slidell had no negotiating partner. Now, at this point, the United States might have pulled back and waited until Mexico got its act together. What right does one country have anyway to threaten war because another country refuses to sell part of its territory? None, but the United States did have a right to protect its borders, which is exactly what Mexico had a right to do. Texas needed to be secured, and waiting for Mexico to get its act together left not only Texas but also the southwest territories at risk. Mexican factions stoked aggressive aims against the United States that they did not have the capability to implement. But European powers had aggressive aims that they did have capabilities to implement and no compunction to exploit Mexico's or America's weakness. Britain meddled in both the Texas and Mexican interventions. And France, Spain, and Britain intervened two decades later during the American Civil War. So Polk's next steps to fortify the disputed Texas territory between the Nueces and Rio Grande rivers were well within the rules of the game, and the question for historians is what would have happened if the United States had withdrawn from the competition and Mexico or other states had occupied the southwest territories and potentially reclaimed Texas as well. These speculations are irresolvable, but they should not be avoided. You can't just stop the analysis simply by morally condemning America, on the one side, or sympathizing with Mexico, on the other.

Polk's second and third forays were less carefully crafted and capable of succeeding. Mackenzie, Slidell's nephew, ran afoul of the same confusion in Mexico that stymied his uncle, and Beach and Atocha were more freelance than deputized negotiators; they operated without written instructions. Even so, Polk never relinquished diplomacy even as he ratcheted up arms, eventually to seize Mexico City. The crowning stroke of his strategic brilliance was how he handled the Trist mission. After investing considerable blood and seizing the capital of Mexico, Polk drew back and accepted a compromised negotiated by an insubordinate emissary, not because he had no other choices but because the deal met his initial objectives and helped him retreat from the heartland of Mexico, which he never coveted. Polk never let arms or diplomacy dictate his policy. It was always the combination of the two that succeeded.

Reagan had the same grasp of the indissoluble link between force and diplomacy. He laid out a road map for ending the Cold War already in

1963: an arms race that would compel the Soviets to negotiate more on his terms than theirs. He followed the script flawlessly, announcing it during his campaign, building up nuclear arms in his first term to build them down in his second term, offering the Soviet Union a middle-class future in the globalized information age, and finally wrestling unsuccessfully with Gorbachev over SDI and how to safeguard a world free of nuclear weapons. Reagan did not resolve the dilemma of force and freedom. And today his acolytes quarrel over whether he was a liberal internationalist after all who saw force as a last and ultimately past resort (his desire to eliminate nuclear weapons) or whether he understood that deterrence through the sharing of missile defense technologies or some other means would still be necessary to safeguard freedom after nuclear weapons were eliminated (his refusal to trade off SDI). Reagan's story is just beginning to be told, and its careful study holds boundless insights into the management of war and peace in a permanently decentralized international community.

Compromise and Consent

The third step toward appreciating better a conservative internationalist perspective on American foreign policy concerns the role of public opinion in foreign policymaking. How does a public accustomed to force playing no more than a deep background role in domestic affairs (Second Amendment) accept the integral role of force in foreign affairs? Conservatives worry about this more than liberals because conservatives are more skeptical of government, even in the national security arena. The keys to this third step are setting priorities to spread freedom and knowing when to compromise.

The presidents studied in this volume knew how to prioritize and compromise even though, in some cases again, they learned along the way. Jefferson's biggest success was the Louisiana Purchase when he prioritized and compromised constitutional principles to expand freedom not war (hence his constitutional objections to war with France but not to the acquisition of Louisiana) and positioned his lap perfectly to catch Louisiana at the moment when Napoleon decided to drop it. By the same token, perhaps, Jefferson's biggest mistake was not to accept the compromise that England offered in 1806 to limit rather than eliminate the hated practice of impressing sailors on American ships into the British navy. At the time, England was weak vis-à-vis its rivals in Europe and ready to make substantial concessions on impressment. Jefferson thought he could get more from an adversary that was weak. He held out and paid the price of a costly embargo and war that followed.

Weak adversaries, however, sometimes make poor negotiating partners. If they can't close on a deal because of their weakness, they create stalemate and may even pull their partners into the dangerous game of direct intervention to effect regime change. England was weak after Pitt's death in early 1806, but it was not so divided internally that it invited regime change. Mexico in the 1840s was. And Polk's experience illustrates some of the problems of reaching closure with failing or failed states.

A constant for Polk throughout his term was Mexico's weakness.[12] Torn by internal divisions, Mexico could neither effectively defend its territory nor make a settlement. In negotiations both sides naturally exploit strengths and weaknesses. That's why they accumulate force as a background factor and use it as leverage inside and outside negotiations. But as important as the relative balance of forces is, the relative capacity of the two sides to make compromises is equally important. Force never resolves anything completely; diplomacy always follows. And if one side is too weak to conduct diplomacy, force persists. Thus the Mexican War began and persisted as much because of Mexican weakness as because of American belligerence.[13]

Was there anything different Polk might have done? Not really. If he could not control the infighting in Mexico—and he tried several times through efforts by Atocha and Beach to influence regime change—he had a better chance of controlling the infighting in the United States. And here he understood the art and timing of compromise. Had he taken a Van Buren–like position on Texas, he may well have never become president. And had he backed off on the southwest territories after Slidell's mission failed in winter 1845–46, he would have very likely lost control of the issue to Congress, either to stalemate or, worse, to the extreme expansionists. He was always ready for compromise, especially before war broke out. Once war began, he knew that Congress would require more by way of territory to compensate for the costs of war. Hence he rejected Beach's willingness to forgo New Mexico after war started, even though he gave Slidell flexibility to forego California before war started. At the same time he did not succumb to the extremist All Mexico Movement in Congress. He grabbed the chance to compromise in February 1848, even though American forces sat comfortably in the Mexican capital, the All Mexico Movement was at a peak in Congress, and his negotiator was not only insubordinate but personally offensive to him.

Truman and Reagan lived in different times than Jefferson and Polk. The franchise was now widespread, and public opinion was more divided and contentious. What is remarkable is that both rallied a skeptical public to implement far-reaching and forceful diplomatic strategies that ultimately contained and defeated the Soviet Union.

In an unlikely victory in the 1948 elections, Truman persuaded the American public to back the Marshall Plan and the Berlin Blockade. Although he muffled the negotiations to establish NATO until the elections were over, the newly elected U.S. Congress strongly backed America's participation in the country's first standing alliance in peacetime. Despite this achievement, Truman was the only one of the four presidents studied in this volume who left office with lower approval ratings than when he entered. That was because of the Korean situation, which he failed to handle in a timely and effective way as he did NATO. Aggressive presidents face stark challenges from their generals—think of Polk's relations with Scott and Taylor—and in the Korean War Truman lost control of his generals at a critical moment when General MacArthur stormed into North Korea and brought China into the war.[14] But consider this in any summary evaluation of Truman. As we noted earlier, the Korean War was a consequence of the failure of deterrence in Asia. There is at least a reasonable likelihood that a similar hot war might have happened in Europe if Truman had not ignited containment and the Cold War. Then Truman's place in history might have rivaled that of James Buchanan or other American presidents whose leadership or failure of leadership invited disastrous wars. Truman's leadership in Europe, even if the Korean War cost him temporarily the support of the American people, was historically exceptional. The year 1952 was no time to compromise, despite the lack of public consent, either in Korea or, more important, in Europe. Retreat in Asia would have muffed the opportunity to galvanize NATO's formation in Europe, while compromise in Europe, responding to Stalin's proposals in 1952 to unify and neutralize Germany, would have gutted NATO altogether.

Reagan, like Truman, rallied the American public from its foreign policy somnolence. He said the Cold War need not go on forever, and the United States could win it. He had extraordinary hurdles to clear. The press and his opponents accused him of war-mongering and inviting the prospect of Armageddon (ABC's film *The Day After*). And he did lead an arms buildup unprecedented in scope and danger and refused to compromise prematurely, rejecting the "walk in the woods" proposal, even in the darkest days of his presidency. Many believed then and still believe that Reagan wanted war, while others believe, conversely and contradictorily, that he wanted to eliminate nuclear weapons. Who was the real Reagan? Even Republicans can't decide.[15] But the American public knew. They reelected him overwhelmingly well before he negotiated and compromised with Gorbachev, and they gave him the benefit of the doubt, even through the politically debilitating Iran-Contra affair. Two-thirds of the public approved his policies when he left office. And when he died, the outpouring was overpowering. But like Polk and Truman, Reagan loomed larger than more popular predecessors—Andrew Jackson, Franklin Roosevelt, and John F. Kennedy, respectively; hence the media and academy quickly dropped him from sight. But Reagan's profile will grow with time, especially as the documentary record accumulates.[16] He understood that Americans grasped the link between force and freedom. They will support an ambitious foreign policy that prioritizes the quest to spread freedom and knows when to compromise.

When Ideas Matter More than Circumstances

Assessments of presidents and public policy are never just factual. They are also affected by theoretical considerations. Scholars, like policymakers, cannot consider everything. They use theories or models of what causes events to happen to guide their selection and assessment of facts. Relatively, conservative internationalism privileges ideas as causal factors, while liberal internationalism privileges institutions, and nationalism and realism privilege power. The case for conservative internationalism therefore hinges on when ideas matter more than institutions and power. In the short rum, power and institutions cannot be wished away. They constrain ideas. That's why conservative internationalism starts with threats. But power and institutions are constantly being pushed around and shaped by ideas. Ideas interpret power and institutions, judge what can be changed or not, and over time move circumstances in directions that increase or decrease power and build or transform institutions. That's why conservative internationalism promotes freedom, not just stability or cooperation. It aims to change the balance of existing domestic regimes, not just manage the external balance of power or strengthen international institutions.

The case studies offer examples of when conservative internationalism is appropriate and when it is not. Jefferson succeeded with this approach in 1803 to purchase Louisiana but failed in 1805 to acquire the Floridas. The difference was Jefferson's assessment of the balance of power and how a U.S.-British alliance might affect it. In 1803 France was weaker and more likely to fear a U.S.-British alliance; in 1805 it was stronger and less threatened by a U.S.-British alignment. From 1805 on, Jefferson came to see Britain as a bigger threat than France. He was right perhaps on the high seas where Britain defeated France at Trafalgar in October 1805, but he was wrong on land in Europe where Napoleon's victories at Austerlitz and Jena in the same period made France dominant. Moreover, Jefferson had less material leverage to work with in Florida than in Louisiana. New Orleans was almost totally dependent on U.S. commerce, and American settlers were pouring into the Mississippi Valley potentially besieging New Orleans. Neither factor operated to the same extent along the southern boundary of the new republic. Florida was sparsely populated and Spanish influence mostly uncontested.

But had Jefferson been a realist mostly and reacted only to circumstances of material leverage, he would have missed the chance to get Louisiana completely. His ideas made him uniquely conscious of possibilities that went beyond existing circumstances. He saw additional land and territory as the future of freedom for yeoman American farmers, their right to own property and trade and thereby to participate in the experiment of self-government. He mobilized the American settlers not only to pressure Spanish and French power but also after the acquisition of Louisiana to reform Spanish and Creole authorities. Until it became a state in 1812, Louisiana was an early experiment in bottom-up nation-building. Jefferson's Federalist rivals, such as Hamilton and Burr, saw land and settlers in more proverbial, geopolitical terms. The western frontier offered opportunities to mobilize armies and lead filibusters to conquer, conspire, or separate one territorial authority from another. They looked at the western territories much the way European powers did: as another pawn on the continental chessboard of power politics. Jefferson's ideas opened him up to the possibility of acquiring all of Louisiana, even though he initially sought only New Orleans and the Floridas, because massive and unknown territories to him were not just a specter of threat but also an opportunity for freedom.[17]

Polk provides another example of when not to push against present circumstances and how to bend future circumstances in your favor. In Oregon, he knew that future circumstances were moving his way. Like Jefferson, he saw that American settlers would secure the conquest of Oregon, "in the bedroom" as the British statesman Castlereagh graphically put it. He also knew, however, that present circumstances would not permit the United States to fight two wars simultaneously. And he had plans to acquire New Mexico and California, which might mean war with Mexico. So he quickly offered his bottom line on Oregon in spring 1845 and, when the British rejected it, looked for a way, like Jefferson, "to palliate and endure" until the British came around. Now domestic circumstances came into play. Congress contained both imperialist types like Lewis Cass (54° 40' advocates) and conciliatory types like John Calhoun (avoid war with Britain at all costs). And Polk's cabinet contained opportunists, like James Buchanan, and ambitious generals, like Zachary Taylor, who constantly sought advantage for personal political gain. He needed some means to hold circumstances at bay. The request for legislation to abrogate the Oregon conventions was the perfect instrument. It bought time with the British while it kept Congress busy and out of the negotiations. By spring 1846, just as war with Mexico loomed, the British capitulated and accepted Polk's original proposal. Polk had anticipated and maneuvered to impose constraints not only on Congress but also on Britain and Mexico, arguably inducing the British not to assist Mexico in the war that followed.

Truman and Reagan offer further examples. Truman failed to use *present* circumstances to his advantage in spring 1945 when he pulled back American forces in Czechoslovakia. But he soon—probably sooner than Roosevelt—recognized that *future* circumstances were moving against him. He therefore created new circumstances by rallying the country and its allies to build up Western economic and military strength. Unlike the situation in Oregon where circumstances favored American settlers, circumstances in central Europe after World War II favored Soviet military forces. These forces were massed and strengthening on the borders of Berlin and Western Europe, while American forces had been rapidly demobilized and returned to the United States. That trend had to be reversed before the United States could expect serious negotiations with the Soviet Union. Hence Truman put negotiations in the deep freeze in the late 1940s and early 1950s and no doubt contributed thereby to the onset of the Cold War. But as events in Asia demonstrated, he also very likely prevented a hot war in Europe; and once future circumstances were more favorable several decades later, the United States eventually won the Cold War.

Reagan also read circumstances accurately while bending them to his advantage. He sensed sooner than other Cold War–era presidents that America could defeat the Soviet Union by mobilizing its inherent advantages as a free and entrepreneurial society. He exploited those advantages and created new circumstances. For a time, that meant no negotiations with the Soviet Union. But he never opposed negotiations or détente per se; he opposed détente from a position of weakness. Once he restored American strength, he pursued détente with a vengeance—elimination of nuclear weapons. His ideas changed circumstances and made possible the end, not just the stabilization, of the Cold War. But his ideas also outstripped future realities. SDI never delivered its technological promise, and Reagan never made clear how deterrence was possible after the elimination of nuclear weapons.

Truman and Reagan exploited the emerging transnational character of ideological politics.[18] In modern times, ideological parties or groups interact across countries through patterned networks or institutions. Democratic and nondemocrative movements compete to shape events. Institutions are not just repositories of expertise and codified rules. They are arenas of ideological contestation. What sorts of expertise, rules, and laws do these networks and movements formulate and execute? Whose ideology shapes the resulting institutions? Under Truman and Reagan, alliances became the bedrock of U.S. foreign policy. Ideological solidarity (democracy), not temporary geopolitical circumstances (balance of power) or universal participation in international organizations (League of Nations or UN), defined friends and enemies.

This picture inverts the more common realist and liberal internationalist portraits of international relations. In realism, relative power determines the ideas countries pursue (great powers always see their interests as common to all) and the tasks common institutions undertake (international institutions do the bidding of great powers). Geopolitical rivalry trumps democracy and interdependence: "even if all the world's countries were democratic, . . . democratic powers may engage in geopolitical rivalry [and] . . . economic interdependence among Europe's great powers did little to avert the hegemonic war that broke out in 1914."[19] In liberal internationalism, institutional cooperation and universal participation establish the common practices that eventually override both power and ideological differences. Institutional arrangements trump power and ideology: "The possibility of an institutional settlement stems from the ability to achieve agreement on institutional arrangements even if the underlying substantive interests [power and ideology] remain widely divergent and antagonistic."[20]

In conservative internationalism the causal arrows are reversed. Competing ideologies drive countries together or apart. The ideological distance between them now determines the extent to which the balance of power operates peacefully and international institutions work to promote common interests. Because conservative internationalist thinking sometimes resists and seeks to change geopolitical and institutional constraints, it is often labeled ideological. But, in fact, present-day constraints are yesterday's ideas. Ideas from the past (present) inspire initiatives that change circumstances and become the geopolitical and institutional constraints of the present (future). Over time ideas are the wellspring of realities no less than exogenous shifts in power or the unintended consequences of repetitive interactions.

In the last two sections of this study, I seek to do two things. First, I take a brief look at how the tradition of conservative internationalism explains the end of the Cold War. I do so to illustrate the reasonableness and defensibility of this tradition. Because conservative internationalism is relatively neglected, realist and liberal internationalist accounts dominate Cold War explanations. Realist accounts credit deterrence and liberal internationalist accounts credit détente. Yet an interpretation based on ideas as causal forces—regime type or democracy—rather than power balancing or diplomatic and economic interdependence offers a perfectly sensible understanding of these unprecedented events. Second, I lay out a strategy of conservative internationalism for the contemporary world.

I revisit the tenets of conservative internationalism in chapter 2 and show what each tenet means in terms of U.S. foreign policy interests and actions for the future. Conservative internationalism does not just focus on nonstate actors and terrorism, as liberal internationalism is prone to do, or counsel a static, state-based tolerance and coexistence with Islamic and other authoritarian ideologies, as realism does. Instead it offers a strategy that integrates state (China and Russia) and nonstate threats (terrorist groups), force and diplomacy, and freedom and peace.

Explaining the End of the Cold War

A plausible case can be made that the competition of ideologies, emphasized by conservative internationalism, ended the Cold War more so than détente, stressed by liberal internationalism, or the balance of power, highlighted by realism.[21] The arms race certainly mattered. Too many accounts ignore the way in which America's and the alliance's military and economic revival in the 1980s challenged Soviet policy and progressively drained Soviet economic strength.[22] Nevertheless, competitive material pressures do not provide a fully satisfactory answer as to what ended the Cold War. If changes in power balances had been primary causes, the Cold War would have ended by the fading away of ideology and a return to balance of power politics as usual. The United States and Soviet Union would have retreated from ideological confrontation but continued their rivalry by protecting their respective spheres of influence in Europe and elsewhere. A moderate balance of power system would operate, much as it did in the nineteenth century. That's what realists such as George Kennan expected. Realists did not expect that the Soviet Union and its empire would break up, let alone evolve toward a Western-style democracy, throughout Eastern Europe and even temporarily under Yeltsin in Russia.

Similarly, if détente and institutional variables had been the decisive factors, the Cold War would have ended by the United Nations assuming the role it was assigned in 1945, a superpower concert in the UN Security Council exercising primary responsibility for global peace and security. Briefly, while the Soviet Union still existed, the UN fulfilled this role. It functioned in the first Persian Gulf war in 1990–91 as a textbook case of collective security. But then the Soviet Union disappeared. Regime change took place, and UN cooperation quickly faded away.

Neither spheres of influence politics nor UN cooperation became lasting feature of world politics after the Cold War ended. Clearly something else was sculpting events at a much deeper level, and that something else was ideological forces. Democracy, not the balance of power or the UN, recast the post–Cold War world. Political revolutions swept across

Europe, starting with Poland and Solidarity in 1981 and culminating with the liberation of the Warsaw Pact countries and the breakup of the Soviet Union itself. Ideological tectonic plates shifted and remolded the geopolitical crust of world politics. Instead of the Cold War ending in a spheres of influence balance of power or UN collective security, it ended in a tidal wave of regime change, political and commercial liberalization that swept across Europe as well as large parts of the rest of the world.

As chapter 7 documents, Reagan's strategy of conservative internationalism was critical for this outcome, albeit not alone determinative.[23] Had anyone else been president (say, Jimmy Carter or Walter Mondale), it is inconceivable that American policy would have consisted simultaneously of three seemingly incompatible parts: a tough ideological stance toward the Soviet Union, a massive arms buildup and economic revival, and a negotiating strategy aimed at reducing nuclear weapons and fostering economic globalization. The tough ideological stance may have been decisive. Reagan inherited military and economic trends that were going against the United States. Consider the situation at the end of the 1970s. The Soviet Union had projected military power for the first time beyond its Eurasian borders in Africa and invaded Afghanistan. The Soviet economy had benefited from significant oil price increases, and Soviet defense outlays had climbed as a percentage of GDP from 13.5 percent in 1976 to 18 percent in 1988. Soviet nuclear warheads had increased from 2,471 in 1961 to 39,000 in 1989 while U.S. warheads flatlined over the same period, around 22,000–24,000.[24] Old thinking drove Soviet policy throughout the 1970s and 1980s, even as Soviet economic prospects sagged when oil prices dropped precipitously in 1985. Meanwhile, during the 1970s, American and Western power was in significant retreat. Political and military morale flagged after Watergate and Vietnam, and economic prospects stagnated while inflation soared. Project these trends forward and there are no inklings whatsoever that the Western and world economies might revive and turbocharge the information revolution of the 1980s and 1990s.

It may be easy *in retrospect* to ascertain that the Soviet economy peaked in the early 1970s and that the American economy rebounded. The Cold War ended, therefore, because economic power shifted. But this kind of rearview mirror analysis is misleading. Events have to be interpreted in real time, and interpretations that proved congruent with and probably helped shape subsequent outcomes are intellectually more compelling than realist accounts that treat economic phenomena as exogenous and unexplained.[25] More likely, political morale and economic policy have something to do with the way societies rallied and grew or didn't grow. If ideas drive material outcomes, some ideas mobilize political consensus and exploit economic efficiencies better than other ideas.

If that's not the case, why do we care at all about leadership and public policy?

Nevertheless, critics dismiss Reagan's ideas as mere rhetoric or worse. Then, in complete contradiction, they credit Gorbachev's ideas and "New Thinking" with the principal role in ending the Cold War.[26] How does that compute? Analysts can't just pick and choose the ideas they like and don't like. They have to measure them against consequences. Reagan's ideas preceded and, in arguable ways, gave meaning to and matched material events that followed. If those ideas did not cause, they clearly reinforced, perhaps decisively, the significant reversal of military and economic trends that took place in the 1980s and presaged outcomes that followed in 1989–91. Surely, in this sense, Reagan's ideas were "consequential." That is not to say that they determined events "all the way down."[27] Reagan exploited conditions in the Soviet Union that existed before he came into office, and he had a lot of help from other Western leaders, especially Helmut Schmidt (who first called for INF missiles before Reagan took office), Margaret Thatcher, Helmut Kohl, and, on the big issues such as INF, Francois Mitterrand. But Reagan's grand strategy, carefully mapped onto observable conditions and consistently executed, tested out pretty well against the moral and material realities that followed. While causation is always impossible to establish definitively, Reagan's ideas mobilized events in certain directions, which then made it possible to exploit other events, such as the arrival of new leadership in the Soviet Union and the pending information revolution.

What about Gorbachev's ideas of "New Thinking"? Did they map out as well onto subsequent events? A few counterfactuals might help. Why did Gorbachev come to power in 1985 and not in 1982 when Brezhnev died, or 1983 when Andropov died? It is not implausible to argue, judging from comments made by Soviet officials themselves (see chapter 7), that Reagan's challenges in the early 1980s had a lot to do with Gorbachev's selection.[28] For the first time, the Soviet leadership reached deep into its pool of younger leaders, convinced that the country needed something different to confront the revitalized West.[29] Moreover, there is evidence, as presented in chapter 7, that changes in U.S.-Soviet relations were under way well before Gorbachev took power. His ascent may not have mattered as much as some accounts suggest. Or, if it did, as another counterfactual, why didn't Gorbachev succeed in reversing the Soviet Union's fortunes, as Reagan and Thatcher did in reversing the fortunes of the West? Exogenous factors such as the information revolution should have benefited him no less than they did Reagan and Thatcher. And his aim, until the very end, was to reform communism, not to give it up. Yet the Cold War ended with the spread of liberal democracy and the expansion of NATO, not the revival of communism and the creation of

Gorbachev's "common European home." If material constraints dictated such outcomes, then at the very least Gorbachev's ideas were inconsistent with those constraints.

None of this is to diminish Gorbachev's contributions. He made courageous decisions, especially to end Soviet imperialism in Eastern Europe and Afghanistan without using force. And those decisions cost him dearly, in terms of both a military coup targeted against him in summer 1991 and a disastrously low approval rating in Russia after he left office. But these decisions were more likely consequences of deeper forces, not the precursors and drivers of events that actually followed.

What about the arguments that institutions matter more than ideas or power, that détente, transnational networks, global economic interdependence, and the onset of the information revolution did the Soviet Union in? These events preceded and therefore too might have caused the end of the Cold War. Begun in the mid-1970s, détente cultivated greater openness and transnational ties involving disarmament, trade, and human rights (Helsinki process); and by the mid-1980s the information revolution took off, accelerating pressures for domestic reform in the Soviet Union. To some extent, transnational bureaucratic networks did play a role, and peace researchers in Western Europe and the Soviet Union collaborated to formulate ideas of common security and economic socialism.[30] But to be persuasive, such accounts have to show that these factors were more decisive and coincided with outcomes better than the ideological and economic ideas of Reagan and Thatcher.

Détente did not strengthen linearly from 1975 to 1985. In fact it weakened substantially in the early 1980s. The so-called new Cold War from 1981 to 1983 gave Moscow little reason to trust in the prospects of détente. U.S. and European leaders rallied support for NATO and went ahead in 1983 to deploy INF missiles despite massive peace protests in Europe backed by Soviet propaganda and money. Secretary of State George Shultz credits the successful INF deployments as the turning point of the Cold War because it signaled to Soviet leaders "the strength and cohesion of the NATO countries."[31] As Gorbachev's remarks to the Politburo in October 1985 suggest (see chapter 7), the strengthened Western alliance was indeed a formidable factor in Soviet calculations.

Moreover, the information revolution did not emerge out of nowhere. Unless economic factors are exogenous, as realist models often assume, the electronics revolution sprang from renewed market-based incentives created by Reagan-Thatcher policies.[32] The Reagan economic program and the so-called Washington Consensus (based substantively on the appendix of the Williamsburg G-7 Summit Communiqué in May 1983) ushered in an unprecedented thirty-year period of world growth based on freer markets. From 1980 to 2007, real world GDP increased by more than 145 percent or 3.4 percent per year, raising the standard of living in the United States *and* lifting hundreds of millions of poor people in China, India, and elsewhere out of poverty.[33] These results were not substantially altered by the so-called Great Recession.[34] After slowing to 2.8 percent in 2008 and then dipping by 0.6 percent in 2009, world growth rebounded by 5.1 percent in 2010, 3.9 percent in 2011, and 3.2 percent in 2012. It is expected to grow by 3.5 percent in 2013.[35]

Thus détente and the information revolution seem to act more as intervening than causal variables.[36] Free-market policy reforms accelerated their prospects rather than their presence being the causes themselves. Détente certainly helped. It facilitated communications between Reagan and Soviet leaders, even as the new Cold War heated up, unlike the situation in the 1950s when arms races accelerated but there was little détente and hence communication. But détente provided the medium, not the message. Reagan rejected the message of détente long before he came into office and made clear that an arms race was integral to successful arms negotiations. His message was competition, not détente, even though his medium was negotiations. He integrated force and diplomacy; he did not separate them.

A conservative internationalist perspective therefore offers the most complete and compelling explanation for the end of the Cold War.[37] The decisive shifts that ended the Cold War were ideological, not material or institutional. The United States and Western countries revived confidence in democratic ideals (after the alleged malaise and governability crisis of Western societies in the 1970s), while the Soviet Union lost further confidence in communist prescriptions. Shifting ideological orientations encouraged government (Helsinki) as well as nongovernmental institutions (e.g., collaboration among peace research institutes) to cultivate cooperative ideas of a non-threatening NATO, human rights, and more open economic markets. Reagan, like Gorbachev, was a visionary. He intensified the Cold War but, as the evidence now abundantly corroborates, he did so not to defeat the Soviet Union in some conventional military showdown but to close off military options favored by hawks in both Moscow and Washington and to empower diplomatic solutions favorable to the West.[38] Reagan's strategy allowed for mutually beneficial outcomes, including a nuclear-free world protected by shared missile defenses and an integrated prosperous world economy open to Soviet participation. The objective was to find common ground not primarily by détente (institutions) or competition (power) but by engineering a convergence of identities (ideas) closer to Western ideals of liberty and markets than communist ideals of police states and command economies.

Conservative Internationalism in Today's World

What does the world today look like from a conservative internationalist perspective? Let's recall the eleven tenets of conservative internationalism summarized under three key features—the disciplined goal of freedom, the integration of force and diplomacy, and the consent of free peoples—and apply them one by one to a contemporary strategy for American foreign policy.

Pursue Disciplined Goal of Freedom

TENET 1: THE GOAL OF AMERICAN FOREIGN POLICY IS TO SPREAD FREEDOM, NAMELY REGIME CHANGE.

The objective of American foreign policy is to narrow regime differences in the direction of more free governments and fewer authoritarian ones. It is, quite simply, to push *freedom forward*. There is no timetable for achieving this goal. But there is also no tentativeness or doubt about it. The world and millions of people, not just Americans, are better-off today because freedom is more widespread. And in the last seventy-five years, no country's leadership has been more important to achieving that goal than that of the United States. That's the sense in which America's contribution is exceptionalist.[39] If the United States does not lead the cause for freedom, who will? Europe may. Today, at least, it is whole and free (if you exclude Russia, Belarus, and a less and less democratic Ukraine), and it is an invaluable partner.[40] But it is not yet united to back freedom with force (no common security policy of consequence), and its commitment to democracy and human rights is more ambivalent and clouded by history. Earlier fascist and communist experiences sour its spirit and trim its aspirations for new freedoms. Europe lacks America's confidence about freedom, just as America needs to remember Europe's hard-learned lessons about freedom.

For a brief moment in 1990–91, the ideological plates of world politics lined up enough to enable the world community to behave just as liberal internationalist models of collective security envisioned. But UN action to expel Iraq from Kuwait reflected a perfect storm of favorable factors. The Soviet Union was preoccupied with what was going on in central Europe. Gorbachev and Soviet leaders clearly gave priority to cooperation with the United States in Europe, not competition with the United States in the Middle East.[41] And, given Soviet weakness, the United States basically called the shots at the United Nations, providing the overwhelming share of forces to accomplish the mission. The United States, of course, could have acted unilaterally. It was suddenly the world's first and, so far in history, only unipolar global power.[42] But to its credit, it did not. The United States followed the codebook of multilateralism to the letter. It acted only with the unanimous consent of the UN Security Council and did not exceed the instructions of that institution, which called for the expulsion of Iraq from Kuwait but not the overthrow of the oppressive Iraqi regime in Baghdad.

UN action in the first Persian Gulf War defended and restored sovereignty; it did not promote human rights or democracy. That is the difference between a realist world order that uses liberal internationalist means for stability and a conservative internationalist world order that uses realist means for regime change. The former prioritizes sovereignty, the latter freedom. Both worlds have costs. The Gulf War was costly enough just to restore sovereignty, but its failure to deal with Saddam Hussein and regime change exacted even further costs ten years later. A world that preserves sovereignty is not necessarily less violent than one that promotes freedom.

The consensus on sovereignty emerged over centuries, and it is changing today only slowly as the world community develops the idea of the "responsibility to protect." This responsibility recognizes the right of international organizations to intervene in the sovereign domain of nation-states to protect the people from genocide or humanitarian disasters if the sovereign government is unable to do so. It constitutes the first beachhead of freedom in the old Westphalian world order, which otherwise permits domestic authorities to do whatever they wish to their own people internally. But even that small beachhead is far from secure, as authoritarian states such as Russia and China consistently oppose UN intervention for human rights reasons, and even the United States defaults as in the case of genocide in Rwanda in 1994.

After 1991, favorable conditions faded, not because of a willful unilateralism on the part of the United States or a *significant* shift in the relative power of the United States but because ideological orientations stopped converging and in critical areas drifted apart once again. By the mid-1990s, Russia was reeling backward from its initial rush to economic and political liberalization. Ethnic divergences in the former Yugoslavia grew and violence escalated, and the United States was reabsorbed by domestic political concerns constraining its unipolar power ("it's the economy, stupid") and causing it to stand down in Somalia, Rwanda, and until 1995 in Bosnia. Thus by the time the world called upon the UN a second time to stop the violence in Bosnia and then a third time in Kosovo, the ideological chasms were too wide to accommodate UN action. Russia vetoed action by the Security Council.

Now NATO took center stage. Democratic convergence persisted in NATO (as well as the EU) to both strengthen and expand it. NATO operations quelled conflicts in Bosnia and Kosovo and created the security framework for nation-building in those areas by the EU and other international organizations. But a price was paid for this success of a freedom-led world; Russia was alienated. Under Vladimir Putin, Russia moved decisively away from the economic and political liberalization policies of Boris Yeltsin and reinstated more traditional policies of authoritarian government at home and spheres of influence policies abroad (e.g., in Georgia, Belorussia, and Ukraine). The specter of traditional great power rivalry reemerged, also in the steady rise of authoritarian China's presence on the world scene.

What is troubling about the future is the recent decline of freedom around the world. From 2005 to 2012 the number of electoral democracies, which include the weakest ones, dropped from 123 to 118.[43] It makes the first tenet of conservative internationalism more relevant than ever. America cannot afford to scale back its support of democracy unless or until there is another country or group of countries (EU) that can provide equivalent leadership toward an ever freer world. On the other hand, until that prospect is in hand, American foreign policy needs discipline as well as dedication in the pursuit of freedom. It cannot be "the policy of the United States to seek and support the growth of democratic movements and institutions in every nation and culture." Threat remains the first though not the final peg of a credible American foreign policy.

TENET 2: FOCUS INITIALLY ON MATERIAL, GEOPOLITICAL THREATS, NOT IDEOLOGY.

Terrorist attacks on the Twin Towers and other targets ended the holiday from history and the absence of a significant global threat. But they did not change everything, as Bush officials asserted, perhaps too often. Instead they added a devilish, complicating factor. They signaled both a new vulnerability of the American homeland that the United States had not experienced since 1814 and a new post-communist, ideological threat to the Western-oriented world: jihadism. Whether either threat was overblown is still hotly debated. But the combination of vulnerability and ideology clearly sidelined international institutions, this time including NATO.

The new threat was not standing armies or missiles in Russia or China, though that threat was growing incrementally particularly in China, but an invisible threat associated with weak, not strong, actors. Terrorist cells incubating in failed states and possibly assisted by rogue states seeking weapons of mass destruction constituted the new danger. This danger had to be either preempted *before an attack* by aggressive intelligence collection, counterinsurgency measures, and potentially preventive war, the argument for the invasion of Iraq, or dealt with *after an attack* by criminal prosecution and counterterrorism measures to punish specific individuals or states responsible for the attacks, the argument for the invasion of Afghanistan. The ideologically united world, that is, the world of NATO, divided over this issue, not enough to resurrect old balance of power suspicions among democratic nations but enough to preclude a consensus on whether and how to use NATO to cope with terrorist groups and states abetting terrorism in the Middle East, southwest Asia, and other parts of the world.[44]

European allies, with the exception of Britain, strongly favored an "after an attack" approach relying primarily on diplomacy and conventional foreign aid to temper terrorism. The United States took a more aggressive "before an attack" approach, waging preventive war in Iraq under the Bush administration and vigorous counterinsurgency campaigns in Afghanistan under both the Bush and initial Obama administrations. The appropriate response probably lies somewhere in between. The jihadist threat does not pose dangers equivalent to communism under Stalin or fascism under Hitler. It has neither a national or imperial center nor a commitment to modernization that those two threats did. But it is also not confined to al-Qaeda or a limited number of specific terrorists that can be killed or captured by unmanned drones and offshore raids under strict observance of guidelines from conventional warfare.

If the Bush administration went too far in making terrorism a war, the Obama administration goes too far in making it a mere crime. The real level of threat lies somewhere in between. Two developments will determine its severity: which way the vast majority of the Muslim world turns, most of it today sitting on the fence in the clash between Western and jihadist ideologies, and whether rogue states and their great power patrons exploit terrorism to mobilize a more significant challenge to Western ideology and power. A clearheaded assessment of this threat suggests that terrorism can be managed below the threshold of global mobilization as long as the United States keeps an eye on the major authoritarian powers that directly and indirectly abet anti-Western terrorism: Russia in the Caucasus, Central Asia, and Middle East, China in Iran, Pakistan, and North Korea, and Venezuela, Bolivia, Cuba, Ecuador, and Peru in Latin America.

Great powers, in this case China and Russia, still constitute the primary challenges to U.S. interests. They hold the key to proliferation of weapons of mass destruction in Iran, North Korea, and elsewhere. And rogue states such as Iran and North Korea hold the key to the deadly convergence of weapons of mass destruction with terrorism. Without these two broader connections, terrorism and violence by nonstate actors are manageable. In this sense, state actors still matter more than transnational terrorists, and it is way too early to declare an end to the state-dominated

Westphalian world order. Liberal internationalism is too inclined to do that, while realism counts too much on rival great power cooperation with Russia and China. Conservative internationalism recognizes that as authoritarian powers, China and Russia remain America's principal challengers and, because they are still too weak to confront America directly, may try to use both rogue states and terrorism indirectly to whittle away at the democracy-dominated world led by the United States.[45]

TENET 3: SEIZE RELATED OPPORTUNITIES TO TILT THE BALANCE OF POWER TOWARD FREEDOM.

For the moment, freedom remains preeminent in the world, and China and Russia are not actual or existential threats to the United States. That means there is more opportunity to change regimes than there is necessity to counter existential threats. Despite recent setbacks, the world of freedom is much more secure today than it was seventy-five years ago or perhaps ever, and that again is largely because of the exceptionalist leadership of the United States.

Unipolar *power* is not the most impressive feature of today's world; unipolar *identity* is.[46] Democracy reigns in the world's only superpower and more than half of all the states in the world, including *all* the world's most industrialized countries. If you doubt that such unipolar identity is more important than unipolar power, imagine what the world would be like today if it were unipolar and fascist or communist identities dominated. In unipolarity, more than any other configuration of power, the domestic regime type of a country or group of countries holding unipolar power matters more than the fact that that country or group is unipolar. Identity suffuses the power structure and to the extent that identity is shared and considered legitimate, countries do not resort to raw power to achieve their aims. International politics acquires a status more like domestic politics in which common law and institutions replace the balance of power and anarchy. Peace reigns, but the character of that peace depends on the substance of the system's identity. The present world is what it is because it enjoys a *democratic* peace; it will be quite a different place if that peace becomes more authoritarian or fundamentalist.

The key question for the future, therefore, is not whether unipolar power is sustainable but whether unipolar *democratic identity* is sustainable. Unipolar power, history suggests, is not sustainable. One empire after the other has been replaced by time. And America since World War II has put in place and led a world in which it has deliberately and progressively shared its power, relatively diminishing that power as defeated and developing states grew faster by joining the American-led globalized economy. However, unipolar democratic identity may be more durable at the international level; as we observe domestically, civil war is the exception rather than the rule, even as material wealth spreads and political power becomes more competitive. But ideological unity, which contains such conflicts at the domestic level, depends on all groups in a country feeling comfortable with the national government's monopoly of force. To what extent will all groups in the world—states and nonstate actors, free and unfree—continue to feel comfortable with democracy's and, in the medium term, America's monopoly of force at the international level, such that they will not seek to reduce or replace it? To what extent will they accept and expand the free world long after the United States is no longer the sole democratic superpower?

TENET 4: PRIORITIZE OPPORTUNITIES TO SPREAD FREEDOM ON THE BORDERS OF EXISTING FREEDOM.

In today's world, there are four sources or settings of discomfort with democracy's and America's political and military preeminence. Each setting involves a different degree of convergence and divergence between democracy and tyranny. As discussed earlier, the distance between these ideologies sets the parameters in which power balances and international institutions operate. When ideologies diverge, conflict increases. When they converge, cooperation increases. The greatest convergence exists among the industrialized nations, all of whom are now durably democratic. The greatest divergence comes from jihad fundamentalists. In between looms the specter of large authoritarian states, such as Russia and China, and smaller rogue states, such as Iran and North Korea, that benefit from Russian and Chinese support and actively support terrorism. If, as noted under tenet 2, the greatest threats come from rogue states and terrorist groups, the greatest opportunities come on the borders of existing freedom with the large authoritarian states of Russia and China—the Balkans, Turkey, and Ukraine in Europe, and the whole of the Korean peninsula in Asia.

The first setting of ideological discomfort involves America's democratic allies in Europe and Asia. These allies are uncomfortable not with America's identity but with America's dominance. Under the democratic peace, they do not fear military attack from the United States, but they do resent America's power. America's dominance is the equivalent of "one-party rule" in the democratic world. There is no effective competing party (country or group of countries) to check and counterbalance U.S. interests. Quite understandably, the allies, both Europe and Japan, prefer a more balanced distribution of power within the democratic world. Imagine how the United States might feel if the balances were reversed. Nevertheless, it's not clear yet whether Europe or Japan is ready to accept the responsibilities of greater power, particularly the need to exercise greater military responsibility. Until they do, their own ambivalence and lack of unity are as much a cause of their continuing unhappiness as American dominance is. And they should worry more about which authoritarian states might rise to counterbalance America if they hesitate to share leadership responsibilities with the United States.

This arena of divergence within today's democratic world order poses no significant threat to America's interests. It constitutes a normal political competition among rival "parties" within the democratic peace, not a potential arena for balancing military power among sovereign states. The democratic peace operates without the realist logic of balancing or the liberal internationalist mechanism of strong common institutions.[47] It comes closest to the conservative internationalist ideal of sister democratic republics living in peace with one another (no anarchy) but not threatened by centralized power (no hierarchy). The challenge for the United States is to stay fully engaged in Europe and Japan and to welcome a gradual equalization of power and responsibility among the allies so that the allies never again resort to balancing power against one another by allying with Russia or China. If, in the twentieth century, Britain found a democratic successor in the United States as British power relatively waned, the United States has to find in the twenty-first century a successor in democratic Europe and Japan, as U.S. power relatively wanes. If it doesn't, it risks ceding a world to authoritarian powers and the greater potential of war. That's what happened when the United Kingdom passed off power to Wilhelmine Germany before America was ready to step in. And it's what happened again in Asia when imperial Japan replaced European colonialists before America was ready to step in. Forward engagement, keeping some U.S. troops in Europe and Japan as long as they want them, facilitates a more hopeful transition. The United States patiently pursues an eventual hand off of power to more responsible and self-confident democratic allies. On this point, conservative and liberal internationalists agree. The skepticism comes from realists and nationalists who believe that forward engagement delays the assumption of responsibility by the allies. They advocate pulling out US troops, being less engaged, and relying more on *offshore* alternatives.[48]

The second setting of ideological discomfort with the contemporary world is from authoritarian states, principally Russia and China (secondarily, Venezuela). This source of rivalry is well-known from traditional international affairs (nineteenth- and early twentieth-century Europe), but it is less dangerous today because of unipolarity. Russia and China, to be sure, seek to counterbalance American power. But unipolarity remains overwhelming in the medium term and buys time in which these countries can assimilate through engagement and integration. The ideological moderation of Russia and China may never occur (see tenet 9); it did not occur in Nazi Germany or Tojo Japan, even though both countries became highly modernized. But the United States and the West have no better pathway to follow. That authoritarian states of today feel as uncomfortable as they do in a democratically dominated world is a good sign. The appropriate response is not to ease that discomfort by lowering America's guard and disarming or abandoning alliances in Europe and Asia but by offering Russia and China the same bargain Reagan offered the former Soviet Union: compete in isolation or get rich through globalization, which makes possible but does not guarantee political liberalization (tenets 9 and 10).

The third setting of ideological rivalry is from rogue states, foremost Iran and North Korea. They, too, seek to counterbalance unipolar democratic power but, unlike Russia and China, do so through more opaque and totalitarian political systems and with less respect for international rules, especially non-proliferation and protection of civilians in combat. The problem is not with the non-proliferation regime. The argument that this regime is hypocritical or not observed by the nuclear powers themselves is not credible. The nuclear powers have systematically and dramatically reduced nuclear arms since the end of the Cold War, from the tens of thousands to less than 1,500. The idea that they now have to reduce them to zero to live up to their non-proliferation commitment is bogus. Non-proliferation never meant abandoning deterrence. As long as nuclear weapons play a deterrent role, they have to exist, unless the world wants to return to massive conventional forces for deterrence or succeeds in developing and sharing missile defense systems that do not deploy nuclear weapons (Reagan's dream). And as long as nuclear weapons exist, it matters in whose hands they exist. Free states (the United States, Britain, France) and stable states (Russia and China) currently manage the nuclear weapons regime. They make concessions to new nuclear states as the latter become free and stable (Israel and India). But they deny nuclear status to the rest. Iran and North Korea are not free, and Pakistan is neither free nor stable. In the case of non-proliferation, as in others, force and freedom cannot be separated. Free or stable states may have nuclear capabilities; unfree or unstable states may not.

The fourth setting of ideological rivalry in today's world is jihadism or Islamic extremism and the failed or failing states in which it breeds and trains. This setting involves the unstable revolutions in the Middle East and North Africa as well as in central, southwest, south, and Southeast Asia and the nonstate terrorist actors such as al-Qaeda who roam these regions and feed like locusts on instability. The problem is the scale of violence that can now be unleashed by small state or nonstate actors. Individual terrorists can bring down the Twin Towers or, with a single nuclear weapon, devastate a whole city. The connection between terrorists and rogue states, therefore, is not imaginary. The Iraq war offers two contradictory lessons: don't be too quick to connect the dots between terrorism and rogue states, *and* don't assume that rogue states are always rational and will never transfer weapons of mass destruction because they care too much about their own survival.[49] Saddam Hussein was not rational. He would still be in power today if he had simply shown the international community what he knew himself, that he had no nuclear weapons. To argue that he could not do so because he needed the myth of nuclear weapons to survive against Iran or among his own associates does not confirm his rationality; it subordinates that rationality to psychology and paranoia.

The greatest worry in this fourth setting at the moment is Pakistan. It is not only unstable and already a nuclear state, but unlike Iran it borders on an existing democratic state, India. If Pakistan came apart, it would endanger freedom in India and draw in the great powers of China and the United States. The same is true of North Korea, which also borders on another free state, South Korea. By this calculus, Pakistan takes priority over Afghanistan; democracy in the whole of Korea is more consequential than in China or Myanmar; and Turkey, which borders on democratic Greece, takes priority over Iraq. Turkey's alienation from both the United States and Israel since the Iraq war has been a high price to pay for that war. Losing freedom in Turkey cannot be compensated for by winning it in Iraq. Having made the investment to free Iraq, however, it seems worthwhile to try to preserve the gains in that country. Iraq is the first breach in the phalanx of authoritarian states rejecting Israel. If Iran now reclaims Iraq for rejectionist purposes, broadens its influence in Afghanistan as the United States leaves, and, backed by Russia, succeeds in saving or putting in place a Syrian regime that sponsors terrorism and opposes Israel, most of the gains won by the United States and Israel since the end of the Cold War will be lost. Add to that the uncertain outcome of the revolutions in the Middle East, especially in Egypt, Jordan, and the Gulf states, and the promise of freedom from the Arab Spring may turn ominously into the perils of despotism from an Arab Winter. American diplomacy needs a firmer grasp of what the priorities are and a strategy that deploys force and diplomacy continuously to address those priorities.

Integrate Force, Diplomacy, Sovereignty, and Markets

TENET 5: ALWAYS ARM DIPLOMACY WITH FORCE, AND EXPECT
TO USE SMALLER FORCE EARLIER AND MORE OFTEN RATHER
THAN LARGER FORCE LATER AND AS A LAST RESORT.

Given the continuing range of threats, the use of force to promote a freedom-forward diplomacy persists. Deterrence, preemption, and prevention before attacks—all remain vital for an effective diplomacy. Defense after attacks cannot suffice, not least because in the case of an attack with weapons of mass destruction it will be too late.

The use of smaller force early to prevent the use of larger force later is a highly controversial topic. Yet it is understudied and likely to remain so. A small amount of force to topple Saddam Hussein in 1991 would have saved the world enormous suffering and loss. But few advocated it then, and after the Iraq invasion in 2003 the public does not support it today. The use of preventive force must be acceptable to be effective, and it's hard to gain approval to prevent something that hasn't happened yet. Nevertheless, the point of scholarship is to raise tough, not easy, questions and ensure a debate of all options, not to pick one. That's why conservative internationalism brings something to the table that should be welcomed even if it is not inherently popular.

The use of force early, before and during negotiations, does not always provoke adversaries, as liberal internationalism believes. At times it denies hard-line adversaries the opportunity to make foreign policy gains outside negotiations and leads them to take more seriously the options being offered inside negotiations. It may also strengthen the hand of domestic groups that oppose hard-line governments in adversary countries. This was certainly the case for Reagan's early policies challenging the Soviet Union to an arms race. Once the costs of a Soviet hard-line response became clear, reformers like Gorbachev came to power and were in a stronger position to argue for disarmament.[50] This outcome is not always the case, however. If reformers control adversary governments, hard-line policies may discredit their détente policies and embolden hard-line domestic opponents.[51] By this calculus, Reagan's policies were perfectly tailored. He pursued hard-line policies toward Moscow during the days of Brezhnev and his hard-line antediluvian successors, Andropov and Chernenko. But he rejected the advice of hard-line advocates on the NSC to do the same after Gorbachev and reformers took office. He wanted to offer soft-line Soviet officials some way out of the box created by an arms race. He did not want just to run over them because even then diplomacy has to follow victory. The key for Reagan was not to win by force without negotiations but to win by negotiations from strength. He opposed détente in the 1970s when the United States was weak; he supported negotiations once the United States had refurbished its military and economic capabilities.

The use of force to arm, ally, and deter therefore continues to be the best solution to today's greatest threats. Those threats, as I have argued, still come from authoritarian states, principally Russia and China. NATO and U.S. alliances with Japan, South Korea, and Australia, and indirectly with Taiwan and India, therefore, remain freedom's firmest fortresses in tomorrow's world. The value of alliances was forgotten in the Afghanistan and Iraq wars, when the United States too quickly dismissed the

Article V appeals of its NATO allies. It must not be forgotten in the future. Force can be used acceptably only if free allies and the American public support it. And even if coalitions of the willing are necessary at times to lead the allies, they should always be designed to be followed as soon as possible by a reengagement of permanent alliance members.

Preemption and prevention gain heightened value to deal with threats from rogue states and terrorists. Deterrence, the threat of force to counterbalance existing capabilities, assumes rogue states have enough at stake in the existing system to act rationally. Like Saddam Hussein, they may not. Moreover, deterrence is not as effective in discouraging countries from acquiring capabilities, like nuclear weapons, as it is in containing countries once they have such capabilities. So if diplomacy doesn't work and the acquisition of nuclear weapons constitutes as U.S. and Israeli officials say a red line for action, preemption and prevention may be the only play to stop the spread of nuclear weapons. A distinction between preempting capability (striking once components are visible) and preempting weapons (striking only after a weapon is assembled) puts preemption on a hairline trigger because the time between the acquisition of capabilities and the acquisition of weapons is miniscule. As Israel has made clear, having the capability is too close to having the weapon. Thus prevention, striking before the capability or weapons are in hand, is the only solution. Otherwise the default position is containment, deterring an existing capability rather than preempting or preventing it. But if containment requires a credible threat to use force no less than prevention, why is the threat to contain believable when the threat to prevent was never forthcoming? Finally, preemption is impossible against terrorists with nuclear weapons because the threat they pose is not visible before it emerges. Here prevention is the only alternative. Yet prevention to use force against something that is not evident is the most difficult option to gain public support. Gaining that support is a function of accompanying diplomacy.

TENET 6: ALWAYS DISCIPLINE MILITARY FORCE WITH DIPLOMACY AND COMPROMISE.

The only way to gain support for the use of preventive force is to persuade the public that that force is disciplined by diplomacy and a willingness to compromise. Using economic and diplomatic sanctions is, of course, a first step. But it is not a separate step from using military force. George W. Bush, despite all the criticism of him by liberal internationalists, did one huge favor for liberal internationalists. He used the positioning and threat of military force to get the UN inspectors back into Iraq in fall 2002. Now the liberal internationalists had a diplomatic option to work with to implement sanctions that had not existed since 1998. They never acknowledged this debt of sanctions to the use of military force and backed continuing UN inspections as if U.S. forces could stay in the Gulf indefinitely.[52] They are not attuned to the use of force to leverage negotiations. They hope that multilateralism will compensate for force; that is, if states are "all in" against the rogue state, the economic sanctions will be strangling and the rogue state will have no choice but to make concessions in negotiations. They hope to shame the rogue state into compliance by isolation. But the rogue state has another alternative, as we have noted in this study: it can achieve its objectives *outside* negotiations while buying time to do that *through* negotiations.

Iran and North Korea are instructive cases. Economic sanctions have never been more complete, especially in the case of Iran, but they are not backed up by forces on the ground and still lack the full support of Russia and China. President Obama left no U.S. forces behind in Iraq, which might have checked Iranian influence in Iraq, Syria, and elsewhere. He gave Russia what it wanted in Europe (reduced emphasis on NATO missile defense) and China what it wanted in Asia (strategic partnership) but did not insist that Russia and China give the United States what it wanted in the Middle East, namely prevention of nuclear weapons in Iran through crippling oil and financial sanctions. Obama does not use leverage in negotiations either to curb the influence of adversaries outside negotiations (Iran) or to bargain with them inside negotiations (Russia and China). He's afraid that leverage disrupts negotiations. But Russia and China use military leverage to achieve results outside negotiations.

For example, Russia prefers the *political* status quo in the Middle East over the *military* status quo (acquisition of nuclear weapons by Iran). Iran and Syria are valuable allies even if they become nuclear powers. Russia gains from their policies to sponsor terrorism, support Russian bases in Syria, and meddle in Iraqi politics—all activities that help counter the influence of Israel, the United States, and moderate Arab regimes in the region. Similarly, on the Korean peninsula, China favors the *political* status quo more than the *military* status quo. The collapse of the Pyongyang regime is a bigger threat to China than nuclear weapons in North Korea. North Korea remains China's best hope for keeping democracy and U.S. alliances in Asia away from China's borders, even if North Korea becomes a nuclear power. In both cases, Russia and China accept the de facto acquisition of nuclear weapons by Iran and North Korea, as long as that status contributes to those countries helping counterbalance Western influence. Moscow and Beijing face two possible outcomes: one *through* negotiations that would prevent nuclear weapons in Iran and dismantle them in North Korea but weaken the capacity of those two regimes to oppose U.S. and Western power in the Middle East and Asia; and a second one *outside* negotiations that concedes a de facto nuclear capability to both Iran and North Korea (as the United States does to Israel) but preserves, indeed strengthens, their ability to oppose Western interests. So far they seem to be seeking the second outcome.

The toughest but most essential task in a conservative internationalist approach is to have a clear diplomatic goal and know when to compromise. That element seems to be missing in U.S. policy toward both Iran and North Korea. The goal is to stop the nuclear programs and have the two countries give them up the way South Africa or South Korea did. Iran and North Korea would retain the right to use nuclear power for peaceful purposes but under full safeguards by the International Atomic Energy Agency (IAEA) including inspections at undeclared locations. So far that prospect is not enough to gain Iranian consent. A broader set of incentives is needed, more on the scale of Reagan's offer to the Soviet Union if it gave up confrontation with the West—inclusion in the global economy and a place in the regional or global political system. Under both Presidents Bush and Obama that larger vision has been missing. Global trade and financial incentives, which wooed the Soviets, are obscured by a troubled world economy and gratuitous anti–free market rhetoric. The global economy and trading system sag under rising protectionist sentiments and soaring national debts. Rather than aggressively leading the global system toward a future of greater freedom and prosperity, as Reagan did, the United States is "leading from behind," retreating from the promotion of democracy and freer markets. Without that more aggressive vision, compromise is unlikely and probably undesirable because it can lead backward as well as forward. Statements by some U.S. officials suggest that steps backward may already be in the offing, namely an acceptance of containment rather than prevention of the spread of nuclear weapons.[53]

TENET 7: CONNECT FORCE AND DIPLOMACY TO DEMOCRATIC NATIONAL, NOT UNIVERSAL INTERNATIONAL, INSTITUTIONS.

If diplomacy is always backed by force and force is never used without diplomacy, the objective of both is to strengthen free national institutions, not universal institutions that include unfree regimes. Franklin Roosevelt's greatest contribution to security after World War II was to start thinking and planning for peace even before the United States entered the war. He understood that victory by force, even total victory, was, at best, only half the matter. The rest was diplomacy and postwar reconstruction. He erred by believing that force and freedom could be connected at the United Nations, an error Truman soon corrected. George W. Bush made his worst mistake not by initiating war against Iraq—a rational, albeit debatable, choice given that intelligence agencies around the world concluded at the time that Iraq had weapons of mass destruction—but by having no apparent plan to follow up the invasion with diplomatic initiatives and alienating both the UN *and* NATO in the process.[54] He had no plans for institutionalizing postwar gains, either at the national or regional level. Instead postwar reconstruction was conducted on the fly, and Iraq as well as Afghanistan drifted without a road map until force had to be used again through surges in both countries to salvage order, at least temporarily.

Some may argue that if you have to plan for every conceivable postwar contingency before you use force, force will never be used. But if that's true then plan quietly and in the background as leadership rallies the country to war. That's how Roosevelt did it. But planning has to be done, and if the expected postwar contingencies are that severe, it has to be done with the help of allies and others. "Coalitions of the willing" must become "coalitions of the enduring," and that means reintegrating temporary coalitions into more permanent alliances as soon as possible.

That would have been the benefit of accepting the Article V appeal of NATO allies in Afghanistan. The objection was that no one wanted to run another war like the one before it in Kosovo, through a committee of NATO members that had to approve every bombing target.[55] But in 2001 NATO had no forces to contribute immediately to the conflict in Afghanistan; hence the United States was free to run the early war as it saw fit. But had the Article V offer been accepted, NATO might have been brought into play a year or so later when it was needed to implement post-conflict reconstruction in Afghanistan (it was eventually anyway); and NATO might have been there in 2003 when the United States and Great Britain sought consensus to widen the war to invade Iraq. The U.S. failure to accept NATO Article V assistance in 2001 is one of the great mysteries and tragedies of the history of 9/11.

As it was, the fortunes of freedom flagged even as the rhetoric of freedom soared. After the Iraq invasion, Bush doubled down on Wilsonianism and declared "the ultimate goal of ending tyranny in the world." Like Wilson he pushed the envelope too far. And he connected the cause of freedom to neither international institutions nor free nation alliances. He wandered off into remote regions of despotism with no lifeline to free institutions anywhere. Iraq and Afghanistan proved that it is extremely difficult to spread freedom in parts of the world that are distant from freedom, especially when there is no plan for how to do so and only grudging support from other distant free countries to help.[56] The problem is not with the rhetoric. Conceivably Bush's rhetoric plucked the heartstrings of Arab citizens that broke out in the rhapsodies of the Arab Spring. The problem is with the application, the details and difficulties of developing democracy. Democracy is a long-term proposition, especially in parts of the world where religious beliefs impede rather than empower individualism (tenet 10). And if there is no realistic plan to follow up in that long-term struggle, the rhetoric disappoints and ultimately reverses itself. Under Obama democracy promotion has gone into hiding.[57]

The cost of not connecting freedom to existing democratic countries and institutions is high. It weakens the prospects of democracy in areas where it is further along and more likely to succeed. Arguably, as noted earlier, America's policies in Iraq and Afghanistan weakened prospects of democracy in Turkey and Pakistan. Turkey refused to allow U.S. forces to invade Iraq from Turkish territory; and Obama widened the war in Afghanistan to include Pakistan, coining the acronym AfPak, but is now leaving Afghanistan with relations with Pakistan at an all-time low. Democracy gained in Kabul will mean very little if democracy is lost in Islamabad.

Perhaps the greatest cost of America's prolonged and indecisive interventions in Iraq and Afghanistan has been borne by countries on Russia's European border. On this border and beyond in Russia, freedom has faltered. The need to secure Russia's support in both the Middle East (sanctions against Iran) and south Asia (supply routes for Afghanistan) led to concessions that endorsed Russia's reassertion of influence in its "sphere of privileged interest." Obama, to placate Russia, modified and delayed missile defense plans in Europe, alienating struggling Eastern European democracies expecting to host missile defense facilities. Through the New START Treaty he gave Moscow great power recognition and effectively condoned the permanent presence of Russian troops in Georgia and Moldova. Most of all, the United States ignored, for all practical purposes, the setbacks to democracy in Russia itself and Moscow's overt meddling in the democratic politics of its neighbors. Moscow-favoring groups are now stronger in the governments in Ukraine, Serbia, and Georgia. If Russia succeeds in strengthening its hand along its European, southwest, and Central Asian borders, while the United States effectively departs from Iraq and Afghanistan, the future of democracy will have taken a significant step back in the case of Europe where it matters the most.

In retrospect, the lessons to be learned from Afghanistan and Iraq are that the United States should be less ambitious to spread democracy in remote areas of the world. If it is necessary to invade these areas to deal with threats, after an attack on the United states or its allies as in the case of Afghanistan or before an attack as in the case of Iraq (and in the future possibly Iran), do so decisively but get in and get out as quickly as possible. Do not prioritize democracy promotion in these areas. Leave behind merely a somewhat more open and humane government than the one that existed before. Ascertain early what political leaders will be acceptable that will at least prevent the behavior that provoked the invasion in the first place.[58] Recognize that there are no ironclad guarantees and that in another two to five years the country may become unstable once again and a second round of intervention may be necessary. But if involvement in the first go-round is limited and the United States gets out while the

American people still support the intervention, the American people will be there when the next round comes. Then the United States can go back in if necessary and move the local government forward another notch toward more humane conditions.

For remote areas, this approach amounts to a *ratchet strategy* for spreading democracy. It calls for modest, incremental steps toward reforming despotic governments when threats and related opportunities arise in remote areas. By contrast, an *inkblot strategy* is reserved for promoting democracy in areas closer to the borders of free countries, such as Ukraine or potentially North Korea. In these cases, the United States and its European and Asian allies bring to bear the full weight of nearby secure and prosperous democratic societies. In competition with Moscow and Beijing, they draw troubled countries like magnets closer toward the free world. Without question the most effective policy to spread and stabilize democracy in central Europe after the Cold War was the expansion of NATO and the European Union. The same was true in Asia, albeit to a lesser extent, as the U.S. alliance with Japan anchored the struggle for democracy in South Korea and Taiwan and both alliances anchor freedom today in the confrontation with North Korea. Obama's "pivot" to Asia was confirmation that U.S. policy in Asia was neglected for too long in favor of south Asia and the Middle East. So too was U.S. policy in Europe, as NATO and economic recovery suffered from allied differences over conflicts in remote regions. America's and the free world's overall weakness diminishes the power of the magnet of freedom.

The danger now is that retreat from Iraq and Afghanistan will involve a more general retreat from Asia and Europe. After ten years of costly and at best uneven progress, the American people are fatigued. They want out, and Obama is getting out regardless, for the most part, of short- or long-term consequences. It is very possible that, as in the case of Vietnam, the governments left behind in Iraq and Afghanistan will fall or shift directions (as Iraq is already doing) in short order after American and allied forces leave, and the U.S. Congress will not permit any further interventions until the next threat or attack from these countries occurs. The United States will go through another military and political malaise like the one that followed Vietnam. Indeed, Obama's second term foreign policy is led by veterans of the Vietnam era who strongly favor retrenchment. If this leaning backward prevails, the American republic is likely to keep getting kicked by the familiar mule of cycling between military misuse and political retreat.

TENET 8: OPEN INTERNATIONAL MARKETS AND BORDERS.

This study has not dealt extensively with international economic measures to implement American foreign policy.[59] It has been a study about the use of force. But no policy has been more important in the construction of the peaceful postwar international system by the United States than free trade. Free trade has empowered one country or group of countries after another to increase their wealth and take their place alongside the United States at the festival table of globalization. China is the latest rising power to be invited to this cornucopia. And it poses today without doubt the greatest potential challenge to the unipolar world of democratic community. But because threats are smaller in a unipolar environment, international institutions have an unprecedented opportunity to assimilate China as well.[60] Russia poses a lesser threat, even though it recently joined the WTO, because it has yet to make the economic changes and embrace foreign investment the way China has. Its prospects of great power status are limited by its largely resource-driven economy. If the price of oil drops again dramatically, as it did in the 1990s, Russia drops with it. And the Muslim world in which jihadism breeds is only beginning to embark on the long struggle to modernize and adapt its institutions and values to participate in global markets.

World markets remain the "ace in the hole" of global hopes of peace. But you would never know it from the malaise afflicting the global economy in 2013. Europe is drowning in a sea of sovereign debt, the United States is slumped in the slowest recovery in history and building up a dam of debt to swamp its future prospects, and the emerging countries that have cushioned global markets in the recent downturn, including China, are slowing down and heading potentially for significant road bumps in the future.

The fault, if you listen to the political rhetoric, lies with global banking. It has spawned an epidemic of risky financial instruments that added nothing to global well-being but padded the bottom lines of "fat-cat bankers." As a result, inequality soared and the middle class dwindled. This partisan-driven rhetoric gets one point right. Private global banking is new; it did not exist before the 1970s. Almost all international finance was provided by governments. The oil crises ended that era and spawned offshore private capital markets that were gradually liberalized during the 1980s. These markets then mobilized the enormous savings from emerging countries like China and India that fueled the unprecedented expansion and growth of world markets noted earlier.

But that's where the political rhetoric misfires. It implies that only capitalists and bankers benefited. Just the opposite is true. The world has never seen a leveling of benefits as large and pervasive as during the recent era of globalization. The mobilization of global savings added enormous wealth to global well-being, and that wealth was spread more equally than ever before. A middle class of nearly one billion people sprouted in China, India, Brazil, Russia, and other developing countries. And American middle-class households jumped into higher income categories, not lower ones.[61] The poor in America also benefited. From 1960 to 2010, poverty in the United States, measured in terms of consumption rather than income, dropped 26.4 percentage points, 8.5 percentage points after 1980.[62]

Was it all wiped out by the global financial crisis of 2008–9? Hardly. Yes, the world did not regulate global financial markets in a timely manner, a joint failing of the Clinton and Bush administrations as well as the world community at large. And now it should. But it should also be careful not to throw the baby out with the bathwater. Trade markets were new in the early twentieth century, and they caused crises. But the world community figured out a way to encourage not strangle trade, and world trade expanded dramatically after World War II. That trade expansion made it necessary in turn to liberalize financial markets. Now those markets have experienced crises. Like trade markets in the 1930s, they need to be regulated but they also need to be nurtured and expanded. Without expanding capital markets, globalization dies.

While global institutions struggle, regional organizations take up the slack. Although divided by the Iraq war, NATO continues to provide vital functions—suppressing genocide in Libya, fighting terrorism in Afghanistan (at least until 2014), and training local forces in Iraq (which terminated in December 2011) and other countries around the world. The European Union marches steadily onward, albeit creakingly, moving past a constitutional crisis in 2005 and assuming greater civilian responsibilities in out-of-area conflicts such as Kosovo and Afghanistan. In 2012 it received the Nobel Prize, a well-deserved recognition of its unprecedented success.[63] Asia is experiencing a renaissance of regional institutions, even though institutional legalism is less common in Asia than in the West.[64] And regional free trade agreements, such as NAFTA, shoulder on in Latin America, although initiatives to expand such as the Free Trade Agreement for the Americas (FTAA) languish amid the "angst" of global recession.

Observe Constraints of Domestic Politics

TENET 9: DON'T EXPECT INTERNATIONAL MARKETS TO LIBERALIZE DOMESTIC POLITICS; ALWAYS KEEP YOUR POWDER DRY.

Since World War II the international system has undergone a spectacular increase of both markets and democracy. Are the two phenomna linked? At some level they undoubtedly are. But cuntries have modernized before and not liberalized. Interwar Germany and Japan are prime examples. There are no guarantees in world affairs. And most recently, the picture is more sobering.

Democracy still dominates but, as already noted, is experiencing a blowback. Recent upheavals in the Middle East—Tunisia, Egypt, Libya, Yemen, and Bahrain—signal renewed aspirations for freedom, and incremental improvements toward more representative governments in that region are possible. Nevertheless, if forces hostile to freedom hijack the Arab Spring and democratic developments elsewhere, power balancing will become more intense and opportunities for international institutions, especially international markets, more limited. At the extreme, the world will drift back toward ideological divisions in which power and institutions rival one another across the globe.

That could happen if China becomes a power equal to the United States, remains authoritarian, and becomes intensely nationalist. Everything depends then on how China evolves internally. Will it liberalize politically?[65] The West has wagered in effect that the global trading and financial system led by the WTO and IMF will mediate economic and political liberalization in China. The bet is that when China reaches a more equitable (and potentially threatening) level of power, it will no longer be so authoritarian or inaccessible that it cannot be integrated into a world system that does not differ significantly in substance from the present one. So far the bet is still on. China is certainly a freer country economically than ever before, but politics, especially local politics, remains harshly corrupt and crushing.[66]

It could also happen if jihadist ideology becomes rooted in a number of important states in the Middle East (Iran, Egypt) or south Asia (Pakistan) and, like communism in Russia, sparks a regional if not global confrontation intensified by the spread of weapons of mass destruction. But the Islamic world is not united or committed to modernization, as China is. It still has a long way to go to establish the prerequisites of modern growth—individual entrepreneurship, employment for women, modern banking systems, openness to foreign investment, and religious pluralism. The West should encourage these developments. A great failing in the Middle East has been not to follow up peace—for example, between Egypt and Israel—with economic and commercial interdependence. But Islam has to come to terms internally with modernization. Until it does, its prospects for wealth and integration with the West are limited.

At the moment, global economic institutions still hold out the best promise of a better life for all. But these institutions could atrophy and decline under the impact of the current economic crisis and leadership gap. Current attitudes, which seem oblivious to unprecedented global growth from 1980 to the present, now favor financial regulation and trade protectionism. Nothing could damage the prospects of future peace more than reversing the commitments of the past thirty years to open market policies.

TENET 10: RESPECT CULTURAL AND NATIONAL DIVERSITY.

The ratchet and inkblot strategies for spreading democracy follow from the conservative internationalist's intuition that it is hard to change a nation's culture, especially in the absence of nearby or relevant models of political freedom. Freedom remains universal. There is no argument here that democracy is unsuitable for certain societies. But the path to freedom is cultural, and culture is procrustean. Like realists, conservative internationalists respect diversity and national sovereignty.

A big part of culture is religion. Some religions may be more helpful to democratic development than others. Protestantism was a big boost for democracy in the West because it emancipated individuals from the hierarchy of the church and it gave a heavenly calling to earthly pursuits, seeing God's hand in the rewards of secular undertakings.[67] But democracy does not always develop as it did in the West, bottom up from individual rights to limited government. It can also develop from the top down through a competition among elites that opens political space for a wider middle class, as it did in Japan, South Korea, and elsewhere.[68] Liberal internationalists spotlight the top-down or government-led approach, conservative internationalists the bottom-up or civil society-led approach. The two groups disagree mostly about when and how to include nondemocratic states.

What is the critical tripwire between democracies and nondemocracies? If culture matters, aren't all countries free to decide for themselves what is democracy?[69] Well, up to a point, yes. But the essence of democracy is widespread participation and rotation of opposing groups in power peacefully. Hence elite systems unless they progressively widen the franchise are not democratic. And one-party systems that rotate power among factions outside the public square are also not democratic. Democracy may bend to culture but it does not break. It rises above culture to affirm the rights of all individuals to govern themselves through opposing political groups that compete fairly and rotate peacefully in power.

TENET 11: ALWAYS TRUST THE PEOPLE TO DETERMINE
THE LIMITS OF BOTH FREEDOM AND FORCE.

The choice lies with the people of free societies. From the perspective outlined in this book, neither institutions nor power substitutes for moral and political leadership. Ideological orientations ultimately trump institutional and material realities. Human beings are free to invent, choose, and evaluate new ideas and make choices that widen or narrow the prospects of both market modernization and democratic development. Modernization is not an elixir nor is it inevitable, and democracy may be corrupted or rejected. Much depends, therefore, on the renewal of ideas in the democratic world. Revolutionaries, like most contemporary terrorists, are not poor or uneducated. They are motivated by rational and moral ideas, which they invent, assess, and choose. They can be defeated only by comparable moral energy and courage in democracies. The balance of such initiatives, not power or institutional momentum, will determine the prospects for future prosperity and global peace.

Coda

The United States still carries the greatest responsibility. It remains the most wealthy and most free country in the world. Its position is exceptionalist. The question is: will its leadership and people continue to choose to be exceptionalist?[70] Conservative internationalism offers a way to think about American exceptionalism that does not ignore moral hubris or material limitations. It unequivocally supports the spread of freedom but does it under the discipline of responding to threats. If threats are smaller, as they are today, it refrains from invoking global crusades. The world is likely to remain threatening enough. On this score, conservatives can listen closely to their realist brethren. But American classical liberals, which include both conservative and liberal internationalists, expect something more than realists offer. The broad consensus in American foreign policy is to support freedom in distant lands, to push the envelope toward more and more democratic nations. That is best done in selected places, not everywhere.

Today's immediate threats come from remote regions, not directly from great powers as during the Cold War. They come from terrorism and rogue and weak states in regions remote from existing free countries—North Africa, the Middle East, and southwest, south, and Southeast Asia. Those threats have to be defeated, but they are not an existential threat to the United States unless they are exploited by the great powers of China and Russia, which exist along the borders of existing freedom. With a ratchet strategy toward terrorism, America can keep its military commitments limited in remote regions while it pursues an inkblot strategy to strengthen democracy closer to Russia and China. Inkblot policies do not require a reconfiguration of American military or civilian agencies for nation-building. They are the policies of free trade and capitalist investment that go on anyway in the world economy of free nations. Thus ratchet and inkblot strategies do not impose an excessive burden on American resources. Nor do they constitute moral imperialism. America and the free world are giving authoritarian powers such as China a chance to develop if they can and liberalize if they choose.

In the end, America's choices are not fundamentally material; they are political. Resources and institutions constrain actions, but ideas expand resources and reform institutions. America corrected what was considered impossible debt in the 1990s by a few "big" budget compromises and a peace dividend that reflected the payoff of conservative internationalist policies that defeated the Soviet Union. It can do so again in the years ahead. Modest adjustments in entitlements would resolve the biggest part of the budget dilemma, and the United States does not face an existential adversary as formidable as the former Soviet Union that requires maximum defense expenditures. That is, *not yet,* which makes even more imperative the forward-leaning policies recommended in this study—dealing aggressively but quickly with terrorist and rogue threats in regions remote from freedom while pressing hard for freedom in regions closer to China and Russia. If freedom fails on the borders of existing freedom, it will do the most harm. And if it succeeds, it will do the most good to alter the long-term balance of freedom and tyranny and to ensure that terrorism and proliferation do not link up someday to pose an existential threat to the West.

Notes

INTRODUCTION: TRADITIONS OF THE EAGLE

1. George McKee Elsey, *An Unplanned Life: A Memoir* (Columbia: University of Missouri Press, 2005), 93–94.

2. For this account, see Clark Clifford with Richard Holbrooke, *Counsel to the President: A Memoir* (New York: Random House, 1991), 102.

3. Already by the late eighteenth century, the United States had a wider franchise and higher standard of living than any European country. See Alexander Keyssar, *The Right to Vote: The Contested History of Democracy in the United States* (New York: Basic Books, 2000), 24; and John J. McCusker and Russell R. Menard, *The Economy of British America, 1607–1789* (Chapel Hill: University of North Carolina Press, 1985), 51–60, 280–81.

4. Thomas Jefferson made this point early on: "We are pointing out the way to struggling nations who wish, like us, to emerge from their tyrannies." Quoted in Robert Kagan, *Dangerous Nation* (New York: Knopf, 2006), 43. In 2012, a survey by the Chicago Council on Foreign Affairs found that "Americans still consider the United States as the greatest and most influential country in the world." *Foreign Policy in the New Millennium* (Chicago Council on Global Affairs, 2012).

5. Quoted in Peggy Noonan, *When Character Was King: A Story of Ronald Reagan* (New York: Viking, 2001), 317.

6. George P. Shultz, *Turmoil and Triumph: My Years as Secretary of State* (New York: Charles Scribner's Sons, 1993), 345.

CHAPTER 1: WHAT IS CONSERVATIVE INTERNATIONALISM?

1. This is not a book about academic or media bias. But the facts are indisputable. Polls show consistently that liberals dominate the two institutions. Liberals don't deny this reality; they just argue that it doesn't matter because they are objective. For one of the most careful studies of liberal bias, see Timothy J. Groseclose, *Left Turn: How Liberal Media Bias Distorts the American Mind* (New York: St. Martin's Press, 2011).

2. Though I am interested in the causal role of ideas, my methods are rationalist, not constructivist. Description, even thick description, provides understanding at some level but not a critical evaluation of alternative ideas.

3. Louis Hartz, *The Liberal Tradition in America: An Interpretation of American Political Thought since the Revolution* (New York: Harcourt, Brace and World, 1955).

4. The original Declaration uses the term "men," as the vernacular at the time meaning "all human beings."

5. Russell Kirk, *The Conservative Mind: From Burke to Eliot*, 7th ed. (1953; Washington, DC: Regnery Publishing, 2001), 72. Samuel Eliot Morison also writes that Americans "fought not to *obtain* freedom but to *confirm* the freedom they already had or claimed." *The Oxford History of the American People* (New York: New American Library, 1972), 1:235. See also Daniel H. Deudney, *Bounding Power: Republican Security Theory from the Polis to the Global Village* (Princeton: Princeton University Press, 2007), 177–78.

6. Alexander Keyssar, *The Right to Vote: The Contested History of Democracy in the United States* (New York: Basic Books, 2000), 24.

7. Daniel Boorstin agrees: "Our history has fitted us, even against our will, to understand the meaning of conservatism. We have become exemplars of the community of history and of the fruits which come from cultivating institutions suited to a time and place, in continuity with the past." See *The Genius of American Politics* (Chicago: University of Chicago Press, 1953), 6.

8. For racial and religious critiques of American liberalism, see, among others, Stephen Skowronek, "The Reassociation of Ideas and Purposes: Racism, Liberalism, and the American Political Tradition," *American Political Science Review* 100, 3 (August 2006), 385–401; Desmond S. King and Rogers M. Smith, *A House Still Divided: Race and Politics in Obama's America* (Princeton: Princeton University Press, 2011); Desmond King and Rogers Smith, "Racial Orders in American Political Development," *American Political Science Review* 99, 1 (February 2005): 75–92; Rogers Smith, *Civic Ideals: Conflicting Visions of Citizenship in the U.S. History* (New Haven: Yale University Press, 1997); and Michael H. Hunt, *Ideology and U.S. Foreign Policy* (New Haven: Yale University Press, 1987).

9. See Peter J. Katzenstein, "'Walls' between 'Those People'? Contrasting Perspectives on World Politics," *Perspectives on Politics* 8, 1 (March 2010): 11–25; and Peter J. Katzenstein, "The West as Anglo-America" and "Many Wests and Polymorphic Globalism," in Katzenstein, ed., *Anglo-America and Its Discontents: Civilizational Identities beyond East and West* (New York: Routledge, 2012), 1–31 and 207–48, respectively. I am especially indebted to Peter, who has kept my feet to the fire with regard to what he considers to be Panglossian interpretations of the American story.

10. Here I side with Seymour Martin Lipset, who affirms the creedal source of American identity, and disagree with Samuel Huntington, who doubts it. See Seymour Martin Lipset, *American Exceptionalism: A Double-Edged Sword* (New York: W. W. Norton, 1997); and Samuel P. Huntington, *Who Are We? The Challenges to America's National Identity* (New York: Simon and Schuster, 2005). Huntington once defined conservatism as a positional not substantive ideology, meaning it stood for defending existing institutions in any era regardless of the ideas those institutions represented. It was therefore principally useful, in Huntington's view, in defense of liberal institutions during the Cold War. See "Conservatism as an Ideology," *American Political Science Review* 51, 2 (June 1957): 454–73.

11. The quotations are from the Douglas-Lincoln debates (emphasis in original). See Doris Kearns Goodwin, *Team of Rivals: The Political Genius of Abraham Lincoln* (New York: Simon and Schuster, 2005), 167.

12. President Lyndon B. Johnson, "To Fulfill These Rights," Commencement Address at Howard University, June 4, 1965, http://www.lbjlib.utexas.edu /johnson/archives.hom/speeches.hom/650604.asp.

13. Aristotle wrote: "equality is of two kinds, numerical and proportional; . . . men agree that justice in the abstract is proportion, but they differ in that some think that if they are equal in any respect they are equal absolutely, others that if they are unequal in any respect they should be unequal in all." See *Politics*, translated by Benjamin Jowett, book 5, part 1, http://classics.mit.edu/Aristotle /politics.5.five.html.

14. Isaiah Berlin once famously identified this difference as "negative" (conservative) versus "positive" (liberal) liberty. See *Two Concepts of Liberty* (Gloucestershire, England: Clarendon Press, 1959). I prefer the more neutral distinction between "individual" and "social" liberty. See Henry R. Nau, "No Enemies on the Right," *The National Interest* 78 (Winter 2004–5): 19–29.

15. These differences are as old as the republic, dating back as we see in chapters 4 and 5 to Republican conflicts with Federalists and Democratic conflicts with Whigs.

16. Two examples are welfare programs, such as the Aid to Families with Dependent Children, which a conservative Congress and liberal president ended in 1996, and entitlement programs today that encourage disability benefits. See Nicholas Eberstadt, *A Nation of Takers: America's Entitlement Epidemic* (West Conshohocken, PA: Templeton Press, 2012).

17. Hillary Rodham Clinton, *It Takes a Village* (New York: Simon and Schuster, 2006).

18. See First Inaugural Address, Washington, DC, March 4, 1801, http://www .bartleby.com/124/pres16.html. The liberal refrain, famously phrased by James Madison in Federalist Paper #51, is: "If men were angels, no government would be necessary." Both individuals (civil society) and government are obviously imperfect and therefore, as this study argues, need competition within and between them to achieve the best balance between liberty and equality. For Federalist Paper #51, see http://www.constitution.org/fed/federa51.htm.

19. As one exhaustive study of religion in America concludes: "While there are notable exceptions, the most highly religious Americans are likely to be Republican; Democrats predominate among those who are least religious." See Robert D. Putnam and David E. Campbell, *American Grace: How Religion Divides and Unites Us* (New York: Simon and Schuster, 2010), 369.

20. Values limit what we study because we can't study everything, what facts we consider because we can't consider all facts, and what causal conclusions we draw because identical facts can be interpreted in multiple ways. For my discussion of this issue, see "The Scholar and the Policy-Maker," in Christian Reus-Smit and Duncan Snidal, eds., *The Oxford Handbook of International Affairs* (New York: Oxford University Press, 2008), 635–48.

21. As Michael Gerson, speechwriter to George W. Bush, notes, "Politics can be studied by methods informed by science. But it remains a division of the humanities . . . the study of justice, moral philosophy and the common good." See "The Trouble with a Silver Lining," *Washington Post*, September 6, 2012, A17.

22. Take a look, for example, at the election of 1800, eventually decided after 36 ballots in the House of Representatives. John Ferling, *Adams vs. Jefferson: The Tumultuous Election of 1800* (New York: Oxford University Press, 2004).

23. President Obama told a House Republican conference in January 2010: "compared to other countries, the differences between the two major parties on most issues is [*sic*] not as big as it's represented." See http://www.pbs.org/news hour/bb/politics/jan-june10/obama_01-29.html.

24. Civility is a separate matter, but it is not unaffected by our understanding of partisanship. If we consider alternatives to be necessary and not polarizing, we are more likely to be civil. See Harvey Mansfield, "Partisanship Isn't Enough (but it is essential)," *The Weekly Standard* 15, 48 (September 13, 2010).

25. On this point, see my discussion with David A. Lake, "Why 'Isms' Are Evil: Theory, Epistemology, and Academic Sects as Impediments to Understanding and Progress" and my response, "No Alternative to 'Isms,'" *International Studies Quarterly* 55, 2 (June 2011): 465–80 and 487–91, respectively.

26. Indeed, it is useful to recall that in this period the Islamic world translated and preserved Western classics.

27. The seminal classical liberal contributions are still John Locke, *Second Treatise of Government* (1690; Indianapolis: Hackett Publishing, 1980, ed. C. B. Macpherson); and Adam Smith, *An Inquiry into the Nature and Causes of the Wealth of Nations* (1776; New York: Oxford University Press, 1993, ed. Kathryn Sutherland).

28. The historian A. J. P. Taylor wrote in November 1945: "Nobody in Europe believes in the American way of life—that is, private enterprise." Quoted in Melvyn P. Leffler, *For the Soul of Mankind: The United States, the Soviet Union, and the Cold War* (New York: Hill and Wang, 2007), 59.

29. This reality explains in part why American conservatives frighten many Europeans and European socialists frighten many Americans.

30. Instead American conservatism uses Enlightenment standards to judge pre-Enlightenment times. As Peter Berkowitz notes, "conservatives look for opportunity to preserve as much premodernity as is good and consistent with modern liberalism." See introduction to Berkowitz, ed., *Varieties of Conservatism in America* (Stanford: Hoover Institution, 2004), xvi.

31. Robert Nash, *The Conservative Intellectual Movement in America: Since 1945* (New York: Basic Books, 1976); Frank S. Meyer, ed., *What Is Conservatism* (New York: Holt, Rinehart and Winston, 1964). For a similar breakdown of traditional, social, and neoconservatism as outlined in this study, see Peter Berkowitz, introduction to Berkowitz, ed., *Varieties of Conservatism*, xiii–xxii.

32. Liberals, for the most part, accept these distinctions between conservatives and liberals. See Sam Tanenhaus, liberal editor of the *New York Times Book Review* and *Week in Review*, "Conservatism Is Dead: An Intellectual Autopsy of the Movement," *The New Republic*, February 18, 2009, http://www.tnr.com /article/politics/conservatism-dead; and a survey of liberal assessments of conservatives by Thomas B. Edsall, "What the Right Gets Right," *New York Times*, January 15, 2012, http://campaignstops.blogs.nytimes.com/2012/01/15/what-the -right-gets-right/.

33. The seminal libertarian works are novels by Ayn Rand, *The Fountainhead* (Indianapolis: Bobbs-Merrill, 1943) and *Atlas Shrugged* (New York: Random House, 1957).

34. On the role of religion, see William F. Buckley, *God and Man at Yale* (Chicago: Henry Regnery Company, 1951); and on the role of natural rights, see Leo Strauss, *Natural Right and History* (Chicago: University of Chicago Press, 1953).

35. There is a distinction between a holder of public office believing and drawing personal guidance from religion, which is acceptable under the Constitution (think of Lincoln who read and quoted the Bible regularly), and using that office to "establish" a particular religion, which is unacceptable under the Constitution.

36. As a result, leading conservatives who reject activist government, such as Friedrich A. Hayek, sometimes identify themselves as liberals. See note 48 in this chapter and Hayek, *The Constitution of Liberty* (Chicago: University of Chicago Press, 1960).

37. The phrase was used most memorably by William H. Seward, the New York senator and Lincoln's secretary of state, in debates before the Civil War. Goodwin, *Team of Rivals*, 146. See also Michael Gerson, "Why Reform Conservatism Deserves a Chance," *Washington Post*, April 30, 2012, http://www .washingtonpost.com/opinions/why-paul-ryans-reform-conservatism-deserves-a -chance/2012/04/30/gIQAikjdsT_story.html.

38. See Kevin Phillips, *The Emerging Republican Majority* (New Rochelle, NY: Arlington House, 1969); and Michael J. Gerson, *Heroic Conservatism: Why Republicans Need to Embrace America's Ideals (And Why They Deserve to Fail if They Don't)* (New York: HarperOne, 2007). As Gerson writes, "[George W.] Bush was willing to use active government as an instrument of reform. . . . The objective, he felt, was not 'small' government or 'big' government, but effective government" (62).

39. In the midst of the Terri Schiavo case in 2005, in which a Republican Congress sought to intervene in end-of-life decisions, the vast majority of conservative voters, in most cases three-quarters, considered such intervention inappropriate. See Mickey Edwards, *Reclaiming Conservatism* (New York: Oxford University Press, 2008), 152. Studies show that Christians, even fundamentalist Christians, are exceptionally tolerant. Putnam and Campbell, *American Grace*, 516–51.

40. Richard Hofstadter, *The American Political Tradition and the Men Who Made It* (New York: Knopf, 1948).

41. In the great debates about slavery, Lincoln took the reform conservative view that some things are right even if a majority thinks otherwise, while Stephen Douglas took the majoritarian view that the people decide by popular sovereignty whether slavery is right or wrong.

42. Many remained Democrats. See Jeane Kirkpatrick, "Why We Don't Become Republicans," *Common Sense* 2 (Fall 1979): 27–35.

43. James Ppiereson, "Conservative Nation," *The National Interest* 110 (November/December 2010): 56. See also Irving Kristol, "A Conservative Welfare State," in Irwin Stelzer, *The Neocon Reader* (New York: Grove Press, 2004), who writes, "the welfare state is with us, for better or worse, and . . . conservatives should try to make it better rather than worse" (145).

44. Again, as Kristol writes, "we should figure out what we want before we calculate what we can afford." See "A Conservative Welfare State," 145. Francis Fukuyama critiques the social engineering zeal of neoconservatism in *America at the Crossroads: Democracy, Power, and the Neo-Conservative Legacy* (New Haven: Yale University Press, 2006).

45. It follows that reform conservatives take Hamilton as their model, while libertarians and economic conservatives take Jefferson as their model. See the different interpretations of these two founding fathers in Walter Russell Mead, *Special Providence: American Foreign Policy and How It Changed the World* (New York: Routledge, 2002), chapter 6 and 331; and Kagan, *Dangerous Nation*, chapter 4, 127–28, 183–84.

46. Andrew Sullivan, *The Conservative Soul: How We Lost It, How to Get It Back* (New York: HarperCollins, 2006). As John Micklethwait and Adrian Wooldridge write, "Libertarians put individual choice at the heart of their thinking; traditionalists cite received wisdom." See *The Right Nation: Conservative Power in America* (London: Penguin, 2004), 252.

47. Edwards, *Reclaiming Conservatism*; Andrew Sullivan, "Crisis of Faith: How Fundamentalism Is Splitting the GOP," *The New Republic* 232, 16/17 (May 2, 2005): 16–23; Gerson, *Heroic Conservatism*, 151–80.

48. This was the reason Hayek always considered himself a liberal (mistakenly as defined in this study because Hayek's redline was clearly limited government); see Friedrich A. Hayek, "Why I Am Not a Conservative," in Frank S. Meyer, ed., *What Is Conservatism?* (New York: Holt, Rinehart and Winston, 1964), 88–107.

49. Some historians use the label "conservative internationalists" to refer to realists, who are internationalist in scope but not in substance, such as Henry Cabot Lodge and other members of the League to Enforce Peace before World War I. See Thomas J. Knock, *To End All Wars: Woodrow Wilson and the Quest for a New World Order* (New York: Oxford University Press, 1992), chapter 4, especially 57. See also Colin Dueck, *Hard Line: The Republican Party and U.S. Foreign Policy since World War II* (Princeton: Princeton University Press, 2010), especially chapter 1 and conclusion.

50. Niccolò Machiavelli, *The Prince*, trans. George Bull (London: Penguin, 1961).

51. Mead, *Special Providence*. Mead explicitly bans realism to Europe. The closest one gets to realism in America, according to Mead, is Hamiltonian economic mercantilism. See also Micklethwait and Wooldridge, who write: "[M] odern American conservatism is a different beast from traditional conservatism: it has strains of individualism, populism, and optimism that would have flummoxed Burke or Churchill." See *The Right Nation*, 252.

52. By contrast, the unification of Germany under the great German statesman Otto von Bismarck was mostly about the balance of power, resolving the old question of whether Prussia or Austria, both aristocratic monarchies (no difference in domestic regimes), would lead the German confederation.

53. That is obvious in repeated debates inside both the Republican and Democratic parties. For example, conservative realists and nationalists opposed U.S. humanitarian intervention in Libya and keeping sizable U.S. forces in Iraq and Af-

ghanistan, while conservative internationalists, including neoconservatives, supported these ventures. Similarly, liberal nationalists and realists urged Obama to end foreign wars immediately, while liberal internationalists prodded him to wage a third foreign war in Libya.

54. The two most prominent ones are generated by Freedom House and the Polity IV Project.

55. G. John Ikenberry, "Introduction: Woodrow Wilson, the Bush Administration, and the Future of Liberal Internationalism," in G. John Ikenberry, Thomas J. Knock, Anne-Marie Slaughter, and Tony Smith, *The Crisis of American Foreign Policy: Wilsonianism in the Twenty-First Century* (Princeton: Princeton University Press, 2009), 16. Multilateralism, synonymous with international institutions, is central to liberal internationalist thought, but unilateralism, which critics associate with neoconservatism, is more central to nationalist than conservative internationalist thought. See chapter 2.

56. President Kennedy noted these limits in a letter to Nikita Khrushchev in 1961: "our respective social systems and general philosophies of life . . . create a great gulf in communications because language cannot mean the same thing on both sides unless it is related to some underlying purpose." Quoted in Marl L. Haas, *The Ideological Origins of Great Power Politics, 1789–1989* (Ithaca: Cornell University Press, 2005), 13.

57. John Owen shows, for example, that military intervention to change domestic regimes is just as common in world politics over the past five hundred years as the use of force to balance power. See John M. Owen IV, *The Clash of Ideas in World Politics: Transnational Networks, States, and Regime Change, 1510–2010* (Princeton: Princeton University Press, 2010), 2–3; for other studies that take into account both ideological and material competition in world affairs, see Haas, *Ideological Origins*; Robert J. Lieber, *Power and Willpower in the American Future: Why the United States Is Not Destined to Decline* (New York: Cambridge University Press, 2012); Thomas Risse-Kappen, *Cooperation among Democracies: The European Influence on U.S. Foreign Policy* (Princeton: Princeton University Press, 1995); Henry R. Nau, *At Home Abroad: Identity and Power in American Foreign Policy* (Ithaca: Cornell University Press, 2002); and Henry R. Nau, *The Myth of America's Decline: Leading the World Economy into the 1990s* (New York: Oxford University Press, 1990).

58. See Elizabeth N. Saunders, *Leaders at War: How Presidents Shape Military Interventions* (Ithaca: Cornell University Press, 2011).

59. Ole R. Holsti, *Public Opinion and American Foreign Policy* (Ann Arbor: University of Michigan Press, 2004), 124–25.

60. These traditions exist in all countries though they may go by different names. See Henry R. Nau and Deepa Ollapally, eds., *Worldviews of Aspiring Powers: Domestic Foreign Policy Debates in China, India, Iran, Japan, and Russia* (New York: Oxford University Press, 2012). The traditions may also be subdivided. The realist school, for example, includes defensive, offensive, classical, and other types of realism. See Henry R. Nau, "Realism," in Steven W. Hook and Christopher M. Jones, eds., *Routledge Handbook of American Foreign Policy* (New York: Routledge, 2012), 61–75.

61. The axes of any matrix spark controversy. The horizontal axis of Figure 1.2 could be multilateralism versus unilateralism, strong versus weak states, or liberal versus conservative. The first alternative does not change the relative propensity of liberal and conservative internationalists to use force because liberal internationalists are constrained by the need to find multilateral consensus. The second alternative simply reflects the realist view that relative power determines a state's goals in foreign affairs. And the third alternative I discuss when I map liberal and conservative positions on the foreign policy traditions. The vertical axis could also be different—for example, status quo versus transformative. But that begs the question of transformative toward what. Spreading freedom makes the direction of transformation explicit and is central to both liberal and conservative internationalism. I am indebted to Michael Desch, David Lake, and Peter Trubowitz for raising questions that helped me clarify these points.

62. For thoughtful reassessments of Reagan coming out of the academic community, see, among others, John Lewis Gaddis, *Strategies of Containment: A Critical Appraisal of American National Security Policy during the Cold War*, rev. ed. (New York: Oxford University Press, 2005); and Sean Wilentz, *The Age of Reagan: A History, 1974–2008* (New York: Harper, 2008).

63. See Henry Kissinger, *Diplomacy* (New York: Simon and Schuster, 1994), 764–65.

64. Claiming Reagan for realist and liberal internationalist traditions are, respectively, Stefan Halper and Jonathan Clarke, *America Alone: The Neo-Conservatives and the Global Order* (Cambridge: Cambridge University Press, 2004); and Ivo H. Daalder and James M. Lindsay, *America Unbound: The Bush Revolution in Foreign Policy* (Washington, DC: Brookings Institution, 2003).

65. Jacob Heilbrunn, "Whose Reagan? A Uniter, Not a Divider," *The National Interest*, no. 90 (July/August 2007), 79–87. Heilbrunn, a realist, calls on conservatives "to get over their Reagan fixation" (87). Michael Gerson counsels Republicans to "move beyond Reagan era nostalgia." See "What's Ailing the GOP," *Washington Post*, February 22, 2013, A21.

66. James Mann, *Rise of the Vulcans: The History of Bush's War Cabinet* (New York: Penguin, 2004); Jacob Heilbrunn, *They Knew They Were Right: The Rise of the Neocons* (New York: Doubleday, 2008).

67. On the Tea Party, see Walter Russell Mead, "The Tea Party and American Foreign Policy: What Populism Means for Globalism," *Foreign Affairs* 90, 2 (March/April 2011): 28–45.

68. For a similar breakdown of conservative foreign policy groups, see Dueck, *Hard Line*, 31; and an earlier discussion in Nau, "No Enemies on the Right."

69. I avoided presidents who were clearly identified with existing traditions, such as Woodrow Wilson and Franklin Roosevelt as liberal internationalists, Richard Nixon and Teddy Roosevelt as realists, and Andrew Jackson and Calvin Coolidge as nationalists. And I did not select presidents identified with any tradition who had conspicuously failed. As scholars know, that amounts to selecting cases on the dependent variable, a methodological no-no. But for an initial plausibility probe of a foreign policy tradition that does not currently exist in the literature, it seemed an acceptable way to proceed.

70. All scholars do this. Some are explicitly known as realist, liberal internationalist (institutionalist), or constructivist (ideas, values) scholars. Or they may practice analytical eclecticism and apply all theories (traditions) simultaneously. If they move beyond selective or thick description, however, they must emphasize in their conclusions one theory or tradition over others. Otherwise there are too many causes and outcomes are overdetermined. These theoretical differences account in good part for the controversies among scholars in evaluating individual presidents. See Rudra Sil and Peter Katzenstein, *Beyond Paradigms: Analytical Eclecticism in the Study of World Politics* (New York: Palgrave Macmillan, 2010); Lake, "Why 'Isms' Are Evil"; and my response, "No Alternative to 'Isms.'"

71. See the conclusion for details.

72. A future study might focus on conservative internationalist strategies that mostly failed. I look at cases that mostly succeeded though I do point out, as noted here, instances of failure within those cases.

73. See, for example, Ikenberry et al., *The Crisis of American Foreign Policy*.

74. See Dmitri K. Simes, "America's Imperial Dilemma," *Foreign Affairs* 82, 6 (November/December 2003): 91–103; and Anatol Levin, "A Trap of Their Own Making," *London Review of Books* 24, 19 (May 8, 2003): 8–11.

75. For the embedded liberalism argument and a critique, see, respectively, John G. Ruggie, "International Regimes, Transactions, and Change: Embedded Liberalism in the Postwar Economic Order," in Stephen D. Krasner, ed., *International Regimes* (Ithaca: Cornell University Press, 1983), 195–233; and Nau, *The Myth of America's Decline*, 71–74, 77–128.

76. See Amity Shlaes, *Coolidge* (New York: Harper, 2013); and Steven F. Hayward, *The Age of Reagan: The Conservative Counterrevolution, 1980–1989* (New York: Crown Forum, 2009).

77. Liberal preferences in the academy tilt the playing field against conservative options in domestic as well as foreign policy. Liberal scholars often write critically about conservative groups such as the Christian Coalition and Tea Party but seldom apply the same scrutiny to liberal or radical movements, such as labor unions, African American organizations, MoveOn.Org, Occupy Wall Street, or climategate scandals. As I have pointed out, social scientists study things they like or dislike. See Theda Skocpol and Vanessa Williamson, *The Tea Party and The Remaking of Republican Conservatism* (New York: Oxford University Press, 2012); and Putnam and Campbell, *American Grace*. For a recent liberal internationalist perspective that explicitly advocates "reversing many of the policies of the Reagan-Thatcher fundamentalist capitalism," see Daniel Deudney and G. John Ikenberry, "Democratic Internationalism: An American Grand Strategy for the Post-Exceptionalist Era" (working paper for the Council on Foreign Relations, November 2012), 8.

78. Peter Trubowitz and Nicole Mellow, "Foreign Policy, Bipartisanship and the Paradox of Post–September 11 America," *International Politics* 48 (2011): 164–87.

79. In the 1950s, as Micklethwait and Wooldridge note, "the conservative movement did not have much bite in Congress" and "even less bark in the intellectual world." See *The Right Nation*, 43. The Democratic Party was considered

the "vital center." Arthur M. Schlesinger Jr., *The Vital Center: The Politics of Freedom* (Boston: Houghton Mifflin, 1949). Vestiges of Democratic dominance persist even after fifty years, such as the control of the Woodrow Wilson International Center for Scholars, a publicly funded institution, by Democratic politicians—Lee Hamilton earlier and Jane Harman today. Would a former conservative Republican politician, such as Vin Weber, be equally acceptable?

80. One study finds, for example, that "while there has been an increase in the polarization of political discourse in the last 30 years, polarization is still low relative to the late 19th and most of the 20th century." See Jacob Jensen, Ethan Kaplan, Suresh Naidu, and Laurence Wilse-Samson, "The Dynamics of Political Language" (conference draft presented at the fall 2012 Brookings Panel on Economic Activity, September 13–14, 2012). And if there is more partisanship in the past thirty years, it is among the political classes, not the broader citizenry. According to another study, "there is little evidence that Americans' ideological or policy *positions* are more polarized today than they were two or three decades ago, although the policy *choices* [that elites propose] often seem to be." See Morris P. Fiorina with Samuel J. Abrams and Jeremy C. Pope, *Culture War? The Myth of a Polarized America* (New York: Pearson Longman, 2005), 8.

81. Dueck, *Hard Line*, 11–39.

82. See Figure 3.1 and National Election Survey data at http://www.election studies.org/. It is part of the partisan process to argue that partisanship is worse on one side or the other. See, for example, Thomas E. Mann and Norman J. Ornstein, *It's Even Worse than It Looks: How the American Constitutional System Collided with the New Politics of Extremism* (New York: Basic Books, 2012).

83. Polls consistently show that conservatives or Republicans favor more defense spending, stronger U.S. leadership, and a more military- or security-oriented approach to the world than do liberals or Democrats. This difference holds even when a majority of Americans are weary of world affairs, as they are today. See *Foreign Policy in the New Millennium*.

84. The Korean War was sanctioned only by the General Assembly in the absence of the Soviet Union from the Security Council.

85. See chapter 3 and Henry Nau, "The Jigsaw Puzzle and the Chess Board: The Making and Unmaking of Foreign Policy in the Age of Obama," *Commentary* (May 2012): 13–20.

CHAPTER 2: AMERICA'S FOREIGN POLICY TRADITIONS

1. The literature developing these grand strategies is large and longstanding. See, among others, Dexter Perkins, *The American Approach to Foreign Policy* (Cambridge: Harvard University Press, 1962); Selig Adler, *The Isolationist Impulse: Its Twentieth Century Reaction* (London: Abelard Schuman, 1957); Felix Gilbert, *To the Farewell Address* (Princeton: Princeton University Press, 1961); and Manfred Jonas, *Isolationism in America, 1913–1941* (Ithaca: Cornell University Press, 1966). Recent updates include Mead, *Special Providence*; and Nau, *At Home Abroad*, especially chapter 2.

2. See, for example, Michael C. Desch, "America's Liberal Illiberalism: The Ideological Origins of Overreaction in U.S. Foreign Policy," *International Security* 32, 3 (Winter 2007–8): 7–43.

3. For revisionist studies, see, among others, Noam Chomsky, *Hegemony or Survival: America's Quest for Global Dominance* (New York: Henry Holt, 2003); and Andrew Bacevich, *The Limits of Power: The End of American Exceptionalism* (New York: Henry Holt, 2008).

4. Mead, *Special Providence*. My classification of Jackson (nationalist) and Wilson (liberal internationalist) generally overlaps with Mead's. But I define Hamilton as an Old World power politics realist, not a New World enthusiast over commerce, and Jefferson as a conservative internationalist, not an economic isolationist or, in today's context, economic stabilizer (Mead uses the metaphor of a gyroscope). Gilbert says Hamilton "tended by inclination to power politics" and believed that "the regulation of commercial relations remained subordinated to power politics." See *To the Farewell Address*, 111, 131.

5. Other scholars define nationalist (neo-isolationist), defensive realist (selective engagement), offensive realist (primacy), and liberal internationalist (cooperative security) grand strategies but omit conservative internationalist strategies. See Barry R. Posen and Andrew L. Ross, "Competing Visions for U.S. Grand Strategy," *International Security* 21, 3 (Winter 1996–97): 5–54. Traditions defined in terms of logic as well as history can be applied to other countries with different histories, as my colleague and I do in Nau and Ollapally, *Worldviews of Aspiring Powers*.

6. These factors are all present in any situation, but the traditions and main contemporary theories of international relations they reflect—realism (power), liberalism (institutions) and constructivism (ideas)—differ in terms of which factor *causes* the others. For example, in realism, relative power determines in large measure the ideas and interests countries pursue and what international institutions can accomplish. See Henry R. Nau, *Perspectives on International Relations: Power, Institutions, and Ideas*, 3rd ed. (Washington, DC: CQ Press, 2011).

7. The best assessment of the isolationist tradition, by far, is Eric A. Nordlinger, *Isolationism Reconfigured: American Foreign Policy for a New Century* (Princeton: Princeton University Press, 1995). For contemporary versions, see especially the writings of CATO Institute foreign policy specialists such as Ted Galen Carpenter, *Smart Power: Toward a Prudent Foreign Policy for America* (Washington, DC: CATO Institute, 2008); and Doug Bandow, *Tripwire: Korea and U.S. Foreign Policy in a Changed World* (Washington, DC: CATO Institute, 1996).

8. Nordlinger, *Isolationism Reconfigured*.

9. Walter McDougall, *Promised Land, Crusader State: The American Encounter with the World since 1776* (Boston: Houghton Mifflin, 1997); and *Freedom Just Around the Corner: A New American History 1585–1828* (New York: HarperCollins, 2004).

10. The quoted phrase is the title of McDougall's last chapter in *Promised Land, Crusader State*.

11. Gilbert, *To the Farewell Address*, 145.

12. Nordlinger, *Isolationism Reconfigured*.

13. For an interwar statement of this position, see Johnson Hagood, *We Can Defend America* (Garden City, NY: Doubleday, Doran, 1937).

14. Quoted in Saul K. Padover, ed., *The Washington Papers* (New York: Harper and Brothers, 1955), 321.

15. McDougall, *Promised Land, Crusader State*, 1.

16. The best exposition of the nationalist tradition I have found is McDougall, *Promised Land, Crusader State*.

17. See Patrick J. Buchanan, *Churchill, Hitler, and the Unnecessary War* (New York: Crown, 2008).

18. Patrick Buchanan, *The Great Betrayal: How American Sovereignty and Social Justice Are Being Sacrificed to the Gods of the Global Economy* (McLean, VA: PJB Enterprises, 1998).

19. For example, McDougall asks if NATO today is an entangling alliance and answers no if it helps "to secure U.S. interests without compromising the constitutional powers of the Executive or Congress." See *Promised Land, Crusader State*, 217–18.

20. See chapter 5. Jackson declined to annex Texas when it first applied for annexation. Jackson's famous quip at the Jefferson Day dinner in 1830 made it clear that union mattered more than expansion: "Our Federal Union; it *must* be preserved." H. W. Brands, *Andrew Jackson: His Life and Times* (New York: Doubleday, 2005), 446.

21. For one of the best expositions of the realist tradition, see Kissinger, *Diplomacy*. For a more detailed discussion of the variations of realism, see Nau, "Realism."

22. John J. Mearsheimer, *The Tragedy of Great Power Politics* (New York: W. W. Norton, 2001).

23. Stephen M. Walt, *Taming American Power: The Global Response to U.S. Primacy* (New York: W. W. Norton, 2005). Brent Scowcroft and Colin Powell took this defensive realist point of view in disputes with Don Rumsfeld and Dick Cheney, who favored a more offensive realist approach, over issues such as the breakup of the Soviet Union and, later, the Iraq war. See George Bush and Brent Scowcroft, *A World Transformed* (New York: Knopf, 1998), 541.

24. Joanne Gowa, *Allies, Adversaries, and International Trade* (Princeton: Princeton University Press, 1994).

25. This is realist John Mearsheimer's complaint about U.S. policy to boost economic development in China. See "The Future of the American Pacifier," *Foreign Affairs* 80, 5 (September/October 2001): 46–62.

26. See Dueck, *Hard Line*.

27. Kissinger commented in 1976, for example, that the Soviet challenge "will not go away" and "will perhaps never be conclusively 'resolved.'" See *American Foreign Policy* (New York: W. W. Norton, 1977), 304.

28. See Samuel Huntington, "Why International Primacy Matters," *International Security* 17, 4 (Spring 1993): 68–83; Charles Krauthammer, "The Unipolar Moment," *Foreign Affairs* 70, 1 (1990–91): 23–33; and a Pentagon study advocating preemption reported by Patrick E. Tyler, "U.S. Strategy Plan Calls for Insuring No Rivals Develop," *New York Times*, March 8, 1992, A1.

29. See Gregory Russell, *The Statecraft of Theodore Roosevelt: The Duties of Nations and World Order* (Dordrecht, the Netherlands: Martinus Nijhoff, 2009).

30. Charles Krauthammer, "Democratic Realism: An American Foreign Policy for a Unipolar World," Irving Kristol Lecture, American Enterprise Institute, Washington, DC, February 12, 2004.

31. Samuel P. Huntington, "The West Unique, Not Universal," *Foreign Affairs* 75, 6 (November/December 1996): 28–46.

32. For excellent expositions of the liberal internationalist tradition, see G. John Ikenberry, *Liberal Leviathan: The Origins, Crisis, and Transformation of the American World* (Princeton: Princeton University Press, 2011); G. John Ikenberry, *After Victory: Institutions, Strategic Restraint, and the Rebuilding of Order after Major Wars* (Princeton: Princeton University Press. 2001); and Ikenberry et al., *The Crisis in American Foreign Policy*.

33. See Margaret MacMillan, *Paris 1919: Six Months That Changed the World* (New York: Random House, 2003), chapter 7. To be sure, Wilson used plenty of national military force in earlier interventions in the Caribbean and Central America. Whether he changed or not is debated, but he was reluctant to enter World War I and became firmly committed later to the replacement of the balance of power by collective security.

34. For a penetrating discussion of republican security concepts, see Deudney, *Bounding Power*.

35. Azar Gat calls this threat "authoritarian capitalism." See "The Rise of Authoritarian Capitalism," *Foreign Affairs* 86, 4 (July/August 2007): 59–71. For analyses of hierarchy in international affairs, independent of ideology, see David A. Lake, *Hierarchy in International Relations* (Ithaca: Cornell University Press, 2009); and Stephen D. Krasner, *Sovereignty: Organized Hypocrisy* (Princeton: Princeton University Press, 1999).

36. See Michael Ignatieff, "Who Are the Americans to Think Freedom Is Theirs to Spread?" *New York Times Magazine*, June 26, 2005, http://www.nytimes.com/2005/06/26/magazine/26EXCEPTION.html?pagewanted=all.

37. Buckley founded the *National Review* in 1955 on this slogan. See Nash, *The Conservative Intellectual Movement in America*, 150–51.

38. These international preferences are consistent with the domestic preferences of conservatives and liberals. See chapter 1.

39. On this point, see Kim R. Holmes and John Hillen, "Misreading Reagan's Legacy," *Foreign Affairs* 75, 5 (September/October 1996): 162–68. As noted in chapter 4, Jefferson scaled back military forces when the threat of war with France abated.

40. Norman Podhoretz, *World War IV: The Long Struggle against Islamo-Fascism* (New York: Vintage Books, 2008).

41. Here is where George W. Bush strayed beyond conservative internationalist sentiments. See chapter 3.

42. In his day, no liberal critic made the argument that Reagan was reluctant to use force. Just the opposite, they charged that he brandished or used force too much.

43. There is historical evidence that most military interventions to promote regime change have followed this inkblot strategy. As John Owen finds, "distant promotions are relatively rare." John M. Owen IV, *The Clash of Ideas in World Politics: Transnational Networks, States, and Regime Change, 1510–2010* (Princeton: Princeton University Press, 2010), 26.

44. The fact that the media and scholars often ignore such obvious cases of the beneficial use of force is one of the motivations of this book.

45. Many realists did as well, but conservative internationalists rejected détente and favored a military buildup, the neoconservatives being most prominent among them.

46. Fred Charles Ikle, *Every War Must End* (New York: Columbia University Press, 2005).

47. Nicholas Trist, who negotiated the end of the war, personally vilified Polk. See chapter 5.

48. These are the same distinctions between liberals and conservatives that exist at the domestic level. See chapter 1. For an insightful summary of conservative principles for aid to the indigent, see Douglas J. Besharov, "The Right Kind of Hand Up," *Washington Post*, November 19, 2007, A17.

49. As Robert Kagan writes, "Democratic progress and liberal economics have been and can be reversed and undone." See *The World America Made* (New York: Knopf, 2012), 21. See also Samuel P. Huntington, *The Third Wave: Democratization in the Late Twentieth Century* (Norman: University of Oklahoma Press, 1993).

50. Fareed Zakaria, *The Future of Freedom: Illiberal Democracy at Home and Abroad* (New York: W. W. Norton, 2007).

51. Larry Diamond, *The Spirit of Democracy: The Struggle to Build Free Societies Throughout the World* (New York: Holt, 2008).

52. Eugene Robinson, "Bring the Troops Home," *Washington Post*, October 27, 2009.

53. John J. Mearsheimer, "Imperial by Design," *The National Interest*, no. 111 (January/February 2011): 16–35; Christopher Layne, "The (Almost) Triumph of Offshore Balancing," *The National Interest*, January 2012; and Stephen Walt, "A Bandwagon for Offshore Balancing?" *Foreign Policy*, December 2011.

54. John Bolton, *Surrender Is Not an Option* (New York: Threshold Editions, Simon and Schuster, 2007).

55. G. John Ikenberry, *Liberal Leviathan: The Origins, Crisis, and Transformation of the American System* (Princeton: Princeton University Press, 2011); Dan Caldwell, *Vortex of Conflict: U.S. Policy toward Afghanistan, Pakistan and Iraq* (Stanford: Stanford University Press, 2011).

CHAPTER 3: RECENT PRESIDENTS: THE PENDULUM SWINGS

1. The discussion and coding of presidents in this chapter follow from the distinctions among the traditions identified in chapter 2.

2. See "Task Force on U.S. Standing in the World," September 2009, http://www.apsanet.org/content_59477.cfm.

3. See National Election Survey data, http://www.electionstudies.org/.

4. Matthew Baum and Henry R. Nau, "Foreign Policy Views and U.S. Standing in the World" (unpublished manuscript, August 2012).

5. Holsti, *Public Opinion and American Foreign Policy*, 124–25.

6. Miroslav Nincic and Jennifer Ramos, "Ideological Structure and Foreign Policy Preferences," *Journal of Political Ideologies* 15, 2 (2010): 119–41.

7. For earlier versions of the analysis that follows, see Nau, "The Jigsaw Puzzle and the Chess Board" and Henry R. Nau, "Obama's Foreign Policy: The Swing Away from Bush: How Far to Go?" *Policy Review* 160 (April/May 2010): 27–47.

8. Derek Chollet and James Goldgeier, *America between the Wars, from 11/9 to 9/11* (New York: Public Affairs, 2008).

9. Quoted in Bush and Scowcroft, *A World Transformed*, 515.

10. Quoted in ibid., 541.

11. The approach was captured by a leaked Pentagon document at the time. See Tyler, "U.S. Strategy Plan Calls for Insuring No Rivals Develop."

12. Mann, *Rise of the Vulcans*, 189–92. See also Donald Rumsfeld, *Known and Unknown: A Memoir* (New York: Sentinel, 2011), 414.

13. Chollet and Goldgeier, *America between the Wars*, 14–15.

14. George H. W. Bush admitted he lacked the "vision thing," and Bush's secretary of state, James Baker, was the quintessential pragmatist and problem solver. See James A. Baker III, *The Politics of Diplomacy* (New York: Putnam, 1995).

15. For excerpts of the "New World Order" speech to Congress on September 11, 1990, see Bush and Scowcroft, *A World Transformed*, 370. For the UN speech, see President George H. W. Bush, "Address Before the 45th Session of the United Nations General Assembly," New York, October 1, 1990, transcript available at http://bushlibrary.tamu. edu/research/papers/1990/ 90100100.html.

16. A UN report issued in 1992 by Secretary-General Boutros Boutros-Ghali called for an expansion of UN peacekeeping activities. See Boutros Boutros-Ghali, *An Agenda for Peace*, 2nd ed. (New York: United Nations, 1995).

17. U.S. Congress, House Committee on Foreign Affairs, *U.S. Participation in United Nations Peacekeeping Activities, Hearings Before the Subcommittee on International Security, International Organizations and Human Rights*, 103rd Cong., 2nd Sess., statement by Madeleine K. Albright, June 24, 1994, 3–21. See also Madeleine Albright with Bill Woodward, *Madam Secretary: A Memoir* (New York: Miramax, 2003).

18. See Stanley A. Renshon, *High Hopes: The Clinton Presidency and the Politics of Ambition* (New York: New York University Press, 1996), 137.

19. See James Bennett, "Clinton in Africa," *New York Times*, March 26, 1998, A1. Clinton omits this apology in his memoirs, *My Life* (New York: Knopf, 2004).

20. President Bill Clinton, "State of the Union," January 25, 1994, http://www .let.rug.ln/usa/P/bc42/speeches/sup94wjc.htm.

21. Michael Mandelbaum, "Foreign Policy as Social Work," *Foreign Affairs* 75, 1 (January/February 1996): 16–32.

22. See Micklethwait and Wooldridge, *The Right Nation*, 120–21.

23. Richard Nixon, in one of the last letters of his life, warned Clinton not to let anything divert him from America's major foreign policy priority: the survival of political and economic freedom in Russia. See Clinton, *My Life,* 593.

24. Bob Woodward, *State of Denial: Bush at War Part III* (New York: Simon and Schuster, 2006), 5–9.

25. For Bush's comments in the debate on October 11, 2000, see 2000 presidential debate transcripts: http://www.debates.org/index.php?page=october-11 -2000-debate-transcript. See also George W. Bush, *Decision Points* (New York: Crown, 2010).

26. See Rumsfeld, *Known and Unknown*, 331.

27. Condoleezza Rice, "Rethinking the National Interest: American Realism for a New World," *Foreign Affairs* 87, 4 (July/August 2008): 2–28.

28. *The 9/11 Commission Report: Final Report of the National Commission on Terrorist Attacks upon the United States,* authorized edition (New York: W. W. Norton, 2004).

29. See Lisa Myers, "Osama Bin Laden: Missed Opportunities," NBC News, March 17, 2004, http://www.nbcnews.com/id/4540958/#.UTSXjo7BTa4.

30. The phrase comes from Stanley A. Renshon, *In His Father's Shadow: The Transformation of George W. Bush* (New York: Palgrave Macmillan, 2004), 75. On revenge, Bush said: "I made up my mind that if America was under attack, we'd get them." See 102, also 142.

31. See Rumsfeld, *Known and Unknown,* 689–90.

32. See Wesley K. Clark, NATO commander during the Kosovo crisis, *Waging Modern War: Bosnia, Kosovo, and the Future of Combat* (New York: Public Affairs, 2002).

33. See Bush's *speech* in Cincinnati, Ohio, October 7, 2002, http://www.gpo.gov/fdsys/pkg/WCPD-2002-10-14/pdf/WCPD-2002-10-14-Pg1716.pdf#page=5. Condoleezza Rice used the same "smoking gun" and "mushroom cloud" imagery in an interview with Walt Blitzer one month earlier, September 8, 2002, http://transcripts.cnn.com/TRANSCRIPTS/0209/08/le.00.html.

34. As Paul Pillar, a sharp critic of the Iraq invasion, wrote: "the Bush administration was quite right: its perception of Saddam's weapons capacities was shared by the Clinton administration, congressional Democrats, and most other Western governments and intelligence services." See "Intelligence, Policy, and the War in Iraq," *Foreign Affairs* 85, 2 (March/April 2006): 15–29; see also Mortimer B. Zuckerman, "Foul-ups—Not Felonies," *U.S. News and World Report,* November 14, 2005.

35. For studies that document the failure to plan, see, among others, Michael R. Gordon and Bernard E. Trainor, *Cobra II: The Inside Story of the Invasion and Occupation of Iraq* (New York: Pantheon Books, 2006) and Woodward, *State of Denial.* Bush himself reflects on whether he might have done the surge earlier, that is, committed more troops to postwar tasks, but concludes that that would have only encouraged war critics. See *Decision Points,* 393. Before the invasion, Donald Rumsfeld laid out a "Parade of Horribles" that could go wrong, including finding no WMD, but he resisted larger troop commitments, favoring the "light footprint" approach, and blamed the State Department and national security advisor for failure to follow up. See *Known and Unknown,* 479ff. See also Douglas J. Feith, *War and Decision: Inside the Pentagon at the Dawn of the War on Terrorism* (New York: Harper, 2008).

36. Mann, *Rise of the Vulcans.*

37. The only traditions that are not implicated are nationalists and liberal internationalists, which explains why those two traditions like the hijack argument so much. See, for nationalists, Pat J. Buchanan, *Where the Right Went Wrong: How the Neoconservatives Subverted the Reagan Revolution and Hijacked the Bush Presidency* (New York: Thomas Dunnes, 2004); and, for liberal internationalists, Daalder and Lindsay, *America Unbound.*

38. See Michael J. Gerson (who wrote the West Point speech), *Heroic Conservatism,* 129–33.

39. Inauguration speech, January 20, 2005, http://millercenter.org/president/speeches/détail/446.

40. Ryan Lizza, "The Consequentialist: How the Arab Spring Remade Obama's Foreign Policy," *The New Yorker*, May 2, 2011.

41. Obama appointed special envoys for the Middle East (George Mitchell), Iran (Dennis Ross), Sudan (Scott Gration), North Korea (Steve Bosworth), and Afpak (Richard Holbrooke), among others.

42. Niall Ferguson, "Wanted: A Grand Strategy for America," *Newsweek* 157, 8 (February 21, 2011): 2–3. The same thing can be said about Obama's domestic policy.

43. See comments, January 29, 2010, http://www.whitehouse.gov/the-press-office/remarks-president-gop-house-issues-conference.

44. http://www.whitehouse.gov/the_press_office/Remarks-by-the-President-to-the-United-Nations-General-Assembly. See also Scott Wilson, "Shared Interests Define Obama's World," *Washington Post*, November 2, 2009, A1.

45. See Obama's speech in Prague, April 5, 2009, http://www.whitehouse.gov/the_press_office/Remarks-By-President-Barack-Obama-In-Prague-As-Delivered/.

46. Thomas Carothers, *Democracy Policy under Obama: Revitalization or Retreat?* (Washington, DC: Carnegie Endowment for International Peace, 2012), 12. For a more critical view of Obama's policy toward democracy promotion, see Joshua Muravchik, "The Abandonment of Democracy," *Commentary* (July/August 2009), http://www.commentarymagazine.com/viewarticle.cfm/special-preview—the-abandonment-of-democracy-15185.

47. Quoted in Lizza, "The Consequentialist."

48. David Sanger, *Confront and Conceal: Obama's Secret Wars and Surprising Use of American Power* (New York: Crown, 2012).

49. See Obama's speech in Oslo, Norway, December 10, 2009, http://www.whitehouse.gov/the-press-office/remarks-president-acceptance-nobel-peace-prize.

50. Comments from Prague speech (see note 45).

51. See Obama's speech in Moscow, July 7, 2009, http://www.whitehouse.gov/the_press_office/Remarks-By-The-President-At-The-New-Economic-School-Graduation/.

52. Obama capped production of F-22 stealth fighter planes and delayed plans for a next-generation long-range bomber. He made deep cuts in missile defenses and did little to expand a navy fleet that is down to roughly half the size it was at the end of the Cold War. Such decisions have consequences, which often turn up only many years later. Containment of China, for example, depends heavily on American air and sea power. Since 1995, China has increased the number of its submarines by thirty-eight, while the United States has cut the number of its submarines by twenty-five.

53. In his accounts, Sanger tells us that Obama always intended to pull out of Afghanistan and used the surges with strict deadlines to protect his flank against the military and charges of endangering the nation's security. See *Confront and Conceal*, 27–28.

54. Lisabeth Bumiller and Thom Shanker, "Obama Puts His Stamp on a Leaner Military," *New York Times*, January 6, 2012, A18.

55. Jennifer Rubin, "U.S. Retreat Means Iran's Influence Grows," *Washington Post*, February 19, 2013, http://www.washingtonpost.com/blogs/right-turn/wp/2013/02/19/u-s-retreat-means-irans-influence-grows/.

56. See progression of Obama's objectives in speeches: March 27, 2009, http://www.whitehouse.gov/the_press_office/Remarks-by-the-President-on-a-New-Strategy-for-Afghanistan-and-Pakistan/; December 1, 2009, http://www.whitehouse.gov/the-press-office/remarks-president-address-nation-way-forward-afghanistan-and-pakistan; and June 22, 2011, http://www.whitehouse.gov/the-press-office/2011/06/22/remarks-president-way-forward-afghanistan.

57. "Of all the countries in the region there," says realist Brent Scowcroft, "our real interests in Libya are minimal." Quoted in Lizza, "The Consequentialist."

58. Michael R. Gordon and Mark Landler, "Senate Hearing Draws out a Rift in U.S. Policy on Syria," *New York Times*, February 8, 2013, A1.

59. Comments from Moscow speech (see note 51).

60. The New START Treaty cuts deployed warheads to 1,550 for each country with a limit on launchers and bombers of 800 deployed and nondeployed (and a sublimit of 700 deployed). Russia was roughly at these limits; the United States had to cut to gain compliance.

61. Walter Russell Mead, "The Carter Syndrome," *Foreign Policy* 177 (January/February 2010): 58–65.

62. "South Korea Seeks UN Action against North," CBS News, June 26, 2010, http://www.cbsnews.com/8301-202_162-6548286.html.

63. See interview with Jeffrey Goldberg, "Obama to Iran and Israel: 'As President of the United States, I Don't Bluff,'" *The Atlantic*, March 2, 2012, http://www.theatlantic.com/international/archive/2012/03/obama-to-iran-and-israel-as-president-of-the-united-states-i-dont-bluff/253875/.

64. Mark Landler, "Biden and Netanyahu Stress Points of Unity in Speeches to Pro-Israel Group," *New York Times*, March 5, 2013, A4.

65. Richard Holbrooke, "The Next President," *Foreign Affairs* (September/October 2008): 18.

66. Obama was photographed carrying and apparently reading the book by Fareed Zakaria, *The Post-American World* (New York: W. W. Norton, 2008).

67. Quoted in James Kirchick, "Squanderer in Chief," *Los Angeles Times*, April 28, 2009, http://articles.latimes.com/2009/apr/28/opinion/oe-kirchick28. At a dinner in 1991, Valerie Jarrett, Obama's close advisor, who like Obama lived overseas as a child, said when she first met Obama: "Barack felt extraordinarily familiar. He and I shared a view of where the United States fits in the world, which is often different from the view people have who have not traveled outside the United States as young children." "Through her travels," David Remnick, Obama's biographer, continues, "Jarrett felt that she had come to see the United States with a greater objectivity as one country among many, rather than the center of wisdom and experience." See *The Bridge: The Life and Rise of Barack Obama* (New York: Knopf, 2010), 273. Obama describes Jarrett as "someone I trust completely. She is family." See Paul Kengor, "Letting Obama Be Obama," *The American Spectator*, July/August 2011, http://spectator.org/archives/2011/07/05/letting-obama-be-obama/print.

68. Comments from his Oslo speech (see note 49).

69. Charles Kupchan and Peter Trubowitz, "The Demise of Liberal Internationalism in the United States," *International Security* 32, 2 (Fall 2007): 7–44.

70. Seven out of ten Americans say that America is the greatest country in the world. See *Foreign Policy in the New Millennium*, 9.

71. The Democratic leadership sponsored a last-minute alternative that failed, calling on President Bush to continue to rely on sanctions. Once again, the greater number of Republicans than Democrats supporting the use of force, even after multilateral consensus, confirms the MI/CI index discussed in chapter 1.

72. *Foreign Policy in the New Millennium*, 8.

CHAPTER 4: THOMAS JEFFERSON: EMPIRE OF LIBERTY

1. Mead, *Special Providence*. On the difference here between a liberal and conservative nationalist, see chapter 2.

2. Robert W. Tucker and David C. Hendrickson, *Empire of Liberty: The Statecraft of Thomas Jefferson* (New York: Oxford University Press, 1990), especially 1–17. Henry Adams offers a similar critique of Jefferson along realist lines: *History of the United States of America during the Administrations of Thomas Jefferson* (New York: Library Classics of the United States, 1986). See also Merrill D. Peterson, *Thomas Jefferson and the New Nation: A Biography* (New York: Oxford University Press, 1970).

3. That is so because the traditions affect the interpretation of policy by scholars no less than the making of policy by statesmen. I am uniquely indebted in this chapter to David Hendrickson for the spirited and constructive criticism of my interpretation of Jefferson. He and I disagree, but I understand Jefferson better because of his alternative view.

4. Robert Kagan argues that this ideological aggressiveness was shared by all of the founding fathers, including Hamilton and Washington. If so, Jefferson was still more cautious than Hamilton, who entertained adventurous, some might say reckless, filibusters to conquer western territories militarily. See *Dangerous Nation: America's Place in the World from Its Earliest Days to the Dawn of the Twentieth Century* (New York: Knopf. 2006), chapters 3–5.

5. To be sure, he was conflicted because every attempt to reform the world risked being corrupted by it through a big or garrison state. Tucker and Hendrickson, *Empire of Liberty*, 247.

6. Adams, *History of the United States*, 543–44.

7. On Jefferson's interactions with revolutionaries in Paris, see Peterson, *Thomas Jefferson*, 377–81.

8. Claude G. Bowers, *Jefferson and Hamilton: The Struggle for Democracy in America* (Boston: Houghton Mifflin, 1925), 110.

9. Quoted in Dumas Malone, *Jefferson and His Time: Jefferson and the Ordeal of Liberty*, vol. 3 (Charlottesville: University of Virginia, 1962), 42.

10. Quoted in Tucker and Hendrickson, *Empire of Liberty*, 82.

11. See Peterson, *Thomas Jefferson*, 480.

12. Tucker and Hendrickson, *Empire of Liberty*, 51. On differences between Washington and Jefferson toward France in this period, see also Dumas Malone, *Jefferson and His Time: Jefferson & the Rights of Man*, vol. 2 (Charlottesville: University of Virginia Press, 1951), 393–405.

13. See Julian Boyd, ed., *The Papers of Thomas Jefferson* (Princeton: Princeton University Press, 1950), 1:426. See also Peterson, *Thomas Jefferson*, 91.

14. For quotations and coverage, see Peterson, *Thomas Jefferson*, 44, 91, 152, 260, 998, 1000–1001. See also Boyd, *Papers of Thomas Jefferson*, 1:426.

15. See Lincoln's Dred Scott speech, June 26, 1857, http://www.virginia.edu /woodson/courses/aas-hius366a/lincoln.html.

16. Jefferson's concept of "sister republics" is an early imagery of the "democratic peace" and, though I found no evidence to this effect, may have been drawn from Immanuel Kant, whose writings Jefferson was undoubtedly aware of.

17. As Tucker and Hendrickson note, "a century later the tonnage carried by American vessels still had not surpassed the level it reached in 1807." See *Empire of Liberty*, 190.

18. Jefferson developed this habit while ambassador in France. In 1787, he wrote a friend: "While there are powers in Europe which fear our views, or have views on us, we should keep an eye on them, their connections and oppositions, that in a moment of need we may avail ourselves of their weakness with respect to others as well as ourselves, and calculate their designs and movements on all the circumstances under which they exist." See Julian P. Boyd et al., eds., *The Papers of Thomas Jefferson* (Princeton: Princeton University Press, 1974), 12:447.

19. Quoted in Tucker and Hendrickson, *Empire of Liberty*, 207.

20. Adams, *History of the United States*, 658

21. Tucker and Hendrickson, *Empire of Liberty*, 93.

22. Peterson, *Thomas Jefferson*, 761.

23. The same paradox affects interpretations of Reagan's use of force. Some today conclude he was a dove. See chapter 7.

24. See Frank Lambert, *The Barbary Wars: American Independence in the Atlantic World* (New York: Hill and Wang, 2007), 29–30. During the Revolutionary War, Jefferson favored a navy of as many as eighteen ships. See Marshall Smelser, *The Congress Founds the Navy, 1787–1798* (Notre Dame, IN: University of Notre Dame Press, 1959), 96.

25. Christopher Hitchens, "Jefferson versus the Muslim Pirates," *City Journal* (Spring 2007): 98–195, http://www.city-journal.org/html/17_2_urbanities-thomas _jefferson.html.

26. Despite these scruples, Jefferson enacted legislation in 1802 to establish a corps of engineers at West Point and constitute that installation as a military academy. Adams, *History of the United States*, 205.

27. Quoted in ibid., 137.

28. For example, Jefferson did not get distracted by supporting slave rebellions against France in Santo Domingo in 1793, less because he feared the impact of these rebellions on slavery in the United States than because his top priority at the time was to encourage the new republican government in France. For a contrary view, see Garry Wills, *"Negro President": Jefferson and the Slave Power* (Boston: Houghton Mifflin, 2003). Nor did he support Spain in 1806–7 when it was being crushed by Napoleon, again because he needed French help to acquire and spread republicanism in Florida.

29. Alexander DeConde, *This Affair of Louisiana* (New York: Charles Scribner's Sons, 1976), 249.

30. Adams, *History of the United States*, 311.

31. Hitchens, "Jefferson versus the Muslim Pirates." See also Joseph Whelan, *Jefferson's War: America's First War on Terror, 1801–1805* (New York: Carroll and Graf, 2003), 40–41.

32. Quoted in Whelan, *Jefferson's War*, 44.

33. Quoted in Gerard W. Gawalt, "America and the Barbary Pirates: An International Battle against an Unconventional Foe," *The Thomas Jefferson Papers*, http://memory.loc.gov/ammem/collections/jefferson_papers/mtjprece.html.

34. Ibid.

35. Christopher Hitchens in "Jefferson versus the Muslim Pirates" concludes that from this period on, "Jefferson had long sought a pretext for war." It is also worthy to note that while in Paris, Jefferson secured a commission for John Paul Jones, the naval hero of the American Revolution, to serve in the Russian fleet in the Black Sea and harass the Ottoman authorities, the nominal master of the Barbary states.

36. Whelan, *Jefferson's War*, 57–59. As Merrill Peterson writes: "Jefferson had always advocated a navy to cruise against the Barbary states; and in fact, Congress had founded the United States Navy in 1794 with this distinct purpose in mind." See *Thomas Jefferson*, 664.

37. Gawalt, "America and the Barbary Pirates."

38. Ferling, *Adams vs. Jefferson*, 109–10; Whelan, *Jefferson's War*, 70.

39. Smelser, *The Congress Founds the Navy*, 146–47.

40. Whelan, *Jefferson's War*, 6. See also Peterson, *Thomas Jefferson*, 664; and Adams, *History of the United States*, 184. Adams ridicules Jefferson for his support of the dry-dock measure, but that measure demonstrated Jefferson's expectation that force and a larger navy would again be necessary. See *History of the United States*, 288.

41. Bowers, *Jefferson and Hamilton*, 444–45.

42. This was not uncommon at the time. Washington had appointees frequently refuse his requests. Peterson, *Thomas Jefferson*, 661–62.

43. For details of this period, see Whelan, *Jefferson's War*, 102ff.

44. Peterson, *Thomas Jefferson*, 664.

45. Adams, *History of the United States*, 354, 397–98.

46. Ibid., 593.

47. Peterson, *Thomas Jefferson*, 665.

48. See Tucker and Hendrickson, *Empire of Liberty*, 21.

49. Adams, *History of the United States*, 593–95.

50. Whelan, *Jefferson's War*, 233.

51. See ibid., 271. The U.S. Navy in the Mediterranean performed erratically, often frustrating Jefferson. See also, for example, 156–57.

52. Curiously, Tucker and Hendrickson devote only a footnote, albeit a five-page one, to the Barbary wars; see *Empire of Liberty*, 294–99. They make the tedious argument that even though Jefferson used force and stretched resources beyond what Gallatin, his secretary of treasury, thought wise, his action was not the equivalent of waging war. If committing almost your entire navy does not constitute war, what does?

53. Peterson, *Thomas Jefferson*, 745. Jefferson repeated this view in his first inaugural.

54. Ibid., 746.

55. Dumas Malone, *Jefferson and His Time: Jefferson the President, First Term, 1801–1805*, vol. 4 (Boston: Little, Brown, 1970), 317. Merrill Peterson agrees: "Liberty was the ultimate value, Union the means." See *Thomas Jefferson*, 772.

56. Quoted in Tucker and Hendrickson, *Empire of Liberty*, 160.

57. Ibid., 161; quoted in Kagan, *Dangerous Nation*, 83.

58. See the blistering and unrelenting attack on Jefferson as the president of "slave power" by Garry Wills, *"Negro President": Jefferson and the Slave Power* (Boston: Houghton Mifflin, 2003). I do not make light of the charges of either racism or imperialism. I simply side with Michael Ignatieff's position that imperialism and liberty cannot be disentangled: "the problem here is that while no one wants imperialism to win, no one in his right mind can want liberty to fail either." See "Who Are the Americans to Think Freedom Is Theirs to Spread?" *New York Times Magazine*, June 26, 2005, http://www.nytimes.com/2005/06/26/magazine/26EXCEPTION.html?pagewanted=all&_r=0.

59. Alexander Keyssar, who is very much aware of the mixed record of American exceptionalism, nevertheless notes, "the United States was indeed the first country in the western world to significantly broaden its electorate by permanently lowering explicit economic barriers to political participation." See *The Right to Vote*, xxiii.

60. Hunt, *Ideology and U.S. Foreign Policy*, 27; and Tucker and Hendrickson, *Empire of Liberty*, 133–35.

61. Peterson, *Thomas Jefferson*, 841–55, 865–72; and Dumas Malone, *Jefferson and His Time: Jefferson the President: Second Term, 1805–1809*, vol. 5 (Boston: Little, Brown, 1974), 215–91.

62. Claude G. Bowers argues that Jefferson was a product of America's first West, the Appalachian ridges in which he lived and went to school, a far cry from the emerging cities of the period in which Hamilton, Washington, and Adams grew up. Bowers believes this association gave Jefferson his passionate attachment to the people, even the uneducated farmers that his version of American democracy championed. See *Jefferson and Hamilton*, 95–97.

63. Quoted in Tucker and Hendrickson, *Empire of Liberty*, 95.

64. This is the argument throughout Tucker and Hendrickson's account, *Empire of Liberty*. "Jefferson believed in the utility of threatening wars and alliances but was exceedingly reluctant to resort to either possibility in fact. . . . Unlike Jefferson, Hamilton was never a man for making threats he was unwilling to carry out" (42–43). Here, as detailed in chapter 2, is the conventional distinction between a liberal internationalist who sees force as a last resort and a realist who is more inclined toward the use of force.

65. Adams writes: "Of all the events at the time, LeClerc's death was the most decisive." LeClerc was the head of the French expeditionary force fighting to suppress the rebel slaves in Santo Domingo. Adams, *History of the United States*, 311.

66. Peterson, *Thomas Jefferson*, 758.

67. DeConde, *This Affair of Louisiana*, 124–25.

68. Peterson, *Thomas Jefferson*, 776.

69. Tucker and Hendrickson, *Empire of Liberty*, 108.

70. Adams, *History of the United States*, 277.

71. Ibid., 293.

72. Whether the sale also included West Florida (the lower part of present-day eastern Louisiana, Mississippi, and Alabama) was much disputed at the time, but the acquisition of the Floridas eventually occurred under separate treaties.

73. Adams, *History of the United States*, 344.

74. Tucker and Hendrickson, *Empire of Liberty*, 117.

75. Ibid.

76. Adams, *History of the United States*, 337.

77. Even Tucker and Hendrickson acknowledge that the American capacity to occupy New Orleans was a factor in French thinking. See *Empire of Liberty*, 106, 116.

78. See *This Affair of Louisiana*, 156, also 251. Malone and Peterson likewise believe Jefferson was ready to use force. See, respectively, *Jefferson and His Time*, 4:271–72, 285–86; and *Thomas Jefferson*, 761–62.

79. Adams, *History of the United States*, 345. Napoleon said of the transfer, seeming to agree with Adams that he intended to strengthen America against England: "I will not keep a possession which will not be safe in our hands, that may perhaps embroil me with the Americans . . . I shall make it serve me, on the contrary, to attach them to me, to get them into differences with the English, and I shall create for them [English] enemies who will one day avenge us, if we do not succeed in avenging ourselves. My resolution is fixed; I will give Louisiana to the United States." See M. J. Louis Adolph Thiers, *The History of the Consulate and the Empire of France under Napoleon*, translated from the French (London, 1875), 1:458.

80. Tucker and Hendrickson, *Empire of Liberty*, 117–22. "Indefinite in time and vague in circumstance, his [Jefferson's] threats to use force were all of a contingent and hypothetical nature," 118.

81. As DeConde reasons, "While Jefferson was willing to use England to threaten France, he still distrusted the British and felt that in command of Louisiana they would be as dangerous as the French." See *This Affair of Louisiana*, 143.

82. Adams, *History of the United States*, 301.

83. The idea of an alliance with Britain was not that fanciful. The U.S. and British navies had cooperated in the quasi-war with France in the late 1790s. See Bradford Perkins, *The First Rapprochement: England and the United States, 1795–1805* (Berkeley: University of California Press, 1967).

84. Adams, *History of the United States*, 304. Jefferson had vigorously opposed the Jay Treaty with England in the 1790s.

85. It is similarly incorrect to equate Jefferson's Kentucky Resolution asserting the right to nullify federal government decisions with later resolutions by John C. Calhoun and other Southerners asserting the right to secede from the Union. Jefferson's resolution was directed against the Alien and Sedition Acts, a clear violation of freedom; Southern secession was advocated on behalf of slavery, a clear rejection of freedom. See Malone, *Jefferson and His Time*, 3:408–9, 414.

86. Malone, *Jefferson and His Time*, 4:106.

87. Jefferson argued: "keep away all show of force, and they [the American

270 • Notes to Chapter 4

people] will bear down the evil propensities of the government, by the constitutional means of election and petition." Malone, *Jefferson and His Time*, 3:414.

88. Tucker and Hendrickson, *Empire of Liberty*, 90.

89. See Malone, *Jefferson and His Time*, vol. 5, chapter 4, especially 58–62.

90. After victories at Austerlitz and Jena in winter 1805–6, Napoleon was dominant on land, even though Admiral Nelson's victory at Trafalgar in October 1805 held France at bay on the high seas.

91. Jackson was in Congress at the time. Brands, *Andrew Jackson: His Life and Times*, 144–45.

92. Quoted in Louis Martin Sears, *Jefferson and the Embargo* (New York: Octagon Books, 1978), 28.

93. Adams, *History of the United States*, 689.

94. Ibid., 632.

95. Ibid., 772.

96. Peterson, *Thomas Jefferson*, 815.

97. Adams, *History of the United States*, 681; and Peterson, *Thomas Jefferson*, 832–39.

98. Adams, *History of the United States*, 728.

99. Ibid., 681–83.

100. Tucker and Hendrickson, *Empire of Liberty*, 206.

101. Peterson, *Thomas Jefferson*, 882.

102. Bradford Perkins, *Prologue to War: England and the United States, 1805–1812* (Berkeley: University of California Press, 1961), 152.

103. Tucker and Hendrickson, *Empire of Liberty*, 211.

104. U.S. shipping "grew by leaps and bounds, . . . as French, Dutch, and Spanish shipping was driven from the seas by Great Britain." American deep-sea tonnage doubled from 1802 to 1810 even during the years of increasing restrictions. Tucker and Hendrickson, *Empire of Liberty*, 190.

105. It's true that Jefferson saw the policy as "an experiment" in "how far an embargo may be an effectual weapon in [the] future as well as on this occasion." But that does not tell us whether he saw it as an effectual weapon without the presence of force or as an effectual weapon because it was backed by force. His comments about the possibility of the embargo leading to war suggest the latter. Peterson, *Thomas Jefferson*, 885.

106. Jefferson sent Monroe to Madrid in 1804 to negotiate for West Florida. Monroe failed and left in 1805. Jefferson then threatened alliance with Great Britain, just as he did in Louisiana Purchase negotiations. And he backed the maneuvering of ground forces, endorsing the recommendations of John Armstrong, American minister in Paris, to occupy disputed territory in Texas. Eventually Jefferson relented, dropped negotiations with Spain, and turned to France for one last effort. Adams, *History of the United States*, 654–57.

107. Tucker and Hendrickson, *Empire of Liberty*, 199. See also Malone, *Jefferson and His Time*, vol. 5, chapter 22, especially 398.

108. For details, see Perkins, *Prologue to War*, 101–40. Weak countries often seem attractive subjects to be pressured further. But weak partners are also less capable of compromise. Polk discovered this fact repeatedly in the case of Mexico. See chapter 5.

109. Bowers, *Jefferson and Hamilton*, vi. By contrast, Hamilton wrote to Gouverneur Morris: "Every day proves to me more and more that this American world was not made for me," 510. And John Adams wrote in *Discourses of Davilla* that "there has never been a democracy that did not commit suicide," 322.

110. Jefferson's faith in the ability of common people to participate in government was utterly incomprehensible to his European counterparts. Here is what Catherine the Great, the "enlightened" czar of Russia, said by contrast in 1789: "I cannot believe in the superior talents of cobblers and shoemakers for government and legislation. It's veritable anarchy. They are capable of hanging their king from a lamppost!" (which of course they did in 1792). See Robert K. Massie, *Catherine the Great: Portrait of a Woman* (New York: Random House, 2011), 539.

111. Bowers, *Jefferson and Hamilton*, quotes from 151 and vi, respectively.

112. Quoted in Adams, *History of the United States*, 138.

113. Quoted in Peterson, *Thomas Jefferson*, 703.

114. Jefferson's first inaugural address in 1801. http://www.princeton.edu/~tjpapers/inaugural/inednote.html.

115. Quoted in Thom Hartmann, *What Would Jefferson Do? A Return to Democracy* (New York: Three Rivers Press, 2004), 78.

116. Quoted in ibid., 66.

117. Peterson, *Thomas Jefferson*, 713.

118. Bowers, *Jefferson and Hamilton*, 108; and Ferling, *Adams vs. Jefferson*, 67.

119. Peterson, *Thomas Jefferson*, 703.

120. Elsewhere, he wrote Governor McKean of Pennsylvania: "They [the Federalists] differ from us but in a shade of more or less power to be given to the Executive or Legislative organ." See Adams, *History of the United States*, 217, also 438–39.

121. Bowers, *Jefferson and Hamilton*, 489–90.

122. Quoted in Bowers, *Jefferson and Hamilton*, 105.

123. Peterson, *Thomas Jefferson*, 703.

CHAPTER 5: JAMES K. POLK: MANIFEST DESTINY

1. Across a dozen academic and citizen polls since 1948, Polk ranks a high of eighth and a low of fourteenth. See Robert W. Merry, *Where They Stand: The American Presidents in the Eyes of Voters and Historians* (New York: Simon and Schuster, 2012), 38.

2. Paul H. Bergeron, *The Presidency of James K. Polk* (Lawrence: University Press of Kansas, 1987), xii. Stephen Skowronek calls Polk a "transformative" president. See *The Politics Presidents Make: Leadership from John Adams to George Bush* (Cambridge, MA: Harvard University Press, 1993), 13.

3. John Seigenthaler, *James K. Polk* (New York: Times Books, 2003), 2.

4. For negative assessments of Polk, see Amy S. Greenberg, *A Wicked War* (New York: Knopf, 2013); Anders Stephanson, *Manifest Destiny: American Expansion and the Empire of Right* (New York: Hill and Wang, 1995), chapter 2; Thomas R. Hietala, *Manifest Design: American Exceptionalism and Empire*, rev. ed. (Ithaca: Cornell University Press 2003); Thomas G. Paterson, J. Garry Clifford, Shane J. Maddock, Deborah Kisatsky, and Kenneth J. Hagan, *American Foreign Relations: A History* (Boston: Houghton Mifflin, 2006), vol. 1, chapter 3;

and William Dusinberre, *Slavemaster President: The Double Career of James Polk* (New York: Oxford University Press, 2003). Presidential Scholar Fred Greenstein ranks Polk high on tactical grounds but, reflecting the weight of the slavery question, low on strategic grounds. In a sense, this chapter makes the strategic case for Polk. See Fred I. Greenstein, "The Policy-Driven Leadership of James K. Polk: Making the Most of a Weak Presidency," *Presidential Studies Quarterly* 40, 4 (December 2010): 725 –33.

5. Sam W. Haynes, *James K. Polk and the Expansionist Impulse* (New York: Longman, 1997), 90.

6. Stephanson, *Manifest Destiny*, 61.

7. Ralph Waldo Emerson compared the conquest of Mexico to swallowing arsenic. Seigenthaler, *James K. Polk*, 145.

8. David M. Pletcher, *The Diplomacy of Annexation: Texas, Oregon, and the Mexican War* (Columbia: University of Missouri Press, 1973), 603.

9. Ibid., 232.

10. Charles Sellers, *James K. Polk: Continentalist, 1843–1846* (Princeton: Princeton University Press, 1966), 214.

11. Pletcher, *The Diplomacy of Annexation*, 605.

12. Walter R. Borneman, *Polk: The Man Who Transformed the Presidency and America* (New York: Random House, 2008), 30.

13. See Sean Wilentz, *The Rise of American Democracy: Jefferson to Lincoln* (New York: W. W. Norton, 2005), 585.

14. For Polk's inaugural address, see http://www.bartleby.com/124/pres27 .html.

15. Borneman, *Polk*, 73.

16. Brands, *Andrew Jackson: His Life and Times*, 508–26.

17. See, among others, Gene M. Brack, *Mexico Views Manifest Destiny, 1821–1846: An Essay on the Origins of the Mexican War* (Albuquerque: University of New Mexico Press, 1975); and Piero Gleijeses, "A Brush with Mexico," *Diplomatic History* 29, 2 (April 2005): 223–54.

18. Some historians blame Mexican nationalism for the war. Mexican leaders were excessively bellicose and hostile to the United States. They used foreign intervention to drive domestic divisions and badly miscalculated Mexico's own weakness. See Justin H. Smith, *The War with Mexico, Volumes I and II* (New York: MacMillan, 1919). Brack refutes Smith's charges, arguing that few Mexicans clamored for war. See *Mexico Views Manifest Destiny*, 175–79.

19. Bergeron, *The Presidency*, 135.

20. Dusinberre, *Slavemaster President*, 11–119.

21. *The Diary of James K. Polk* (Chicago: A. C. McClurg & Co., 1910), 2:350.

22. See Paul Johnson, *A History of the American People* (New York: HarperCollins, 1999), 158.

23. See Stanley L. Engerman and Kenneth L. Sokoloff, *Economic Development in the Americas since 1500: Endowments and Institutions* (Cambridge: Cambridge University Press, 2012), 111.

24. As Michael Morrison writes, "expansion attracted Democrats because it would mean the addition of thousands of square miles of uninhabited arable land to a nation of independent, self-sufficient, and restless yeomen." See "Westward

the Curse of Empire: Texas Annexation and the American Whig Party," *Journal of the Early Republic* 10, 2 (Summer 1990): 244.

25. Sellers, *Continentalist*, 345.

26. In his first speech in Congress, Polk called slavery "a common evil." Seigenthaler, *James K. Polk*, 86. Washington declared "that nothing but the rooting out of slavery can perpetuate the existence of our union, by consolidating it in a common bond of principle." Quoted in Henry Wieneck, *An Imperfect God: George Washington, His Slaves, and the Creation of America* (New York: Farrar, Straus and Giroux, 2003), 352.

27. Jackson, for example, wrote in March 1844 that the annexation of Texas positioned the United States to "enlarge the circle of free institutions." Quoted in Robert W. Merry, *A Country of Vast Designs: James K. Polk, the Mexican War, and the Conquest of the American Continent* (New York: Simon and Schuster, 2009), 74.

28. Pletcher, *The Diplomacy of Annexation*, 32.

29. Samuel Flagg Bemis, the noted American historian, reaches a similar conclusion. See "American Foreign Policy and the Blessings of Liberty," *American Historical Review* 67, 2 (January 1962): 291–305. As a young student at the University of Texas, John Lewis Gaddis recalls Bemis acknowledging American aggression against Mexico and then asking his audience whether in retrospect anyone would want to give it all back and trace an alternative path led by other powers. See *Surprise, Security and the American Experience* (Cambridge, MA: Harvard University Press, 2004), 32.

30. Dusinberre, *Slavemaster President*, 154.

31. Pletcher, *The Diplomacy of Annexation*, 599, 602. The same might be said of Ronald Reagan, suggesting the historical lineage of conservative internationalism. See chapter 7.

32. Sellers, *Continentalist*, 226.

33. Pletcher, *The Diplomacy of Annexation*, 101.

34. Dusinberre, *Slavemaster President*, 172.

35. As Wilentz argues, "Polk's vision of Manifest Destiny was an emollient on sectional discord, and not a sectional ploy." See *The Rise of American Democracy*, 585.

36. Pletcher, *The Diplomacy of Annexation*, 526.

37. In an insightful exercise in counterfactual history, Gary J. Kornblith argues that "had Clay been elected in 1844 and the Mexican-American War thus avoided, the Nebraska territory would have been organized on the basis of the Missouri Compromise with little congressional debate." He sees the war causing the inflammatory emergence of the Wilmot Proviso and the concept of popular sovereignty, but the unanswerable question is whether the war caused these ideas or these ideas would have appeared in other crises even if the Mexican War had not occurred. See "Rethinking the Coming of the Civil War: A Counterfactual Exercise," *Journal of American History* 90, 1 (June 2003): 98.

38. Pletcher, *The Diplomacy of Annexation*, 581.

39. Ibid., 577.

40. Haynes, *James K. Polk and the Expansionist Impulse*, 72.

41. Arthur M. Schlesinger Jr., *The Age of Jackson* (Boston: Little, Brown, 1946), 441.

42. Skowronek, *The Politics Presidents Make*, 157.

43. Dusinberre, *Slavemaster President*, 139.

44. Bergeron, *The Presidency*, 37.

45. Texas first applied for annexation in summer 1837 but President Van Buren and Congress never acted on the request. Congress did recognize Texas independence, and Jackson, on his last day in office, appointed a chargé d'affaires to the new country.

46. According to one historian, Polk's immediate response offered "telling evidence of Polk's strong commitment to principle above politics." See Borneman, *Polk*, 87.

47. Polk clearly had a strategy to become the presidential nominee. The story of how he rebooted his career after his second defeat in 1843 to regain the governorship of Tennessee (a post he held from 1839 to 1841) is ample testimony to the political skills and instincts Polk possessed. See Merry, *A Country of Vast Designs*, especially chapter 4.

48. The popular vote was 49.6 versus 48.1 percent. Sixteen thousand votes in New York State went to the Liberty candidate, who strongly opposed Texas annexation. Schlesinger, *The Age of Jackson*, 440.

49. Sellers, *Continentalist*, 207; and Pletcher, *The Diplomacy of Annexation*, 183.

50. Sellers, *Continentalist*, 220.

51. The quote is from Calhoun's account; see ibid., 216; and Pletcher, *The Diplomacy of Annexation*, 183.

52. Borneman, *Polk*, 146.

53. Pletcher, *The Diplomacy of Annexation*, 183. Bergeron agrees: "Polk was content to let Tyler take some of the heat off him." See *The Presidency*, 57.

54. Sellers, *Continentalist*, 219–20.

55. Ibid., 221.

56. On August 23, 1843, the Mexican government warned: "The Mexican Government will consider equivalent to a declaration of war against the Mexican Republic, the passage of any act for the incorporation of Texas with the territory of the United States." Pletcher, *The Diplomacy of Annexation*, 126.

57. This proposal had been around for some time and was supported in summer 1844 by Sam Houston, then president of Texas, when Britain and France agreed in the so-called Diplomatic Act to guarantee Texas independence. See Pletcher, *The Diplomacy of Annexation*, 164–65.

58. Borneman, *Polk*, 147.

59. Sellers, *Continentalist*, 222; and Pletcher, *The Diplomacy of Annexation*, 255.

60. Sellers, *Continentalist*, 227.

61. Ibid., 228.

62. On these details, see Pletcher, *The Diplomacy of Annexation*, 255–56.

63. See also Bergeron, *The Presidency*, 59. For an account that gives greater credence to Jones's narrative, see Richard R. Steinberg, "The Failure of Polk's Mexican War Intrigue of 1845," *Pacific Historical Review* 4, 1 (March 1935): 39–68. For a later development of the same argument, see Glenn W. Price, *Origins of the War with Mexico: The Polk-Stockton Intrigue* (Austin: University of Texas Press, 1969). The case is based on the assumption that Polk must have known and approved of what his emissaries in Texas were doing. But given Polk's repeated

disputes with emissaries, most glaringly Nicholas Trist, that assumption without proof is unwarranted.

64. Pletcher, *The Diplomacy of Annexation*, 200.

65. Ibid., 270. Bergeron, *The Presidency*, 59; and Sellers, *Continentalist*, 225, agree.

66. Haynes, *James K. Polk and the Expansionist Impulse*, 109.

67. Nationalists and defensive realists argue, of course, that Polk, defying prudent behavior, was inviting two wars simultaneously. And indeed from this perspective, Polk's actions seem to be those of an offensive realist or imperialist.

68. Pletcher, *The Diplomacy of Annexation*, 270. Bergeron, *The Presidency*, 59 and Sellers, *Continentalist*, 225, seem to agree.

69. Bergeron, *The Presidency*, 67.

70. Haynes sums it up best: "Few presidents ever had so clear a view of their goals at the outset of their terms; fewer still can claim to have left office having fulfilled them." See *James K. Polk and the Expansionist Impulse*, 194.

71. Sellers, *Continentalist*, 232. Polk's vision to think outside the box was reminiscent of Jefferson's.

72. Merry, *A Country of Vast Designs*, 194.

73. Sellers, *Continentalist*, 229.

74. Ibid., 261.

75. Pletcher, *The Diplomacy of Annexation*, 256.

76. Sellers, *Continentalist*, 229–30. Bergeron agrees: "Aggression, like beauty, may often be in the eye of the beholder, but Polk sincerely interpreted his policies as nonaggressive, basing that view partly upon his belief that the Rio Grande rightly constituted the southern and western boundary of Texas." See *The Presidency*, 63. See also the conclusions of Eugene Irving McCormac, *James K. Polk: A Political Biography* (New York: Russell & Russell, 1965), 380–81; and Haynes, *James K. Polk and the Expansionist Impulse*, 116.

77. *The Diary*, 1:437–38.

78. Sellers, *Continentalist*, 336; and Pletcher, *The Diplomacy of Annexation*, 289.

79. Sellers, *Continentalist*, 336.

80. See speculation by Sellers, *Continentalist*, 336; and Pletcher, *The Diplomacy of Annexation*, 291.

81. *The Diary*, 2:16.

82. Ibid., 2:76.

83. In July 1845, the leader of the French government, Francois Guizot, said to the Chamber of Deputies: France's interest in the New World is "that the independent states remain independent, that the equilibrium of forces between the great masses which divide America continue, that no one of them become exclusively dominant." Pletcher, *The Diplomacy of Annexation*, 267; and Sellers, *Continentalist*, 342.

84. Pletcher, *The Diplomacy of Annexation*, 294–95, 593. Pletcher believes that European activities in California were "mostly sound and fury" (98); and it is true that British prime minister Peel actually rejected a proposal by British merchants to establish a colony in California (96–97). But these assessments are made with the benefit of hindsight.

85. Sellers, *Continentalist*, 336–37.

86. In the less than two years of war, eight men served as president of Mexico, with eleven different changes in office. See Krystyna M. Libura, Luis Gerardo Morales Moreno, and Jesus Velasco Marquez, translated by Mark Fried, *Echoes of the Mexican-American War* (Toronto: Groundwood Books, 2004), 159.

87. Brack describes Herrera's situation: "federalists, centralists, the commercial class, the Church, the army, and outright monarchists comprised the opposition. All invoked the Texas issue against Herrera. None would therefore support his efforts to reach an accord first with the Texans, and, later in 1845, with the United States itself." See *Mexico Views Manifest Destiny*, 136.

88. Pena told John Black, the U.S. consul in Mexico City, in early December: "you know the opposition are calling us traitors for entering into this arrangement with you." Smith, *The War with Mexico*, 1:96. *Puros*, or extreme federalists, as well as centralists opposed Herrera. See David S. Heidler and Jeanne T. Heidler, *The Mexican War* (Westport, CT: Greenwood, 2006), 53–56.

89. Pletcher, *The Diplomacy of Annexation*, 358; and Brack, *Mexico Views Manifest Destiny*, 144.

90. As Norman A. Graebner concludes, "it was the weakness of the Herrera regime . . . that proved the undoing of the Slidell mission." See *Empire on the Pacific: A Study in American Continental Expansion* (New York: Ronald Press Company, 1955), 120.

91. As Seigenthaler writes, "The Mexicans gave Slidell short shrift and sent him packing." See *James K. Polk*, 126.

92. Pletcher, *The Diplomacy of Annexation*, 364.

93. Ibid., 365–66.

94. Brack, *Mexico Views Manifest Destiny*, 179. Brack also argues that, given the intense nationalist animosities, many Mexicans may have also feared extermination by American racism, like the American Indians.

95. Pletcher, *The Diplomacy of Annexation*, 439.

96. Sellers, *Continentalist*, 422; and Pletcher, *The Diplomacy of Annexation*, 398. The language "hold until peace was made" was indicative of Polk's view of territory as a bargaining chip for peace rather than a permanent military conquest.

97. Pletcher, *The Diplomacy of Annexation*, 410, 593.

98. "Polk . . . wished to press as far south as the twenty-sixth parallel but would accept a boundary as far north as the thirty-second parallel. Flexibility seemed to be his motto, as long as Upper California as well as New Mexico, became a part of the United States." See Bergeron, *The Presidency*, 82.

99. Polk also had Buchanan send a letter directly to Mexico's foreign minister offering negotiations "to terminate . . . the present unhappy war." Merry, *A Country of Vast Designs*, 279.

100. Bergeron, *The Presidency*, 83. Mackenzie, against instructions, had written down his communications with Santa Anna, creating a document Congress later demanded during the final debates of the war. See Merry, *A Country of Vast Designs*, 411–12.

101. Pletcher, *The Diplomacy of Annexation*, 445.

102. During this period, the British had no better luck negotiating with a fragmented Mexico. Aberdeen wrote in June 1846: "[the Mexicans] have at last plunged down the precipice from which the British Govt. spared no efforts to

save them." Lord Palmerston, the Whig foreign minister who replaced Aberdeen that same month, offered mediation, but neither Mexico nor the United States accepted. Pletcher, *The Diplomacy of Annexation*, 451–53.

103. Sellers, *Continentalist*, 434.

104. Polk wanted to put Senator Benson in charge as a freshly minted lieutenant general but Congress refused. A bizarre idea, Polk's preference reflected constant difficulties with his generals, not unlike Lincoln or Truman in subsequent wars. At this stage, Calhoun opposed the expedition to Mexico City, as did Buchanan, Taylor, and Marcy. The alternative Calhoun proposed, as a defensive realist, was a chain of defensive posts across northern Mexico to hold territory for indemnification. Bergeron, *The Presidency*, 88; and Pletcher, *The Diplomacy of Annexation*, 469, 472.

105. Pletcher, *The Diplomacy of Annexation*, 476–77.

106. The notations were made on April 14, 1847, when Polk learned of Beach's potential agreement. *The Diary*, 2:476–77.

107. See *The Diary*, 2:477.

108. Pletcher, *The Diplomacy of Annexation*, 478.

109. Ibid., 479.

110. Beach subsequently met with Polk in May 1847 and, as Polk says in his diary, "had a long conversation with me . . . and gave me valuable information," 3:22. Given the two tracks on which Polk was negotiating (the Beach proposal including the northern provinces, the Atocha offer excluding it), it is clear that Polk was not bent on acquiring Mexico's northern provinces but, as he indicated in his April entry, would have taken such an arrangement to Congress if Beach had brought it off.

111. Bergeron, *The Presidency*, 97.

112. Pletcher, *The Diplomacy of Annexation*, 481. Pletcher concludes that the disarray in Mexico was once again the principal culprit for the failure of negotiations: "Mexico was a sick country, with the national equivalents of dropsy, intermittent fever, and creeping paralysis," 31. And there is "no convincing evidence . . . that [Santa Anna] ever seriously intended to reach an agreement with the United States," 604.

113. As Bergeron reports: "Informing the cabinet of Scott's successes, the president indicated his desire to dispatch a peace commissioner at once to Mexico." See *The Presidency*, 97.

114. *The Diary*, 1:495–96.

115. Many years later, "Trist revealed what Polk and Buchanan had not known: He had considered the war with Mexico an 'abuse of power' by the United States. Trist had had his own agenda, which influenced his negotiations with the Mexicans. . . . [He] considered himself guilty not of violating presidential orders but of violating Mexico." See Robert W. Drexler, "Sent by President James K. Polk to End the War with Mexico, Nicholas Trist Soon Embarked on His Own Agenda," *Military History* 14, 6 (February 1998): 10–12.

116. *The Diary*, 2:477–78.

117. Pletcher, *The Diplomacy of Annexation*, 500–501. For Polk's own understanding of these instructions, see *The Diary*, 2:472–74.

118. For both quotations, see *The Diary*, 3:164.

119. Pletcher, *The Diplomacy of Annexation*, 510.

120. Ibid., 517–19.

121. Pletcher, *The Diplomacy of Annexation*, 529.

122. Bergeron, *The Presidency*, 102.

123. Ibid., 103; and Pletcher, *The Diplomacy of Annexation*, 540.

124. Pletcher, *The Diplomacy of Annexation*, 601.

125. Dusinberre, *Slavemaster President*, 139, argues to the contrary: he "had no firm ground on which to reject the work of his insubordinate emissary."

126. Pletcher, *The Diplomacy of Annexation*, 527.

127. On the personal side, Scott answered to a court of inquiry but retired with honor. Trist was arrested and deported by Butler, and Polk, in the one outburst of personal pique, refused to pay his salary after his dismissal. Congress eventually remedied that insult, awarding him full salary in 1871.

128. Pletcher, *The Diplomacy of Annexation*, 219.

129. Bergeron, *The Presidency*, 113.

130. In 1818, Castlereagh, the British foreign minister, made this point to an American negotiator: "You need not trouble yourselves about Oregon, you will conquer Oregon in your bedchambers." See Pletcher, *The Diplomacy of Annexation*, 103.

131. Calhoun, according to the British foreign minister, negotiated in "fairness and good humor," even at the height of the presidential campaign. Pletcher, *The Diplomacy of Annexation*, 221.

132. Pletcher, *The Diplomacy of Annexation*, 226.

133. Sellers, *Continentalist*, 236.

134. Ibid., 248–49; and Pletcher, *The Diplomacy of Annexation*, 248–49.

135. Pletcher, *The Diplomacy of Annexation*, 247, argues that McLane "was selected deliberately . . . since he was known to oppose fifty-four-forty."

136. Bergeron, *The Presidency*, 118; Pletcher, *The Diplomacy of Annexation*, 243. Pletcher concludes that "Pakenham violated the spirit of Aberdeen's instructions," 248. Aberdeen later told McLane in extensive discussions in October 1845 that he would have accepted such a proposal as a basis of discussions and possible agreement, 297.

137. Pletcher, *The Diplomacy of Annexation*, 248.

138. Ibid., 249.

139. Sellers, *Continentalist*, 377–78.

140. Bergeron, *The Presidency*, 126; and Pletcher, *The Diplomacy of Annexation*, 328.

141. Sellers, *Continentalist*, 377.

142. Pletcher, *The Diplomacy of Annexation*, 306. Polk was willing to accept *temporary* rights for the Hudson Bay Company, as his 1845 negotiating offer suggested. See Sellers, *Continentalist*, 248–49.

143. Bergeron, *The Presidency*, 125.

144. For both quotes, see Sellers, *Continentalist*, 392.

145. Ibid., 387.

146. Pletcher, *The Diplomacy of Annexation*, 408.

147. Sellers, *Continentalist*, 332.

148. Britain's interest in the Oregon Territory had been ebbing for some time. At the beginning of 1845, the Hudson Bay Company, induced in part by the mas-

sive influx of American settlers in 1843–44, moved its headquarters from Fort Vancouver on the north bank of the Columbia River to the newly constructed Fort Victoria on the southern tip of Vancouver Island, suggesting, according to Pletcher, that "it regarded the territory between the river and Puget Sound as expendable." See *The Diplomacy of Annexation*, 588.

149. Pletcher, *The Diplomacy of Annexation*, 409.

150. Seller, *Continentalist*, 410, argues that Aberdeen's willingness under McLane's guidance not to insist on full navigation rights on the Columbia River and Polk's willingness to accept temporary rights were the telling concessions: "By this narrow margin was possibly averted a double war that would surely have been disastrous to the United States." But this argument ignores the fact that the U.S. concession of temporary rights was part of Polk's negotiating instructions already in May 1845. See Sellers, *Continentalist*, 248–49.

151. *The Diary*, 1:453.

152. Ibid., 1:460.

153. Sellers, *Continentalist*, 415.

154. Ibid.

155. Sellers excuses the manipulation by arguing that "if Polk's diplomatic bluff with Great Britain were to succeed, he could hardly take the country into his confidence" See ibid., 414.

156. See Polk's inaugural address at http://www.bartleby.com/124/pres27 .html. All subsequent quotes are from this address unless otherwise noted.

157. Polk accepted Christianity only on his deathbed. Merry, *A Country of Vast Designs*, 470.

158. Schlesinger, *The Age of Jackson*, 421.

159. As Sellers writes: "Polk was not remotely equipped to understand the emotions men brought to the emerging slavery controversy. Even to ask whether this rapidly industrializing, urbanizing nation could remain half slave and half free seemed to him wildly irresponsible and unpatriotic." See *Continentalist*, 487.

160. Bergeron, *The Presidency*, 45.

161. Pletcher, *The Diplomacy of Annexation*, 232, quotation from 230.

162. Sellers, *Continentalist*, 447.

163. Pletcher, *The Diplomacy of Annexation*, 602.

164. Ibid., 232.

165. Polk had plenty of encouragement to seek a second term. See Merry, *A Country of Vast Designs*, 422.

CHAPTER 6: HARRY S. TRUMAN: LIBERTY IN WESTERN EUROPE

1. Spoken at a White House dinner on November 10, 1945. *Memoirs by Harry S. Truman*, vol. 1, *Year of Decisions* (Garden City, NY: Doubleday, 1955), 540.

2. For an insightful comparison of Truman and his Democratic predecessors, see Elizabeth Edwards Spalding, *The First Cold Warrior: Harry Truman, Containment, and the Remaking of Liberal Internationalism* (Lexington: University of Kentucky Press, 2006), 84.

3. See John Lewis Gaddis, *George F. Kennan: An American Life* (New York: Penguin, 2012). See also Louis Menand, "Getting Real: George F. Kennan's Cold War," *The New Yorker*, November 14, 2011, 76–83.

4. "Ideology is a product and not a determinant of social and political reality," Kennan wrote in 1947. See Gaddis, *Strategies of Containment*, 33.

5. Spalding finds these comments in Kennan's papers at Princeton University. See *The First Cold Warrior*, 107.

6. Walter Lippmann was another realist who sharply criticized Truman for his anti-communism. He called containment a "strategic monstrosity." See *The Cold War: A Study in U.S. Foreign Policy* (New York: Torchbooks, 1947), 444–45.

7. Quoted in Gaddis, *Strategies of Containment*, 3.

8. Truman wrote in his diary on June 7, 1945: "I'm not afraid of the Russians. They've always been our friends and I can't see any reason why they shouldn't always be." Quoted in Walter Isaacson and Evan Thomas, *The Wise Men: Six Friends and the World They Made, Acheson, Bohlen, Harriman, Kennan, Lovett, McCloy* (New York: Simon and Schuster, 1986), 287.

9. David McCullough, *Truman* (New York: Simon and Schuster, 1992), 445. For perhaps the most thorough and careful treatment of the differences between Roosevelt and Truman, see Wilson D. Miscamble, C.S.C., *From Roosevelt to Truman: Potsdam, Hiroshima, and the Cold War* (Cambridge: Cambridge University Press, 2007).

10. As Robert Dallek writes, "Truman's interactions with Stalin and his Soviet colleagues . . . in Potsdam deepened his suspicions and doubts about his ability to get along with them." *Harry S. Truman* (New York: Time Books, 2008), 22.

11. Robert H. Ferrell, ed., *Dear Bess: The Letters from Harry to Bess Truman, 1910–1959* (New York: W. W. Norton, 1983), 521–22. See also Robert H. Ferrell, *Presidential Leadership: From Woodrow Wilson to Harry S. Truman* (Columbia: University of Missouri Press, 2006), 128.

12. In fact, he did just the opposite. Later, during the 1948 campaign, Truman depicted Stalin as "a prisoner of the Politburo"; the political controlled the personal. See Clifford, *Counsel to the President*, 200–201.

13. Robert J. Donovan, *Conflict and Crisis: The Presidency of Harry S. Truman, 1945–1948* (New York: W. W. Norton, 1977), 86.

14. *Memoirs by Harry S. Truman*, 1:71. See also Isaacson and Thomas, *The Wise Men*, 262–63.

15. Quoted in Spalding, *The First Cold Warrior*, 15.

16. Ferrell, *Dear Bess*, letter of April 30, 1942, 474.

17. Quoted in Spalding, *The First Cold Warrior*, 26.

18. *Memoirs by Harry S. Truman*, 1:537.

19. Quoted in Spalding, *The First Cold Warrior*, 20. As Gaddis notes, Roosevelt felt that communism was not as prone to the use of force as fascism and expected that "as fears of Germany subsided, the Russians would moderate the severity of measures" needed to maintain their position in central Europe. See *Strategies of Containment*, 10–12.

20. Spalding, *The First Cold Warrior*, 40.

21. See, for example, Marc Trachtenberg, who concludes "the policy of containment, as it came to be called, was adopted at the beginning of 1946." *A Constructed Peace: The Making of the European Settlement 1945–1963* (Princeton: Princeton University Press, 1999), 41. See also Paul C. Avey, "Confronting

Soviet Power: U.S. Policy during the Early Cold War," *International Security* 36, 4 (Spring 2012): 172.

22. "Truman had been given a copy of the text on the train ride west." See Elsey, *An Unplanned Life*, 137. According to Clark Clifford, another top aide: "The President said he would not read the text, in order to be able to say later that he had not endorsed or approved it in advance." See *Counsel to the President*, 102. Donovan says Truman changed his mind and read the text on the train. See *Conflict and Crisis*, 191.

23. Quoted in Spalding, *The First Cold Warrior*, 246. See also Truman's unsent letter of August 30, 1947: "if we had held the line which we attained in Germany our troubles in that country with Russia would now be over." Monte M. Poen, ed., *Strictly Personal and Confidential: The Letters Truman Never Mailed* (Boston: Little, Brown, 1982), 37.

24. Spalding, *The First Cold Warrior*, 43.

25. On Wallace as "the most insistent liberal," see *The Price of Vision: The Diary of Henry A. Wallace, 1942–1946*, edited and with an introduction by John Morton Blum (Boston: Houghton Mifflin, 1973), 233. Clifford writes: "With the exception of Eleanor Roosevelt, Wallace was the leading liberal of the nation in 1946" (*Counsel to the President*, 114).

26. Quoted from original letter of July 23 in Spalding, *The First Cold Warrior*, 51.

27. *The Price of Vision*, 664. Joseph Davies, another soft-line Roosevelt advisor, held similar views: "when approached with generosity and friendship, the Soviets respond with even greater generosity. The 'tough' approach induces a quick and sharp rejoinder that 'out toughs' anyone they consider hostile." See Isaacson and Thomas, *The Wise Men*, 279.

28. Quoted in Isaacson and Thomas, *The Wise Men*, 666.

29. Ferrell, *Dear Bess*, 538–39. Truman later identified Wallace publicly with the Communists (Donovan, *Conflict and Crisis*, 360). But in his memoirs he retracted, calling Wallace an "honest man" who "was apparently unaware of the purposes to which the Communists were putting his 'progressive' movement." *Memoirs by Harry S. Truman*, vol. 2, *Years of Trial and Hope* (Garden City, NY: Doubleday, 1956), 185.

30. Quoted in Spalding, *The First Cold Warrior*, 228.

31. *Memoirs by Harry S. Truman*, 1:552.

32. Anne R. Pierce, *Woodrow Wilson and Harry Truman: Mission and Power in American Foreign Policy* (Westport, CT: Praeger, 2003), 151.

33. Ibid., 124.

34. Miscamble, *From Roosevelt to Truman*, quotations from 68 and 47, respectively.

35. Davies was a former U.S. ambassador to Moscow who wrote a popular book in the 1930s, *Mission to Moscow*. The book drew a rather benign portrait of the Soviet regime, which was then engaged in mass atrocities against Russian peasants and bourgeois military officers. See Robert Conquest, *The Great Terror* (New York: Macmillan, 1968).

36. Truman shaped the speech in significant ways. See *Memoirs by Harry S. Truman*, 2:105.

37. See Joseph M. Jones, *The Fifteen Weeks (February 21–June 5, 1947)* (New York: Viking, 1955), 154–55. See also Menand, "Getting Real," 83. Within a year, Kennan, like Lippmann, whose criticism of Kennan stung, felt that "he had created a monster" with containment. Isaacson and Thomas, *The Wise Men*, 435.

38. Quoted in Spalding, *The First Cold Warrior*, 94.

39. *Memoirs by Harry S. Truman*, 2:242.

40. Quoted in Spalding, *The First Cold Warrior*, 102.

41. Ibid., 142.

42. Ibid., 144.

43. Ibid.

44. Ibid., quotes from 183, 185, 186, 189, and 190, respectively.

45. See, among others, Dallek, *Harry S. Truman*, 100ff, who blames Republican anti-communists more than Truman; Leffler, *For the Soul of Mankind*, 71; and Ernest B. May, *"Lessons" of the Past: The Use and Abuse of History in American Foreign Policy* (London: Oxford University Press, 1973), 44–45. For the debate at the time, see Isaacson and Thomas, *The Wise Men*, 395–99; and Daniel Yergin, *Shattered Peace: The Origins of the Cold War and the National Security State* (Boston: Houghton Mifflin, 1977), 275–302.

46. For the "Martial Plan" comment, see McCullough, *Truman*, 595; for the "declaration of war" comment, see Spalding, *The First Cold Warrior*, 73.

47. See Acheson's responses to Congress in Jones, *The Fifteen Weeks*, 194–95.

48. Miscamble, *From Roosevelt to Truman*, 52.

49. Isaacson and Thomas, *The Wise Men*, 260–61.

50. Miscamble, *From Roosevelt to Truman*, 53.

51. Stalin had given a speech in February 1946, even before Churchill's Fulton speech, that foresaw inevitable conflict between capitalism and communism. Kennan in Moscow was asked to comment on this speech, precipitating the Long Telegram. Donovan, *Conflict and Crisis*, 187.

52. Thomas Risse-Kappen, "Collective Identity in a Democratic Community: The Case of NATO," in Peter Katzenstein, ed., *The Culture of National Security: Norms and Identity in World Politics* (New York: Columbia University Press, 1996), 372.

53. Ibid., 374. As Donovan writes: "For ideological as well as strategic reasons, Truman and his advisors did not wish to see communism installed beyond the Soviet borders because it then appeared a threat to democracy itself and not simply an instrument of Soviet security." See *Conflict and Crisis*, 43.

54. See Colin Dueck, *Reluctant Crusaders: Power, Culture, and Change in American Grand Strategy* (Princeton: Princeton University Press, 2006). See also Henry R. Nau, "Ideas Have Consequences: The Cold War and Today," *International Politics* 48 (July/September 2011): 460–81. For a realist argument that a sharp increase in Soviet relative power during 1946–48 is sufficient to explain the onset of the Cold War, see Avey, "Confronting Soviet Power," 159. My account, as mentioned above, is that the Soviets had to increase their relative power precisely because they did not feel safe *given* the ideological disparity. See also the conclusion.

55. For a fuller development of how ideas drive power and diplomacy, see Henry R. Nau, "Rethinking Economics, Politics, and Security in Europe," in Richard Perle, ed., *Reshaping Western Security: The U.S. Faces a United Europe* (Wash-

ington, DC: American Enterprise Institute, 1991), 3–41 and Nau, "Ideas Have Consequences," 462–67.

56. Pierce, *Woodrow Wilson and Harry Truman*, 263.

57. Elsey, *An Unplanned Life*, 68.

58. See, respectively, Gaddis, *Strategies of Containment*, 5–6; and Miscamble, *From Roosevelt to Truman*, 70.

59. Ferrell, *Presidential Leadership*, 127.

60. See Donovan, *Conflict and Crisis*, 11, 35.

61. Spalding, *The First Cold Warrior*, 28. Donovan, too, concludes that "in the passage from Roosevelt to Truman the presidential attitude [toward the Soviet Union] hardened." *Conflict and Crisis*, 42.

62. According to Gaddis, Truman embraced a tougher quid pro quo approach advocated by Harriman rather than the open-handed or integration approach practiced by Roosevelt. See *Strategies of Containment*, 14–15.

63. *Memoirs by Harry S. Truman*, 1:81–82. For an eyewitness account of this meeting, see Charles Bohlen, the translator, in *Witness to History, 1929–1969* (New York: W. W. Norton, 1973), 212–14. Bohlen, who visited with Roosevelt on the Polish issue just days before he died, believes Roosevelt would have conveyed the same message but "smoother."

64. Ferrell, *Dear Bess*, letter to Bess, July 31, 1945, 522.

65. Isaacson and Thomas, *The Wise Men*, 281.

66. *Memoirs by Harry S. Truman*, 2:11.

67. Wilson D. Miscamble, C.S.C., *The Most Controversial Decision: Truman, the Atomic Bomb, and the Defeat of Japan* (Cambridge: Cambridge University Press, 2011), 45. See also *Memoirs by Harry S. Truman*, 1:419–20; Donovan, *Conflict and Crisis*, 97; and Truman's unsent letter of August 5, 1963, in Poen, *Strictly Personal and Confidential*, 36.

68. For Truman's account of this period, see *Memoirs by Harry S. Truman*, 1:211–19.

69. *Memoirs by Harry S. Truman*, 1:262.

70. Ibid., 301–2.

71. Ibid., 305.

72. Quoted in Spalding, *The First Cold Warrior*, 17; she cites McCullough, *Truman*, 399, who offers no original citation. For further evidence, see Poen, *Strictly Personal and Confidential*, 37.

73. *Memoirs by Harry S. Truman*, 1:307.

74. Ibid., 2:55.

75. Quoted in Pierce, *Woodrow Wilson and Harry Truman*, 1:133.

76. *Memoirs by Harry S. Truman*, 1:509.

77. Ibid., 2:345.

78. Miscamble, *From Roosevelt to Truman*, 66.

79. Ibid., 293.

80. Jones, *The Fifteen Weeks*, 48–58; see also *Memoirs by Harry S. Truman*, 2:93–94.

81. Miscamble, *From Roosevelt to Truman*, 274–75. For Truman's account, see *Memoirs by Harry S. Truman*, 1:552. Whether Truman read the letter to Byrnes or not is immaterial. According to Donovan, he had expressed similar concerns to

Byrnes on previous occasions. *Conflict and Crisis*, 190. The letter "was obviously a calm, deliberate attempt by [Truman] to define his thoughts," 161.

82. When Molotov told Stalin that the West would not accept Soviet-Turkish control of the Dardanelle Strait, Stalin replied: "demand it." Miscamble, *From Roosevelt to Truman*, 294.

83. When he made these decisions, Truman pulled out a map of the Middle East and eastern Mediterranean and gave his aides—Eisenhower, Acheson, and others—"a brief lecture on the strategic importance of the area," fully understanding that his actions could lead to war. See Dean Acheson, *Present at the Creation: My Years in the State Department* (New York: W. W. Norton, 1969), 195–96. See also Jones, *The Fifteen Weeks*, 66.

84. Miscamble, *From Roosevelt to Truman*, 295–96.

85. For Clifford's account, see *Counsel to the President*, 109–30. Elsey actually wrote most of the report. See *An Unplanned Life*, 144.

86. Spalding, *The First Cold Warrior*, 55. See also Clifford, *Counsel to the President*, 126.

87. Elsey, *An Unplanned Life*, 162.

88. Clifford, *Counsel to the President*, 123. The existence of the report did not surface until twenty years later.

89. McCullough, *Truman*, 547.

90. Spalding, *The First Cold Warrior*, 130.

91. Isaacson and Thomas, *The Wise Men*, 457.

92. *Memoirs by Harry S. Truman*, 2:107.

93. Quoted in Ferrell, *Dear Bess*, 550.

94. See Spalding, *The First Cold Warrior*, 91; and *Memoirs by Harry S. Truman*, 2:114.

95. *Memoirs by Harry S. Truman*, 2:119.

96. General Lucius Clay, who led the negotiations in the field, blamed himself for not insisting on confirmation of the agreement in writing. See *Memoirs by Harry S. Truman*, 2:122–23. Also Donovan, *Conflict and Crisis*, 363ff.

97. *Memoirs by Harry S. Truman*, 2:248.

98. Ferrell, *Presidential Leadership*, 1340.

99. Isaacson and Thomas, *The Wise Men*, 458.

100. *Memoirs by Harry S. Truman*, 2:130.

101. Isaacson and Thomas offer such an appraisal: "Frightened by the Western Alliance, the Soviets began to rebuild their forces after 1948 and to develop their own nuclear weapons." See *The Wise Men*, 503.

102. Quoted in Spalding, *The First Cold Warrior*, 189.

103. *Memoirs by Harry S. Truman*, 2:244–45.

104. For an elaboration of this argument, see Henry R. Nau, "Ideas Have Consequences: The Cold War and Today," *International Politics* (July 2011): 1–22.

105. Miscamble, *From Roosevelt to Truman*, 31.

106. Ibid., 47.

107. McCullough, *Truman*, 489.

108. *Memoirs by Harry S. Truman*, 1:352.

109. Donovan, *Conflict and Crisis*, 50.

110. *Memoirs by Harry S. Truman*, 1:289.

111. Ibid., 1:290.
112. Ibid., 1:273.
113. Ibid., 1:292–93.
114. Quoted in Spalding, *The First Cold Warrior*, 75.
115. *Memoirs by Harry S. Truman*, 1:292–93.
116. Miscamble, *From Roosevelt to Truman*, chapters 6–7. The one exception perhaps was the Truman Doctrine, which was heavily criticized for bypassing the United Nations. But for Truman, ideology trumped institutions; there was no way the Soviet Union was going to cooperate with the United States to prevent communist takeovers in Greece and Turkey.
117. Spalding, *The First Cold Warrior*, 101.
118. Ibid., 77.
119. Ibid., 98. See also Clifford, *Counsel to the President*, 3–26; and Donovan, *Conflict and Crisis*, 382.
120. Robert H. Ferrell, *Harry S. Truman: A Life* (Columbia: University of Missouri Press, 1994), 323.
121. For example, see Kissinger, *Diplomacy*, 471: "Containment allowed no role for diplomacy."
122. President Kennedy dramatized the lack of contacts between the superpowers by speculating whether the Cuban Missile Crisis might have been avoided if the United States and Soviet Union had had a hot line to communicate with one another.
123. Secretary of State Dean Acheson speculated in a letter to Truman in February 1954: "how much did Stalin change his plans about China and Korea when, to what must have been his utter amazement, our army, navy and air force simply melted away." See *Affection and Trust: The Personal Correspondence of Harry S. Truman and Dean Acheson, 1953–1971*, with an introduction by David McCullough (New York: Knopf, 2010), 48.
124. Three years earlier, Kennan had made a similar proposal. Isaacson and Thomas, *The Wise Men*, 471–72.
125. Quoted in Pierce, *Woodrow Wilson and Harry Truman*, 26.
126. For details, see chapter 7.
127. *Memoirs by Harry S. Truman*, 2:173.
128. Truman was the first president since Grover Cleveland and the last president to date not to have a college degree.
129. Ferrell, *Dear Bess*, 524.
130. Ibid., 519.
131. Quote from Donovan, *Conflict and Crisis*, 15.
132. Elsey, *An Unplanned Life*, 145.
133. Donovan, *Conflict and Crisis*, 27.
134. For all quotes in this paragraph, see *Memoirs by Harry S. Truman*, 1:12.
135. Quoted in Spalding, *The First Cold Warrior*, 208 (emphasis in original).
136. Ibid., 219.
137. Ibid., 213.
138. Ibid., 215–16.
139. Ibid., 217.
140. Ibid., 209.

141. Truman identified with Polk and considered him "one man who has been very much overlooked in the history of this country." See *Memoirs by Harry S. Truman*, 2:195. Truman's grandmother was a niece of President Tyler, Polk's predecessor, and Tyler had also come to the presidency early in his vice presidency after the sudden death of William Henry Harrison.

142. *Memoirs by Harry S. Truman*, 1:328.

143. Ferrell, *Presidential Leadership*, 118–26.

144. Merle Miller, *Plain Speaking: An Oral Biography of Harry S. Truman* (New York: Berkeley Publishing, 1974), 308.

145. Elsey, *An Unplanned Life*, 206.

146. For both quotes, see Spalding, *The First Cold Warrior*, 19.

147. *Memoirs by Harry S. Truman*, 1:527.

148. Elsey, *An Unplanned Life*, 82–84. See also William D. Leahy, *I Was There: The Personal Story of the Chief of Staff to Presidents Roosevelt and Truman*, (New York: McGraw Hill, 1950).

149. Ibid., 144. For the "white sepulcher" comment, see Ferrell, *Dear Bess*, 523.

150. *Memoirs by Harry S. Truman*, 1:328.

151. Ibid., 2:196.

152. Ibid., 2:200.

153. The Republicans had a 58-seat margin in the House and 6-seat advantage in the Senate.

154. The Democrats, in an unprecedented reversal, seized a 92-seat advantage in the House and a 12-seat advantage in the Senate. In 1950, the Democrats retained majorities in both houses but with much slimmer margins—2 seats in the Senate and 12 in the House.

155. Donovan, *Conflict and Crisis*, 144–45.

156. The Korean War was in large part the cause. As Elsey writes, Truman "failed to nail down congressional support as he had in 1947 for Greece and 1948 for Berlin." See *An Unplanned Life*, 194.

CHAPTER 7: RONALD REAGAN: LIBERTY IN EASTERN EUROPE

1. In this chapter, as others, I investigate and ultimately classify Reagan's views using the analytical distinctions among traditions developed in chapter 2. I served in the Reagan administration and do not discount this fact. But my conclusions should be criticized on the basis of my analysis of Reagan's record, not my association with him. As the endnotes suggest, I am particularly indebted to Martin and Annelise Anderson (who also served in the Reagan administration) and their book, *Reagan's Secret War: The Untold Story of His Fight to Save the World from Nuclear Disaster* (New York: Crown, 2009). This book is based *entirely* on NSC and other declassified documents released in recent years. The Andersons generously gave me copies of the NSC minutes they used. In only two cases did I find something in the documents that I wanted to use that did not appear in their book. For the rest, I happily cited their splendid volume. They deserve full credit for bringing to light a Reagan record that many scholars continue to ignore.

2. Quoted in Anderson and Anderson, *Reagan's Secret War*, 248–49. Nationalists and realists, by contrast, tend to see America more as a geographic and cul-

tural reality rather than an idea. Skeptical of American internationalism, Walter MacDougall refers to America as "a delightful spot." See McDougall, *Promised Land, Crusader State.*

3. Noonan, *When Character Was King,* 317.

4. Reagan was what political scientists today call a constructivist, someone who constructs the meaning of the material world through ideas. But Reagan was a classical liberal constructivist who sees individuals as the makers of society, not a social constructivist who sees society as the molder of individuals. For the social constructivist perspective, see Alexander Wendt, *A Social Theory of International Politics* (New York: Cambridge University Press, 1999). For a more classical liberal constructivist perspective, see Haas, *Ideological Origins.*

5. Quoted in Anderson and Anderson, *Reagan's Secret War,* 233. I take Reagan quotes from this book throughout this chapter. It contains the best record to date of declassified and other documents on the Reagan presidency. The Andersons were kind enough to give me a copy of all the NSC minutes they used, but I found little of significance in those minutes that they had not already included and saw no reason not to give their book the full credit.

6. Quoted in Shultz, *Turmoil and Triumph,* 762.

7. Then Reagan quipped: "But it isn't true that I don't trust anyone under 70" (Anderson and Anderson, *Reagan's Secret War,* 207).

8. Quoted in Anderson and Anderson, *Reagan's Secret War,* 313.

9. Quoted in ibid., 357–58.

10. Ronald Reagan, *An American Life* (New York: Simon and Schuster, 1990), 569.

11. Ibid., 570.

12. Anderson and Anderson, *Reagan's Secret War,* 122.

13. "Religious conservatives regarded evil as real; for Reagan, it was rhetorical." See John Patrick Diggins, *Ronald Reagan: Fate, Freedom, and the Making of History* (New York: W. W. Norton, 2007), 2.

14. Ibid., 373–74.

15. Quoted in Hayward, *The Age of Reagan,* 337.

16. Ibid., 606.

17. Ibid., 605.

18. Ibid.

19. Quoted in Noonan, *When Character Was King,* 213.

20. Quoted in Peter Robinson, *How Ronald Reagan Changed My Life* (New York: ReganBooks, HarperCollins, 2003), 71–72.

21. Quoted in Lou Cannon, *President Reagan: The Role of a Lifetime* (New York: Public Affairs, 2000), 272.

22. Ibid., 711.

23. Quoted in Noonan, *When Character Was King,* 317. Reagan's view is more widely shared than critics recognize. In 1986, Mitterrand, a European socialist, reflected on his trips to America and American exceptionalism: In America "very progressive young people . . . were reproachful toward Europeans like us . . . who seemed to them timid. . . . Liberty had fired their spirits. . . . It is a metaphysical quest. . . . Although no system will ever be able to satisfy those who harbor such a desire, I think that American democracy guarantees that the

greatest number will enjoy liberty that is genuine, lived, practical. That isn't so bad, even if it remains . . . very imperfect." See Martin Anderson, *Revolution* (New York: Harcourt Brace Jovanovich, 1988), 20.

24. Quoted in Robinson, *How Reagan Changed My Life*, 88–89.

25. Quoted in Noonan, *When Character Was King*, 207.

26. Quoted in Anderson and Anderson, *Reagan's Secret War*, 42.

27. Lou Cannon, "Arms Boost Seen as Strain on Soviets," *Washington Post*, June 18, 1980, A3.

28. Quoted in Anderson and Anderson, *Reagan's Secret War*, 102.

29. Quoted in Hayward, *The Age of Reagan*, 255.

30. As Stephen Hayward muses, "it remains difficult to square in the same person the seemingly contradictory positions of, on the one hand, pursuing a large arms buildup and employing aggressive rhetoric about an adversary and, on the other, a sincere desire for productive negotiations to *abolish* nuclear weapons." See *The Age of Reagan*, 330.

31. Ibid., 114.

32. Ibid., 123.

33. Quoted in Noonan, *When Character Was King*, 207.

34. Quoted in Hayward, *The Age of Reagan*, 255–56.

35. See Henry R. Nau, "President Reagan and Democracy Promotion," in Michael E. Cox, Timothy J. Lynch, and Nicolas Bouchet, eds., *US Presidents and Democracy Promotion* (New York: Routledge, 2013), 138–59.

36. This document and over one hundred other NSDDs were produced by Reagan's national security advisor, William Clark, during his tenure from January 1982 to October 1983. Clark was an astonishingly effective organizer of Reagan's foreign policy initiatives. The NSDDs, many recently declassified, scripted Reagan's actions for the rest of his administration and demonstrated clearly the continuity between his first- and second-term policies. For revealing insights into Clark's time in office, see, among others, Paul Kengor and Patricia Clark Doerner, *The Judge William P. Clark, Reagan's Top Hand* (San Francisco: Ignatius Press, 2007); Peter Schweizer, *Reagan's War: The Epic Story of His Forty-Year Struggle and Final Triumph over Communism* (New York: Anchor Books, 2002); Steven R. Weisman, "The Influence of Bill Clark: Setting a Hard Line in Foreign Policy," *New York Times Magazine*, August 14, 1983; and Thomas G. Mahnken, "The Reagan Administration's Strategy Toward the Soviet Union," in Williamson Murray and Richard Sinnreich, eds., *Successful Strategies* (New York: Cambridge University Press, forthcoming). On the NSDDs dealing with the Soviet Union, see also Richard Pipes, *Vixi: Memoirs of a Non-Belonger* (New Haven: Yale University Press, 2006); and Thomas Reed, *At the Abyss: An Insider's History of the Cold War* (New York: Presidio Press, 2005).

37. Paul Lettow, *Ronald Reagan and His Quest to Abolish Nuclear Weapons* (New York: Random House, 2006), 70.

38. Jack F. Matlock Jr., *Reagan and Gorbachev: How the Cold War Ended* (New York: Random House, 2005), 53–54.

39. Quoted in Anderson and Anderson, *Reagan's Secret War*, 249. Richard Reeves, a liberal reporter for the *New York Times*, wrote that "Reagan just

cleaned his clock" in the debate. Kennedy apparently responded by telling his staff: "Don't get me alone with this guy again," 249.

40. Ronald Reagan, *The Reagan Diaries*, ed. Douglas Brinkley (New York: HarperCollins, 2007), 57.

41. Quoted in Laurence J. Barrett, *Gambling with History: Ronald Reagan in the White House* (New York: Doubleday, 1983), 298.

42. Quoted in Cannon, *President Reagan*, 414.

43. Quoted in Paul Kengor, *The Crusader: Ronald Reagan and the Fall of Communism* (New York: HarperCollins, 2006), 220. The Yalta message was carefully targeted. Over the previous year, Gromyko complained to Shultz (and no doubt the president as well) that "no one—no one—can change the reality of the situation in Europe" and called "shocking" the administration's talk about the "artificial division" of Europe. See Shultz, *Turmoil and Triumph*, 484–85, 467–68.

44. Quoted in Cannon, *President Reagan*, 404.

45. Ibid., 422.

46. Quoted in ibid., 706. By contrast, Gromyko once called human rights issues a "tenth rate question." Shultz, *Turmoil and Triumph*, 122.

47. Anderson, *Revolution*, 71.

48. Anderson and Anderson, *Reagan's Secret War*, 94. This is one year before Shultz hears it in February 1983.

49. Ibid., 94.

50. Haynes Johnson, *Sleepwalking through History: America in the Reagan Years* (New York: W. W. Norton, 2003). Johnson had the good grace to admit later that he was wrong. Hayward, *The Age of Reagan*, 16.

51. Quoted in Anderson and Anderson, *Reagan's Secret War*, 129.

52. Quoted in ibid., 102.

53. Quoted in Hayward, *The Age of Reagan*, 255.

54. Quoted in Anderson, *Revolution*, 36.

55. Seweryn Bialer and Joan Afferica, "Reagan and Russia," *Foreign Affairs* 61, 2 (Winter 1982): 263.

56. For example, in 1984, Henry Kissinger ridiculed the idea that the Cold War might end: "There are no final 'happy endings.' . . . Ideological hostility will continue. Specific precise arrangements can, indeed must be made. But they are more likely to ameliorate tensions than to end them." See "Reagan Must Seize the Middle Ground," *Los Angeles Times*, November 18, 1984, E-1.

57. Cannon, *President Reagan*, 760. The CIA concluded in November 1984 that "Soviet economic problems were unlikely . . . to cause them to limit their strategic programs." See Anderson and Anderson, *Reagan's Secret War*, 182. And the Soviets did continue to increase their military budget right through 1988. At Westminster Reagan noted the decline in the rate of growth of the Soviet economy since the 1950s (not the same as a decline of the economy), which was now half what it was then. See Hayward, *Age of Reagan*, 255. Oil price increases propped up Soviet fortunes in the 1970s, and oil price drops probably had a lot to do with its precipitous decline after the mid-1980s.

58. Cannon makes this point repeatedly in *President Reagan*.

59. Shultz, for example, thought SDI was "lunacy." See Strobe Talbott, *The Master of the Game: Paul Nitze and the Nuclear Peace* (New York: Knopf, 1988), 193. He told Reagan two hours before the speech, "I have to say honestly that I am deeply troubled." See Hayward, *Age of Reagan*, 294. See also Wilentz, *The Age of Reagan*, 165. Once it existed, however, Shultz recognized the bargaining value of SDI and worked hand in hand with Reagan to use it for maximum effect with the Soviets. Later Shultz embraced Reagan's goal of eliminating nuclear weapons but without Reagan's insurance policy of something like SDI to deter the reacquisition of offensive systems. See *Turmoil and Triumph*, 536.

60. Reagan, *Diaries*, 142.

61. Cannon, *President Reagan*, 321.

62. Diggins, *Ronald Reagan*, 196.

63. See Beth A. Fischer, *The Reagan Reversal: Foreign Policy and the End of the Cold War* (Columbia: University of Missouri Press, 1997); James Mann, *The Rebellion of Ronald Reagan: A History of the End of the Cold War* (New York: Penguin, 2010); and Diggins, *Ronald Reagan*, 354.

64. I elaborate this explanation further in the conclusion.

65. See Richard Reeves, *President Reagan: The Triumph of Imagination* (New York: Simon and Schuster, 2006).

66. Kenneth L. Adelman, *The Great Embrace: Arms Summitry—A Skeptic's Account* (New York: Simon and Schuster, 1989).

67. Anderson and Anderson, *Reagan's Secret War*, 188.

68. See George P. Shultz, Steven P. Andreasen, Sidney D. Drell, and James B. Goodby, eds., *Reykjavik Revisited: Steps toward a World Free of Nuclear Weapons* (Stanford: Hoover Institution Press, 2008).

69. In his first year it was frequently said that he had no foreign policy because he gave priority to domestic military and economic revitalization. But domestic revitalization was foreign policy, and Reagan worked from the very beginning to plan how he would use it. In six weeks between February and the end of March in 1981, he chaired ten national security meetings. Anderson and Anderson, *Reagan's Secret War*, 34.

70. Alexei Arbatov, "What Lessons Learned?" in Kiron Skinner, ed., *Turning Points in Ending the Cold War* (Stanford, CA: Hoover Institution Press, 2009), 57.

71. Quoted in William C. Wohlforth, ed., *Witnesses to the End of the Cold War* (Baltimore: Johns Hopkins University Press, 1996), 14.

72. Hayward, *The Age of Reagan*, 450.

73. Quoted in Stephen G. Brooks and William C. Wohlforth, "Power, Globalization, and the End of the Cold War," *International Security* 25, 3 (Winter 2000–2001): 29.

74. Reagan, *Diaries*, 30.

75. Caspar W. Weinberger with Gretchen Roberts, *In the Arena: A Memoir of the 20th Century* (Washington, DC: Regnery, 2001), 280.

76. Shultz, *Turmoil and Triumph*, 663. I asked Shultz what the title of this article was and where I might find it but he and his assistant Charles Hill could not recall.

77. Ibid., 489.

78. Support for freedom fighters in central America, south Africa, and Afghanistan was another important element of ground leverage in Reagan's strategy, but this assistance was covert and cautious not because "Reagan was reluctant to take major military risks" but because his central priority was Europe, not Nicaragua, Afghanistan, or Namibia. Reagan also used overt ground force in Grenada and Lebanon. See Cannon, *President Reagan*, 293. A comprehensive NSC study, NSSD 1-82, discussed at an NSC meeting in April 1982, stated emphatically: "Priorities are North America, NATO, Southwest Asia, Pacific, Latin America, and Africa, in that order." See NSC 00045 04/16/1982 in Executive Secretariat, NSC: NSC Meeting Files, Records, 1981–88, box 91284, Ronald Reagan Presidential Library, Simi Valley, CA.

79. Soviet foreign minister Gromyko told West German officials in January 1983 on the eve of German elections that INF deployments would limit war to Europe; he was clearly trying to split the alliance. See Jay Winik, *On the Brink: The Dramatic, Behind-the-Scenes Saga of the Reagan Era and the Men and Women Who Won the Cold War* (New York: Simon and Schuster, 1996), 212.

80. Ibid., 175, 178.

81. Anderson and Anderson, *Reagan's Secret War*, 68–69. Why this flexibility in Reagan's negotiating position never leaked may be explained by the fact that both hard-liners and soft-liners opposed it, the latter because the INF issue drew attention to foreign policy when economic policy had priority.

82. See Strobe Talbott, *Deadly Gambits: The Reagan Administration and the Stalemate in Nuclear Arms Control* (New York: Knopf, 1984), chapter 6.

83. Winik, *On the Brink*, 203.

84. Anderson and Anderson, *Reagan's Secret War*, 117–18. In February 1983, the Soviet Union maneuvered surface ships with nuclear missiles in the mouth of the Mississippi to suggest how the Soviets might counter Pershing deployments. The Soviets were still more serious outside the negotiations than they were inside. Winik, *On the Brink*, 211.

85. The Able Archer story was based primarily on one Soviet source. A subsequent intelligence community study in 1984 determined that "there was insufficient evidence to conclude that the Soviets had been worried about a possible attack because of 'Able Archer.'" See Robert M. Gates, *From the Shadows: The Ultimate Insider's Story of Five Presidents and How They Won the Cold War* (New York: Simon and Schuster, 1996), 272–73.

86. Reagan, *Diaries*, 203.

87. Cannon, *President Reagan*, 270.

88. Hayward, *The Age of Reagan*, 349.

89. Anatoly Dobrynin, *In Confidence* (New York: Random House, 1995), 556.

90. Anderson and Anderson, *Reagan's Secret War*, 183.

91. Quotes from Reagan and Chernenko in ibid., 198, 199.

92. Ibid., 201.

93. Gromyko allegedly said of Gorbachev: "Comrades, this man has a nice smile but he's got iron teeth." Cannon, *President Reagan*, 667.

94. Cannon, *President Reagan*, 282. See also Robert C. McFarlane and Zofia Smardz, *Special Trust* (New York: Cadell and Davies, 1994).

95. For the early history of SDI, see Anderson, *Revolution*, 94–100. See also Lettow, *Ronald Reagan and His Quest to Abolish Nuclear Weapons*, 37–42; and Gates, *From the Shadows*, 262–66.

96. Anderson and Anderson, *Reagan's Secret War*, 129.

97. Ibid., 144.

98. Ibid., 188.

99. Ibid.

100. Ibid., 197.

101. Ibid., 297.

102. Ibid., 187.

103. Reagan, *Diaries*, 288.

104. Anderson and Anderson, *Reagan's Secret War*, 187.

105. Ibid., 189.

106. These provisions were outlined in a letter Reagan sent to Gorbachev in July 1986 and suggest that the negotiations at Reykjavik were not as ad hoc as some reports claimed.

107. The Soviets had a radar station at Krasnoyarsk, which was not confirmed incontrovertibly until 1983 because of persistent cloud cover. Located inside the Soviet Union rather than on the border, the station arguably violated the ABM Treaty.

108. For Reagan and Gorbachev quotes respectively, see Anderson and Anderson, *Reagan's Secret War*, 311, 308.

109. Shultz, *Turmoil and Triumph*, 773. The CIA reported at the time that Gorbachev had to succeed at the summit or he would be overthrown. See Shultz, *Turmoil and Triumph*, 757. Anatoly Chernyaev, Gorbachev's aide, said there were death threats from the military in spring 1986. See Hayward, *Age of Reagan*, 485. And Gorbachev himself doubted at Reykjavik that "I will still have it [the capability to compromise] in a year or 2–3 years." See Hayward, *Age of Reagan*, 502.

110. Reagan terminated the meetings. The Soviets had apparently agreed to negotiate for another day. Cannon, *President Reagan*, 690.

111. Reagan, *Diaries*, 598.

112. Hayward, *Age of Reagan*, 478.

113. Marshall Sergei Akhromeyev, chief of the Soviet General Staff who participated in the coup against Gorbachev in 1991 and then committed suicide, told Shultz at the INF Summit in December 1987: "I am fighting alongside Mikhail Sergeyevich to save it [my country], and that is why we made such a lopsided deal on INF, and that is why we want to get along with you. We want to restructure ourselves and to be part of the modern world." See Shultz, *Turmoil and Triumph*, 1012.

114. Hayward, *Age of Reagan*, 589. The reference is to Britain's capitulation to Germany in 1938 on the Sudetenland issue.

115. Winik, *On the Brink*, 515.

116. Anderson and Anderson, *Reagan's Secret War*, 66.

117. On Reagan's briefing about SIOP, see Hayward, *The Age of Reagan*, 329 and footnotes, 680. The Andersons asked Reagan directly in an interview in July 1989 if he would have pulled the nuclear trigger, and Reagan replied firmly "yes." See *Reagan's Secret War*, 151.

118. Anderson and Anderson, *Reagan's Secret War*, 61. On the Cronkite comment, see page 34.

119. Matlock, *Reagan and Gorbachev*, 50.

120. Anderson and Anderson, *Reagan's Secret War*, 41.

121. Hayward, *The Age of Reagan*, 144; Anderson and Anderson, *Reagan's Secret War*, 50.

122. All quotes from Anderson and Anderson, *Reagan's Secret War*, 78–79.

123. The visit with the pope was dismissed by the press when Reagan was thought to be napping during the pope's public remarks.

124. On the reversal theory, see Fischer, *The Reagan Reversal*; Diggins, *Ronald Reagan*; and Mann, *The Rebellion of Ronald Reagan*.

125. Shultz, *Turmoil and Triumph*, 139. On the pipeline controversy, see Nau, *The Myth of America's Decline*, 293–326; Bruce W. Jentleson, *Pipeline Politics: The Complex Political Economy of East-West Energy Trade* (Ithaca: Cornell University Press, 1986); and Michael Mastanduno, *Economic Containment: CoCom and the Politics of East-West Trade* (Ithaca: Cornell University Press, 1992).

126. Anderson and Anderson, *Reagan's Secret War*, 159.

127. Reagan, *Diaries*, 222–23.

128. Jack Matlock, then serving on the NSC, observed: "The Soviet leadership had obviously decided not to deal seriously with Reagan . . . lest they inadvertently help his campaign for reelection." Quoted in Hayward, *The Age of Reagan*, 349.

129. Cannon, *President Reagan*, 258.

130. Bessmertnykh, the Soviet foreign minister, said the following about Reagan's performance: "Reagan handled negotiations very, very well. . . . He would try to rush through this formal part, and then he would throw away the cards and . . . start talking the direct way. I sat across the table at all the summits and . . . if it were not for Reagan, I don't think we would have been able to reach the agreements in arms control that we reached later." Cannon, *President Reagan*, 762–63.

131. On this point, see the careful empirical account by Mark Haas, "The United States and the End of the Cold War: Reactions to Shifts in Soviet Power, Policies or Domestic Politics?" *International Organization* 61, 1 (2007): 145–79.

132. See Leon Aron, *Yeltsin: A Revolutionary Life* (New York: St. Martin's Press, 2000), 177.

133. See Brooks and Wohlforth, "Power, Globalization, and the End of the Cold War," 24; Robert S. Norris and Hans M. Kristensen, "Global Nuclear Stockpiles, 1945–2006," *Bulletin of Atomic Scientists* (January–February 2006): 66; and Shultz, *Turmoil and Triumph*, 702.

134. Reagan, *Diaries*, 66.

135. Cannon, *President Reagan*, 407.

136. Ibid., 417.

137. Brooks and Wohlforth, "Power, Globalization and the End of the Cold War," 29.

138. Democrats on the Hill, many of them liberal internationalists, reacted very differently and urged that Lichtenstein be fired. Hayward, *The Age of Reagan*, 312.

139. Reagan, *Diaries*, 33, 110. See also Anderson and Anderson, *Reagan's Secret War*, 90.

140. See Nau, *The Myth of America's Decline*, especially chapter 7.

141. Shultz, *Turmoil and Triumph*, 186.

142. This is Cannon's conclusion from his short-term view of history. See *President Reagan*, 413.

143. Reagan's economic foreign policy was almost as revolutionary as his strategic program. See Henry R. Nau, *International Reaganomics: A Domestic Approach to World Economy*, Significant Issues Series, vol. 6, issue 18 (Washington, DC: Center for Strategic and International Studies, Georgetown University, 1984); Henry R. Nau, "Where Reaganomics Works," *Foreign Policy*, no. 57 (Winter 1984–85): 14–38; and Robert L. Paarlberg, *Leadership Abroad Begins at Home: U.S. Foreign Economic Policy after the Cold War* (Washington, DC: Brookings Institution, 1995).

144. Shultz, *Turmoil and Triumph*, 982.

145. Quoted in Cannon, *President Reagan*, 408.

146. Kissinger, *Diplomacy*, 764–65.

147. Gaddis, *Strategies of Containment*, 375.

148. Cannon, *President Reagan*, 710.

149. Robinson, *How Reagan Changed My Life*, 240.

150. Cannon, *President Reagan*, 106.

151. See Louis Hartz, *The Liberal Tradition in America*, and my discussion in chapter 1.

152. Quoted in Adams, *History of the United States*, 137.

153. Anderson and Anderson, *Reagan's Secret War*, 51.

154. Noonan, *When Character Was King*, 307.

155. Cannon, *President Reagan*, 197.

156. Ibid., 705.

157. Paul Kengor, *God and Ronald Reagan: A Spiritual Life* (New York: HarperCollins, 2004).

158. See Reagan, *A Life of Letters*, 280.

159. Anderson and Anderson, *Reagan's Secret War*, 48.

160. Ibid., 374.

161. Cannon, *President Reagan*, 704–5.

162. Robinson, *How Reagan Changed My Life*, 203.

163. Cannon, *President Reagan*, 92.

164. Ibid., 712.

165. Hayward, *The Age of Reagan*, 204.

166. Cannon, *President Reagan*, 90.

167. Shultz, *Triumph and Turmoil*, 1135.

168. Minutes of the National Security Council Meeting, classified Secret, January 28, 1983, 073-1. Private copy obtained from Martin and Annelise Anderson.

169. The phrase belongs to Martin Anderson, who knew him well. See *Revolution*, 288.

170. The comment is attributed to Bud McFarlane. See Shultz, *Turmoil and Triumph*, 1134. "The root of the problem," Lou Cannon observed in the case of

chief of staff James Baker, "was Baker's feeling that he was insufficiently valued by the president." See *President Reagan*, 492.

171. The press reinforced this point of view: "Too often, Reagan was a performer and presidential leadership an empty shell." See Cannon, *President Reagan*, 351. "There is no gainsaying that his success was often a reflection of the prowess of his White House staff," 749.

172. "Weinberger was convinced he knew what Reagan would do if left to his own instincts, and Shultz behaved as if he knew what was best for the president." See Cannon, *President Reagan*, 352.

173. Cannon, *President Reagan*, 374. As Cannon states elsewhere in his book: "The view that Reagan needed protection from himself was an axiom among the veteran Reaganites, whatever their ideological persuasion," 617. Dick Darman, James Baker's aide, was particularly contemptuous of the president's abilities: "Don't you understand? It's our *job* to protect the President from himself." See Robinson, *How Reagan Changed My Life*, 198.

174. Cannon, *President Reagan*, 753.

175. Ibid., 130.

176. Anderson and Anderson, *Reagan's Secret War*, 197–98.

177. Cannon, *President Reagan*, 718.

178. Ibid., 37, 125.

179. Robert D. Putnam and Nicholas Bayne, *Hanging Together: Cooperation and Conflict in the Seven-Power Summits*, rev. ed. (Cambridge, MA: Harvard University Press, 1987).

180. Cannon, *President Reagan*, 265. Fred Ikle, a top Defense Department official, agrees, noting that Reagan's stories "amazingly always had some connection with the meeting," 350. I agree as well, recalling one meeting in particular when staff discussed exchange rates with the president, and a top economic advisor complained after the meeting that Reagan's story about consulting a book in the 1930s to find exchange rates made no sense. But exchange rates printed in a book did not change every day; the president was clearly telling us he wanted more stable exchange rates.

181. See Annelise Anderson et al., *Reagan: In His Own Hand* (New York: Free Press, 2001); Annelise Anderson et al., *Reagan: A Life in Letters* (New York: Free Press, 2003); and Reagan, *Diaries*.

CONCLUSION: FREEDOM AND FORCE

1. Deudney, *Bounding Power*; and David C. Hendrickson, *Union, Nation, or Empire: The American Debate over International Relations, 1789–1941* (Lawrence: University Press of Kansas, 2009).

2. Steven Pinker, *The Better Angels of Our Nature: Why Violence Has Declined* (New York: Allen Lane, 2011).

3. Whatever its limitations, the evidence of the "democratic peace," that democracies do not fight one another, confirms the proposition that most violence originates in nondemocratic ideologies. No study has shown empirically that America's watch has been more militant or less restrained than that of previous hegemons: Spanish Hapsburgs, Louis XIV, Napoleon, imperial Japan, Nazi

Germany, and the Soviet Union. Just the opposite. By any measure, the world today is less violent, more prosperous, and more free than ever before.

4. John Mueller, *The Remnants of War* (Ithaca: Cornell University Press, 1984).

5. On the fragility of nascent democracies, see Jack Snyder, *From Voting to Violence: Democratization and Nationalist Conflict* (New York: W. W. Norton, 2000).

6. The evidence of the democratic peace, while still disputed, provides ample reinforcement of the argument that democratic publics are more peaceful than nondemocratic ones. While revisionist traditions may see it differently, they offer few comparative studies to show persuasively that America's watch has been more militant and less restrained than that of imperial Japan, Nazi Germany, Napoleon, Louis XIV, or any other historical hegemon.

7. Gaddis, *Surprise, Security, and the American Experience.*

8. See, for example, Richard Ned Lebow and Janice Gross Stein, *We All Lost the Cold War* (Princeton: Princeton University Press, 1994), 24–27.

9. As Gaddis writes, Polk was acting under the premises set by John Quincy Adams that "Americans . . . have generally responded to threats—and particularly to surprise attacks—by taking the offensive." See *Surprise, Security, and the American Experience*, chapter 2, quote from page 13.

10. For an in-depth account of this episode, see Igor Lukes, *On the Edge of the Cold War* (New York: Oxford University Press, 2012).

11. Whelan, *Jefferson's War*, 271, 311.

12. During the fifty-five years from 1821 to 1876, Mexico had seventy-five presidents, with one strongman serving as president on eleven different occasions. See Stephen Haber and Victor Menaldo, "Do Natural Resources Fuel Authoritarianism? A Reappraisal of the Resource Curse," *American Political Science Review* 105, 1 (2011): 1–26.

13. This is a hard truth to accept because it seems like blaming the victims. But then don't blame Britain, France, or the United States for Nazi aggression before World War II or Soviet aggression after World War II. They were just victims.

14. Struggles between statesmen and generals are a recurring problem in international affairs. See Eliot A. Cohen, *Supreme Commanders: Soldiers, Statesmen, and Leaders in Wartime* (New York: Free Press, 2002).

15. Heilbrunn, "Whose Reagan?"

16. For an assessment of Reagan's economic legacy, see Henry R. Nau, "The 'Great Expansion': The Economic Legacy of Ronald Reagan," in Paul Kengor and Jeffrey Chidester, eds., *Reagan in a World Transformed, 1989–2011* (Cambridge, MA: Harvard University Press, forthcoming). A very different picture is painted by partisan politics. At Osawatomi, Kansas, in December 2011, President Obama characterized the previous three decades as an era of Wall Street greed and Main Street inequality. See http://www.whitehouse.gov/the-press-office/2011/12/06/remarks-president-economy-osawatomie-kansas.

17. Mark Haas shows how such differences in domestic ideas (ideological distance) among political leaders influence international outcomes. Parties, such as the early Republican and Federalist parties in the United States, adopt diverging or converging ideological orientations toward power and institutions, both within

and between countries. Jefferson emphasized commerce and decentralized expansion; his rivals favored armies and territorial conquest. These differences cause leaders to react to foreign countries differently. From this perspective, Jefferson was not just the beneficiary of random French actions; he anticipated and perhaps even helped bring them about in ways that might never have occurred to his rivals. See Haas, *Ideological Origins* and *The Clash of Ideologies: Middle Eastern Politics and American Security* (New York: Oxford University Press, 2012).

18. In *Clash of Ideas*, John M. Owen IV stresses and develops this role of transnational ideological networks.

19. See Charles A. Kupchan, *No One's World: The West, the Rising Rest, and the Coming Global Turn* (New York: Oxford University Press, 2012), 185.

20. G. John Ikenberry, *After Victory: Institutions, Strategic Restraint, and the Rebuilding of Order after Major Wars* (Princeton: Princeton University Press, 2001), 59.

21. See the supplementary special issue of *International Politics* 48, 5 (July/September 2011), which published results of a Princeton University project comparing alternative explanations of the origins and end of the Cold War. What follows comes from my contribution, "Ideas Have Consequences: The Cold War and Today," 460–81.

22. For one account that does not ignore the material competition, see Brooks and Wohlforth, "Power, Globalization, and the End of the Cold War," 5–54; and William C. Wohlforth, "No One Loves a Realist Explanation," in Daniel Deudney and G. John Ikenberry, eds., "The End of the Cold War after Twenty Years: Reconsiderations, Retrospectives, and Revisions," *International Politics*, special issue, 48, 5 (July/September 2011): 441–59.

23. Gaddis, *Strategies of Containment*.

24. Robert S. Norris, "Global Nuclear Stockpiles 1945–2006," *Bulletin of Atomic Scientists* (July/August 2008): 64–66.

25. In realist accounts, economic and technological change occur randomly and unevenly, shifting material wealth and triggering the competition for power. See Paul Kennedy, *The Rise and Fall of Great Powers: Economic Change and Military Conflict from 1500 to 2000* (New York: Random House, 1987); and my critique of Kennedy's book, "Why the 'Rise and Fall of the Great Powers' Was Wrong," *Review of International Studies* 27 (2001): 579–92.

26. See, among others, Robert D. English, "'Merely an Above-Average Product of the Soviet Nomenklatura'? Assessing Leadership in the Cold War's End," *International Politics* 48, 5 (July/September 2011): 607–26.

27. The phrase refers to the argument between realists and idealists (constructivists) as to how much of reality is ideological and how much material. See Wendt, *Social Theory of International Politics*.

28. On this point, see, in particular, the work of Peter Schweizer, *Victory: The Reagan Administration's Secret Strategy That Hastened The Collapse of the Soviet Union* (New York: Atlantic Monthly Press, 1994) and *Reagan's War: The Epic Story of His Forty-Year Struggle and Final Triumph over Communism* (New York: Anchor Books, 2002).

29. Bill Clark, then secretary of the interior after leaving the NSC in late 1983, wrote a personal letter to President Reagan in January 1984 that predicted with

uncanny foresight that, because of Western pressure, a new more agreeable Soviet leader might soon emerge: "Another few months of 'standing tall' should restore the arms balance in Europe and very likely influence the rise of a less dangerous Soviet leader than the dying Andropov." See Kengor and Doerner, *The Judge*, 280–81.

30. See Matthew Evangelista, *Unarmed Forces: The Transnational Movement to End the Cold War* (Ithaca: Cornell University Press, 2002).

31. George P. Shultz, "A Perspective from Washington," in Kiron Skinner, ed., *Turning Points in Ending the Cold War* (Stanford: Hoover Institution Press, 2009), xix–xxiv. See also Shultz, *Turmoil and Triumph*, 510.

32. I assembled voluminous statistical data and analysis to support this conclusion in *The Myth of America's Decline*. Sadly, the sources of revival of the American economy then, as well as perhaps today, remain obscured in the repetitive media fascination with America's decline. See also Nau, "The 'Great Expansion.' "

33. See Gary Becker and Kevin Murphy, "Do Not Let the 'Cure' Destroy Capitalism," *Financial Times*, March 19, 2009, http://www.ft.com/cms/s/0/98f66b98 -14be-11de-8cd1-0000779fd2ac.html and Henry R. Nau, "Lessons from the Great Expansion," *Wall Street Journal*, January 26, 2012, A15. From 1980 to 1988, measured in constant 1980 dollars, the percentage of American families with incomes above $29,070 rose from 20 percent to 38 percent, a phenomenal increase. Much of this increase benefited minorities—African Americans and women—who filled many of the twenty million new jobs created during the 1980s. Much of this progress was evident already at the time but ignored by the mainstream media and academy. See Cannon, *President Reagan*, 747.

34. The "Great Recession" is a misnomer. It is part of the partisan battle among scholars over the legacy of various policies and periods. By many measures, the recent recession was not as severe as the recessions of 1974–75 or 1981–82. In 1981–82 unemployment reached 10.8 percent compared to 10.2 percent in 2009, and inflation reached double digits, forcing monetary policy to contract, whereas in the recent recession monetary policy expanded in an unprecedented manner to cushion recession. See Allan Meltzer, "What Happened to the Depression?" *Wall Street Journal*, August 31, 2009, A14 and Nau, "Lessons from the Great Expansion."

35. International Monetary Fund, *World Economic Outlook* (Washington, DC: IMF, October 2012), Table A1, p. 190; *World Economic Outlook Update*, January 23, 2013, http://www.imf.org/external/pubs/ft/weo/2013/update/01/pdf /0113.pdf.

36. For a view that credits greater causality to institutional forces, see Daniel Deudney and G. John Ikenberry, "Pushing and Pulling: The Western System, Nuclear Weapons and Soviet Change," *International Politics* 48, 5 (July/September 2011): 496–544.

37. Others will disagree. The differences are not issues of fact but directions of causal arrows, although conflicting causal interpretations can and should always be tested against further facts.

38. See Reagan, *Diaries*, 142. The Reagan diaries, together with other voluminous writings by the former president (over ten thousand letters uncovered so

far), put to rest the partisan canard that Reagan was an actor not a strategist. As George Shultz writes in the foreword to the Andersons' book, "the act of writing is fundamentally an act of thinking. Reagan was a thinker as well as a doer." See Shultz, foreword to Anderson and Anderson, *Reagan's Secret War*, x.

39. Robert Kagan, *The World America Made* (New York: Knopf, 2012).

40. Roy H. Ginsberg and Susan E. Penska, *The European Union in Global Security* (New York: Palgrave Macmillan, 2012).

41. For one insider's account, see Anatoly Chernyaev, *My Six Years with Gorbachev*, trans. and ed. Robert English and Elizabeth Tucker (University Park: Pennsylvania State University Press, 2000). For an account from the U.S. side, see Philip Zelikow and Condoleezza Rice, *Germany Unified and Europe Transformed* (Cambridge, MA: Harvard University Press, 1995); for a comprehensive account, see Mary Elise Sarotte, *1989: The Struggle to Create Post–Cold War Europe* (Princeton: Princeton University Press, 2011).

42. William C. Wohlforth, ed., *Cold War Endgame: Oral History, Analysis, Debates* (University Park: Pennsylvania State University Press, 2003).

43. Arch Puddington, *Freedom in the World, 2013: Democratic Breakthroughs in the Balance* (New York: Freedom House, 2013).

44. See Henry R. Nau, "Iraq and Previous Transatlantic Crises: Divided by Threat, Not Institutions or Values," in J. Anderson, G. Ikenberry, and T. Risse, eds., *The End of the West? Crisis and Change in the Atlantic Order* (Ithaca: Cornell University Press, 2008), 82–111.

45. For a clear-headed assessment of China as a "partial power," see David Shambaugh, *China Goes Global: The Partial Power* (New York: Oxford University Press, 2013).

46. For background on this discussion of poles of identity as well as poles of power, see Nau, *At Home Abroad* and Haas, *Ideological Origins*.

47. Even the arch-realist Henry Kissinger now realizes that the North Atlantic area defies the logic of anarchy. See *Does America Need a Foreign Policy? Toward a Diplomacy for the 21st Century* (New York: Simon and Schuster, 2001), chapter 2. Realism in general talks about "soft" balancing to acknowledge that anarchy among democracies no longer involves the prospect of the use of force. See, among others, Robert A. Pape, "Soft-Balancing against the United States," *International Security* 30, 1 (Summer 2005): 7–45.

48. This view is growing today by leaps and bounds. See Barry R. Posen, "Pull Back," *Foreign Affair*, 92, 1 (January/February 2013); Mearsheimer, "Imperial by Design"; Christopher Layne, "The (Almost) Triumph of Offshore Balancing," *The National Interest*, January 2012; and Stephen Walt, "A Bandwagon for Offshore Balancing?" *Foreign Policy*, December 2011.

49. See Henry R. Nau, "Why We Fight Over Foreign Policy: Different Perspectives Yield Different Conclusions," *Policy Review* 160 (April/May 2007): 25–42.

50. An earlier case was the Clinton administration's hard-line policies toward Iran during 1995–97, which helped reformers take over the government in Tehran in 1997. See Haas, *The Clash of Ideologies*, 113–15.

51. Mark Haas finds that under conditions of ideological bipolarity, hard-line policies by outside powers hurt hard-line governments in target states and help reformer groups take power, while soft-line policies by outside countries work

best after reformers are in control in target states. See Haas, *The Clash of Ideologies*, 106–19.

52. For liberal internationalist views of Bush's foreign policy, see G. John Ikenberry, Thomas J. Knock, Anne-Marie Slaughter, and Tony Smith, *The Crisis of American Foreign Policy: Wilsonianism in the Twenty-First Century* (Princeton: Princeton University Press, 2009).

53. Secretary of State Hillary Clinton spoke in 2009 of extending a "defense umbrella" in the Middle East if Iran acquired nuclear weapons. Mark Landler and David E. Sanger, "Clinton Speaks of Shielding Mideast from Iran, *New York Times*, July 22, 2009. http://www.nytimes.com/2009/07/23/world/asia/23diplo.html?ref=global-home&_r=0.

54. For evidence to support this conclusion, see chapter 3.

55. General Wesley K. Clark, *Waging Modern War: Bosnia, Kosovo, and the Future of Combat* (New York: Public Affairs, 2001).

56. John Owen finds that across the centuries, "distant promotions [to support regime change] are relatively rare." Most promotions take place on the borders of the promoting state or across a narrow body of water from it. See *The Clash of Ideas*, 25–26.

57. See Nau, "Obama's Foreign Policy"; Muravchik, "The Abandonment of Democracy"; and Jackson Diehl, "Obama's National Security Agenda Is Light on the Human Rights Agenda," *Washington Post*, May 31, 2010, http://www.washingtonpost.com/wpdyn/content/article/2010/05/30/AR2010053003299.html. For a defense of Obama's policies, see Carothers, *Democracy Policy under Obama*.

58. I once heard a four-star American general describe an elaborate data bank developed to track prospective warlords and leaders in Afghanistan, largely to account for where U.S. military money was going to placate Afghan elites. I asked if the White House had ever inquired as to which elites the United States might find acceptable in an Afghan government after U.S. forces left. He said without hesitation and a wry grin, "No."

59. My earlier work focused on international economic issues. See, among others, *National Politics and International Technology: Nuclear Reactor Development in Western Europe* (Baltimore: Johns Hopkins University Press, 1974); *Domestic Trade Politics and the Uruguay Round* (New York: Columbia University Press, 1989); and *Trade and Security: U.S. Policies at Cross-Purposes* (Washington, DC: American Enterprise Institute, 1995).

60. For an optimistic assessment of China's eventual inclusion in the liberal world order, see G. John Ikenberry, "The Rise of China and the Future of the West," *Foreign Affairs* 87, 1 (2008): 23–38.

61. See the counterconventional statistical work of Stephen J. Rose, *Rebound: Why America Will Emerge Stronger from the Financial Crisis* (New York: St. Martin's Press, 2010), 102–26.

62. See Bruce D. Meyer and James X. Sullivan, "Winning the War: Poverty from the Great Society to the Great Recession," *Brookings Papers on Economic Activity* (Fall 2012): 133–200.

63. It might have been appropriate if the award had footnoted NATO because

the EU would have never existed, let alone succeeded, if NATO had not protected its security.

64. See Alastair I. Johnston, *Social States: China and International Institutions, 1980–2000* (Princeton: Princeton University Press, 2008).

65. For insights into China's domestic reforms, see Jie Chen and Bruce J. Dickson, *Allies of the State: Democratic Support and Regime Support among China's Private Entrepreneurs* (Cambridge, MA: Harvard University Press, 2010); and Bruce J. Dickson, *Wealth into Power: The Communist Party's Embrace of China's Private Sector* (New York: Cambridge University Press, 2008).

66. In spring 2012, the Chen Guangcheng story illustrated once again the overweening oppression of China's political system. A blind Chinese dissident, Chen earned prison and perpetual house arrest for, among other things, defending women against the one-child policy. He escaped and eventually took refuge in the United States.

67. Max Weber, *The Protestant Ethic and the Spirit of Capitalism*, trans. Talcott Parsons (Mineola, NY: Dover Publications, 2003).

68. Diamond, *The Spirit of Democracy*.

69. Vladislav L. Inozemtsev makes the case for an elite-dominated democracy in Russia. See "Neo-feudalism Explained," *American Interest*, March/April 2011, http://www.the-american-interest.com/article.cfm?piece=939.

70. See Lieber, *Power and Willpower in the American Future*.

Index

assimilation, 45–46
Atchison, David, 139
Atocha, Alexander, 128–33, 211, 213
authoritarian capitalism, 248n35
authoritarian states, 244, 295n3;
  regime change goals for, 52, 204,
  224–26, 300n56; as threats, 5–9,
  25–26, 215, 229–34; use of force
  and, 203, 209–10. *See also* Soviet
  Union

Bachmann, Michelle, 20, 29
background leverage, 179, 181–82,
  208–12
Bahrain, 242
Baker, James, 261n14, 294n170
balance of power, 11, 23, 40, 41, 70–71,
  252n52; conservative internationalism on, 25–26, 53–54; in future sce-
  narios, 242; great power orientation
  of, 70–71; international institutions
  and, 156–57; militant nationalist
  views on, 44; old-world paradigm
  of, 82–83, 85, 161, 266n18; realist
  views on, 46–48, 60, 78–79, 205,
  218, 299n47
Balkan wars. *See* Yugoslavia
Barbary pirates, 82–93, 206, 210,
  267n35, 267n52
bargaining leverage, 179, 185–90,
  208–12
Barrett, Lawrence, 177
Barron, Samuel, 93
Bay of Pigs invasion, 204
Beach, Moses, 32, 130–33, 211, 213,
  277n110
Bemis, Samuel Flagg, 273n29
Bendetson, Karl, 186
Benghazi attack, 76
Benson, Thomas Hart, 120, 145,
  277n104
Bergeron, Paul, 110, 113, 123,
  131–33, 139, 275n76
Berkowitz, Peter, 250n30
Berlin, Isaiah, 249n14
Bermudez de Castro, Salvador, 128

Bessmertnykh, Alexander, 181,
  293n130
Bevin, Ernest, 163
Bialer, Seweryn, 179
Biden, Joe, 77
Bin Laden, Osama, 6, 37, 62, 71, 208
Bismark, Otto von, 252n52
Black Hawk Down, 68
bluffing, 77, 95, 142–43, 180
Bohlen, Charles, 155, 283n63
Boorstin, Daniel, 248n7
Borah, William, 50
Borneman, Walter, 112
Bosworth, Steve, 263n41
Bowers, Claude G., 105, 268n62
Brack, Gene, 128, 272n18, 276n87,
  276n94
Bretton Woods, 37
Brezhnev, Leonid, 190, 191, 221, 233
BRIC countries, 194
Britain, 8, 206, 230; abolition of
  slavery in, 114–15; on Barbary pi-
  rates, 89–90, 92; evolution of self-
  governance in, 12–13; Hudson Bay
  Company trade for, 136–37, 140,
  278n142, 278n148; Jefferson's
  embargo against, 85–88, 100–105,
  210–11, 270nn104–5; Oregon conflict of, 110, 122–23, 135–43, 216–
  17, 278n136, 278n148, 279n150,
  279n155; Polk-era rivalry with U.S.
  of, 113; potential intervention in
  California of, 125–27, 276n102;
  sailor impressment policies of, 33,
  90, 100, 103–4, 212; ship seizure
  laws of, 101; Texas proposal of, 118–
  19, 121, 126–27, 211, 274n57; on
  U.S. expansion and Civil War, 117,
  126–27; wars with France of, 90,
  96–98, 100, 105, 215, 269n83,
  270n90
Brussels Pact, 162
Bryan, William Jennings, 170
Brzezinski, Zbigniew, 74
Buchanan, James, 31–32, 144, 214;
  Mexican War and, 116, 126, 127,